# Paradise Blues

# Paradise Blues

Travels Through America's
Environmental History

**Christof Mauch**

*Translated from German
by Lucy Jones*

*Paradise Blues: Travels Through American Environmental History*
© Christof Mauch 2024

Translated from the German by Lucy Jones

Published by:
The White Horse Press, The Old Vicarage, Main Street, Winwick, PE28 5PN, UK

Original German edition:
*Paradise Blues: Reisen in die Natur und die Geschichte der USA* (dtv, 2022).

Set in 12 point Adobe Caslon Pro and Neue Haas
Printed and bound by CPI Group (UK) Ltd, Croydon, CR0 4YY

Open Access sponsored by BMBF and Rachel Carson Center, Munich

British Library Cataloguing in Publication Data
A catalogue record for this book is available from the British Library

ISBN 978-1-912186-78-5 (PB)
978-1-912186-79-2 Open Access ebook CC-BY-NC-ND 4.0

doi: 10.3828/63831596608648.book

Maps by Stephanie Schuster and Peter Palm. Cover photo by Bernhard Lang; all other photographs by the author.

Illustrations and Maps may not be reproduced. Translations for commercial use are not permitted.

Cover and interior layout by Stefania Bonura Graphics Web & Books.

# Contents

| | |
|---|---|
| Prologue | 7 |
| Wiseman, Alaska. 'The Happiest Civilization' | 13 |
| Malibu, California. Stranger than Paradise | 41 |
| Memphis, Tennessee. Mississippi Blues | 63 |
| St Thomas, Nevada. The Ghosts Return | 91 |
| Dodge City, Kansas. The Windy Wild West | 117 |
| Niagara, New York. The Second Greatest Disappointment | 145 |
| Walt Disney World, Florida. At Least Two Natures | 173 |
| Portland, Oregon. Into America's Green Future | 207 |
| Afterword | 237 |
| Acknowledgements | 248 |
| Notes | 251 |
| Index | 291 |

The USA

# Prologue

America is a country of dreams, desires and longings. Millions of visitors from all over the world flock to the USA to experience its extremes – from city adventures to the vast wilderness, the plunging Niagara Falls to towering skyscrapers, the glitz of Las Vegas to the glaciers of Alaska, Memphis blues to Florida's swamps, from giant sequoias to canyons and rivers. A trip from coast to coast by car or campervan is still considered the ultimate pilgrimage through America's great outdoors.

My work as an environmental historian has involved exploring the USA for decades. Washington D.C. was my home for fifteen years and the jumping-off point for my travels all around the country. For all its contradictions, it's a nation close to my heart: a paradise of unlimited possibilities on one hand and, on the other, the epitome of political megalomania. For some, it's the land of the free, for others, the land of slavery, role model and cautionary tale rolled into one. But it wasn't until I experienced the USA at first-hand and studied traces of its inhabitants that have been inscribed in the landscape down the centuries that I discovered a country beyond the common clichés and well-known dichotomies.

To understand America, it's helpful not to focus solely on its politics and economy, its presidential office and its almost uninterrupted succession of wars since 1945 but, rather, to survey its people's relationship with and handling of their environment. Trying to grasp a nation's identity as a whole by travelling to its very different parts might seem like an odd idea at first but, by doing this, I gained a range of unexpected insights – and *Paradise Blues* lays these out.

'Any good history begins in strangeness', said the American historian Richard White. Things we find strange but not daunting make us curious to discover more. However, exploring landscapes – the crux of this book – can unearth new mysteries. The scars left on the topography of rural America reveal some grim stories lurking beneath its breathtaking façade. On my detours through nature, I frequently discovered the familiar in unfamiliar places – and found the unfamiliar in places I thought I knew. This realisation opened my eyes, for example, to the tight link between one of America's most popular tourist attractions, Niagara Falls, and one of the most infamous toxic waste scandals in US history, the Love Canal disaster. Similarly, Florida's transformation into a paradise for leisure and citrus fruit is slowly but surely destroying its fragile ecosystems and water supply.

America is often called 'nature's nation', as if its landscape were homogenous.[1] The comparable architecture in each state capital and the similar appearance of many suburbs disguise regional differences. Clipped, lush lawns in suburban Philadelphia and Denver, for example, look surprisingly alike although these two cities are further apart than Brussels and Moscow. Philadelphia has a temperate climate with frequent rainfall while Denver's arid atmosphere means that a well-kempt lawn is only possible with intensive irrigation and fertilisation.[2] Homogeneity in America is rare, especially in terms of climate, which ranges from Florida's subtropical zone to arctic Alaska. You'll find alligators in the south and reindeer in the north. Along the Mississippi and in the southeast, the population has to battle with floods and hurricanes while dry periods and droughts ravage the region west of the Mississippi and California is endangered by terrible wildfires.

The common language connecting America's people, along with the national highway system, the omnipresence of fast food, supermarket and hotel chains, and phrases like 'the American way of life' suggest that a national uniformity exists: but, in terms of the country's physical geography, this is an illusion. To understand America, as I learned on my travels, you have to grasp its diversity.

America's different landscapes have also produced distinct cultures since time immemorial. Indigenous communities spoke up to a hundred languages and built over twenty types of dwellings, from simple brushwood shelters to multi-storey pueblo buildings, nomadic tepees and subterranean pit-houses that serve as models for modern ecological housing.[3]

Unlike 'nature', the word 'environment' conjures few positive images where the USA is concerned. Americans are known for emitting more $CO_2$ per capita than citizens of any other nation. The country produces more waste, uses more packaging and exploits more surface area to construct houses than any other. Over the past 200 years, no other nation has tapped its natural resources – water, forests and earth – as rigorously as the United States. Especially from a European perspective, the details and differences of how America treats the environment stand out all too clearly, both in the negative and positive sense. After all, the United States can lay claim to the invention of large nature reserves and national parks, a model that has been

## Prologue

successfully copied throughout the world, from the Kruger National Park in South Africa to the Bavarian Forest in Germany. With the non-profit Sierra Club, America benefits from a politically influential conservation association. And activists like Julia 'Butterfly' Hill, members of groups like Earth First and environmental thinkers like Henry David Thoreau, Aldo Leopold and Rachel Carson are among the most important pioneers of movements that have gained traction far beyond the USA.[4]

Americans' relationship with nature is unique. An account that took a national historical standpoint, therefore, would have its appeal. At the same time, a bird's eye view of national politics and abstract environmental thinking is missing a crucial element: the 'down-to-earth' aspect of being on-site, an approach that takes in landscapes and natural phenomena, including the feeling of mud on one's shoes that environmental historians pride themselves on.[5]

Over the past few years, I've visited all the places mentioned in this book. My search for American nature has resulted in a travelogue through culture and history in these selected locations that comments on their transformation over long periods. Even though they were selected subjectively, they are an attempt to represent the whole. What interests me about each place is that it is symptomatic. Dodge City, Kansas, for example, with its vast plains, sandstorms and huge cattle herds stands for a Midwestern prairie. St Thomas, Nevada represents the desert and artificially irrigated and militarised landscape in America's South West. Wiseman, Alaska, embodies the exploitation of natural resources like gold and oil, but also wilderness preservation. Memphis, Tennessee is a stand-in for other places along the Mississippi that have spawned their own cultures entirely. And Malibu, California, is an example of those towns on the southern Pacific coast that live in our imaginations like paradise on earth but are in reality plagued by natural disasters of all kinds.

I visited the places and people in this book at different points in time. In some cases, my last encounter dates back many years. It may well be that my impressions would be different if I were to visit a particular place again today. History is fluid, and I can by no means claim that my observations are timeless. In fact, they represent just a snapshot in time.

*Paradise Blues* was inspired by William Faulkner's *Requiem For a Nun*. In it, one of his protagonists says, 'The past is never dead. It's not even past.' On my travels through America's nature and history, I worked like a detective to discover the past and future hidden behind the present and what immediately meets the eye. Travelling, driving and walking are amateur activities. This way, I came across things I'd never have found out but which I could systematically research using my professional craft as a historian.

This book spans an arc from the Brooks Range in Alaska all the way to Portland, Oregon in the final chapter, although each section can be read independently. I start by exploring a region where humanity's interventions are minimal and I finish with a portrait of a city that was once dubbed 'the most sustainable town in the USA' and whose environmental politics and campaigns have resonated throughout the world. While searching for traces in America, I wanted to counteract the ubiquitous story of 'the end of nature' with something positive.[6] I didn't always manage but sometimes my wish was granted. This history of the American environment unearths grand hopes and bitter disappointments. Even in paradise, the blues are sometimes playing.

Alaska

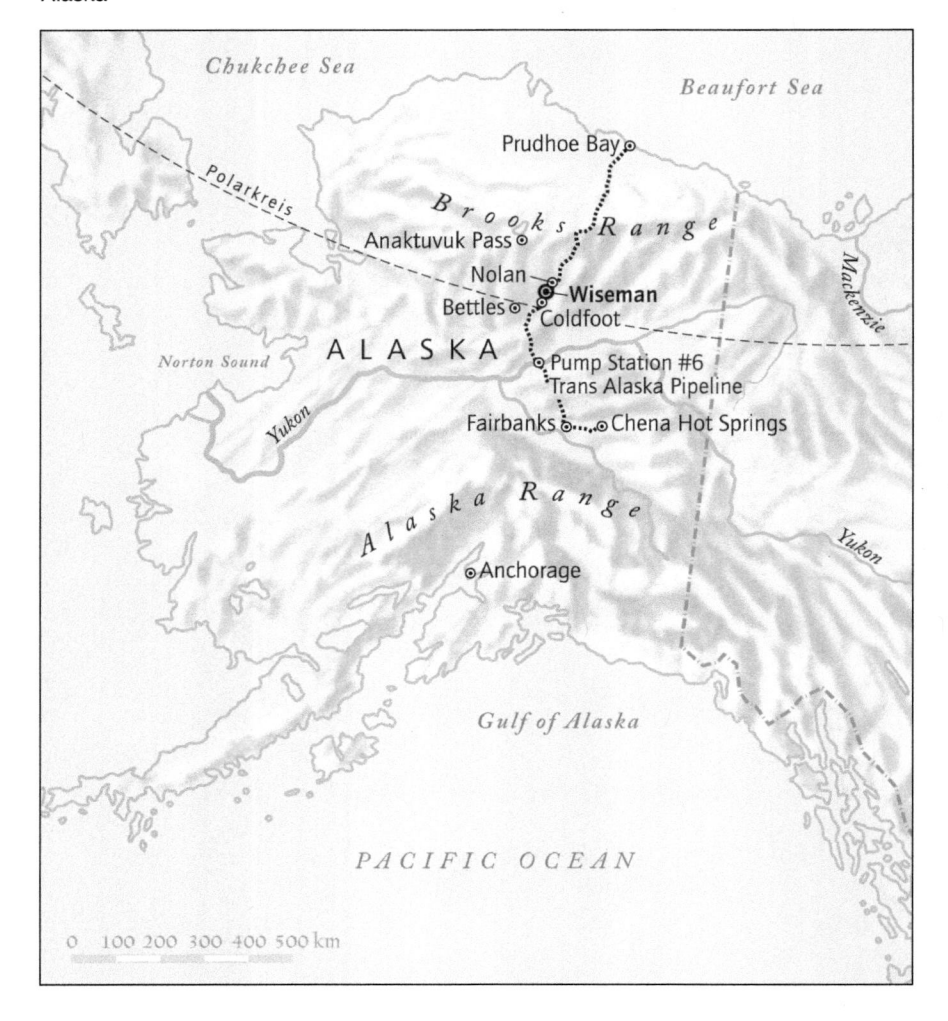

# Wiseman, Alaska.
## 'The Happiest Civilization'

### The 'happiest civilization'

Wiseman is in the Arctic, a hundred kilometres north of the polar circle. In summer, the sun does not set there and, in winter, it's pitch black for days. According to the census, the former gold-rush boomtown had just fourteen inhabitants in 2010: seven men and seven women. In the farthest northern region of the USA where Wiseman lies, wild animals have outnumbered humans several times over since time began. Herds of caribou, the reindeer's North American relative, migrate along centuries-old routes through the Gates of the Arctic National Park. Grizzly and black bears roam here too, as well as Dall sheep and wolves. Alaska, or *Alyeska* in the language of the indigenous Aleut people, means something like 'great unknown country'. Marks on the landscape bear witness to its volcanic and glacial origins. A few hundred kilometres from Wiseman, glaciers formed by the sun trace the movements of the Ice Age like living fossils. Here you will find forests of black spruce and an endless tundra of mosses, lichens and ferns. When the snow melts, nature explodes. Plants shoot up out of the ground, mosquitoes multiply and the birds arrive – over a hundred species, of which some, especially terns, have flown halfway across the globe to breed in Alaska. Nowhere else in the USA is nature so present, and nowhere else has humanity left such a faint trace on the landscape.

I decide to travel to Wiseman because, when settlers of European descent immigrated to America, the mountains and valleys in this area remained barely touched; there are still historical cabins from the gold-rush era and this region is far off the beaten track for crowds of tourists. As an environmental historian, Wiseman also interests me because of the tension caused by the nature of its geology that is expressed in its landscape. The town itself only exists because of the exploitation of one natural resource: gold. Yet, in the immediate vicinity is one of the largest wildernesses on the American continent.

Wiseman in particular interests me because I happened to read a book by Robert Marshall called *Arctic Village*. Marshall, a forester and plant pathologist and the son of a wealthy family of New York lawyers, flew to Wiseman in a sports plane for the first time at the end of 1929. The village and the outstanding beauty of the Brooks mountain range and Koyukuk River made such an impression on the 28-year-old that he decided to return in the summer of 1930. He stayed for fifteen months, officially to investigate the growth of trees at the timberline. In truth, he was interested in the lives of the 127 Inuit, American Indians and white settlers in Wiseman. He described them as 'the happiest civilization of which I have knowledge'.[1] I pack *Arctic Village* to read on my trip, not least to gain insight into the changes that have taken place in the northern United States over the past century. The effects on the forty-ninth state – on its economy, landscape, nature and culture – were radical when vast oil resources were discovered about fifty years ago in Prudhoe Bay, its farthest northern tip.

## Alaska – a very different side of America?

This journey to the extreme north of the USA is not my first. In 1999, I visited Anchorage, the most populous town in Alaska. Back then, I knew practically nothing about the state. It usually features in history books because in 1867, the US Foreign Minister, William H. Seward, bought it from the Russians for a ludicrously low price. Elsewhere, it crops up in the context of the early twentieth-century gold rush and the Cold War because, during those periods, Americans feared an attack from the nearby Soviet Union. On US land and weather maps, Alaska is nearly always placed in the Pacific Ocean like an enormous island because it does not share a border with the USA, but with Canada. So the image of the isolated, unique 49th state has inscribed itself deep into the collective consciousness. Clichés about the predominance of men and the lack of women also abound, as well as its half-yearly total darkness. Americans don't associate the fast-food restaurants and skyscrapers that I saw in Anchorage with Alaska; they think of polar bears, Inuits and a population that lives in the wilderness. But, in reality, almost three-quarters of the Alaskan population live in towns. In 2016, 740,000 people lived in Alaska, and 300,000 in Anchorage alone. Only a tiny section of the state's 1.723 million square kilometres is inhabited, and over half the towns have fewer than 500 inhabitants.[2]

Alaska could not survive on its own. The region depends on the state of Washington and its capital city, Seattle. Seattle's business world has maintained close ties to Alaska since the gold rush. Almost everything consumed in the North is either shipped or flown from Seattle.[3] In economic terms, Alaska is undoubtedly an integral part of the United States.

Despite this, the state has a variety of characteristics that makes it fundamentally different from all others. Nature and culture are governed by their own unique rhythm. 'Only in Alaska', writes the journalist Roxanne Willis, 'does daily life ebb and flow with the caribou migration, the midnight sun, the Iditarod [dog sleigh race], and the Iñupiat whaling season. Only in Alaska are bear maulings, bush plane crashes, and hypothermia common threats to life and limb'.[4]

Only in Alaska does a 10,000-year-old indigenous population made up of Inuits, American Indians and Aleut still exist, still living in their ancestral habitat, not persecuted or driven out like the indigenous populations in the rest of the USA.

Alaska's geography is extreme, incomparable and virtually immeasurable. It is four times bigger than California. Its rocky, rugged coast stretches for 550,000 kilometres and is significantly longer than the coasts of the forty-eight other states taken together. Its territories lie between the arctic and subarctic range on a northern latitude of between 51 and 72 degrees. At the farthest northern point, 560 kilometres north of the Arctic Circle, the sun does not rise for 77 days a year and does not set for 84. In the northernmost region of Alaska, permafrost prevails. The ground there has been frozen for thousands of years.[5] These things all make Alaska an exceptional place, fascinating to visitors.

## The fascination of the wild

I am not travelling alone. My wife, an American, thinks that Alaska is too dangerous: 'It's a vast wilderness. I want you back alive', she says. So, a friend of mine, the painter Johannes Heisig from Berlin, is accompanying me. We meet in Fairbanks, Alaska's second-biggest town. Unlike during Marshal's times, you can drive to Wiseman these days. Before we set off, we wonder why most car rental companies don't allow trips along the Dalton Highway, which is the route to Wiseman. But once we're on the road heading north, it becomes clear why (and why almost all the cars here are four-wheel-drives): most of the 666-kilometre-long Dalton Highway from Fairbanks to Prudhoe Bay is a deeply potholed gravel track.[6] Long, straight sections alternate with winding, often steep segments. The oncoming traffic churns up stones that glance off our car. 'Be careful that a moose doesn't end up on your windscreen', says the man in the car rental agency, only half-joking, as he hands us the keys. We have reason to be cautious. The Alaskan Department of Fish and Game estimates that there are easily 700 collisions a year between moose and vehicles.[7]

Our Alaskan number plates say 'Alaska: The Last Frontier'. Fairbanks people laugh about it. But outside of Alaska, a reality TV show called *The Last Frontier* has been running on the Discovery Channel for years, with over 120 episodes and high audience ratings. Why do Americans never grow tired of choreographed scenes of film crews subjected to freezing temperatures and starvation, coyote and wolf attacks, illness and floods on the Kenai Peninsula? Why was Werner Herzog's *Grizzly Man* such a success, a documentary featuring a young man who spends many summers living among grizzly bears in Alaska, only to be mauled to death with his girlfriend at the end?

And where does the fascination with Christopher McCandless' story come from, a 24-year-old Californian who hitchhiked to Alaska in search of answers to life's big questions, but only found mosquitoes, freezing

On the Dalton Highway, Alaska.

temperatures and a lonely demise? During winter, McCandless starved to death in a decommissioned bus from the Fairbanks City Transit System and was only found months later by hunters. Hundreds of Americans used to make the pilgrimage every year to retrace McCandless' journey into the wild, having read Jon Krakauer's eponymous biography or watched Sean Penn's movie. McCandless' cult status led to camps being set up next to his bus before it was taken away, camps where people starved like he did. One female tourist drowned swimming in the nearby river and others had to be saved from dire situations. The film *Into the Wild* was a box-office hit in the USA and on video distribution channels. But in Alaska, McCandless is regarded as 'a poacher' and 'a thief', a 'noble, suicidal narcissist' and 'a bum'. For the Alaskan journalist Craig Medred, McCandless and his imitators represent 'self-involved urban Americans … more detached from nature than any society of humans in history'.[8]

Perhaps, I think, as we drive from Fairbanks into the wilderness, the fascination stems from a longing for another world, one where people have not yet controlled and tamed nature, exploited and built over it, and sealed or excavated the earth. Today, in the Anthropocene, the tides have turned and nature seems completely exposed to the impulses, for good or ill, of people; so we long for it to regain its old power and strike back, at least sometimes, with force. In the vastness of Alaska, a person is a mere speck. It is an extremely remote place where men (there is barely any talk of women) show their strength and courage in the face of ruthless nature. This is reflected in Robert W. Service's poetry and Jack London's *Call of the Wild*.[9]

## Hot springs in Frigidia

The highway that takes travellers north from Fairbanks is asphalted for the first few kilometres. There's not a trace of wilderness around here. Instead of travelling straight to Wiseman, we take a detour to Chena Hot Springs northeast of Fairbanks. We hadn't planned it but at the hotel in Fairbanks, they had called after us: 'Chena Hot Springs! It's a must for you! A must for historians!' At first glance, the tiny village is far from spectacular. There's an airstrip for planes, a few wooden cabins and a lake. Its special feature is the hot springs. Over a hundred years ago, Robert and Thomas Swan, two brothers looking for gold, came across the springs by chance when they were canoeing on the Chena River. The water healed Robert Swan's rheumatism and so the history of today's spa resort began.[10]

At the turn of the twentieth century, what must have been the tallest trees and the best source of wood in the interior of Alaska grew between the hot springs and Fairbanks. And they were needed in large quantities in the frontier town of Fairbanks. The wood was used to build houses, heat open fireplaces and power the steam engines of locomotives and ships carrying goods and food to Fairbanks.

To our astonishment, we not only find hot springs in Chena but also a vegetable garden with enormous lettuces, tomatoes, beans and peppers, zucchini and potatoes, cucumbers and all kinds of herbs. The apples from the Chena Hot Springs plantation measure almost ten centimetres in diameter. Who would have thought there would be a fruit and vegetable paradise near the Arctic Circle? The endless daylight and relatively mild climate help all kinds of fruit to thrive; in a highly modern, geothermally heated greenhouse, more than 100,000 cut flowers are harvested every year. In fact, agricultural produce in Alaska has set world records: there are reports of a nineteen-pound carrot, a 76-pound rutabaga and a whopping 107-pound cabbage.[11]

Right near Chena Hot Springs, we come across a collection of rusting farm vehicles, among them a McCormick-Deering harvester from the 1930s. They bear witness to the immigrants' dreams in the first half of the twentieth century, when it was hoped that Alaska could become a large-scale agricultural state. Especially during the Great Depression, when many regions of North America suffered from unemployment, poverty and hunger, Alaska was considered an insider tip where the luckless might strike lucky. The territory that had previously been mocked with nicknames like 'Walrussia', 'Icebergia' and 'Frigidia' slowly underwent a positive makeover. The US government invested five million dollars in 1935 to bring 200 farming families from the Midwest to the Matanuska Valley in Alaska.

The experiment was not a great success. Contrary to the expected dry climate of sun and blue skies, resulting in gigantic yields of crops, severe rains fell in the first spring and summer. Six families gave up in the first six months and over half that number again within five years. It might have been possible to grow enormous pumpkins and ears of corn in Alaska: but unexpected snowstorms could also wipe out the entire harvest. The soil was less fertile than expected and the short planting period and harsh climate conditions did the rest. A market barely existed for agricultural produce and the infrastructure could not meet demand. Even the construction and expansion of the railway network was a mixed blessing in Alaska: the tracks might have opened new markets to Alaskan farmers, but, most of all, they

## Gold prospectors

We're barely back on the highway heading north when a gigantic gold dredge comes into sight. Like a metal dinosaur, the Goldstream Dredge No 8 hunkers in the middle of a compound made up of gravel, grass and sand. In its heyday, the towering monster, with its long steel bucket line, inched seven kilometres across the compound shovelling gold-bearing earth, day in, day out, from 1928 to 1959 with a total excavation of over 212 tons of gold.[13] Harry A. Franck, a travel writer who observed the gold dredge in 1939, describes it with fascination as being similar to 'a large scow with heavy machinery and housing on it, flowing in a little pond of water which it opens ahead by digging in, and closes up behind as it edges slowly along a creek bottom – like some prehistoric monster reaching out its long neck of chain-and-buckets, rooting in the earth with its metal snout, and drawing in enormous daily meals of golden gravel'.[14]

The principle of the gold dredge is incredibly simple. These machines were set to work in the twentieth century in any place where traces of gold were found in rivers and creeks. Interspersed in thin layers of stone, the gold was released through weathering and deposited itself as 'river gold' or 'alluvial gold', if you use the geological technical term, in gravel, sand or dirt. The gigantic gold dredges crawled along the rivers throwing up water-saturated soil and separating the heavy gold from the excavated earth with sieves and grooved water channels. Mining dredges like the No 8 worked very well: they combined effective digging with low operating costs. In the year 1935, the Fairbanks Exploration Company paid over 900 employees an annual total of 1.9 million dollars – at a time when the rest of the USA was still suffering from the consequences of the Great Depression. Fairbanks, too, has gold mining alone to thank for its wealth. In the mid-1930s, when the town had a population of approximately 2,700 people, the administration removed the wooden pavements and built concrete houses, as well as the first paved roads in northern Alaska.[15]

The craving for gold changed the face of Alaska from the end of the nineteenth century on, and the machinery of the Goldstream Dredge No 8 has left deep marks on the landscape. Historic photos show a desolate landscape, destroyed and full of artificial mounds and deformations. Most contemporaries saw the gold dredges as the arrival of a new, benevolent era and few anticipated the destructive potential of gold mining. One of them, a journalist and successful writer from a German-American family, John Gunther, went in search of the Goldstream Dredge No 8 in 1947. For him, the gigantic machine was nothing more than 'a big, ugly gray dredge [that] squats in a dirty pool of its own creation, eats out the earth to the water in and then floats on the scum it makes'. It left behind 'the kind of furrow that an enormous obscene unhouse-broken worm might leave – an encrusted seam of broken earth with mud and rocks lying across a winding trail like excrement'.[16]

John Gunther fretted about the unsightliness of the landscape; today, however, we know that the great gold dredges disturbed not only the appearance but also the ecology in many parts of Alaska. Mountains were literally moved to create enough water to mine gold, and large quantities of water were redirected. Goldstream Dredge No 8 benefited from the construction of a ninety-mile conduit, the Davidson Ditch, which was dug in the 1920s especially for gold mining. Where prospectors believed there was gold, water was entirely at the service of hydraulic gold mining. Once excavation began, the water used became useless. Any method was fair game to gold prospectors to separate gold from sand and rocks and so mercury was used unscrupulously because it settles and combines with gold, making it easy to extract. Then the amalgam was heated, and the mercury evaporated, leaving only molten gold.[17]

As we travel north, our conversations revolve around questions of time and place. Heisig, a painter, and so attuned to the visual world, suggests that the gold prospectors' disturbance of nature is barely visible half a century after the last dredges were shut down. However, this period imposed enormous *invisible* damage that is much more far-reaching than tourist places like Chena Hot Springs. Indeed, traces of the mercury used in gold mining have found their way into the soil, creeks, rivers, oceans, fish and our bodies. There has rarely been a phenomenon equivalent to gold mining that has risked such long-term harmful effects on people and the environment for the sake of fast profit.

## On the road

One hundred and thirty-four kilometres north of Fairbanks, we reach the stretch of the Dalton Highway that goes all the way to the northernmost tip of Alaska: the Prudhoe Bay Oil Field on the coast of the Arctic Ocean.

## Wiseman, Alaska. 'The Happiest Civilization'

Our travel guide says that Dalton is the only highway in Alaska that crosses the Arctic Circle, the only one that crosses the Yukon River via bridge, and the only one that takes you to the arctic Beaufort Sea.[18]

Roads in North Alaska are rare. The indigenous population did not have them and the explorers and researchers who explored the interior of this region did not build any. They arrived by ship, and mostly covered long distances by river.[19] That the Dalton Highway exists despite this – a road that crosses the whole of northern Alaska – is down to one reason alone: the discovery of oil in Prudhoe Bay.

This took place in February 1968 and hailed the beginning of a radically new era for the region, which had hitherto been spared major crises and wars. Oil fields were not a new thing in Alaska per se (Inuits had already made use of smaller oil deposits over a hundred years earlier). But estimates by scientists in 1968 that ten billion barrels of 'black gold' in Prudhoe Bay were just waiting to be drilled and pumped prompted a scramble for oil that captured the imaginations of investors, thrill-seekers and politicians in every state in America. Overnight, the 300,000-person state was flooded with money. Alaska's newly elected governor, Republican businessman Walter Hickel, immediately set about constructing roads to the oil fields. But the Hickel Highway (Dalton's forerunner) was only navigable in winter. Then its course was marked in the snow by long, vertical wooden stakes. In spring, however, when the snow melted, the 'ice road' transformed into a river of mud. A 'battlebook' was published by the Sierra Club, America's biggest nonprofit environmental organisation, with the title *Oil on Ice* that described the Hickel Highway 'from an environmental point of view' as 'the biggest screwup in the history of mankind in the Arctic'.[20] If they didn't get trapped in the mud, the powerful rigs with their long, heavy tractor-trailers, used to transport equipment and supplies north from Fairbanks, inflicted often irreparable damage onto the already susceptible permafrost. For Alaska's natural world, this disaster was a stroke of luck. The destruction of a previously untouched landscape brought to the scene at lightning speed environmental associations and politicians who prevented the highway from being converted into a paved road without first taking full stock of the ecological as well as the technological, economic and political factors. Five years later, and after a fierce battle between the various interest groups, politicians decided against transport routes that would lead through Canada and underground oil pipelines (such as those in Texas and Oklahoma). What they decided on was a haul road – a one-to-two-metre-high gravel surface that would follow the overground trans-Alaskan pipeline. The Dalton Highway (named after the Alaskan engineer and oil researcher, James W. Dalton) was built in just five months and the pipeline in three years (from 1974 to 1977).[21]

Even though the Dalton Highway has been officially open to the public since 1994, there aren't many reasons for tourists to travel this gravel road. Dalton doesn't offer charming restaurants, marked hiking paths or spectacular views along the way, nor does it pass idyllic villages, stylish gift shops, banks, food or medical supplies stores. Deadhorse, the biggest of three villages along the Dalton Highway with 25 permanent residents, is nothing more than a large oil-industry plant that employs thousands of seasonal workers.

Our first stop is near Pump Station No 6, where the highway crosses the vast Yukon River. Here there are a couple of tumbledown wooden huts selling all kinds of burgers: big burgers and teriyaki burgers, mushroom and vegetarian burgers, BBQ and boo-boo burgers. We are in America, after all! 'We're in the wilderness, but we still need burgers', explains George, who tells us he's an ex-trucker. George is travelling in a small four-wheel-drive Chevrolet truck to show his girlfriend the route he used to drive with his tractor-trailer 'for almost twenty years'. During that time, he lost eighteen fellow truckers. 'When we were coming from different directions', George explains, 'we'd let each other know via walkie-talkie that we were coming round the bend.' Full-frontal collisions were rare, he says, but in winter, some of the drivers plunged down the big embankments and flipped over. That was fatal. 'I'll never forget those pictures.' When George is telling us his stories, it's as if he and his fellow truckers gave every bend in the road and every embankment a name: 'Oil Spill Hill', 'Beaver Hill', 'Roller Coaster' and 'Oh Shit Slide'. George is a dry kind of guy, but when he gets going on the subject of the highway, he transforms into an eloquent travel reporter. As he talks, it's hard to separate the stories he lived through from the ones he's retelling. They were going to build a dam near here, he tells us. 'They wanted to create a big lake and produce energy. But the Eskimos and environmentalists prevented it.'[22]

There was indeed going to be a big dam construction near here at one point, but George must have been a child when the planning for the Rampart project began, just a few kilometres from the Yukon crossing. In the 1960s, a massive wall was supposed to be erected in the Rampart Valley to accumulate water from the Yukon and surrounding creeks and lakes to use for Alaska's energy supplies. The US Army Corps of Engineers was commissioned to carry out a feasibility study for this huge undertaking. The dam, had it been realised, would have put 25,000 square kilometres underwater, equivalent to around two per cent of Alaska's landmass. Spawning grounds for salmon, a refuge for waterfowl, biotopes for mammals and the gravel bed of the Yukon would likely have been flooded by the biggest artificial lake in the world. George Sundborg, an external advisor for the Rampart project, described the floodplains of the Yukon as a worthless area containing 'no more than ten flush toilets'. One could 'search the whole world over', he continued, and it would be difficult to find 'an equivalent area with so little to be lost through flooding'. It is only thanks to the objections by nature conservation authorities, especially the US Fish and Wildlife Service, as well as the nascent protests by the indigenous population – seven native Athabaskan settlements would have fallen victim to the dam project – that the unique habitat of the Yukon Flats was maintained.[23] However, gigantic projects like the Rampart Dam and the oil pipeline to Prudhoe Bay made the indigenous population realise that 'white men' were not only interested in individual areas but were a grave danger to traditional landscapes and ways of life in general, such as hunting and fishing. In contrast to the American Indians in the rest of the USA, however, Alaska's indigenous population were not forced to live on reservations. In December 1971, Inuits and American Indians were granted 962 million dollars and more than sixteen million hectares of land (roughly a ninth of Alaska's entire surface area) as compensation in the most comprehensive settlement of territorial claims in US history. Indigenous territories and village communities could, according to the wording of the settlement, choose territories for their own use.[24] As a result, their vote became highly significant when implementing major projects or protecting nature and the wilderness.

On the journey further north, we pass through the region that was supposed to be flooded in the 1960s – the Yukon Flats. Birch, spruce and aspen trees grow here. There are many ducks, tits, woodpeckers and screech owls. We see a moose. But we can only surmise the great expanse and diversity of nature at home here, with over 36,000 lakes, ponds and backwaters. Countless migratory birds use the plains as their summer habitat. Lux and muskrats live here, alongside mink and ferrets, grizzly bears and wolves. We hike a short way through the quiet landscape. Heisig makes tape recordings all along our tour. Years later, the sounds and birdsong evoke images of a remote and incomparably beautiful landscape. How lucky, we say, that, during Jimmy Carter's presidency in 1976, the Rampart Dam was halted, and the Yukon Flats became a national nature reserve.[25]

## In Wiseman

By the time we reach Wiseman, we've covered over 600 kilometres. The town is only two kilometres from the Dalton Highway. On the outskirts, a wooden sign hangs on a tree: 'Wiseman was founded in 1908 and since then has always been able to survive on its own. Huts and property are private. So please respect the property of the people here.' The fact that the former gold-rush village is described as 'able to survive' has a deeper meaning. In the first half of the twentieth century, there were hundreds of villages like Wiseman where gold prospectors settled. Most of them are now weather-beaten or have disappeared altogether. They were never even drawn on a map. Just a few archaeological traces and relics remind visitors of the golden era. Why is Wiseman an exception? Why did the village survive? We spend a few days here looking for the answer in conversations while we explore.

We find a room at the Boreal Lodge, run by Heidi Schoppenhorst. Heidi grew up in Wiseman, was home-schooled and works part-time as a park ranger in the environmental education department of the National Park Service.[26] Heidi's mother, June Reakoff, and one of her brothers, Jack Reakoff, also live in Wiseman. The Boreal Lodge dates to 1910. It stands in the middle of some old cabins that are all at least half a century old. Around two-thirds of them have long since disappeared: they were eventually turned into firewood. Of those that are still standing, most are crooked. The soft earth swallows them up. 'In the last twenty years, my cabin has sunk twenty inches into the tundra. The bottommost logs have disappeared into the ground', explains Jack Reakoff, who works as a hunter, gatherer, trapper and guide, and who used to be a pilot. Bernie Hicker from Freising, Bavaria, whom we are surprised to find running a bed-and-breakfast here with his wife Uta, has taken precautions and mounted concrete blocks into the earth. The house in which he, Uta and their three Arctic-born children live used to be a gold prospector's inn called the Silverly and Bowker Saloon. For a long time, it served the Pioneers of Alaska, an organisation that preserves Alaska's gold-prospecting history, as its northernmost clubhouse, or 'Igloo No 8'. Elections used to be held here, Uta Hickers tells us. There was a library, a chapel and a dance hall; today there is still an old piano in the guesthouse. A few metres from the Arctic Getaway, as the B&B is called, there is a cabin where the post office used to be. Post has not been delivered to Wiseman for a long time. But inside the hut, the original counter, post sacks, post box and scales have been preserved.[27]

# Wiseman, Alaska. 'The Happiest Civilization'

Some of the original goldminers' cabins can be seen around Wiseman.

Many of the huts are decorated with moose antlers. Wiseman's remote location produces some interesting results and cultivates inventiveness. There are tall, homemade antennas and satellite dishes, small trucks with eccentric modifications, walls and roofs improved with corrugated iron and aluminium from long-forgotten construction sites. Hardly anything is thrown away in Wiseman. At the edge of the village, an ancient caravan covered in yellow lichen is hidden away. Perhaps a tourist left it behind? Or was it home to a pipeline worker, a prospector or a thrill-seeker? One time we stumble across a pile of tens of thousands of old aluminium cans: Miller beer and Budweiser, Pepsi and Sprite. The locals ironically refer to this local artwork as 'The Totem Pole of the White Man'. A little further up, overlooking the village, there is a completely overgrown cemetery. Over forty people and some dogs are buried here. Most of the grave markings are made of wood, weather-beaten and no longer decipherable. One of the few gold prospectors here with a gravestone – Harry Ross (1939–1975) is decorated with an American flag and an artificial red flower. He didn't even make it to his 36th birthday. 'You can tell the value of a man from the sharpness of his knife', says the not untypical epitaph for a frontier town cemetery.

The characteristics of remote places as conceived by the British anthropologist Edwin Ardener all apply to Wiseman: They are 'full of ruins of the past … There is always change and intervention', 'no stagnation'. Remote areas are 'full of strangers. People in remote areas have a wide definition of "strangers", so that, whatever the real numbers of the latter, there will always appear to be a lot of them. Lastly, remote areas are obsessed with communications: the one road; the one ferry; the tarring of the road; the improvement of the boat; the airstrip' etc.[28]

Wiseman has access to radio, TV and the Internet; nevertheless, the relevance of its history and gold rush past are in evidence. Among the houses, we find gold pans and bowls, rusty wheelbarrows and gold sluice boxes, winches and buckets, boilers and other steam-powered machinery once used to transport gold. The former colonial goods store on the southern outskirts of Wiseman – the only two-storey cabin – conjures up its long-gone past. When we go inside the building that dates to 1927, it's as if we've gone back in time to Wiseman's boomtown era. On the shelves, there are all kinds of bottles, enamel plates and cups, baking tins, little sacks of salt and metal pots containing vanilla extract and gelatin. On the walls hang flags and adverts for Winchester rifles and ammunition. The most precious find, however, is a pair of golden cast iron scales and a shining, wood-burning stove made by the Lang company in Seattle, patented in the year 1911 and fittingly named 'Arctic'.[29]

I remember a passage in Robert Marshall's book in which he describes the Wiseman Trading Company: it had 129 different foodstuffs, according to his account, from flour to split peas, tea to olive oil, prunes to figs and macaroni to corned beef. Marshall evidently loved tables and lists, because next to the prices, he noted what you would pay for the same goods in Baltimore: products in the Arctic were twice to eight times as expensive. In spring, Marshall writes, even fresh apples and oranges were delivered via river from the south – for astronomical prices, of course. And for 'those who had a special taste or a lot of money', there was crab, lobster, shrimp and asparagus although it was all canned.[30] Today Wiseman no longer has a shop. Just a corner of Heidi's Boreal Lodge sells some items of food and souvenirs to tourists.

Heidi's brother Jack and his family almost exclusively live off fishing, hunting, trapping, fur selling and Arctic handicrafts. Jack grew up in the wilderness. 'I once went to Anchorage ... but I realised the city isn't for me', he explains. The Reakoff family rhythm is determined by the weather and the migration of the animals. Every summer, Jack goes to Bristol Bay where he works as a commercial salmon fisher. He's paid in cash. He brings back between seventy and ninety kilos of frozen fish – as much as he can take on the plane – to Wiseman. Then it's time to weed and work in the garden. In the fall, he hunts Dall sheep and moose and, during the rainy month of October, he saws wood and cuts meat before the trapping season begins in November. Everything is used: either the family keeps or sells the furs, while they share lux, beaver and wolverine meat with their dogs. In April, Jack hunts bears: 'We love fresh bear meat!' Then the annual changing of the seasons starts all over again. His income is low but in Wiseman, you need less than half of the official minimum wage to lead a good life.[31]

One afternoon, Jack's mother shows us two large buckets of blueberries that she has picked in just a few hours. 'They've never been as big as they are this year', she explains. And then she tells us about the wolf that is doing its rounds in the little village. Early in the morning, it turned up in Wiseman, and while looking for something to eat, it ran into her daughter-in-law's (Jack Reakoff's wife's) cat. But the cat scared it off. Thank goodness! We don't meet the wolf, but its paw prints are clearly visible in the damp, sandy earth.[32]

We're slightly surprised to come across a little church in Wiseman (without a steeple or a bell). The Kalhabuk Memorial Chapel was originally a gold prospectors' cabin from the 1910s and belonged to an Inuit called Big Jim. It was considered the social and spiritual centre of Wiseman's indigenous population. The transformation of the Inuit hut into a chapel traces back to June Reakoff, Jack and Heidi's mother – a petite woman with sharp features, silvery-white hair and a peaceful smile on her lips. June has held sermons here for over twenty years. They might tell the story of John the Baptist calling into the wilderness, the promises and the lamentations of the prophets, Christian redemption and the imminent end of the world. Sometimes, June's daughter is the only person in the congregation. The handwritten sermons lie in large piles in the cabin, like an archive in the wilderness. June christened the Kalhabuk Memorial Chapel in honour of Florence Jonas whose Inuit name was 'Kalhabuk'. Robert Marshall wrote that Kalhabuk was 'the strongest woman' he had ever met. Many times, he claimed, he saw her 'with a hundred-pound sack of flour on her back and a fifty-pound sack under her arm'. For June Reakoff, on the other hand, she was 'certainly the wisest woman' she ever met in her life. 'Kalhabuk knew the mystery of the mountains. And she understood nature's soul.'[33]

By chance, Kalhabuk's granddaughter, Ruth Williams, arrived in Wiseman a few days ago and is planning to spend her retirement in a little house here where she grew up. Her partner, Francis, is sawing a couple of planks outside. Ruth invites us into her home. It consists of one room with a homemade bed and a simple metal shelf stocked with tins. Both Ruth and Francis belong to the indigenous population. Ruth's ancestors are Inuits, and Francis's are American Indians. His father, he said, had 'Swedish and German forebears'; and, to prove it, he quotes a Swedish proverb about silver and gold. Because his father married an American Indian, Francis spent his entire childhood and youth in a Native American village. Later he moved away, fought as an American soldier in Korea, and then acquired his pilot's licence. Ruth wants to stay in Wiseman for good. Francis finds Wiseman too remote, too dark in winter and too far from the civilised world. Perhaps the little hut will only be their summer retreat.

Ruth's life story clearly shows how rapidly and radically the Arctic world has changed within one generation. Born in a tent near Big Lake, Ruth belonged, like her grandmother Kalhabuk, to a group of nomadic Inuits who made their living from hunting. For millennia, the indigenous people of Alaska hunted Dall sheep, mountain goats, brown bears or migrating caribou. In spring, the caribou move from the forested regions in the south to the fodder-rich meadows at the foot of the Brooks Range to calve. In Wiseman, Kalhabuk lived in an adobe house whose roof reached the floor like a tent. Before that, she had only known teepees that could easily be put up and taken down while hunting. Tables and chairs were things she'd only heard about.[34] At the age of seven, when the USA entered the Second World War, Ruth tells us that she was put in a boarding school of the Church of the Brethren missionaries in Fairbanks. This meant that all of a sudden, she 'arrived in civilisation'. After the war, she visited her grandmother regularly, sometimes several times a year, in Wiseman, where only nine people lived in 1945. Ruth constantly compares current times with her childhood. Spring now comes two or three weeks earlier, she says, and summer lasts longer. 'The trees grow faster, and the meadows higher.' There are more laws to observe nowadays, 'especially from the Bureau of Land Management' which even regulates the planting of trees. 'There are more mosquitoes', says Ruth 'and fewer caribou.' She sounds rather sad when she says this, even when

## Wiseman, Alaska. 'The Happiest Civilization'

she mentions her grandmother Kalhabuk 'who always looked towards the mountains', as if 'waiting for the herds of caribou to return' – the sign of better times.

Robert Marshall assumed that the area around Wiseman was not populated before the trappers' and gold panners' cabins were built. Archaeological explorations from the mid-1980s have revealed, however, that mountain Inuits and their prehistoric ancestors hunted, carved animals and camped in the region from at least 6,000 but more likely 12,000 years ago.[35] A permanent settlement has only existed in Wiseman since the beginning of the twentieth century. If gold fever had not gripped the American Northwest, Kalhabuk would have not come across the mountains to settle here with her three children to hunt (and prepare) meat for gold prospectors; Ruth would not be here either and the Inuits would still live in harmony with the rhythms of nature. Without gold, Wiseman would not exist.[36]

An abandoned caravan.

## Fortune and gold

Wiseman's heyday (if a frontier settlement of wooden cabins can have a 'heyday') lasted just seven years from 1908 to 1915. During this period, plenty of whiskey flowed. In 1915 alone, sixty tons of alcohol for 300 white settlers and 75 indigenous people were shipped northwards. 'Whiskey', wrote Marshall, 'had the priority over everything else, and the trail never got so bad they couldn't haul whisky up here, no matter how scarce the food might bethe road was never in too bad a condition not to transport whiskey, even when food became scarce.' The number of prostitutes in Wiseman reached a record high in 1915 when there were fourteen. From 1920, the number sank back down to zero. Between 1907 and 1911, gold prospectors near Wiseman (Nolan Creek and its tributaries) dug more gold here than in the whole of remaining northern Alaska. And just when mining in Nolan was starting to decline, a small group of gold prospectors excavated a million dollars worth of gold from great depths in the nearby Hammond River Valley in just five years from 1911 to 1915.[37]

When we find out that there is still a working gold mine some sixteen kilometres away from Wiseman in the Nolan Valley, we set off to visit it. The route takes us partly by car and then on foot through an indescribably beautiful taiga landscape with lakes and brooks and stagnant bodies of water, as well as low spruce trees, birch and aspens, lichens and mosses, tussock grasses and Arctic cotton. Then we suddenly come to a locked barrier, a stop sign and a notice warning us, 'Danger. Do not enter. Authorized personnel only.' Permitted visitors should register in the mining office. We aren't authorised, yet continue on our way until a voice shouts: 'What are you doing here? There's no way through!' In the middle of the Nolan River a woman in a red anorak, high gumboots, a headband and sunglasses stands with a bear whistle around her neck, an old leather belt and a gun stuck in her holster. The longer we talk, the friendlier she becomes. 'I live here', says Sheriar Erickson. There is no one up at the mine at the moment. Sheriar takes us, one at a time, across the river on her quad, the bed of which glitters goldenly. She invites us into an old gold prospector's cabin and introduces us to her partner Jeff, whom she met seven years ago on a trip around the world. In Nolan, her travels came to an end. She thinks that us walking kilometres on foot is 'reckless'. 'Why didn't you come by car? You can drive to the mine. Did you see the grizzly? A grizzly mother with her cubs?' Jeff waves his hand dismissively. Grizzly bears are shy, unlike brown bears. But

## Wiseman, Alaska. 'The Happiest Civilization'

when the mine is in operation, they come because the mineworkers always have barbecues. And the bears smell the meat. This summer the bears have been especially hungry. Even so, in the north, they're not as big as they are in the south, where they can fish to their heart's content.[38]

We'd expected the Nolan goldmine, which is ironically called 'Silverado', to be in full operation. But no one has been mining here for a year and a half. From descriptions by the American writer Philip Caputo, we knew that, until a few years ago, thirty miners and a bulldozer driver had worked in the Silverado mine and excavated 'half a mountainside'. Jeff shows us his 'personal bulldozer', which arrived in Wiseman and Nolan in the 1920s. The vehicle, now completely covered in rust, is an International and bears the weather-beaten skull of a mountain goat on its cooler.[39] 'When I came here in 1975 after returning from Vietnam', says Jeff Lund, 'I moved into the chapel in Wiseman. Back then, there were three old-timers still living there.' By that, he means Charlie Breck, Ross Brockman and Harry Leonard, all gold prospectors who had looked for gold before the Second World War. Right at the beginning, shovels were still used in Nolan. But with new technology and mechanical shovels, great mounds of earth could be moved, Jeff explains, 'thousands of yards a day'. The old mines could be scoured again and deeper deposits sought. After a boom in gold prices, investments in old mines became attractive once again 'to mine the rest of the gold'. This meant that business started up again in Nolan in the 1990s. Jeff didn't come to the Arctic as a gold prospector but as a pipeline construction worker. 'What does gold mean to me?' He shows us a lump of gold that he found by chance. 'It feels warm', says Jeff, 'not cold, like metal usually does. Luckily I never got bitten by the gold fever bug. Perhaps I'll strike lucky one day. There are people here who make a living from it.'[40] Nolan's gold mine was known for nuggets worth more money than just their value per weight. 'Rich people like to put things like that on their desks and in one casino in Las Vegas, there's a Nolan nugget on display.'

Most gold mines, Jeff reports, have been abandoned. There are 'bad guys' at the old mines, 'especially in remote parts'. Drug dealers, black-market brokers, importers. Marihuana is grown in old mining settlements. In the past, the government didn't check the mines at all because they didn't have enough money to do so. Now, a state official drops in on Nolan from time to time.

I try to imagine how the old 'sourdoughs' (the name for experienced gold prospectors) used to live in Wiseman and Nolan. Black-and-white photographs and Super-8 films from the Elmer E. Rasmuson Library at the University of Fairbanks vividly conjure up their stories, such as that of Harry Leonard. He came to Alaska from Maine in 1928 and settled in Fairbanks with his fiancée. First, he worked in the machine hall of a gold company and then as a suit-wearing salesman for a Chevrolet dealer. But from one day to the next, he left behind his creased pants and tie, his partner and the whole of civilisation and dedicated the rest of his life to searching for Arctic gold. In 1934 he ended up near Wiseman. He lived here for half a century with his dogs, tirelessly prospecting, felling trees, hunting wolves and building gold sluices, bought himself a Jeep in 1950, which was flown in on a DC-3, shot Super-8 films and renovated abandoned cabins to resell them (which earned him the derisive nickname of 'the Capitalist').[41] In many photos, Leonard – who was described by his friend George Lounsbury as 'eccentric' and 'unapproachable' – is almost always grinning, toothless and in a hat, alongside Inuits and other miners, a sand and gravel pump in one hand and, more than once, a pan full of nuggets in the other. Harry Leonard didn't strike it rich, but that was the case for most gold prospectors in Alaska. He spent his retirement in the Pioneers of Alaska old folks' home in Fairbanks.[42]

I try and imagine the landscape seen from a bird's eye perspective and with the mindset of an environmental historian. The gold fever that started in the mid-1800s in California and surged via Canada's Klondike gold rush up through Alaska is considerably responsible for today's map of Alaska. Camps, settlements and small towns sprang up everywhere that gold was found. But this wasn't the case in the mid-1800s. In 1850, when Alaska was still part of Russia, the mining engineer Peter Petrovich Doroshin discovered gold on the Kenai Peninsula. But the Russian czar was more interested in the 'soft gold' of furs from polar foxes, beavers, river and sea otters. The last thing he needed was a barely controllable gold rush that would bring countless fortune-seekers to Alaska. That's why the discovery of gold deposits there was kept secret.[43]

After the acquisition of Alaska by the USA in 1867, however, the situation changed completely: gold mining in the new territory was viewed favourably and, at the end of the nineteenth century, Alaska experienced a stampede. The first settlements appeared in the far south, near Juneau, and spread northwards. Juneau was the first American town to be established in Alaska and was almost named Pilztown, after the German mining engineer George Pilz, who was supplied gold and other minerals by Chief Kowee of the Auke tribe of the Tlingit people. Because of these findings, the fjord town of Juneau, which is still inaccessible by road today, became the capital of Alaska. Fairbanks and Nome, too, were founded and owe their continuing importance today to gold mining alone: they are still the most populous cities in Alaska. Only the administrative and industrial city of Anchorage is significantly larger.

Over the last hundred years, engineers and miners from all over the world have disrupted the Alaskan landscape far more radically than in the 15,000 years before. Despite the relatively sparse population of Alaska, man-made changes to its surface over the last century are certainly greater than the transformations caused by nature, such as volcanic eruptions or erosion. A railway line from Fairbanks to the southern coast near Seward was built at great expense. And in the north, gold-mining camps and settlements were created right up to the Brooks Range. Like in Nolan and Wiseman, the earth was excavated in thousands of places, mountains heaped up, and streams diverted. The only exceptions were the swampy Yukon floodplain and the North Slope – the mountain slopes in the far north. Most minor excavations were unsuccessful. They often only left ghost camps behind. The lion's share of gold production in Alaska is handled by four giant industrial gold mines. The Fort Knox mine northeast of Fairbanks, Alaska's largest gold mine, produces approximately 250 kilograms of gold every day. Over 1.5 billion dollars in gold was mined in the record year of 2013 alone, and 1.3 million tons of gold between 1880 and 2017 – an inconceivable amount. To transport this quantity of gold in railway wagons would require at least 220 freight trains, each with fifty of the most modern railway wagons fully loaded with gold.[44]

Gold prospecting was never carried out on a large scale in Wiseman and the surrounding area. From their historic gold mining hut, Jeff Lund and Sheriar Erickson have a view of the Silverado mine, the rubble mountains, offices and vehicles and the vast areas that have been levelled. What keeps them in Nolan is not the mine but the indescribable beauty of nature. Just a few kilometres from the border of the Gates of the Arctic National Park, a spectacular panorama unfolds. Initially, Jeff only wanted to use his gold mining hut in the summer. But then he realised that up here near the mine, he doesn't have to pay rent, unlike in Wiseman. There is no property tax, no telephone, no computer, no television, no garbage fee and no sales tax.[45] With a visibly cheerful expression on his face, he continues: 'You catch a moose, you have a small garden, and a hole in the ground as your refrigerator. And suddenly life doesn't cost much anymore.' 'We have plenty of time to read', adds Sheriar. And indeed, the walls of their small log cabin are lined with bookshelves from top to bottom, stocked primarily with classic novels and philosophers like Descartes. 'In winter', says Sheriar, 'it's all ours.' There are a few animals, like Boreal chickadees, Canada jays and ravens. They have to ski six kilometres to fetch water. And they have to use the two and a half to three hours of semi-darkness in the winter to go out. Then 'the snowmelt is incredible, an onrush of new life in spring. The birds have chicks. Everything has to be done quickly.' As we listen to them, my thoughts turn to Robert Marshall. Perhaps Sheriar and Jeff in Nolan and Jack Reakoff, Uta and Bernie Hicker are some of the 'happiest folk', like those he found in Wiseman ninety years ago.[46]

## The Gates of the Arctic

Wiseman's happiness has a name: The Gates of the Arctic National Park. Just beyond the Nolan gold mine, west of the sixteen-kilometre-wide Dalton Highway corridor, where all roads end and the wilderness takes over, the area of the northernmost national park on the North American continent starts: the Gates of the Arctic National Park and Preserve. Wiseman's hinterland has remained largely untouched because of the huge nature reserves in northern Alaska. Without them, the region would look very different today: due to its mineral resources, development would have been difficult to avoid.

The Gates of the Arctic National Park spans part of the Brooks Range, named after geologist Alfred Hulse Brooks. The mountain range, which was originally twice as high and has been eroded over long periods, is geographically a continuation of the Rocky Mountains, but a separate geological formation. Hundreds of thousands of years ago, a prairie existed here, which was driven upwards by tectonic shifts and formed mountain peaks. Since the continental plates were once below sea level, you can still find marine fossils on the peaks of mountains in the middle of the Arctic. It was only in recent geological times that an ice age began. Glaciers, whose meltwater shifted and changed the landscape, now sustain a variety of streams and rivers. Six major rivers have been declared protected areas by the National Wild and Scenic Rivers Act.[47] Parts of the Gates of the Arctic National Park have been declared a preserve; together with the adjacent Noatak area, it forms the largest 'wilderness area' in the USA. The name of the park, established by President Jimmy Carter in 1980, goes back to Robert Marshall. He thought that two mountains (Frigid Crags and Boreal Mountain) looked like a natural portal and so he named it the Gates of the Arctic. Marshall was fascinated by terra incognita – and nowhere in North America at the time was there such a huge unchartered area as the Brooks Range. Owing to Marshall's trip to Wiseman and his writing, the region had already been discussed for decades as a potential area for a national park.

From a European perspective, the scale of the Gates of the Arctic National Park is gigantic. At 30,448 square kilometres, it covers an area larger than the whole of Belgium; yet only just over 10,000 visitors come every year. Only in specially designated areas are hunting enthusiasts with a permit allowed to shoot game. The people of Wiseman once resisted closing parts of the national park to hunters and turning them into reserves.[48] But overall, those we speak to are happy that the US federal government has protected extensive areas of northern Alaska. Hunting and fishing are only allowed for the local population in many places to make a living, but even here restrictions apply.[49] People from outside also have some advantages. In the summer, Susan Holly works for the National Park in Bettles (a couple of hours by snow sledge from Wiseman) and spends from October to March with her husband hunting and trapping in a cabin in the park; she is disappointed that tourists are allowed to travel by sports aircraft to some areas of the Gates of the Arctic National Park, whereas residents have to use traditional means such as dog sledges, snowmobiles and boats to transport solar panels, batteries and dog food (1.5 tons per year!) to remote hunting areas.

The establishment of the national park and wilderness areas is the result of conflicts of interest and political disputes that go back a long way. The extremely short version of the story is: two camps with opposing ideologies have always existed in Alaska. In one camp, some see economic benefits from gas and oil extraction, and subordinate everything to progress, playing down environmental damage. In the other camp sustainability advocates acknowledge that the long-term consequences of exploiting nature are hazardous: they support ecological protection measures. Arguments of both groups have a particular tradition in the USA. Many American pioneers saw the expansion and development of the vast North American continent as 'divine destiny'. But when national parks – starting with Yellowstone in 1872 – were created, nature conservation representatives also established a specifically American institution. In Alaska, these two philosophies have taken up irreconcilable positions, more so than in other parts of the USA. The majority of Alaska's inhabitants represent the ideology of progress. This camp also receives support from proponents of the raw materials industries, commercial interests, the Juneau government and most Republican deputies.

It is opposed by environmental associations, the government in Washington, especially when led by Democrats (it is responsible for setting up most protected natural areas), the national press and the majority of Democrats.

The promoters of the doctrine of exploitation appear to have an advantage because they can appeal to the short-term economic needs of citizens and outbid their opponents financially – through advertising, lobbying, campaigns and court proceedings. Especially in underdeveloped Alaska, which owes its wealth to natural resources such as gold, oil and gas, the pioneering concept of Manifest Destiny still finds fertile ground today.[50] Emptiness and cold, seclusion and the sparse population had led many scientists and politicians to push radical plans and infrastructure projects, often in the name of national security, without exploring the ecological consequences. One example was Project Chariot, a proposal that would have created a gigantic crater and an underground port using thermonuclear bombs in 1958 in the far north of Alaska – ironically close to a place called Point Hope. Advocates of the project downplayed, if not completely denied, the effects that nuclear contamination would have on Inuit bodies.[51]

Dalton Highway and oil pipeline, north of the Gates of the Arctic National Park.

Environmental protectionists were able to stop Project Chariot and push through a series of initiatives that were not of high interest to large corporations: programmes to rescue polar bears and Greenland whales, as well as the protection of bald eagles and waterfowl in the Yukon Delta. However, environmental associations were often powerless to stop oil extraction in Prudhoe Bay, the construction of the Dalton Highway or underground nuclear tests on the uninhabited Aleutian island of Amchitka – projects all backed by the federal government. (Nonetheless, the Amchitka nuclear project led directly to the creation of Greenpeace.)[52] Protests against projects on national territory are occasionally successful. If, however, the land belongs to the state of Alaska, the chances for sustainability advocates are almost always worse; and environmental associations are the least effective against the economic interests of indigenous people. Nevertheless, environmental awareness has increased overall across the board in recent decades, and ecology advocates have been able to delay or halt several major projects. In general, the dispute over Alaska's almost untouched nature resembles an ongoing tennis match, in which the opponents watch each other closely, constantly adjust their technique, and coordinate and improve their movements. Each successful strike may be followed by a barely preventable counterattack. Following Donald Trump's presidency, for instance, supporters of oil and gas production suddenly gained the upper hand, while environmentalists found themselves in the role of deflection and defence. The administration of Joe Biden in turn suspended oil drilling leases in the Arctic National Wildlife Refuge, thereby reversing a signature achievement of the Trump presidency. Had it been up to the Trump administration, the gates of the arctic would have been flung wide open for drilling rigs in the northern tip of Alaska.[53]

## Past and future

Why did Wiseman survive? We asked ourselves that when we arrived there. It is astonishing that it still exists when you think of the fate of other gold-mining locations. What kept the village's inhabitants in the Arctic? Here, as elsewhere, people have always lived off the resources that secured their survival. The indigenous population hunted animals that regularly migrated through the area; and, with the discovery of gold, some rugged men were able to eke out a reasonably secure existence. 'In the Wiseman area, gold is not simply extracted from streams and rivers, but usually from deep-hole drilling', Jack Reakoff explained. 'The get-rich-quick types didn't like this area.' Civil engineering requires time and patience. In Wiseman, therefore, the people who settled were industrious, stubborn and tenacious. Those who lived here could not rely on regular deliveries of food and equipment. Instead, many became hunters, gatherers or trappers, and like the Reakoff or Hicker family they continue this way of life today as a part of their livelihood. When gold supplies ran low, the construction of the oil pipeline brought work to all those who could prove residence in Wiseman. Again, a natural resource and its high value drew people to the north. The opening of the Dalton Highway also contributed to Wiseman's survival. Since the village can be reached by car, tourists – not in droves, but from all over the world – have visited the remote village, many of them to see the spectacular Northern Lights. As a result, an abstract value – the beauty of nature and the untouched expanse of the surrounding protected areas – has become a consumable natural resource.[54]

Wiseman is not Alaska. But our visit to the region and an attempt to understand the reality of people's lives and the dynamics of nature in a larger historical context brings to light tensions and challenges, realities and opportunities that are important not only for Wiseman but far beyond. What surprises us on our journeys north from Wiseman (towards the oil fields of Prudhoe Bay, the largest in the USA) and finally back to Fairbanks, is the concurrent existence of things that are non-concurrent: the remoteness of the Arctic world and its connection to the global economy (via pipelines, tankers and the Internet); satellites and subsistence economy; nature conservation and oil spills (of which only the large ones grab media headlines); the apparent constancy of a landscape and its change during the present climate crisis; the simultaneity of past and present.

Fifty million years ago, Alaska had a hot, humid climate, similar to present-day Florida. It took millions of years for the once vast tropical forests to evaporate and be ground into oil and natural gas. What was irreplaceably produced by nature over millions of years has been consumed almost completely within three generations of humans. Was it worth it? If so, for whom?

Here in the north, unlike in Anchorage, where almost all tourists end up, the extreme contradiction of Alaska becomes visible: the contrast between radical protection and the perilous exploitation of nature. This is where the controversy over the meaning of protected areas arises 'where man is only a visitor' (in the wording of the US Wilderness Act of 1964). How important is it to preserve areas that are largely untouched by humans? Indigenous groups and the inhabitants of Wiseman claim that hunting should not be ruled out. Others make a plea for extracting resources 'to a limited extent'.

But there is also criticism of preserving the wilderness. The environmental historian William Cronon once warned against perceiving untapped nature, especially in Alaska, as divine and the epitome of a perfect, primitive past, a place where people (often men) can discover their true (bestial) nature. Doesn't this imply, Cronon thought, that elsewhere, the places people live in are tainted and unworthy because they have lost their original natural resources? And doesn't it follow that less spectacular places are automatically judged as disposable and played down in importance?[55]

When Johannes Heisig and I leave the north and return to air-polluted cities built on sealed ground, we're convinced that it is valuable per se to leave parts of the globe to their own devices. The fact that ancient subsistence practices and ecologies have been preserved north of the Arctic Circle, alongside technological oil-producing landscapes of the twenty-first century, is of global interest today. The wilderness of Alaska has become an emblematic place, both nationally and internationally. It conveys a message: even if you can, human beings, don't subjugate every corner of the globe to your power! For many, this slogan may not be enough in the age of man-made global warming – and rightly so. Rising temperatures have long since caused glaciers to melt, permafrost to thaw, tree lines to move higher faster, and animals and plants to migrate or die out. What failed miserably almost a hundred years ago – sustainable vegetable production in the Matanuska Valley – is no longer a utopia. Wiseman's future and happiness won't be decided locally. Both oil interests and conservation initiatives have their most effective lobbies in national and international centres of power. But what becomes of Wiseman (in particular) and the Arctic North (in general), and which historical and ecological decisions come to reign in the future, will be a barometer of how Americans deal with their continent and how humans deal with the planet as a whole.

Malibu

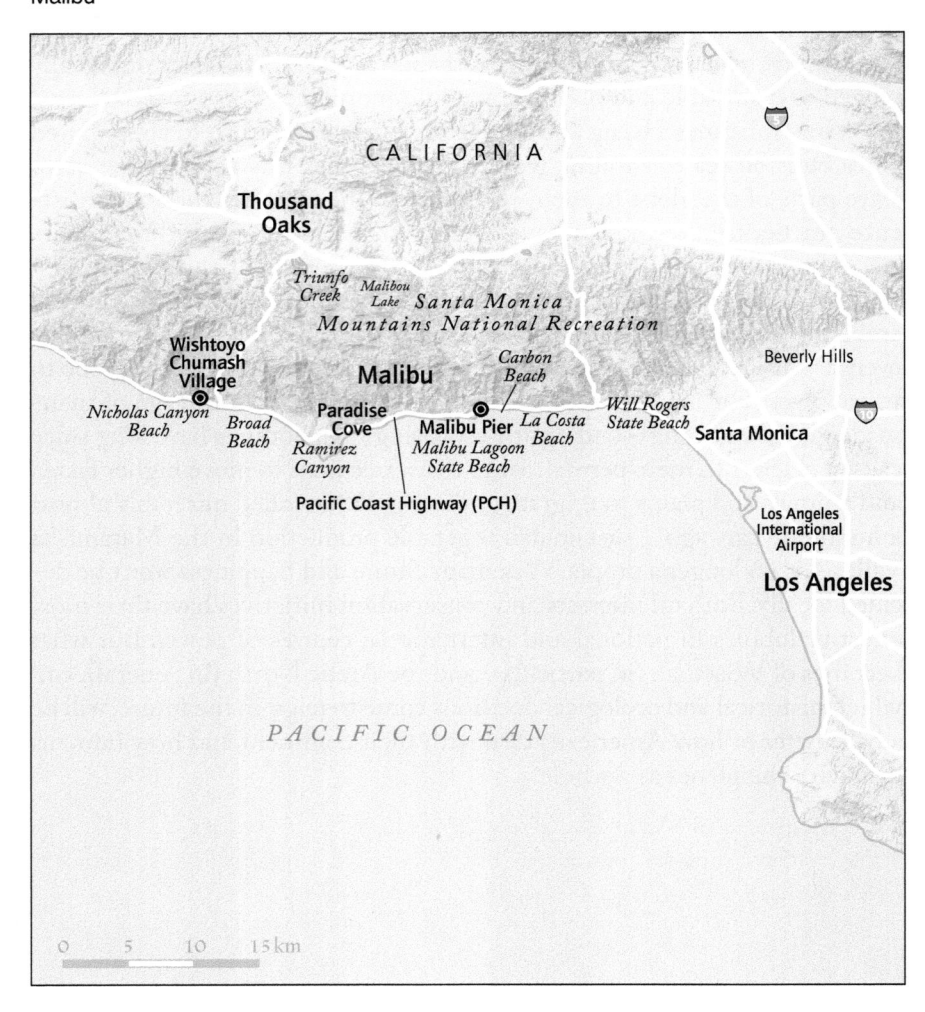

# Malibu, California.
## Stranger than Paradise

### Stranger than Paradise

On postcards, Malibu looks like paradise on earth. It's a haven of beaches and palm trees with idyllic sunsets and wave-riding surfers. A refuge for multimillionaires and Hollywood celebrities. A secluded wonderland of earthly delights. A Garden of Eden made in America.

Since the nineteenth century, the most attractive properties with stunning ocean views have belonged to a small, wealthy elite. Tension between private entitlement and public interest has shaped disputes in this city; debates initially centred on the construction of a coastal road whereas, today, access to the beach is a crucial bone of contention.

Many consider Malibu a Pacific paradise of the highest calibre, although the city regularly hits the headlines when it is struck by countless natural disasters, from wildfires to landslides and winter storms to floods. Most of the celebrities who live in this region cultivate eco-friendly images and consider themselves environmental activists. But how sustainable is life in Malibu in truth? What drew people here? Throughout history and in the present day, how have they accommodated the environment and the frequent natural disasters that occur in the region into their lives?

If you've ever taken the train from San Francisco to Los Angeles, you'll never forget the spectacular views of the Pacific Ocean from the Coast Starlight. Strangely, just before reaching Malibu, the train takes a turn inland and begins to ascend a steep incline. No engineer would voluntarily build a railroad through mountains when there is a coast nearby. So why does the train turn off here and avoid Malibu? And why is the hinterland so unspoiled in comparison to nearby Los Angeles?

Malibu is an odd place. Here, the sky seems a shade bluer, the sand whiter and the sea fresher than elsewhere. And yet, all three of these aspects belong to a paradise with pitfalls. There's more to this land of milk and honey than meets the eye. On my journey through this landscape and through research, I'm off to find out why.[1]

# Paradise Blues

Malibu sunset.

## Arriving in Malibu

On the way from Los Angeles to Malibu, I see more joggers and cyclists than anywhere else in the USA. There isn't much traffic – which is, I know, a rare thing. Normally on sunny days, an endless stream of traffic edges its way along the southern Californian coastal road for miles. But when I arrive in Malibu, it's midweek in January.

'Malibu – 27 miles of scenic beauty', says a sign at the city limits. It's a bold proclamation of the city's beauty. Soon, I discover an Eco Auto Spa – what might that be? On the forecourt next to a row of sports cars, none with less than 400 hp under their hoods, stands a man called Ed with a chamois leather. 'Not exactly the most eco cars you've got there', I can't help saying. Although I'm grinning, Ed doesn't appreciate my joke. Instead, I receive a lecture on how ecological Malibu is. 'Residents here pay for conservation', he says, going on to explain the assets of his car hand-wash services, emphasising the care he uses. 'People want to do their cars a good turn. And we think it's important that no oil gets washed off into the water run-off.' My first impression, then, is that Malibu wants to pass itself off as a paradise for nature and ecology, a sunny spot for the rich and beautiful – and for twelve-cylinder cars.

One of my first ports of call in Malibu is the beach bar in the Paradise Cove bathing spot where countless Hollywood films and TV series have been filmed. Admission to the bar costs two dollars per passenger, five dollars per pedestrian, twenty-five dollars per car, and fifty dollars per bus. 'Sorry, no pets, surfing or fire!' This is how the bar owner keeps mass tourism at bay. On the walls of his establishment, I discover photographs that tell the story of Malibu's early years. Many feature May Knight Rindge, aka the Queen of Malibu, sometimes sporting a long dress, sometimes walking along railroad tracks. So, there *was* once a railroad here; and in the course of my visit and research, I make it my mission to find out about it.

## The Rindge ranch

Mary Knight Rindge arrived in Malibu in 1892 with her husband, oil millionaire Frederick Rindge. The couple bought one of the biggest ranches in the USA, whose boundaries are almost identical to today's Malibu district limits. From the beginning, the Rindges did everything in their power to keep undesirables – that is, tourists, settlers and Chinese smugglers who used the caves along the coast to stash opium – off their property. Frederick Rindge, from Cambridge Massachusetts, had made his fortune as the vice president of the Union Oil Company in Los Angeles. When he offered ten dollars an acre for the Malibu ranch, a hundredfold increase from the previous owner, he didn't just do it so that he could breed cows. He was looking for an unspoiled idyll, a 'farm near the ocean', protected by the mountains', where it would 'not be too hot in summer'.[2]

California was one of the most remote areas in the world until 1848 when the discovery of gold in Sacramento changed almost everything overnight. Gold seekers from every country flocked to the American West. Between 1848 and 1854 alone, the number of immigrants to California grew twentyfold, from around 5,000 to over 300,000, while the numbers of the indigenous population vanished at almost the same pace.[3] For the Frenchman Leon Victor Prudhomme, from whom Frederick Rindge took over Rancho Malibu, the surge of gold seekers and speculators meant good business because they rapidly drove up demand for high-quality beef. In retrospect, it's astonishing that cattle were driven across 700 kilometres from Malibu to the newly discovered goldfields in northern California, even if they fetched incredible prices.[4]

Although much less money was to be made with Rancho Malibu around the turn of the twentieth century than a few decades earlier, cattle breeding was still profitable – even though large regions of California had long been overgrazed, including the Rindge family ranch. Cattle hooves had damaged the soil and, as cattle driver Richard Gird noted in his journal in 1881, 'all kinds of weeds' had sprung up in place of indigenous grasses.[5] Before European settlers arrived, nutrient-rich grasses made up 95 per cent of all plants; by the 1930s, this was reduced to one third.[6] Frederick Rindge, however, was not very interested in ecology. He was far more drawn to the breathtaking beauty of Malibu. He praised 'the lee of the mountains, with a trout brook, wild trees, a lake, good soil, and excellent climate'. He christened Malibu's coast 'the American Riviera'. His friend John Harvard cried 'Ah Italy, thou hast a rival', when he paid Frederick a visit on his Malibu ranch.[7]

There are historical reasons why Malibu turned into a beach paradise, and Los Angeles into a megalopolis. An oil boom had already swept through Los Angeles in the 1890s, which continued apace between the two world wars on the West Coast. The fact that oil was discovered in LA of all places, where the population was growing faster than anywhere else in the USA, led to levels of real estate speculation that were hitherto unheard of, as well as unplanned construction and accelerated suburbanisation. Los Angeles developed very slowly in the nineteenth century, at first from an area of Mexican ranches whose population predominantly consisted of mestizos and mixed-race families, to a place with extensive orange groves. It broke through the million mark in around 1930 thanks to railroad construction, the location of the petroleum industry and the emergence of the film and aviation industries. In virtually no other place in the world in the early twentieth century was the physical structure of the earth so rapidly and permanently changed as in LA. Within the shortest time, extreme practices that were deemed necessary due to geological formations ruined the original landscape completely, transforming it, as contemporaries described, into a 'Stygian landscape'.[8] Inhabitants in the surrounding town of Torrance even went as far as claiming that their city had been 'sacrificed on the altar of oil'.[9]

## The Rindge story

If Los Angeles reminded people of the underworld, the view across Malibu bay had a 'divine' element, at least for Frederick Rindge.[10] Because his search for oil in Malibu ran, literally, into the sand, Malibu was spared the fate of Los Angeles.

'Here, protected from the wearing haste of city life', as he wrote in his memoirs Happy Days in Southern California, 'here, time flies.' He praised the 'holy hills' and 'calm and sweet retreat', musing upon the fact that the Californian climate promotes longevity and more incentives for a healthy, happy life outdoors than any other place in the world. It had a regenerative and restorative effect, ensuring a long life. For Rindge, California was a 'holy land'. Here, one could live, 'like Victorianno, a native chief', to a biblical 'one hundred thirty-six' years. Like many later residents of Malibu, almost everything turned out differently for Frederick Rindge than he expected. His happy days were soon over. The alleged moderate climate promptly showed its teeth: violent storms and wildfires swept through the canyons towards the sea and were, as Rindge was forced to admit, not the exception but the rule. In 1903, a devastating fire engulfed the family's dream castle in flames. At first, Rindge replaced it with just tents and a wooden hut. Two years after the disaster, he died, aged only 48, from an acute illness. On his deathbed, he urged his wife, May Knight Rindge, who now had three teenagers to bring up on her own, to keep the Malibu ranch intact. Under no circumstances should the Southern Pacific Railroad lay its tracks through their property.

The fact that May Knight Rindge managed to stop the railroad moguls from building along the coast was a feat comparable to David slaying Goliath. The 'Queen', who was prepared to go to any lengths, discovered that the Southern Pacific Railroad only had the right to lay tracks through her property if one did not previously exist. Without hesitation, Rindge resolutely had her own 24-kilometre track built and called it the Malibu and Port Los Angeles Railroad, of which she herself was president. Now and then, grain and cow hides would be shunted as cargo along the route, or she took visitors for walks along the tracks.[11]

When, in the 1910s, the state of California began to plan a coastal highway from Los Angeles to San Francisco, Rindge readied herself for the next battle. She defended her ranch, with violence if necessary. She hired herself a lawyer and made sure that armed cowboys patrolled the barbed wire fences that marked the border to her property. The legal battle of the Queen of Malibu – one of the most legendary in Californian history – finally went to the Supreme Court in Washington. After a long trial between unequal parties, Rindge lost in 1923 and, with her defeat in court, she also lost millions.[12] She was no longer able to live off the income produced by the ranch and saw no alternative but to sell off part of her property. Rindge decided to part with La Costa, an idyllic beach near Malibu lagoon. The sale earned her a staggering sum of $6 million back in 1928.

## Hollywood in Malibu

May Knight Rindge's coastal land was bought by Art Jones, a construction manager, who built rows of modern beach huts on the sand at lightning speed. As it took less than one and a half hours to reach Malibu by car from Hollywood after the highway was built, Jones could let the exclusive properties to Hollywood stars. He set the lease on the ten-metre-wide properties to ten years apiece, hoping to recoup the construction costs within just seven years.

Hollywood, originally a small, nondescript town with citrus groves, evolved into the global capital of the film industry by the end of the 1920s. Because of its moderate climate, the Californian town managed to nudge the former film capital of New York into second place within no time. Unlike the East Coast, southern California's mild weather meant that filming could take place all year round. The length and reliability of daylight were also advantages in the movie business because, in the early days, film producers relied on natural light not only for outdoor scenes but also in studios with their glass roofs. Most of all, movie people were very taken with the variations of the Californian landscape as a backdrop. On the same day, the sinking of the Titanic and a Western could be shot. Mountains and deserts, cliffs, oceans and beaches all lay within easy reach of Hollywood. [13]

Illustrious celebrities such as Jack Warner, the head of Warner Bros Studios, and Clara Bow, the sex symbol of the silent film era, were among the first residents of the Malibu Film Colony. Legendary Western hero Gary Cooper also bought a beach hut on the former Rindge estate on Malibu beach. His neighbours included fashion icon Gloria Swanson, Oscar prizewinner Warner Baxter and actress Dolores del Rio, the 'Princess of Mexico'. British actor Ronald Colman introduced Duke Kahanamoku, the pioneer of modern surfing and surfboard culture, to Malibu from his native Honolulu. From then on, the stream of movie-industry people, from gaffers to paparazzi, never let up. By the late twentieth century, actors like Tom Hanks and Larry Hagman, Bill Murray and Tatum O'Neal, Mel Brooks and Roma Downey, singers Sting and Linda Ronstadt, comedian Harry Mandle, director Rachel Ward, and many others all had pads on Malibu Colony Road or nearby. Since the 1990s, the spotlight of the media and celebrity gossip has never left the bays of Malibu. And yet the story bears a certain irony. By selling a part of her land, May Knight Rindge, the very same woman who fought her whole life to keep her sanctuary in seclusion, inadvertently ensured that Malibu found world fame. The tranquillity she had felt on this patch of earth was well and truly over.

Hollywood's influence was noticeable up past Rindge's ranch, too, in the rocky hinterland of the Santa Monica Mountains. At the end of the Second World War, two investors dug an enormous fifteen-metre pit to create an artificial lake at the confluence of the Medea and Triunfo Creeks. For years, the lakebed remained dry, causing the investors to go bankrupt. But in April 1926, after a devastating spring storm, several million litres of water flowed within a few hours into the pit – and a formidable mountain reservoir was created, which was christened Malibou Lake.[14] Film personalities like Arthur Edeson and actors like Strother Martin, not to mention Ronald Reagan later, settled near the lake. Paramount Pictures and Twentieth Century Fox purchased sizeable estates there, and dozens of directors used the lake and its surroundings as a backdrop for their film sets. Paramount Picture's Western Town, a motion picture set right on the lake, stood in for locales as diverse as Dodge City, Laredo and Salem. The mountains and valleys doubled up for the Ozark mountains and Tom Sawyer's Missouri, the island of Java and mediaeval China. Charlie Chaplin marched around the lake in his hunting uniform in *The Great Dictator*, and the monster from James Whales' horror classic *Frankenstein* drowned a small girl in it. When Hollywood produced *The Adventures of Marco Polo* with Gary Cooper in 1938, herds of elephants and 2,000 costumed horses trampled through Paramount's landscape; a few decades later, on the same site, a post-apocalyptic city was filmed, the primates' habitat in *Planet of the Apes*. It wasn't until the 1970s that the glamour of Malibou Lake began to fade. In the long run, the never-changing landscape could no longer be peddled to increasingly discerning audiences. The Californian backdrop gave way to real-life locations.[15] These days, Paramount's Western Town, and sites such as the legendary Peter Strauss Ranch, are under the administration of the National Park Service.

## The Streisand effect

Just like the Queen of Malibu during her time, Hollywood stars came to Malibu to escape from the outside world. Instead of patrolling cowboys, however, there are now modern alarm systems and walls, fences and warning signs. As I drive through Malibu, I keep on coming up against iron gates at the end of streets with signs that say 'Caution. Armed response'. In the Coen brothers' film *The Big Lebowski* (1998) the fictional Malibu Chief of Police says, 'Now we got a nice, quiet little beach community here, and I aim to keep it nice and quiet.'[16] Yet the seclusion of Hollywood celebrities has only increased movie fans' curiosity and piqued their interest in Malibu. It's known as the 'Streisand effect'. Actress Barbra Streisand lost a $50 million lawsuit against a photographer in 2003 when she tried to sue him for taking photos of her new beach villa on a cliff near Malibu and uploading them onto the Internet. The attempt to suppress the aerial shot that he took to document coastal erosion for the California Coastal Records Project had the opposite effect: it drew attention to Barbra Streisand's luxury property from hundreds of thousands of people, who then downloaded the photographs and caused the said effect.[17]

Before Streisand moved into her villa on the eroding cliffs, she lived in Ramírez Canyon in Malibu. But after a major fire destroyed parts of her house, the actress left the area and bequeathed the property to a landscape conservation organisation, the Santa Monica Mountains Conservancy. During one of my visits to Malibu, I'm lucky to be invited by the Conservancy to do a tour of Streisand's former property behind gates that are normally closed to the general public. Only two cars a day are allowed access. A private street winds along a creek, on both sides of which there are villas with parks in which numerous gardeners are carrying out their work. Enormous oaks, walnut trees, sycamores and exotic plants line the path. At the end of the street, where the Canyon is overgrown with brushwood and becomes steeper, Streisand's property begins. It consists of a total of five residences in five different styles: an art deco house in black, grey, pink and burgundy, a barn with colourful glass windows, a Mediterranean Peach House, a janitor's hut and a wooden lodge with a vaulted roof called Barwood, former residence of a film production company. Then there is a tennis court surrounded by a rose pergola. Mallard ducks waddle around the property. Trumpet-shaped *Eschscholzia californica*, otherwise known as Californian poppies or cups of gold, bloom in the garden. So, *this* is how the stars live behind high metal gates in Malibu.[18]

The residents of Ramírez Canyon Road have successfully fought to keep Streisand's former property out of the public eye – even though it is the headquarters of the non-profit Santa Monica Mountains Conservancy, and access to the organisation should be a matter of course. But where the rich live, other laws apply. The exotic world of parks, gardens and villas in

Malibu, California. Stranger than Paradise

The former Streisand property,
Ramírez Canyon, Malibu.

Malibu's canyons is only accessible to a rarefied elite. The mock Spanish castle on Laudamus Hill, former residence of the Queen of Malibu, which was never completely rebuilt after a disastrous fire in 1931 and sold for a paltry $50,000 in 1942 to the Franciscan Order, is not open to the public either. But after enquiring several times at the Serra Retreat, as it is now called, a place of spiritual contemplation, I am allowed to visit. It is an astonishing mix of lush labyrinths, fountains, statues and a magnificent view across the Pacific. The buildings, outhouses and staircases of the mansion are all adorned with beautiful ceramic tiles. The Queen might not have found oil in Malibu, but she did find rich deposits of yellow-brown and red clay, and an abundance of water that gushed from a source in Sweetwater Canyon. So, for a few years, Rindge operated the Malibu Potteries on this site. After they were destroyed in a fire, however, 9,000 boxes of ceramic tiles were transported up the Laudamus Hill. Over 100 ceramicists, engineers, designers and draughtspeople, administrators and vendors used to work in the factory where three kilns produced more than 2,500 square metres of tiles a month. The potteries had their own showroom in Los Angeles and tiles in Saracen, Moorish and Spanish styles did a roaring trade in California. In the 1920s, those who could afford it had Turkish smoking rooms and simulated tiled Persian carpets constructed. The most spectacular architectural testimony to this time is the Adamson House in Malibu, which used to be the home of the Rindge family's daughter. The villa on the beach displays all the characteristics of Spanish Colonial Revival style: red tiled roofs, arched doorways, windows with wrought-iron grilles, Mexican-style tiled open fireplaces, numerous balconies and terraces, bathrooms, swimming pools and fountains.[19]

On the former site of the Malibu Potteries on Carbon Beach in Malibu, there is now a gathering of stars from the film and music industries. And, while the entrances to the villa communities in Malibu's canyons remain strictly closed to unbidden visitors, activists have been rattling the gates to Malibu's beach properties for several years, first and foremost, the environmentalist Jenny Price.

In January 2010, I have a meeting with Jenny. It takes me a while to decipher the email message: 'Let's meet tomorrow. PCH 22126. 3 pm'. 22126 is the number of the house along the Pacific Coast Highway. The Carbon Beach villa belongs to multimillionaire music and film producer David Geffen. No parking is allowed in front of the house. Geffen has made sure of this by having four fake garage doors built. It seems unlikely to me that Jenny Price, the activist who has declined invitations to university professorships out of principle, is a friend of Geffen's. As it turns out, I'm right. When I meet Jenny, she shows me a narrow passageway to the beach right next to Geffen's property. For years, the Los Angeles Urban Rangers, an environmental organisation that she co-founded, have been patrolling the beach. From afar, the uniforms of the young women could be mistaken for National Park Rangers, the only difference being their badges. 'The public thinks this is a private beach', Jenny says. 'In truth, only a small part of the beach belongs to the residents. And we Rangers are fighting to make public beaches accessible not just for residents but also for everyone.' The Urban

# Malibu, California. Stranger than Paradise

Rangers organise what they call safaris: in upbeat language, safari participants are informed about their rights and duties on the beach. Together they survey the public section of the beach and engage in 'beach activities' as conspicuously as they can. Their subversive antics include arranging deckchairs, doing gymnastics, drinking lemonade, applying sunscreen, reading trashy magazines and building sandcastles. In doing so, the Urban Rangers simply want to reverse prevailing perceptions: rather than seeing the beach as a private space with an adjacent ocean, they try to show that it is public land with adjacent private properties. It's no wonder that some residents in their luxury villas feel provoked by the beachgoers. Verbal attacks on the safari participants are not uncommon.[20] But the Rangers don't give up. And since Jenny and her colleagues have developed an app called Our Malibu Beaches, marking public access to the Pacific, tens of thousands of visitors have started using what were formerly considered strictly private beaches.[21]

For years, David Geffen also opposed public use of 'his' beach, employing tricks and the best lawyers – but in vain. In 2015, Geffen put villa No 22126 on the Pacific Coast Highway up for sale for $100 million and eventually sold it for $85 million. A drop in the ocean for Geffen, who owns countless other villas.[22]

## Chumash

Not far from Geffen's villa, at No 33904 on the Pacific Coast Highway, I meet Mati Waiya in Chumash Village, a guy who has a postcode but little else in common with Hollywood stars. Mati, with whom I arranged a meeting by email, lives in a trailer. Long before I see him, I hear his dogs, who hurtle across his fenced-off property directly towards the locked garden gate I'm standing behind. When he comes to greet me, he teases a little, saying 'Haven't you bought me a present? In our culture, it's customary for guests to bring a present for their host.' Mati is in his mid-fifties, with long, tightly combed-back hair and a bone stuck through his pierced nose. His clothes smell very strongly of burnt sage. 'My ancestors', he explains, 'used sage to disguise their body odour when hunting as a way to become one with nature.' Mati Waiya presents himself as a Chumash Indian. 'The Chumash lived where there is water nowadays. The land and ocean formed the basis of their lives. They lived off fishing, hunting, and gathering. They were afraid of the natural world, but they also respected it.' Mati reminds me that the name Malibu, originally *Humaliwo*, comes from the language of the Chumash. It means something like 'where the surf is loud'.

Twenty-five years ago, Waiya was working as a building contractor and wearing a suit. But in the 1990s, he began to reflect on the cultural values of the Chumash, which his mother had taught him. Today he lives on public land provided by the Los Angeles County Department of Beaches and Harbors, and represents the Wishtoyo Foundation, which sees itself as a bridge between 'the wisdom of the old Chumash culture' and 'present-day environmental issues'. 'There are at least eight Chumash sites in a radius of half a mile around here', Waiya says. On his property, there are several domed Chumash dwellings, known as *aps*, each about seven meters in diameter, made using simple tools and curved willow branches. One of them is a sauna, an *apa'yik*. In a fireplace in the earth, rocks are 'heated to extremely high temperatures', Mati explains 'so that the hot air can drive toxins out of your body as you sweat'.

Mati is particularly proud of his replica of a *tomol* – a canoe at least twice as long as a regular one – which is made of redwood planks, fibre ropes and

Mati Waiya, voice of Malibu's Chumash natives; domed dwelling reconstruction in the background.

pine resin. The Chumash were able to sail quickly from village to village along the coast in these boats with a capacity of up to ten people. Fishermen caught prey using harpoons and curved hooks.[23] Even today, there are more than two dozen different species of whale off the coast of California – among them dolphins, tooth whales and beaked whales – as well as seals, sea lions and sea otters. However, the profusion of marine life must have been incalculable during the golden age of Chumash culture, which lasted from 4,000 to 6,000 BCE. In their religion, both the dolphin and the orca played leading roles. Early soapstone carvings by the Chumash always show a smiling orca.[24]

Among the almost 3,000 inhabitants registered in the Malibu census of 2010, only twenty declared their ethnicity as Native American. Place names like Lompoc, Ojai, Pismo Beach, Point Mugu, Piru, Castaic, Saticoy and Simi Valley testify to the population of Chumash people that spread from San Luis Obispo to Los Angeles, an area of several hundred kilometres.[25] Explorers and missionaries who advanced to southern California in the sixteenth century depicted the indigenous population with a mixture of fascination and alienation. Juan Paez, for example, objected to the long hair of the tribespeople as well as their various trinkets made of flint, bone and wood. Pater Pedro Font was very taken in 1776 by the 'good-looking women' and the tribesmen's perforated ears into which they stuck small rolls of wild tobacco. He was also fascinated by the barge boats he saw, decorated with small shells, and sometimes painted red. In 1769, Brother Crespi took notes on their preparation of meals, observing that fish and seeds were cooked in a hole in the ground and fried.[26] Mati Waiya spends half the day with me strolling around his property, often glancing at the horizon as if looking for the legacy of the Chumash. Admiration expressed in early documents did nothing to avert the fate of the Chumash once outsiders arrived. Based on conservative estimates, the number of Native Americans in California sank in the mid-nineteenth century by eighty per cent. Those who were not eradicated mixed with settlers from other parts of the world and took on their religions and names.[27] *Humaliwo*, the former culture of the Chumash, renamed Malibu, fell prey to the inexorable tide of change.

## Renaturing

Just a few paces from Chumash village, Mati Waiya shows me Nicholas Canyon Creek. There, the Wishtoyo Foundation has restored an extensive wetland biotope with substantial funding from state and private institutions.

They have radically removed all non-native plant species because, they claim, these deplete the soil of moisture and nutrients. Hordes of volunteers – from primary school children in Santa Monica to youth organisations in Oxnard and helpers from the National Park Service – lend a helping hand, clearing rubble and weeds to free up the bed of Nicholas Canyon Creek. In contrast to the opulent, exotic and invasive flora that can be found in the gardens of the rich and famous in Malibu, where pines and palms grow, in the small area of Nicholas Canyon Creek just a few kilometres from Paradise Cove, unassuming and rare plants such as Alkali heath (*Frankenia salina*), bulrushes (*Juncus*) and saltbushes (*Atriplex*) grow. These used to dominate broad swathes of southern California, thereby protecting the soil, which is susceptible to erosion. The fact that hydrologists and environmental engineers rather than the likes of Mati Waiya designed this landscape to regulate rainwater drainage and control flooding is not evident from the landscape.[28]

'Nature knew her business when she developed the chaparral', wrote Francis M. Fultz, an early Californian conservationist and member of the Sierra Club. 'Without their coat of chaparral', the 'mountains [would be] defenceless against the elements.'[29] Several hundred years ago, almost all southern Californian hillsides were overgrown with underbrush, once known as an elfin forest. Without human intervention, the oily brushwood naturally burns away every fifteen to thirty years. For centuries, in fact, wildfires that occurred periodically kept California's unique ecosystem alive with chaparral, oaks and sage brushes.

The Chumash cleared areas to cultivate arable crops, interfering with the cycles of nature, and then regularly burned the underwood more often than it would naturally occur. This kept grizzly bears at bay, increased the wildlife population and ensured the long-term preservation of soil structure by recycling nutrients. But most of all, it kept in check the devastating wildfires that occur when scrubland grows into large bushes.

The contrast between the flora around Nicholas Creek and the well-maintained lawns, palms and exotic plants of the private villas could not be any greater. On the one hand, you see the rugged, dark green carpet and on the other, garish colours and large blossoms. When you stand on the land of the Wishtoyo Foundation, you could even forget that this is the twenty-first century. The image becomes completely surreal when Mati Waiya, in full Indian regalia of deerskin and feathers, performs ritual songs and dances or speaks up for the protection of dolphins or condors, or protests to audiences of school classes or politicians against the urban sprawl of Malibu.

Malibu, California. Stranger than Paradise

## Paradise in flames

When the Spanish colonised California and the *vaqueros* arrived, the forerunners of cowboys, Malibu's landscape slowly began to change. When the Rindge family bought their land, and the influx of Hollywood stars began, interference with native flora and fauna rose rapidly. Malibu's new residents did not have visions of hunting grounds and certainly not of fire to clear scrubland. Their vision was a multi-coloured world with gardens and palms like on the Riviera. They brought with them many Mediterranean and South American plants, or even South African plants, such as plumbago, coral and flame trees.[30] In the twentieth century, the dark thicket of the Canyon receded and was replaced by grand villa estates where roses, camellias and azaleas grew along picturesque roads. From then on, smaller wildfires were routinely extinguished, and the ancient scrubland grew unimpeded. When I meet the chief of the Malibu Fire Department, Andrew Gosser, he explains: 'Malibu is highly flammable. The trees brought by the settlers from Europe go up in flames like matches.' In Malibu, Gosser says, the devastation is so great because of the unprecedented accumulation of oily biomass.[31] Fire always has the potential to destroy, but the combination of strong desert winds, a high proportion of essential oils in chaparral and the conglomeration of luxury villas in Malibu's spectacular landscape is unrivalled elsewhere in the USA. When a fire breaks out here, hundreds of millions of dollars of destruction are threatened in no time.

Fire has spared nothing and no one in the history of Malibu. In 1929, just in time for the housewarming of the Malibu movie colony, thirteen Hollywood huts went up in flames. A year later, Decker Canyon in Malibu's hinterland was destroyed by fire and more than a thousand firefighters could do nothing but stand and watch the spectacle as Santa Ana winds fanned the flames. Six years later the Malibu Lake clubhouse fell victim to a terrible fire. And so on, and so on.[32] In November 1993, a fire in old Topanga Canyon blazed out of control. The flames destroyed the over-sixty-year-old shrubbery and old huts, which were completely exposed. At incredible speed, the Great Malibu Fire sped towards the Pacific and consumed more than eighty hectares of land in ten minutes; within an hour, according to official reports from the Fire Department of Los Angeles, the figure had already reached 400 hectares.[33] Santa Ana winds reached speeds of over 110 kilometres per hour, and turbulence caused by the fire exacerbated the disaster. Three people lost their lives, and 400 private and business buildings were destroyed, causing insurance damage costs of $540 million. Despite Malibu's sparse population, the Old Topanga Fire became one of the most costly wildfire disasters in American history. This caused enormous damage, consuming not only buildings in other parts of southern California, but also two of Malibu's landmarks, Castle Kashan and the Presbyterian Church.[34]

With each major fire, calls from Malibu's residents for safeguarding and support grow louder. The sums of state funds, tax reliefs and subsidies that Malibu and its residents have received in recent decades are hard to estimate. But the amount is certainly in the billions. The state spends far less money on fire prevention than on compensation. One day, when Adamson House is closed to the public, I meet a group of young women in orange suits. The words 'CDC Prisoner' are printed in large letters on their uniforms, the abbreviation for California Department of Corrections and Rehabilitation. 'We're the lucky ones', explains one of the convicts to me. 'We get to work in the open air and help the fire department fight fires, here in Malibu and everywhere in Los Angeles County.' The convicts are members of the Malibu Conservation Camp CC #13, who cut hedges and clear brushwood to reduce fire hazards under the supervision of prison officers and firefighters.

The State of California has an extra budget to spend on firefighting. To protect Malibu's villas, the regional fire department operates the largest civil air force in the world. When the Santa Ana winds fan the flames, the hills of Malibu are transformed into a battlefield, in which gigantic airplanes fight against the elementary forces of nature. Blackhawk helicopters and Sikorsky aerial crane helicopters then appear in the skies. The bigger the disaster, the greater the commando fleet. For years, the Los Angeles Fire Department has rented Canadian Super Scoopers and Helitankers to dump water from the Pacific onto the blazing Canyon. The Scoopers from Quebec take just twelve seconds to pick up more than 6,000 litres of water from the ocean, and the Helitankers can even fill 10,000 litres per minute. To fight the biggest wildfires, Andrew Gosser tells me proudly, the Californian fire department deploys wide-bodied aircraft such as DC 10s and Boeing 747s, which can deposit over 75,000 litres of flame retardants onto the burning chaparral. However, if nature does not play along, and winds do not die down or suddenly turn, even whole troops of firefighters and the largest emergency fleet in the world can do little to stop natural forces.[35] Then there is only one option: to flee the raging flames and evacuate Malibu's residents as quickly as possible. Hiking through Corral Canyon in January 2010 where a fire had raged 26 months earlier, consuming houses and causing the evacuation of thousands, I discover in places the traces of the bushfire.[36] Countless oaks in the Canyon have been burnt to a cinder. Interestingly, however, most of the houses have already been rebuilt. Just one property is up for sale: '1/4 acre ready to build'. Singed tree stumps encircle the plot where a new bigger housing estate is earmarked for construction.[37] 'In the future, too', prophesises Andrew Gosser, 'there will be devastating fires in Malibu. Houses will burn down and be rebuilt.' He then lists a few canyons as if wildfires are something that will not take place in the future but are consigned to the past. 'Wherever vegetation is old, fires will rage especially fiercely', he explains. 'But wildfire won't destroy Malibu. The much greater problem is the erosion of the beach.'[38]

## Erosion

Americans are fond of uniforms. In Malibu, I come across uniformed female prisoners, prison officers, private security staff, firefighters and police officers in rapid succession. There are even people in fake uniforms. Apart from the environmental activists disguised as Rangers, I see several bands of uniformed workers on the narrow two-kilometre strip of Broad Beach one day. When I take photos and ask some of them who their boss is, discovering that they only speak Spanish, the entire crew disappears behind a garage in a flash. Their uniforms suggest they belong to local authorities, but in fact they are illegally digging up sand, filling it into sacks and building a fortifying wall to protect private villas from floods.

Some of the groups are using bucket wheels and conveyor belts to speed up their work. Broad Beach, the legendary Malibu spot which made Frank Sinatra famous in his felt hat, has suffered from extreme erosion in just a few decades. For years, residents like Pierce Brosnan, Robert Redford, Stephen Spielberg and Dustin Hoffman have all pitted their strength against the destruction of the beach which used to be fifty metres wide at low tide. A high rock sea wall has been built, berms have been created to stabilise embankments, foundations and caissons have been sunk into the subsoil and houses built on sand have been anchored into underground concrete with steel girders. But even the most sophisticated engineering feats can only guarantee a partial victory against winter storms, floods and the risk of tsunamis. It is just a question of time until the beach properties and their luxury villas one day – perhaps in two or three generations – are completely swept up by the ocean.

## Green veneer

'I will tell you that 90% of the people living here are environmentally conscious', explains Gil Segel, an actor known for *The Last Supper* who lives in

Paradise Blues

Building a flood protection wall at Broad Beach, Malibu.

Carbon Beach and happens to be the president of the Santa Monica Bay-Keeper environmental group.[39] When I drive through Malibu city centre, I notice how many outlets (both here and in other southern California coastal resorts) put a high value on their green image, whether it's the organic food store Pacific Coast Greens or the Eco Auto Spa, all the way to the sustainable Eco Malibu Clothing store. Most of Malibu's residents are likely to declare that they love nature – the ocean, the sun and the mountains. And hardly an opportunity goes by without a Hollywood star laying claim to environmental protection: Leonardo DiCaprio is the chairman of a family foundation that fosters awareness for a sustainable future. He also sits on the boards of many environmental, nature and animal protection associations, such as the World Wildlife Fund, Oceans 5, Pristine Seas and the International Fund for Animal Welfare. Pierce Brosnan, who was named 'Best-dressed Environmentalist' in 2004, is committed to the protection of wetlands and marine life. Julia Roberts shows off energy-efficient appliances and recycled tile in her mansion while actively promoting the use of solar energy. Robert Redford, meanwhile, is an advocate for wilderness reserves in Utah and, on his Sundance festival channel, he promotes ecological projects and 'green' living. Tom Hanks is known to support the environmental organisation The Nature Conservancy. After the Hurricane Katrina disaster, Brad Pitt had 150 'green' houses built in New Orleans from funds raised by the Make It Right Foundation, created for just that purpose. Barbra Streisand bequeathed her property to the Santa Monica Mountains Conservancy and actress Charlize Theron, who is famous for appearing at the Oscars in ecological clothing, is an active campaigner for the creation of a liquid natural gas terminal off the coast of Malibu.

The list of well-known and lesser-known residents in Malibu who appreciate the charm of the southern Californian backdrop and are visibly committed to environmental causes could easily continue.[40] It is therefore even harder for outsiders to understand why for decades a central wastewater treatment system in Malibu has been rejected. The beach East of Malibu Pier has the dubious claim of being 'one of the longest polluted' beaches on the list of national 'repeat offenders'. On my first visit to Malibu, I was surprised by the smell of the ocean – the notorious 'Malibu smell' – and the fact that people sunbathe on the beach, but don't swim. The explanation is simple: intensive rainfall and flooding make private septic tanks overflow regularly, swilling sewage and human faeces into the ocean.[41]

When speaking to the residents of Malibu, I begin to notice how important septic tanks have been for the town's history and identity. The reason the town registered itself in 1991 is even connected to these tanks: they were regarded by Malibu's residents not so much as cesspits but more as a symbol of resistance to efforts by Los Angeles county to introduce a central wastewater treatment system. Back then, fear weighed heavily that Malibu might simply become a suburban appendage to Los Angeles. Outraged residents prophesied that mammoth hotels such as those in Miami Beach West might spring up and replace Malibu's villas.

In the early twenty-first century, Malibu's water quality has slightly improved – even though the environmental organisation Heal the Bay continues to find breaches of environmental regulations and increased concentrations of bacteria in the water. Meanwhile, an enormous rainwater retention basin has been created in Malibu's Legacy Park, and various stores and households have been encouraged to connect to the central wastewater treatment system.[42]

Things are slowly starting to change. But self-declared environmental protectionists in Malibu have often been the decelerating rather than the accelerating force when it has come to reinforcing stricter environmental regulations. The irony is that the 'eco-barons' – a term coined by journalist

Edward Humes – may have been very vocal in their warnings about climate change as well as the fact they drive hybrid cars and have solar panels installed on their villa roofs; yet they guzzle energy for air conditioning, insist on retaining septic tanks in their gardens, spend holidays on yachts, fly around the world on kerosene-fuelled private jets and increase beach erosion by building sea walls. The history of Malibu's eco-barons appears to be just as eccentric as the history of the city itself.[43]

## A paradise of delusion

Why do people live in Malibu in the first place? Why do they build their houses in canyons that are repeatedly ravaged by wildfire? Or at the edge of the ocean? Malibu isn't the only coastal resort in America beleaguered by natural disasters. The nature of the ocean – erosion and the risk of tsunamis from the West, and hurricanes from the East – makes the frontier between land and sea a fragile place everywhere in America. Coasts are exposed to increasingly rapid changes in the era of global warming. Nevertheless, surf and turf hold an enduring fascination. In 2020, the proportion of residents in coastal regions made up more than one per cent of the entire American population. Especially in places particularly known for hurricanes – Florida and Texas – numbers of residents are growing faster than anywhere else in the USA. Perhaps the reason for this is a mixture of temptation and denial. Sea air and ocean views enhance our mood, according to psychologists, and we tend to suppress potential catastrophes or quickly forget about them. Besides this, risks to life and limb have actually fallen from one century to another.[44] The Chumash people knew they had to locate their dwellings further inland when flooding threatened, and they burnt the chaparral to keep the constant threat of wildfire at bay. Protecting their own lives was the highest priority. In contrast, goods and chattels were expendable. Today, immense wealth has accrued on the coasts of America. Here, people are transportable. In emergencies, helicopters are used to evacuate them from exclusive residences like in Malibu. The prices that Hollywood stars pay for their villas are astronomical but, when catastrophe strikes, the costs of rebuilding the infrastructure, firefighting and clean-up campaigns are carried by insurance and reinsurance companies – and, not least, by taxpayers, who are proportionately not wealthy. In this way, social discrimination and environmental justice are hidden behind Malibu's wealthy, green façade.

Jim Jarmusch's film *Stranger than Paradise* from 1984, which he called

## Malibu, California. Stranger than Paradise

a 'neo-realistic black comedy', shows the American landscape to be something other than it appears at a distance – just like in Malibu.[45] Palms and exotic flora were transplanted here in California from all over the world in the past hundred years. After heavy rains, the beaches teem with bacteria. And even Malibu's legendary seclusion is nothing more than an illusion at a closer look. Twelve million cars per year motor through this paradise. Every year for a few days, heavy rain turns the streets into creeks and rivers; mighty waves and winds erode dunes and shores; landslides and rock falls shift the subsurface of canyons; and the dry 'devil's winds' from the Mojave Desert fan disastrous wildfires. What's worse, natural disasters exacerbate each other. Almost half of Malibu's luxury villas have been built on cliffs threatened by mudslides. Wherever wildfires sweep through the landscape and burn vegetation, the risk of floods, landslides and erosion rises. Highly flammable creosote from native brushwood leaves behind oily deposits that turn canyon escarpments into veritable water and mud chutes. Malibu is beautiful and at the same time terrible. Where else in the world are beginning and end, paradise and apocalypse, so close together?[46]

Malibu's history reminds us that nature can only be controlled to a limited extent. We can regulate temperatures in our homes and fight one fire after another; but fires, landslides and floods will always return to the Californian paradise. Malibu is neither the biblical promised land nor the prelapsarian Garden of Eden. Instead it is a garden harbouring a mighty snake (or two): natural forces threatening humans and human culpability.

In Malibu, nothing is permanent and there is no harmony; there is not even the sustainable joy that Frederick Rindge once dreamed of. Even the seclusion for which so many residents of Malibu have always yearned is an illusion. Fortunately, an increasing number of people are finding out that they have the right to use formerly exclusive beaches. Malibu is intricately tied to the world – economically, ecologically, politically and culturally.

Maintaining Malibu's exclusivity as a place to live and stopping its beach and canyon residencies from being wiped out is a costly undertaking. Only a select few will profit from it. In the Garden of Eden, the first people were innocent and could devote themselves to leisure until they were morally tested and driven out of paradise. Malibu – and other places like it in the world – might be a further test: of our readiness not to settle in every place in the sun, to maintain the wildness of nature, to share its beauty fairly and to come to terms with its temperament.

Memphis

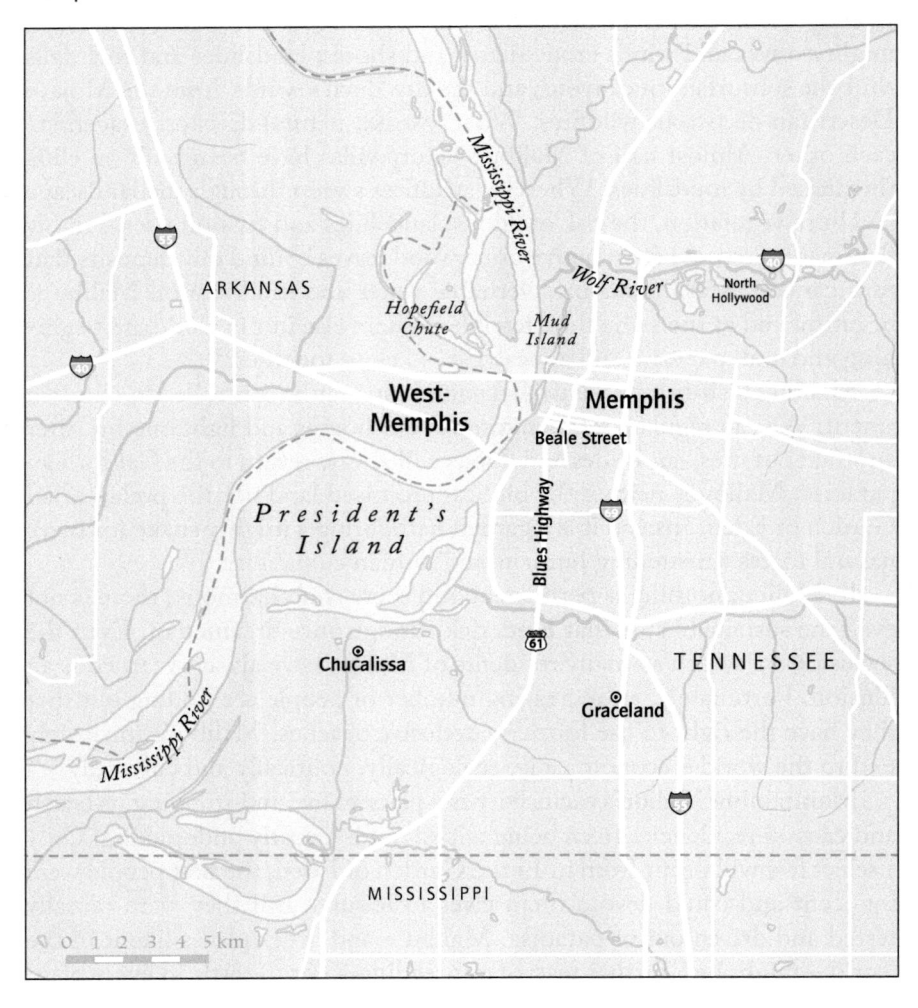

# Memphis, Tennessee.
Mississippi Blues

### Mississippi blues

Memphis is the biggest city on the Mississippi and the cradle of American music. Blues, which started its triumphal procession in renowned Beale Street, took the world by storm in the 1920s. It was in Memphis that B.B. King's elegiac guitar licks were recorded, as well as Howlin' Wolf's rasping protests against racial segregation. The music of Johnny Cash, Jerry Lee Lewis, and Elvis Presley was all produced in Memphis. In 1977, US Congress declared the town on the Mississippi the official home of the blues.[1]

Founded in 1819, Memphis developed over the nineteenth century into the world's biggest trade centre for cotton. The founding fathers envisaged a shining future for their town and chose a suitably glorious namesake – the capital of ancient Egypt. Trade required a port, neighbourhoods and depots. But, most of all, it needed the Mississippi River, which linked 'the metropolis on the American Nile' with Canada and the Gulf of Mexico, and thereby the entire world.[2]

Ever since it was founded, Memphis has been a city of contradictions. Besides being a stronghold for African American music, it's the heartland of the Ku Klux Klan. It used to be a trading hub for cotton, but also slaves. Its location on the banks of the Mississippi has favoured it with wealth, as well as fatal floodings. It's home to Elvis's shrine Graceland, as well as to the Lorraine Motel, where Martin Luther King was shot dead in 1968. Lively African American culture and racism jostle for space. And, to top it all, for centuries people have attempted to dominate its landscape and have polluted the environment. Triumph and tragedy lie closer together here than in most other cities in the USA. The history of Memphis is a history of the exclusion of Black people. No wonder, then, that the blues – the music of Black American labourers and the disempowered – was born in Memphis.

Rum Boogie Cafe's Blues Hall features live music every night of the week.

## To Memphis

I pick up a rental car at the airport. 'It might be difficult to take public transport', writes Tait Keller, my contact in Memphis. 'True, there are railroads, but they take everything except people.' On the way to my hotel downtown, I cruise down wide streets, through rundown neighbourhoods and past Sun Studio with its Gibson guitar sign.

The contrast between these sights and Rhodes College, where I am to give a lecture, is almost surreal. 'It looks like Hogwarts, doesn't it?' says Tait, a professor of history there. And he's not wrong. At the centre of perfectly mowed lawns reminiscent of English parks, rise walls and towers with neo-Gothic windows. The college campus is idyllic. Yet Memphis has a reputation for being particularly dangerous. The year I visited the city, it was No 4 on the list of US criminal statistics.[3] This is a world of contrasts.

On my trip through the history and nature of Memphis, I'm interested in grasping its many facets. I'm interested in the way it presents itself to

## Memphis, Tennessee. Mississippi Blues

tourists and its hidden sides. I plan to see the attractions as well as the areas not mentioned in any travel guide. I want to trace the origins of the blues and explore industrial areas and Black neighbourhoods; I want to visit the city and the surroundings that have contributed to its wealth. So my itinerary includes the rural areas of West Memphis, Arkansas on the opposite side of the river, where cotton is still cultivated today.

But first of all, I plan to find out where and how the indigenous population lived in this area a thousand years ago – on the river banks that have burst many a time.

## The river

*In the beginning was the river.* When I see the Mississippi for the first time in downtown Memphis, I understand why Americans so often add the word 'mighty' to its name. Docked in the port of the 'mighty, mighty Mississippi', as Delaney Bramlett sang, is a three-storey paddlewheel steamboat, the Memphis Queen III.[4] Huge cargo cranes crawl across the water and a gigantic bridge stretches from one riverbank to the other. The Mississippi holds more water than any other river in the USA. Its catchment area delivers drinking water to one-third of all Americans; it crosses 31 US states, from the Rocky Mountains in the West to the Alleghenies in the East. In Memphis, its high waterbed is over four kilometres wide. Every day, in the words of Mark Twain, this 'magnificent river' is 'rolling its mile-wide tide' at an unfathomable rate of 18.4 million litres of water per second into the ocean.[5]

Five thousand years ago, the Mississippi began life as a melting glacier. The valley in which it lies is much older than the river. Millions of years ago, when the continents of Africa, Europe and America collided, sweeping the Atlantic into extinction for a fraction of a geological moment, the Appalachian Mountains emerged from the bedrock. This created the depression into which the Mississippi flowed. In contrast to the Grand Canyon Valley, which is continually sinking due to erosion, the Mississippi Valley rises every year due to the mud deposited by its water and the fact that its heavy bed is continually reforming. So, the Mississippi is its own landscape designer: it swerves about wildly, changing course, its water levels sinking before they swell unpredictably and break its banks. The entire region around the southern Mississippi was formed by its waters. Four hundred thousand tons of sand and silt are shifted by the tide every day into the bay of the Atlantic. New terraces are continually shaped, canals dug and lakes and oxbows formed.

A single Mississippi flood can create dykes over a metre high.[6]

Historical maps of the Mississippi appear to show that the reason for Memphis's location is the river itself. From the North, it flowed at high speed in a straight line to the city. But shortly before it reached the spot, it ran into high ground – the Fourth Chickasaw Bluff, named after the Chickasaw indigenous people – and slowed down, before continuing in a south-westerly direction. Wolf River also joins the Mississippi very close to Memphis. The city founders were in no doubt that they had found the ideal place for their city, as Baird Callicott, a Memphian philosopher and writer, tells me.[7] After all, the heights of Chickasaw Bluff that stretch from Lauderdale to the north of Memphis at a height of fifteen to thirty metres along the Mississippi offer more protection from floods than river regions further south. The temperature is somewhat cooler too and fewer insects live there. The bluff kept the river in check and slowed it down, while Wolf River connected Memphis with the eastern hinterland where cotton was grown in large quantities. In fact, in the forty years from the city's foundation in 1819 to the beginning of the Civil War in 1861, Memphis evolved into a riverboat city of the finest kind and the largest inland centre for cotton in the USA. The founding fathers could not suspect that nature's idiosyncrasies and the wilfulness of the Mississippi would cause the city grave environmental problems over time, from disease to devastating floods.[8] While travellers and contemporary witnesses did give accounts of rapids, wolves howling in the nearby tropical jungles, shipwrecks and the 'climate fever that befalls almost everyone who sails down the Mississippi', Memphians mistakenly believed they were safe.[9]

The brutality of the river, meanwhile, exceeded everyone's imagination. The loess deposited primarily by wind over long geological periods in the Memphis region, creating fertile arable land and bluffs, was by no means an impenetrable obstacle for the mighty Mississippi. The river burrowed its way into the bluffs and city shores so deeply that more than thirty metres of the harbour walls were lost in the 1870s. From 1850 on, the shop fronts on Market Street were flooded with increasing frequency. More worryingly, strong eddies in the river meant that it was an adventurous, if not risky, undertaking to dock steamships, rafts and boats. These eddies were caused by sand, silt and gravel from a protruding cape, loosened in large chunks by the current and piled into deposits at the mouth of the port, causing a gigantic sandbank to form – today's Mud Island. For this reason, the flow of the river changed direction and created an enormous whirlpool. Ships trying

## Memphis, Tennessee. Mississippi Blues

Mississippi River Cobblestone Landing and Mud Island.

to enter the port risked running aground on the sandbank. Driftwood, such as branches and pieces from shipwrecks carried along by the Mississippi, turned into dangerous projectiles at the mouth of Memphis port. The river gave anything but a warm welcome to captains and raftsmen. At the end of the nineteenth century, experts from the US Army Corps of Engineers first tried to shore up the banks of the Mississippi, not with dams but with 'mattress work', as was used in Germany back in the early Middle Ages. The mattresses of Memphis, over 300 metres long and 45 metres wide, were bigger than any previously known reinforcements; but the river current swept them away before they could be completed and fulfil their function.[10]

While being next to the river was a mixed blessing for Memphis as a trading hub, it spelt the downfall of the village of Hopefield, directly opposite Memphis, because Hopefield Point, its cape, was always being damaged and hollowed out by the Mississippi. A court, a railroad station and a small settlement had been set up one after the other; contemporaries considered it a 'healthy, moral, and intelligent' place.[11] But, within a few years, Hopefield lost more and more land. Devastating floods in the years 1887 and 1888 sealed the town's fate. The railroad was consumed by water. Finally, heavy flooding in 1912 buried the town in the mud forever, along with its residents' hopes. Nowadays only the cornerstone of the Mississippi bridge can be found on Hopefield's former site.

On my first day in Memphis, I walk along the banks of the American Nile to the pyramids of Memphis, an impressive building made of glass and steel. Originally conceived as a sports arena, the Great American Pyramid now houses a mega outdoor store experience that exceeds all expectations. Among hunting equipment, sports clothing and boats, all of which you can buy, a Bass Pro Store contains live alligators, artificial habitation for ducks, an archery range and replicas of Southern State swamplands, as well as countless aquariums that contain over two million litres of fresh- and saltwater. In the middle of the building, a freestanding glass elevator takes you to the top of the pyramid. Although it's raining, from the top, which is 100 metres high, I have a spectacular panoramic view across the valley. Only three Egyptian pyramids are higher than that of Memphis.

On the opposite side of the river, which is in the state of Arkansas, the terrain is conspicuously flat. From the Memphis side, I can see the Wolf River and Mud Island. I wonder whether the wealthy Memphians of Mud Island know that they live on a sandbank whose base used to be part of Hopefield. In Memphis tourist guides, the myth is perpetuated that Mud Island was created by a sunken canal boat during the Civil War, which the river then inundated with sand.[12] From the tip of the American Pyramid, the yachts moored on Mud Island look adorable and the Mississippi seems tame. But without the river's force and the flooding in 1913, Mud Island would never have been formed; and, were it not for extreme interventions in nature, it would no longer exist either. Mud Island and Memphis are part natural, part manmade projects. Only the redirection of Wolf River and prohibiting the countless sawmills along its banks from tipping sawdust into its waters prevented the island from being connected to the mainland. Temporarily, at least.[13] Although Memphis is positioned on a bluff, its banks slope gently. The port area is not resistant to flooding. Later I find out that during the great Mississippi Flood of 1937, even the site of the Pyramid was submerged by water. Back then, there were still oil refineries operating here, all of which had to pack up and leave because of the constant threat of flooding.[14] That downtown Memphis still stands today is only thanks to the interests of businesspeople and the expertise of engineers, who went to great lengths to ballast the riverbanks in the twentieth and twenty-first centuries, with flood barriers of increasing height that saved the city from going under in the truest sense of the word. Mark Twain was perhaps right in saying: 'One who knows the Mississippi will promptly aver … that 10,000 River Commissions, with the mines of the world at their back, cannot tame that lawless stream, cannot curb it or confine it, cannot say to it, "Go here", or "Go there", and make it obey; cannot save a shore which it has sentenced; cannot bar its path with an obstruction which it will not tear down, dance over, and laugh at.'[15]

## The early history of Chucalissa

Over 10,000 years ago, the Mississippi Valley was already the site of an indigenous settlement, long before the Spanish, French and English explored the region and quarrelled over its spoils. On my first day in Memphis, I decide to drive to the place where relics and traces of earlier villages exist – to Chucalissa, the site on the southern border of Memphis, where earth mounds and archaeological finds bear witness to the culture of regional tribes. Their heyday was during the era of the European high Middle Ages, a time when no one in North America envisioned cultivating cotton.

I enter the Chucalissa site, which is run by the University of Memphis and offers insights into a long-lost world that profited from its proximity to the Mississippi, fertile loess sediment and a climate that stays temperate all year round. Chucalissa sits on a steep bluff a good thirty meters above the Mississippi Valley. An enormous plaza and flattened earth mounds, on which a temple and dwellings for priests and shamans once stood, reflect the site's former significance. The river offered residents the opportunity to fish and they hunted wild animals in the nearby hills. The bluff protected the settlement from floods, and the surrounding deep ravines offered natural protection from invaders.[16] Standing on a sloping ledge known as Bluff Edge, I look across a valley through which the Mississippi flowed 1,000 years ago directly below the Chucalissa settlement. Today its course is several kilometres further north and the valley is dense with trees. I wonder whether the indigenous population moved away when the river's path began to change. Was there any contact between these people and the first white settlers? Did Spanish seafarers and the conquistador Hernando de Soto, who died of a fever on the shore of the Mississippi in 1542, come into contact with the native

Chucalissa? No one can answer these questions with any certainty today.

What's sure is that Soto claimed he was an immortal Son of the Sun, because he knew that native Mississippi communities were sun worshippers. What's also sure is that the fleet of war canoes or *pinnaces* headed by Chief Quigualtam, who lived in the vicinity of Chucalissa, instilled respect in the Spaniards. Spanish officers secretly swathed de Soto's body in cloth, weighted it down and dumped it into the river to hide their leader's mortality. In Chucalissa, you can see a canoe fashioned from cypress wood covered in moss as well as earthenware remains in the museum that demonstrate the craftsmanship of Mississippi tribes. Indigenous tribes could travel northward in their canoes as far as today's Ohio River, westward as far as the edge of the Great Plains, southward to the Gulf of Mexico and eastward to the Florida Panhandle.[17]

But the native population in the Memphis area was best known for cultivating maize. This, green beans and squash were the staples of their diet. Other than this, they experimented with a wide range of plants and grain types including sumpweed, goosefoot and sunflowers. Herbs, such as lemon balm, passion flower, echinacea and bergamot, were grown for their healing properties.[18] Countless medicinal herbs, in fact, that were greatly revered by Mississippi tribes can be found in a sanctuary on the Chucalissa site, among them, celandine poppy used to cure sleeplessness and fever, black cohosh that was once used as an insect repellent, wormseed as a remedy for parasites, sassafras for measles and wild lily as an antiseptic.[19]

Chucalissa survived several centuries. It is unknown what led to its downfall along with other towns in Mississippian culture. Indigenous tribes did not pass down written testimonies and evidence from archaeological sources points in different directions – to sickness, war or climate change. But perhaps it was also the rapid growth of the population, excessive demands on the soil from maize farming or the deforestation of hardwood trees to meet the demand for housing. The European conquest of the continent, whose people brought fatal diseases to the indigenous population, also played its part.[20]

Although indigenous groups held out longer than those further south in the Mississippi Delta near Memphis, including members of the Choctaw and Chickasaw tribes, the Louisiana Purchase in 1803 – the greatest sale of land in world history, which doubled the size of US territory and brought the whole of the Mississippi Valley under the control of United States – ultimately sealed the native population's fate. The French, with whom Thomas Jefferson agreed the Louisiana Purchase, were more familiar with the environmental conditions of the New World than the British. They had explored the continent inland mostly via waterway and had opened it up for trade; in doing so, they'd always found ways to live alongside native peoples. And although they cultivated rice fields in southern Mississippi, dried out smaller areas and farmed sugar, the large-scale transformation of the region's landscape only began with Napoleon's retreat. From then on, nothing stood in the way of rapid expansion and the colonisation of the American continent.[21] European explorers and colonisers had always regarded the double continent as a treasure trove whose resources could be used profitably – in other words, exploited. During their military campaigns and raids, Spanish conquistadors might have mainly been interested in gold and, to a lesser extent, animal furs, but they did not see themselves as permanent settlers. The national government in Washington D.C., however, set about ordering the North American continent according to new neo-European ideals. The fact that century-old habitats and traditions existed in the Mississippi Valley, safeguarding the continuation of the indigenous population and culture, played no part in the white settlers' machinations. Whereas natives had learned to live with the river and knew how to protect themselves from floods by building settlements on high ground, the European settlers, together with their black slaves, built new living areas next to the river. A culture of control emerged. The settlers were primarily interested in taming the river, keeping it in predefined channels and, by creating dry areas and cultivating lucrative crops, exploiting it economically.

When I drive back from Chucalissa to Memphis, I wonder whether the founders of Memphis in the early nineteenth century realised that the river next to which they established their town had a tremendous energy and history of its own. Members of the Mississippian culture in Chucalissa had lived for over half a century in a relatively sheltered way. But when Memphis was founded, a radically new chapter in human dealings with nature began.

## King cotton

A crop belonging to the mallow family provided the impulse for thousands of people from all over the world to move to Memphis in the nineteenth century. These included Jewish textile workers and haberdashers, Black American slaves and tenant farmers, Italian labourers, Syrian grocers and Chinese vegetable sellers. And the crop they came for was cotton.[22] Without 'white gold', Memphis would never have been founded. Anyone with a job in the Mississippi Delta and central Mississippi Valley during the nineteenth and early twentieth century was working in the cotton business. 'Cotton is king' was a common expression.

Since the turn of the nineteenth century, it had emerged that 'the new material', as George Washington prophesised in a letter to Thomas Jefferson in February 1789, would be 'of almost infinite consequence to America'.[23] Despite this, America's first president could not suspect that the United States would quickly become Europe's biggest importer of cotton – a consequence, among other reasons, of a slave uprising in 1791 and the subsequent collapse of the cotton industry in the French colony of Saint Dominique. The uses of cotton were legendary. In India, it was processed to produce dye and, in China, a male contraceptive. In North and South America and Europe, cottonseed oil was used in fertiliser, fodder and food. Most of all, however, cotton fulfilled Europeans' demand for clothing.[24] As machine textile production in England expanded and the population grew on an unprecedented scale, cotton prices rapidly increased, making it an extremely attractive crop, especially on the floodplains of the lower and central Mississippi, where fertile soil mud had been deposited for centuries and cotton was able to grow faster than anywhere else in the world. In 1789, the USA produced some 3,000 bales of cotton; by 1857, the figure was almost 5.4 million. By then, the USA had outstripped all other nations.[25]

There were at least two reasons why enterprising farmers and politicians set their sights on the Mississippi and the region surrounding Memphis in the first half of the nineteenth century. On the one hand, technological developments, prompted by the invention in 1793 of the cotton gin (a machine that separated cotton fibres from their seeds) accelerated the speed of cotton production so much that speculators and politicians began searching feverishly for new cultivable land.[26] On the other, like tobacco, cotton leached the soil in the eastern part of the United States so rapidly that, in 1860, three-quarters of cotton production no longer took place in the state of Georgia and South Carolina, but further west instead.[27] Ports with direct access to the sea – New Orleans, Charleston and Savannah – were very important because cotton could be shipped from them to Western Europe and New England. But the more cotton was picked along the Central Mississippi, the more important the inland port of Memphis became for national and international markets. In 1859, forty years after Memphis was founded, the city had a national market share of over ten per cent; in the course of history, this tripled. The appearance of Memphis was completely shaped by the cotton trade. It featured oil mills,

## Memphis, Tennessee. Mississippi Blues

warehouses and cotton presses. Freight transportation boomed for as long as cotton was harvested in the Mississippi region. And in no other American city was the proportion of employees in trade and transport as high as in Memphis.[28]

When Memphis proudly celebrates its origins and history as a centre of the cotton industry, the fact that this required the almost complete expulsion of the indigenous population to acquire enough land for cotton growing nearly always goes unsaid. One of the founding fathers of Memphis, military commander and later US President Andrew Jackson, together with the banker and constitutional judge, John Overton, set their sights at an early stage on growing cotton in the area of modern-day Memphis and from there, shipping it to the world. The contracts Jackson signed in his official capacity with the Choctaw and Chickasaw Nation opened up not only the entire area west of the Mississippi for the cotton industry, but also a further two million hectares in the Mississippi delta of the Yazoo. Native Americans living there were 'compensated' with inferior land further west: in other words, they were expelled. Long before the southern US dedicated itself to the cotton industry, there were cotton plantations in other regions of the world; but nowhere else – not in China, the Ottoman Empire, India or Brazil – did cotton farming go hand in hand with comparatively brutal actions and the expulsion of indigenous peoples.[29]

Driving through the older parts of Memphis, I see a row of elegant Victorian mansions with splendid façades among less prestigious buildings and empty lots. These used to belong to the captains and bankers, lawyers and business people, cotton agents and growers. The high society of Memphis had exquisite taste. They led luxurious lives, attending symphony concerts and balls, enjoying sumptuous banquets and eating out in Floyd's Restaurant while moving only in elite circles; their lives did not overlap in any way with those of the predominantly Black Memphians, whose labour had generated the wealth they enjoyed.[30]

The centre of the cotton industry in the city was the Memphis Cotton Exchange. On my tour through the city, I make a stop at the corner of Union Avenue and Front Street, a few hundred yards from the river at most. Here, in the former exchange salon with its high ceilings and an enormous board on which sales offers were once noted, a museum has been set up, visited by school classes and tourists alike. During the heyday of the cotton trade, the exchange was a male domain where dominoes were played, whiskey knocked back and cigars puffed. In the showrooms of the cotton companies that lined Union Avenue in Memphis in rows, the city bristled with business people. In historical photos, the protagonists can be seen in three-piece suits, ties and hats like any other businessmen, yet tell-tale cotton fluff clings to their trousers. The main thing in the cotton business was to scrutinise and classify the quality of the fibres, which was standardised. In contrast to its counterparts in New York and New Orleans, the cotton exchange in Memphis was not a futures but a spot market: nearly every exchange of money took place on the spot after the goods had been checked, and decisions were final. A terse phrase like 'I'll take it', or 'that's okay, put that down', was enough for transactions involving exorbitant sums to change hands. Only members of the exchange were allowed to do business. Those who did not stick to the rules could have their membership revoked. The higher the profits in the cotton business, the quicker the population grew. Half a century after its founding, Memphians totalled 40,000; in 1900, the population had already grown to 100,000 and, by 1950, to nearly 400,000.

## Land reclamation

Even if Memphis's economic success in the nineteenth and early twentieth century was primarily thanks to cotton, it coincided with other businesses, especially the wood trade. Up until the nineteenth century, ancient swamp forests grew in the Memphis region, with exotic trees including hornbeams, persimmons, tupelo and mulberry trees. Shrewd entrepreneurs made a profitable business out of chopping down, processing and trading in wood, because the hardwoods from the Mississippi region were perfectly suited to making barrel staves, furniture and vehicle chassis. Millions of metres of cypress and ponderosa pine trees were used every year for levees and railroad sleepers, while gigantic quantities of hardwood were processed to make flooring. In 1925 alone, forty sawmills produced over nine million linear metres of floorboards, coining the capital of cotton the singular title, 'Hardwood Capital of the World'.[31] Forestry work in the Mississippi swamps was neither easy nor risk-free, and the shipping of logs, first carried out using five-span ox-drawn vehicles, was anything but agreeable.[32] It left behind an immeasurably large, deforested area, which in turn piqued the interest of cotton growers. Businessmen in Memphis barely registered that their natural surroundings were undergoing a radical transformation. On Front Street and Union Avenue, what mattered was profit. This in turn – according to a simple economic formula – was based on tapping natural resources; because those who tapped natural resources could take credit for promoting progress and therefore the common good.

The late nineteenth-century belief that nature could be manipulated for the benefit of forward-looking American people proved to be the driving force for many large-scale drainage and land reclamation projects. Uncultivated land, according to leading voices in new America – mainly crop growers, politicians and water engineers – was considered worthless. Pumping off 'surplus water', developing plantation business and extending America's gigantic railroad system, on the other hand, were regarded as milestones of progress and improvement. Republican Senator John S. Harris, a New Yorker who himself owned a cotton plantation in Mississippi, summed up the never-ending optimism of his time when he told members of the US Congress in 1870 that the $2 billion trade in the Mississippi region 'captured one's imagination'. He went on: 'In this age of great engineering enterprises, when Pacific railroads and Suez canals dwarf the old Egyptian pyramids, it may well-nigh be said of such efforts "nothing is impossible". … The civilisation of our age … and its network of railroads, its steamships and telegraphs, and its clearing of forests are triumphs full of utility to all, and this changing of watery waste to a smiling expanse of cultivated lands unequalled in fertility is in accord with its other useful undertakings.'[33]

He didn't consider the transformation of backwaters into cultivated land a mere passionate vision, but an objective appeal to common sense. Harris's appeal and those of his entrepreneurial contemporaries were an attempt to kick off a large national project to dam the Mississippi from Missouri to Louisiana. To strengthen his argument, he added that the ancient Romans and later the Dutch and Italians had achieved similar things in less favourable conditions. The mission to tame the Mississippi would be 'great and difficult' but it was 'possible to achieve'. Americans did not need to know any more, Harris believed.

Towards the end of the nineteenth century, land reclamation in the Mississippi Valley took on an industrial character. Horse and mule-drawn equipment was replaced with steam-driven water pumps, and the US State Army Corps of Engineers began building and extending ever higher levees intended to protect agricultural planes from the uncontrollable river. Around the turn of the twentieth century, most forests and wetlands from Memphis to New Orleans had disappeared. Drainage and deforestation also had an impact on the fauna. While there had still been an incalculable number of beavers, otters, deer and rabbits up until the mid-nineteenth century, the

Mississippi soon lost its wealth of native animals. The separation of the Mississippi from lakes, smaller rivers and the few remaining swamplands robbed its waters of the nutrients deposited over thousands of years that were necessary for survival, as nature conservationists, biologists and later ecologists alarmingly discovered from the mid-1920s on. Its ecosystems were transformed beyond recognition. Invasive plants and animals became widespread and some of them, such as beaver rats from South America and the notorious Mexican boll weevil – the subject of many a Mississippi blues song – caused terrible plagues in rice fields and cotton plantations.[34] And with the rise of pest infestations, the use of insecticides also increased.

## Toxins

For over a hundred years, toxic substances have been used to eliminate boll weevils from cotton. In the beginning, field labourers dusted the cotton plants with poisons that were carted in flour sacks by mules. Later on, pesticides were sprayed from the air. In the beginning, arsenic compounds such as lead and calcium arsenates were highly popular. But 'mopping' the cotton flowers with a mixture of molasses and arsenic proved to be 'a terrible job', as former US President Jimmy Carter, who came from a farming family, wrote in his memoir: molasses also attracted swarms of bees and mosquitoes. While the use of highly toxic substances – organochlorides like DDT, Endrin and Toxaphen – killed off the insects, this in turn led to bollworm infestations that also had to be tackled with DDT. The National Cotton Council whose headquarters were in Memphis recommended a deadly five pounds of DDT per hectare in the 1950s as an adequate amount of pesticide. At times, up to 94 per cent of the nation's DDT and eighty per cent of Endrin and Toxaphen were used on the cotton plantations of the southern states. The poisons found their way via the groundwater into rivers, so that, in many places, masses of fish died out. Soon, fish-eating birds, including America's national symbol, the Bald Eagle and the state bird of Louisiana, the brown pelican, threatened to become extinct. It wasn't until DDT was banned in 1972 as a result of Rachel Carson's spectacular publication, *Silent Spring*, that much worse was prevented. But even today, high levels of DDT can be found in the fish stocks of the cotton states; people living in the lower Mississippi region are advised not to eat more than two meals a month containing fish.[35]

The transformation of forests and swamplands into agricultural regions inevitably had an impact on people too. Almost all those affected were Black

## Memphis, Tennessee. Mississippi Blues

Americans, who, when spraying crops, came into direct contact with insecticides like Parathion, Malathion and Endrin. At the end of the 1950s, Dr Mary E. Hogan, who had a surgery in Glen Allan, was very vocal about the dire health consequences including 'chemical pneumonia', which could be traced back to inhaling insecticides. These days, she has faded into oblivion. She called it 'appalling' that in the 'insecticide season' of 1957, up to 125 Black American workers would turn up each day in her surgery with often serious symptoms of poisoning.[36]

Black Americans – slaves and indentured servants – were on the frontline during the conversion of the Mississippi Valley's natural landscape into a gigantic cotton imperium, which returned high yield and profits. But in the end, it was Black Americans in nearly all regions who were the losers in the great environmental transformation of the American South. The exploitation of nature and that of people were very closely linked.[37]

Near the city centre of Memphis, too, in a district with the affluent-sounding name of North Hollywood, there are concrete reminders of soil toxification that resulted from the cotton industry. Here, on the shore of Wolf River, a waste disposal site known as the North Hollywood Dump was created in the 1930s. Its early history is unremarkable. But in the 1960s, it became one of the most toxic waste disposal sites in the USA from one day to the next. Before this, there had been investigations in 1964 by employees of the regional health authority who had who waded a kilometre through Wolf River in rubber suits taking water samples. As they did, they came across a metre-deep, toxic, muddy sediment with inordinately high concentrations of organochlorine pesticides. The manufacturer, Versicol, had the river dredged and shipped the material to the disposal site in North Hollywood. The toxins in Wolf River came from the cotton fields east of Memphis where they had been washed into the water.[38] It took decades until the highly poisonous residues in North Hollywood were included in the Superfund, America's national environmental sanitation programme.[39] What makes the case of waste dumping in Memphis so perilous and gruesome is the double exploitation of the Black population and the environment: it has left an unspeakable stain on the region's history which, to the present day, has not found its way into the history books of Memphis.

## Black blues

One afternoon I meet Wayne Dowdy at his desk in Memphis library. Dowdy, wearing a bow-tie and rimless spectacles, is a historian who has written numerous books on the political and social history of Memphis.[40] 'Memphis', Dowdy bemoans, 'is caught in a black-and-white trap.' The gap here between Black Americans and all other members of society is 'too difficult to bridge', he explains and 'greater than in other places'. Chinese, Jews and Irish, according to Dowdy, were welcomed to Memphis after the Civil War. In contrast to the state of Mississippi, people with Asian heritage counted as white in Memphis, Tennessee, and were permitted to attend 'white schools'. This meant that Black Americans, who were already ostracised, ended up being pushed to the very margins of society. The social topography of the city reflects this segregation. In the western areas of the city, the population is mostly Black American; in the East and on the eastern outskirts, such as Germantown, on the other hand, the population is almost uniformly white. During my visit to Memphis in autumn 2016, the US presidential election campaign was at its height. The division of Memphis showed in election posters for both candidates: Hillary Clinton was the preferred candidate in downtown Memphis and districts with a high percentage of Black Americans, while Trump had the support of those living in bungalows and villas in the East. Racial segregation is quite clearly inscribed in the social and party-political topography of Memphis, and it pervades the city's history like a curse.

In the census of 2010, 63.3 per cent of Memphis residents were Black Americans, most of whom were descended from the slaves herded into the Mississippi Valley in the nineteenth century to take on the heaviest workload in the swamps, cotton plantations, rice fields warehouses and the port of Memphis. In the mid-nineteenth century, people in Bremen and Liverpool feared that the price of cotton would double or triple when US American slaves were set free. Over 275,000 Black slaves were registered back then in Tennessee and more than 1.2 million in the five biggest slave states along the Mississippi (Missouri, Kentucky, Tennessee, Louisiana and Mississippi). The physical and psychological violence endured by Black Americans is one of the most tragic chapters in the history of the Southern United States. What's more, they lived in flood-prone districts of Memphis and stayed in the city – unlike the majority of the white Memphians – when fatal waves of yellow fever and malaria in the Mississippi Valley followed on the heels of the Civil War.[41] Historical sources leave no doubt that Black Americans developed a higher resistance to malaria than their European contemporaries. Although they were not immune, the death rate of the Black population was significantly lower – ten times, in fact – than among white inhabitants. Since the seventeenth century, mosquitoes introduced from Africa had led to the rapid spread of yellow fever and malaria on the American continent. When forests were cleared, however, and the associated bird populations began to disappear, mosquitoes' natural enemies died out. The combination of environmental factors, economic interests and cultural prejudices spelt doom for those who lived in swampy and flood-prone areas, namely the Black population. Urgent need for their labour kept them subjugated.[42] Even after the official abolition of slavery in 1865, structures of feudal paternalism persisted in places like Wilson, Arkansas, on the opposite bank of the Mississippi. Even in the 1920s, the Wilsons, a single family, owned a cotton plantation the size of Lichtenstein. The marketplace was bordered by pretty Tudor-style houses, and everything except the post office and railroad station belonged to this one family – including the bank, drugstore, gas station, hospital, cleaners and slaughterhouse. Eleven thousand predominantly Black workers were set to work in the fields and at companies belonging to the Wilsons; they did not receive wages for their work, but coupons that could only be used in the Wilsons' stores.[43]

To get an idea of how contemptuously Black people were treated by the white bourgeoisie in Memphis until late in the twentieth century, the photos of the first years of the Cotton Carnival, founded in 1931, give a pretty accurate account. Back then, Black Americans pulled large carnival floats through the streets like workhorses while privileged white people waved from the sidelines. The Memphis elite voted for a cotton king and queen every year and they even imported British red foxes, even though North American foxes were perfectly adequate, to carry out fox hunts in the tradition of the English aristocracy.[44]

How fitting that a city which publicly paraded its elitist posturing, racism and discrimination was also the site of vibrant Black American counterculture. Beale Street in downtown Memphis, stretching eastwards from the steamboat dock for a kilometre and a half, is considered by many historians as the hub of this counterculture. Here, the blues, a Black American music genre that inimitably expresses pain, suffering and longing, found a home in images and music for the whole of America. Beale Street was originally called Beale Avenue, but the 'Beale Street Blues', composed by W.C. Handy in 1917, was one of the reasons that its name was changed. At the time, Beale Street was widely known as the 'Main Street of Negro America'.[45] Black Americans and immigrants looking for work and adventure lived here cheek-by-jowl. There were clubs, gambling houses and saloons, jewellers and pawnshops, picture-frame and arms stores, operators of cultural events and brothels, banks and billiard salons, theatres and cinemas. The Black activist George W. Lee described Beale Street in the 1930s as a place full of 'carefree people' with 'midnight serenaders twanging on their guitars'. This was a street where 'it was always Saturday night', 'a main street of Negro America where its pulse beat highest, where richly red, dark brown women, hang-jawed country rubes mixed with spruce urban negroes in an atmosphere pungent with barbecued pig'. Lee explained that Beale Street 'belonged to the Jews', was 'controlled by the white police, while Blacks entertained themselves there'. Its guitar music 'blended with the traffic noise to create a sound triumphant'. And 'back of the sound of this red-hot syncopation', he claimed, 'lies the plantation Negro who if he was sometimes lost in the vast apathy of a decaying system was also often impelled to seek Beale Street'.

Nobody really knows where the blues was born.[46] Some say it was the Dockery plantation, 160 kilometres south of Memphis, where music legends like Charlie Patton, Robert Johnson and Howling Wolf picked cotton and made music. But in reality, the yearning, gloomy music with its simple and characteristic diminished chords – blue notes – was sung on dozens of cotton fields, timber yards and farms. The pulse of work delivered the rhythm accompanied by a call-and-response technique. A lead singer would set the melody and a group of workers would answer, overlaying the monotony of cotton picking with music. 'not a day went by', explained Sam Phillips, founder of the legendary Sun Studio in Memphis, 'when I didn't hear Black people singing in the cotton fields. ... They could pick faster than me. They could stay in key. They made a great impression on me. ... If I hadn't tried to capture (this music), then I would have been the biggest dam coward that God ever put on this earth.'[47] The blues might have originated from the country but found its audience in the city – in places like Beale Street, on Black radio broadcasting stations like WDIA and on millions of records, many of which were recorded in Memphis.

That Beale Street hit rock bottom in the 1960s and was slated to make way for a modern business complex is inconceivable today. Around that time, *Time Magazine* depicted Memphis as 'a decaying Mississippi River town' and a 'Southern backwater'.[48] The murder of Martin Luther King Jr

## Memphis, Tennessee. Mississippi Blues

in Lorraine Motel, two blocks from Beale Street, caused such riots in the city that it was inconceivable for the administration to continue the project. Instead, the street was restored in the 1980s and transformed into an entertainment district.[49] Even today, blues musicians from all corners of the USA come to Memphis, some in search of jobs. Every morning in front of the Peabody hotel, a small dark-skinned man asks passers-by for a few cents. He comes from Michigan and plays the organ, he explains, but has been living for twelve weeks in a homeless shelter on Poplar Avenue. 'I came to Beale Street', he explains, frustrated. 'I played there for three evenings – keyboard, blues and rock – but then they didn't need me no more.'

I arrange to meet my colleague Tait Keller at the top end of Beale Street where roadblocks and police cars from the Memphis Police Department block vehicle access of all kinds and tourists stroll en masse. On the corner of Second Street, in the second storey of B.B. King's Blues Club, the speakeasy-style Itta Bena restaurant, with wooden floors and vaulted ceilings, can be entered via a hidden passageway. The menu lists dishes from the Mississippi Delta: shrimp and corn grits, spicy crab soup and Andouille hash. Through

Late-Night Beale Street.

the shimmering blue windows, the street noise drifts through the eatery, and from the ground floor, the blues band can be heard. The name Itta Bena was made famous by Martin Luther King and one of the leaders of the Black Panther movement, Stokely Carmichael: it was during a march of civil rights activists near the small town of Itta Bena led by King and Carmichael that the battle cry 'Black power!' was coined. In the restaurant, Black and white people sit tightly packed together, families and couples, all elegantly dressed. This is where the high society of Memphis gathers.[50] When Tait and I leave the restaurant late that evening, the nightlife in Beale Street is only just getting going. Music can be heard everywhere.

It's difficult to imagine that Beale Street was once known as the most dangerous street in America. The Monarch, a building at number 340, now accommodates the police. It used to be a club known for its notorious fights, with a funeral parlour in the backyard crematorium that earned the moniker of the Castle of Missing Men. Con artists and other unpopular types who tried their luck in the bar allegedly disappeared there. But in the twenty-first century, the world of Beale Street seems to be in order. I remember the words of the filmmaker Dee Garceau whom I met a few days ago at Rhodes College. 'We have a complex history of violence here in Memphis', she explained, 'but we repress it.'[51] Memphis's music mile is, I think, one of the places where the repression takes place.

## The other side of the river

To understand the relationship between Memphis and its agricultural surroundings, I take a trip across the Memphis-Arkansas Bridge from Memphis, Tennessee to West Memphis, Arkansas. The river marks more than just the border between two states; the town on the East side is an industrial metropolis while the West is mostly a chain of farms. In the East, the bluff rises; the land in the West is flat. Memphis is an urban area, and Arkansas strictly rural. Memphians call Arkansas a 'delta', although the actual Mississippi Delta is hundreds of kilometres further south. It's October. On some of the cotton fields, fleecy cotton flowers glitter in the sunshine. Most of them, however, have already been harvested. I drive past thousands of cotton balls, first on Interstate 55 and then on the famous Blues Highway 61 towards Wilson, Arkansas. Highway 61, made famous by Bob Dylan's folk-rock album *Highway 61 Revisited*, was the historical starting point for US musicians on the road to somewhere better. 'Pack up and go' is a common

Memphis, Tennessee. Mississippi Blues

phrase in blues lyrics. Dylan himself, and almost every great blues musician, was born and lived along Highway 61. In bars and at small markets, I meet rural labourers and farmers, amateur musicians and mechanics. The elderly tell me how it was in the old days – that their fathers didn't used to have combine harvesters for soya, rice and cotton. 'Nowadays everyone works with combines and all of them have air-conditioning in their cabins', Reynolds says, whose father-in-law began growing rice in the early 1950s. 'Today, five guys do what a hundred used to. The combines cut, thresh and clean the rice. And then trucks transport the whole harvest to elevators in large silos.' Pesticides haven't been sprayed by hand for a long time, Reynolds explains. 'We have pilots who fly so low you have to duck when they drive over you. Five or six feet above the ground.' Reynolds dismisses my suggestion that pesticides might be dangerous and end up in the groundwater. 'Costs are skyrocketing', he laments, 'and profits are getting smaller all the time.' I find out that the rice harvested at the beginning of September is not for human or pet consumption, but is fed to cattle, and goldfish, which are used as living bait by anglers. I also find out that most of the water that floods the

Cotton roll, Jericho, Arkansas.

rice fields comes from underground, not the Mississippi.

More rice is grown in the East of Arkansas than anywhere else in the USA, not least because the biggest US brewery, Anheuser-Bush in St Louis, Missouri, a few hours north of Memphis by car along the Mississippi, is also the largest bulk buyer of rice in the country. American Budweiser beer is produced using up to thirty per cent rice. In the 1990s, Anheuser-Bush's Wildlife Edition beer steins were advertised with the phrase 'brewed with rice'. Back then, adding rice was considered a quality seal. Only when Greenpeace reported that Anheuser-Busch beers were tainted with genetically altered rice produced by the German company Bayer Crop Science did the brewery hush things up. Greenpeace's campaign brought to light that Anheuser-Busch in Wuhan, China and Europe explicitly eschewed genetically modified rice; but not their branch in the USA. Greenpeace then parodied a Budweiser advert on YouTube, showing a couple of deadbeat men drinking genetically engineered rice instead of beer.[52] Anheuser-Busch owns rice fields west of the Mississippi, but the brewery is ubiquitous in Memphis – in pubs and restaurants, as a political lobby and a sponsor of sporting events.

On the way back to Memphis, I take a side road that passes a cemetery. The town it belongs to is called Jericho, and this is no coincidence. Biblical Jericho was the first town captured by the Israelites after crossing the Jordan River. Jericho, Arkansas was also captured by white settlers, a riverboat captain called Stephen Stonewall and his brother James. James set up a farm, cleared its wood, then built a sawmill and grew fruit. The cemetery in Jericho, which slowly becomes cotton fields, has evidently been flooded in the past: some of its gravestones stick halfway out of the loess. In nearby Marion, Arkansas, a West Memphis suburb, I talk to the manager of Journey Inn, a motel on Interstate Highway 55. He tells me that the freeway was flooded the year previously, and that water seeped into the motel apartments. He shows me the ditch next to the street which ran over and flooded the parking lot. 'We're a good way off the Mississippi, but we're part of the floodplain.' Unlike downtown Memphis, rural areas west of the river don't receive financial support to build large dams. Reflecting on the disaster of the previous year, the manager grins as he says, 'Here in this region, enormous areas of soybean fields were flooded. But it did mean we could go fishing in the fields for bream, catfish, perch, and crappies with their nice white meat.'[53]

Memphis, Tennessee. Mississippi Blues

## President's Island

The ascent of Memphis is directly linked to the transformation of the Mississippi region into an agricultural landscape. But, around the turn of the twentieth century, leading opinions in the area shared the view that the future of the city, in Wayne Dowdy's words, 'lay in industry, not nature'. As a result, 'the city was divorced from its river a hundred years ago'.[54] But, in fact, the river with its historical Mississippi steamboats and Pyramid is still the showcase of the tourist city of Memphis. Industry and trade take place in a hidden 'backyard', on President's Island. Without Dowdy's tipoff, I'd never have found it. Tourists don't come across it by accident and no travel guide mentions the island, which used to be the largest in the Mississippi. On old maps, it was still divided in two, a smaller northern section (Vice President's Island) and a larger southern section (President's Island). After the devastating Mississippi flood in 1937, when President's Island was submerged by almost three metres of water, both islands were connected and so was the mainland. So President's Island is no longer an island at all,

River port and industrial park as seen from President's Island.

but a peninsula. Even the first part of its name is misleading: despite many legends, US President Andrew Jackson never owned land on the island.

On Interstate Highway 55 which cuts through Memphis, I take the McLemore Avenue exit towards Channel Avenue. On the map, the peninsula with its twenty-five-kilometre shore looks idyllic. I can make out the Mississippi and a long lake. But when I take the causeway to the peninsula, it's immediately obvious that President's Island is nothing more than an industrial port complete with industrial buildings.

Endlessly long cargo trains inch forward at snail's pace parallel to the shore. The International Port of Memphis transports oilseed, soybeans, cattle feed, wheat and rice, scrap iron and metal, petroleum and gasoline. It's also home to one of the highest cranes in the world, the Ichabod Crane, named after the lanky giant in Washington Irving's short story, 'The Legend of Sleepy Hollow'. Over 150 companies have their headquarters on Channel or Harbor Avenue. I drive past scrapyards, wire-drawing mills and smelting works, past a sweetener manufacturer called Cargill, an Italian cement company called Buzzi Unicem, past the Tomsin steel processing works, and Heritage Crystal Clean, a company that disposes of chemical solvents and waste products. You'll also find the Phoenix Manufacturing Co., which manufactures forestry equipment, and Great Plains, which produces seed planting machines. I see at least fifty grain silos, and the US Army Corps of Engineers has a maintenance facility known as the Ensley Engineer Yard, with over thirty water vehicles. Firms with confidence-inspiring names have surrounded their properties with barbed wire: Food Protection Service, a specialist firm for pest control and Vertrauen Chemie, a company that packages dangerous substances. Many of them display the American flag. But in the part of the island that looks most natural, with green areas, trees and shrubs, signs warn that the water might be contaminated. President's Island is both a gigantic transport hub in central USA and Memphis's secret industrial backyard.[55]

It has always been a strange place. The small farmers who ended up here on this mound of drift sand covered in poplars were regularly hit by floods before industrialisation. Some buildings stand on stilts. The small forest used to be populated with rabbits and squirrels; there were duck ponds, and farmers grew cotton, maize, vegetables and pecan nuts. After the Civil War, Nathan Bedford Forrest, the first leader of the Ku Klux Klan, bought a site on the island. Forrest, whose mounted figure I come across, to my outrage, in the middle of an idyllic park in central Memphis (it was removed in December

2017), built the biggest farm of all, hoping to settle his debts with the profits. The KKK leader, who was responsible for the use of bedsheets as capes, the racist alignment of the group and its oath of secrecy, took prisoners from the local jail to work for him as forced labourers. He paid the county ten cents a day for every healthy prisoner. The sick and injured received the most basic medical care and those who were not willing to work were punished, including by whipping. After the deadly yellow fever epidemic of 1878, the city purchased a section of Presidents Island and set up a quarantine centre there. A short time later, the island became a refuge for moonshine sellers and gamblers and, during prohibition, bootleggers smuggled their wares across the water on flat boats. Today nothing remains of the secret history of smugglers and the island's sinister past under the leader of the KKK. The radical transformation of the island 'from bog to boom' has wiped out all historical traces. Instead, the international airport and the presence of five companies symbolise the meteoric rise of Memphis to one of the most important and central transport and logistics hubs of the USA.[56]

## Glimmers of hope

One afternoon, I meet Bob Wenner, the CFO of the Wolf River Conservancy conservation organisation. Wenner suggests that we meet in the legendary Peabody hotel in downtown Memphis, a noble, Renaissance-style building. There, Wenner says, we can follow the curious March of the Peabody Ducks over coffee. Since the early 1930s, at least four ducks, led by a duck master, waddle each morning at 11 o'clock across a red carpet to the hotel fountain made of Italian marble. From there, they take the hotel elevator to the Royal Duck Palace, a penthouse with a pool and panoramic view of the city. The Peabody ducks celebrate that the area around Memphis, especially in the duck capital of Stuttgart, Arkansas, is a paradise for these birds. After they almost died out in the first half of the twentieth century, the population has grown steadily since the 1960s, thanks to the introduction of seasonal hunting regulations.

While watching the duck spectacle from a distance, Wenner tells me about an initiative to buy private plots of land, to systematically restore the Wolf River and to build a paved hiking route of almost forty kilometres from Beale Street (at the confluence of the Wolf and Mississippi Rivers) all the way to suburban Germantown in the East. The property owners who offer their land for this project receive tax breaks and the city is giving it financial support, while the employees of the initiative are involved in ecological clean-up programmes. In the 1970s, the press reported that the Wolf River was 'dead'. But nowadays, fish swim in its waters again and one day, Bob Wenner says, people won't just be able to fish them out but eat them too. The Wolf River Trail aims not only to unearth the crimes done *to* nature but also the history of violence *in the setting of* nature that hangs over the river like a curse. In 1917, a white armed mob was accused but never found guilty of the murder of Ell Persons, who was dragged out of the train, doused in petrol and, as publicly announced beforehand, set on fire in broad daylight. Around 5,000 white spectators stood and watched the grisly spectacle; children were given the day off school, and the mob took parts of his charred, dismembered body to Beale Street and threw it at Black pedestrians. Even weeks later, Memphians were sending postcards showing a picture of Ell Persons' head.[57] In May 2017, exactly 100 years after the lynching, schoolchildren in Memphis collected $2,500 for a plaque commemorating the atrocity.

Restoring the river and bringing to light the city's brutal history – projects carried out by schoolchildren and activists in connection with Wolf River Conservancy – are a glimmer of hope in the dark history of Memphis. On my last day there, I, like thousands of others, visit Elvis Presley's former house and grave, Graceland. Afterwards, I sit in the bar of Marlowe's Barbecue Restaurant on 4101 Elvis Presley Boulevard. Apart from the white barkeeper and myself, the clientele is entirely black. Fifty years ago, a Black person in Memphis could not be served by a white barkeeper. This is also a small glimmer of hope, I think.

Blues, folk and rock, as well as the music of Elvis Presley, whose ancestors were indigenous people, helped deconstruct some racial prejudices. Perhaps the history of Memphis can also be interpreted positively. The fact that a group of activists in the city prevented Overton Park, with its natural arboretum, and one of the last primeval forests in Tennessee, from being destroyed by the construction of a highway, is a further reason to be hopeful. Is it a coincidence that the children of the Overton Park activists were the ones who erected a memorial plaque for Ell Persons? As a scientist, I know that there is no such thing as karmic justice. Yet it feels like justice to learn that the KKK leader Nathan Forrest, who spread fear and terror, died in 1877 after drinking the water on President's Island. Or when I find out that River Park, directly opposite the island, was renamed Martin Luther King

## Memphis, Tennessee. Mississippi Blues

Jr Riverside Park after its namesake was assassinated.[58] The more glimmers of hope we can discover in the history of Memphis, the more likely it is that the future will be brighter than its past.

St Thomas, location map

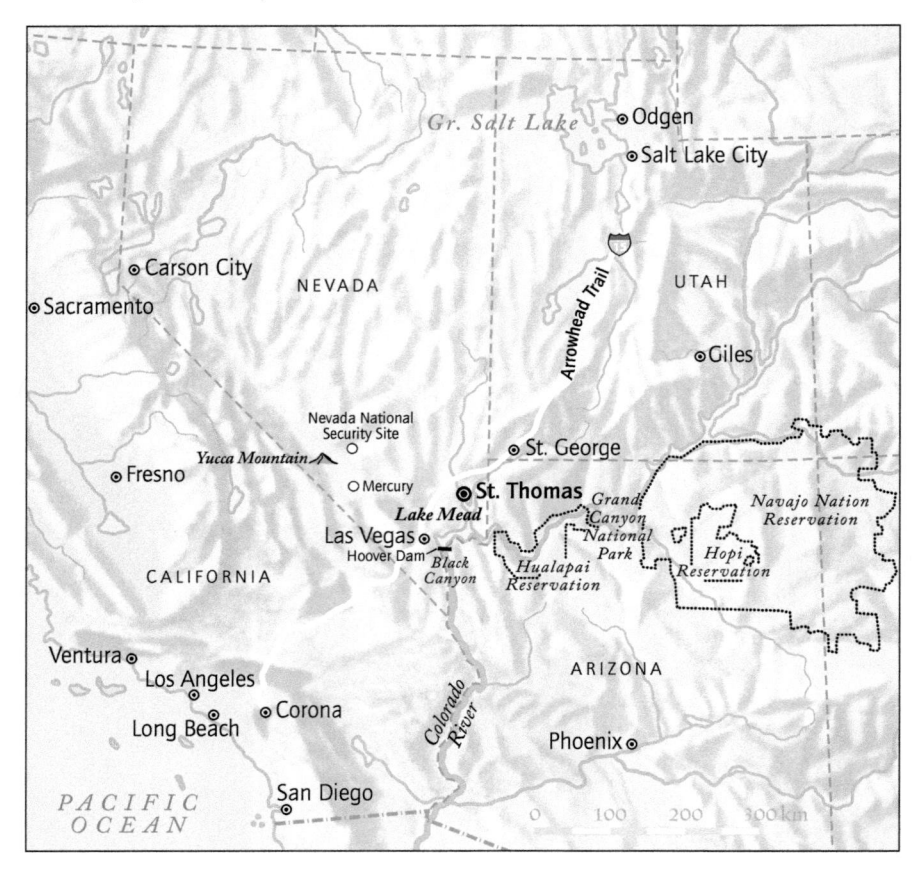

# St Thomas, Nevada.
## The Ghosts Return

### The ghosts return

There is no hairdresser or hotel in St Thomas, and no general store or gas station either. Not a single soul lives here – there's not even a house. St Thomas is long gone. Ironically, the only signs of life are at the cemetery where, year after year, relatives of the deceased lay flowers on the graves of their loved ones. These artificial blooms are a splash of colour in the otherwise brown-grey desert of southern Nevada.

St Thomas is a ghost town. It's not a magnet for tourists, but the history of the town and nearby Las Vegas reflects the enormous challenges of settling and surviving in the arid climate of the American Southwest.

The Valley of Fire State Park, Nevada.
A geological wonderland.

On my trip into the desert, I'm interested in finding out how, over the centuries, people dealt with the region's limited water resources and how major desert projects, such as the Hoover Dam and nuclear testing, had often unintentional consequences for the ecology and local population.

## In the Valley of Fire

Driving eastwards from Las Vegas shortly before arriving in St Thomas, I pass the Valley of Fire. It is one of North America's most spectacular desert landscapes and derives its name from the red sandstone outcrops that look as if they are aflame when the sun rises and sets. The 150-million-year-old volcanic rocks and formations of limestone, sandstone and conglomerates have eroded over the centuries into fantastical shapes: in the middle of the desert, you can find an elephant, a beehive and a grand piano.

In the Valley of Fire, it's barely conceivable that here, where the temperatures in summer climb to fifty degrees Celsius, humans once hunted and gathered. Nonetheless, countless petroglyphs – rock carvings – testify to a group of Puebloans, the Anasazi, who farmed the Muddy River Valley from around 300 BCE to 12 CE and used it as a place of worship.[1]

The Valley of Fire feels so alien that it's as if I've time-travelled to another era. Hollywood directors have often used the eerie scenery as a backdrop for sci-fi movies and prehistoric sagas, from the 1940s Stone Age love story *One Million B.C.* to *Star Trek*.[2]

The dramatic landscape surrounding St Thomas has attracted people for centuries. Those who come in the summer months justifiably wonder how the Puebloans and, later, white settlers buried in St Thomas's cemetery were able to survive in this inhospitable, desolate region. It's even more remarkable when you consider that heat is not the only hazard. Besides mice, rats, and toads, rattlesnakes, beaded lizards, tarantulas and scorpions live in today's deserts in Nevada, Utah and Arizona.[3] On my drive to the cemetery in St Thomas, warning signs from the US Department of the Interior alert me to the danger of drowning too. Because the desert earth can only absorb very little water, heavy rainfall can cause tidal waves of up to ten meters that sweep drivers off the road with a fatal force.

St Thomas, Nevada. The Ghosts Return

## St Thomas

Who were the settlers who founded St Thomas in this hostile environment in the nineteenth century? And what happened to this town that was far more significant than nearby Las Vegas back in 1900? Wandering around the cemetery in the deserted landscape, I see a car that must be at least three-quarters of a century old: a Ford Model T with its wheels, motor and roof missing. Who did it belong to? Who abandoned it here? I find a sign saying: 'Dedicated to those stalwart pioneers who forged an oasis out of the desert sands'. And an explanation for the town's disappearance is below:

The St Thomas Cemetery was established in the 1860s in the town of St Thomas, Nevada. Anticipating the inundation of the town by the waters of Lake Mead, the graves were moved to this point in 1935. Only past residents of the buried towns of St Thomas and Kaolin and their decendants (sic) are buried here.

When I drive along the old St Thomas Road, now a dirt path, out of the cemetery towards the sunken town, I can't believe my eyes. The reservoir that once submerged St Thomas – at depths of up to twenty metres in

St Thomas, Nevada. Ford Model T.

some places – has receded to a large extent. The water table of Lake Mead, America's largest reservoir, has diminished enormously in past decades. It provides water for over twenty million people and countless agricultural enterprises. When it was completed in 1936, it spanned over 180 kilometres from east to west. But where St Thomas used to be, you can now walk on the former lakebed and keep your feet dry. At the spot where the road to St Thomas ends, I discover a sign with a hiking symbol and the inscription 'Site of historic St Thomas, 1865–1938'. I am the only person there and the atmosphere is uncanny. I hear two coyotes howling at one another from two different directions. When I discover relics from the former town among the brushwood, stone and shells, it's as if the spirits of St Thomas have returned: there are foundation walls, wells and metal grids. There used to be a wide, tree-lined avenue here too, a modest hotel with a small tower, a school, whose entrance steps have survived to this day, a church, a post office, grocery stores and, as becomes a happy town in the desert, an ice-cream parlour. And St Thomas was a happy town. No matter how hot, dusty, windy and dry it was in the summer, the little town had an advantage over the neighbouring places: it was spring-fed by the nearby Muddy River, which ensured an all-year-round water supply. Hundreds of years ago, the place that was renamed St Thomas in the nineteenth century was an important way station because the next stop on the Old Spanish Trail with a decent water supply was a good 200 kilometres away.[4]

## Mormons and indigenous peoples in the desert

The founders of St Thomas were Mormons, otherwise known as members of the Church of Jesus Christ of Latter-day Saints, or LDS. Brigham Young, one of the first apostles, sent his followers into the arid West to look for suitable places where the church's congregation could settle. The Mormons had been accused of racism, isolationism and polygamy in the eastern United States. This led to harassment and persecution and, in 1844, their founding member Joseph Smith was murdered in prison in Carthage, Illinois. The Mormons believed that God wanted to test their people in the desert wasteland and that those who turned the barren landscape into a garden would find deliverance.[5] St Thomas should become an oasis and a green refuge for the righteous.

The Mormons were probably the first society in the western hemisphere to develop a modern economy using a large-scale irrigation system. Salt

Lake City, which Young dubbed 'the Kingdom of God on earth', was built in 1847 on salt flats.[6]

The members of Young's church were able to fall back on the wisdom and methods of the Puebloans, who had located springs and built irrigation channels in the dry areas of western North America, often in adverse conditions. When the first Mormon scouting parties arrived in St Thomas, they met descendants of the Paiute people who had lived there for hundreds of years. 'On the Muddy', noted the Mormon apostle Parley P. Pratt, 'our camp was thronged with near sixty Indians, in a state of nudity, bringing with them green corn, melons, and dressed skins for sale, or exchange for clothing'.[7] The Mormons were impressed by the abundance of the Paiute's harvest and ascribed it to how they cultivated their crops. Individual wheat crops stood at great distances apart and were regularly irrigated but never stood in water. The white explorers were less understanding of the Paiute practice of baking bread from ground mesquite beans and searching for edible roots in the desert; they were especially sceptical of their custom of eating lizards, locusts and ants.

Admirers of the Mormons' way of handling scarce water resources and those who consider them to be early environmentalists might want to bear in mind that the Muddy River appeared so inviting only because the indigenous population had subtly transformed the landscape over long periods.[8] The gradual transformation by Native Americans of the desert into farmland, their practice of mining salt for trade and their use of fan palms to weave baskets and build huts were all cultural practices that resulted from prolonged, complex learning processes. The pitfalls and opportunities presented by life in the desert had been understood by the indigenous population over centuries. In contrast to the white settlers who steamrollered their way through the American West in the late nineteenth century, the indigenous Americans learned to avoid places where nature could fully unleash its destructive power. Many a Mormon group founded a town in what they thought was a perfect location, only to have to abandon their settlement when it was flooded.

One flash flood disaster after another took place in Giles, Utah, for example, after several Mormon families set up their homes and built wells there.[9] Today the ghost town of Giles is no longer marked on North American roadmaps and can only be found online. The land there and the ruins are occasionally put up for sale at the bargain price of two to three hundred dollars a plot.[10]

So the Mormon settlers in St Thomas were lucky. They met the indigenous population who, if historic reports are to be believed, shared their wisdom with the newcomers and even let themselves be christened by them. Soon a colony had sprung up in the Muddy River Valley, its fruit trees and cotton fields giving it an idyllic appearance.

The explorer and cartographer Frederick S. Dellenbaugh, who stopped in the Muddy River Valley in 1871 on his way to the Grand Canyon, was impressed. 'As pioneers', he wrote in his travelogue, 'the Mormons were superior to any class I have ever come in contact with, their idea being home-making and not skimming the cream off the country with a six-shooter and a whiskey bottle.' Mormon towns were undoubtedly quieter than those in the legendary Wild West, with their 'ghastly hodge-podge of shacks in the midst of a sea of refuse'.[11]

## Paths to St Thomas

St Thomas steadily grew in size. In the early twentieth century, the settlement and its greater area comprised almost 2,000 inhabitants.[12] A few years later, up to 520,000 pounds of salt were being mined there daily (almost a quarter of the Pacific Coast's entire salt requirements), as well as potter's clay, plaster, copper, and even silver and gold. Farmers, mining enterprises, and operators of irrigation systems had an impact on railroad companies and drove forward the project of a rail connection. On 1 June 1912, the final nail was hammered into the track. Leading Mormon apostles came to the inauguration, and the official ceremony was followed by a ball game, barbecue, rodeo and other entertainment.[13] The importance of the railroad, telegraph system and national roads cannot be underestimated for St Thomas and places like it. The railroad did not just bring in tourists: when the cooling van was invented, it also brought ice blocks to the desert, making it possible to transport goods swiftly towards the Pacific Coast.

More quickly than other countries, the USA became an 'asphalt nation' for automobiles. The 1910s heralded the construction of a network of 'auto trails' – the forerunners of today's highways.[14] Less than a year after the railroad was opened, lobbies urged for a 'trail' to be built to St Thomas. Automobiles were more flexible than railroads but, without roads, they were useless. The first truck to arrive in St Thomas belonged to the Grand Mulch Mining Company. On its maiden voyage, the company driver wore a black dustcoat, safety goggles and fashionable breeches. The entire town thronged around the gigantic vehicle and children climbed onto its flatbed. But its wheels sank into the desert sand, horses had to haul it out, the motor overboiled, its brakes started smoking when driving downhill and the sharp rocks along the route to the mine destroyed its tyres. After a few trips, the vehicle was deemed unsuitable for desert journeys, and it was shipped back to civilisation.[15]

Nevertheless, the expansion of the road network soon followed. At the end of May 1915, three years after the railroad had opened, the first automobile trip took place from Las Vegas to St Thomas. After four hours, the drivers reached their destination over ninety kilometres away without mishap and were greeted with iced water, lemonade and a cheering crowd. In contrast to the railroad, which always remained a spur route, the road was navigable in all weathers and connected the small town to the big wide world – Salt Lake City west of the Rocky Mountains and the major hub of Los Angeles on the coast. Many a tourist who traversed the North American continent by car passed through St Thomas; and on their way, they admired the eroding sandstone formations and the cotton plantations, filled up with gas at the Red Crow Gasoline pumps, bought groceries at the Arrowhead Store, stopped by the ice-cream parlour and spent the night at the Gentry Hotel.[16] The residents of St Thomas did everything they could to make visitors feel welcome. Together with the men from nearby Bunkerville, they even shovelled and raked free a sixty-kilometre section of the Arrowhead Trail to make the little oasis town as accessible as possible.[17]

## The birth of America in the desert

From 1924 on, St Thomas and neighbouring Overton made headlines all over the USA.[18] The governor of Nevada, J.G. Scrugham, had invited the eminent archaeologist, Mark Raymond Harrington, to determine the age of painted clay fragments that had been found in the Muddy River Valley. What Harrington discovered was revolutionary: the ruins of a 2,000-year-old town that stretched along the river for about eight kilometres. No researcher had thought it possible for a Pueblo culture to exist so far west. Harrington named the town 'Pueblo Grande de Nevada'. But the press, with its tendency towards corniness and sensationalism, dubbed the place the 'Lost City' from the first moment. The origin of North American Pueblo culture had not sprung up in the modern-day states of New Mexico and Arizona as people had hitherto believed; it had come instead from the Muddy River Valley in Nevada. Earlier than elsewhere, the indigenous population of Pueblo Grande had built mostly subterranean housing, woven fine cloth, made pottery, farmed the land and mined and traded with salt.[19]

A replica Anasazi pueblo in the Lost City Museum, Overton, Nevada.

When Harrington found a building complex of ninety rooms, ten years after his first visit to Muddy River Valley, headlines in the *Los Angeles Times* read: 'Chicago Was Built in Nevada 1,500 Years Ago'.[20]

The Mormons of St Thomas were involved in the archaeological project from the very beginning. They built a road to the excavation site for Mark Harrington and his team and, in May 1925, they produced a large-scale stage show with musical numbers on the history of the Lost City. The Union Pacific Railway offered festival visitors from Los Angeles inexpensive return tickets to St Thomas. Several schools were involved in preparations for the Pageant Pueblo Grande de Nevada, a professor from Brigham Young University took on the role of programme director and members of the University of Nevada helped reconstruct and sew historic costumes. The spectacle started with scenes from prehistoric times, showed episodes from the Spanish era and ended with the Mormons' arrival. There was also a large exhibition showing regional resources and products.[21] St Thomas was a small boomtown in the desert. In the early 1920s, however, economic difficulties began to emerge. First, the price of copper fell so low that ore mining was no longer profitable and numerous miners left the region. Not long afterwards, the bridge across the Virgin River burned down. The Arrowhead Trail no longer led to St Thomas but ran north past the town, meaning that automobile tourists no longer visited.

## Hoover Dam

The ultimate demise of St Thomas began, however, when the US Congress passed a bill in 1928 to build a gigantic dam in the Black Canyon to safeguard supplies of water and electricity in the southwest and to regulate the Colorado River. St Thomas's fate was sealed in one fell swoop: the plans for the Hoover Dam included the flooding of the town. An average compensation of 2,000 dollars per capita was offered to the townsfolk, who gradually left because of the imminent eradication of their hometown. In 1935, as water levels from the nearby reservoir rose, the cemetery was relocated to Overton where it can still be found today. Some inhabitants stayed until the very end, among them the owner of the local service station, Hugh Lord. Those who remained didn't want to believe that the floods would wipe out their homes. But when Hugh Lord woke up on 11 June 1938 with water washing around his bed, he too packed his bags and left – the last resident of St Thomas to do so.[22]

Hoover Dam was celebrated by its contemporaries as one of the world's greatest architectural feats and an embodiment of modern engineering. It was the biggest dam in the world at the time, redirecting the Colorado River into an artificially created basin and erecting a monument to a self-confident American nation. The taming of an untamable river that, at times, threatened to trickle away and, at others, burst its banks with devastating consequences, signified for most people nothing other than the triumph of technology over nature. After geologist John Wesley Powell's exploratory research trip on behalf of the US government, he announced that two-fifths of western America was not exploitable as regular farmland due to the extremely dry climate. But the government in Washington did not react to his assessment by considering forms of agriculture suited to these climate conditions or by recommending the sparing use of water. Instead of adjusting to suit environmental circumstances, North American policies were geared toward the missionary slogan of the journalist William E. Smythe, whose cause was the 'The Conquest of Arid America' as his optimistic pamphlet of that name proclaimed.

Since its founding in 1902, the Bureau of Reclamation, America's highest-level water management authority, has followed the aim of turning the western American desert into an enormous, irrigated garden. To this end, the authority supported the construction of an almost 25,000-kilometre-long canal system during the twentieth century. Hundreds of reservoirs and dams were built. But no construction transformed the economy and landscape of the USA more radically than Hoover Dam. Lake Mead and the adjoining hydroelectric power plant made it possible for the sparsely populated Southwest, from Los Angeles to Las Vegas and Phoenix, to develop economically. Without Hoover Dam, there would be no fruit and vegetable plantations in California's Imperial Valley or central Arizona. Today twenty million people receive their water supply from the reservoir.[23]

## The construction workers from Boulder City

On my way from the ghost town of St Thomas to the Hoover Dam, I stop in Boulder City. This town, built from scratch in the middle of the desert by the US government during the Great Depression, housed the workers who constructed Hoover Dam. I am just one of many tourists taking a walk around the town. Its pleasant shops are a magnet for day-trippers escaping the hectic pace of Las Vegas, and for those who want to eat pizza and ice cream in a cosy atmosphere or drink coffee at Starbucks and browse thrift shops. Even though many of the historic buildings from the early days remain, and gambling is still prohibited – a leftover from the construction workers' period – the town has little in common with the 1930s settlement. From here, enormous trucks with several flatbeds in tow used to set off every day for the Black Canyon – 150 workers per cartload, thousands of people per day. Most of them did not know each other before they ended up in the desert. Nowadays Boulder City has an airport, fully air-conditioned hotels and its own brewery; but, when it was founded, it was sixty kilometres from the nearest railroad station and over 300 kilometres from the nearest power plant. The heat was diabolical – air-conditioned housing still lay in the distant future. Two ambulances stood on constant standby to transport exhausted and injured workers to Boulder City's sixty-bed hospital. Between 1931 and 1935, 69 workers died according to official records, most of them killed by tumbling boulders or by falling into the canyon. The real figures, however, were much higher. Workers were also exposed to high carbon monoxide levels in badly ventilated areas; these deaths were officially attributed to pneumonia.[24]

St Thomas, Nevada. The Ghosts Return

## A gigantic project

Hoover Dam was finished in 1936. Every year, over a million people visit the reservoir and power plant. For me, it's an overwhelming sight. Hanging in the enormous turbine halls, which convert hydropower into electricity, is a star-spangled banner. A bas-relief in the elevator depicts muscled men in dramatised scenes of the dam's various uses: as a flood barrier, a navigable body of water and a source for irrigation, water storage and electricity. Two nine-metre bronze statues of angels elevate the achievements of the American engineers into the realm of the divine.

When I look out across Lake Mead, the Black Canyon and the enormous reservoir, I still have the historic exhibition photos in mind – sepia images of dynamite explosions, workers in helmets abseiling down the steep canyon walls to clear loose rocks, gigantic caterpillar trucks and diggers, multi-storey machines for tunnelling, 'jumbo' drill heads over fifteen metres in diameter, steel pipelines manufactured on-site, workers covered in canyon dust and enormous pillars cast from liquid concrete. Each pillar required 6,000 litres of liquid concrete, 20,000 tons of mounting iron and five million barrels of cement. The dam is 220 metres high but only a short section is visible above water. The calm of the reservoir hides the secret of how it was built and the story of its constructors.

## The goats of the Navajo

On rocks near the dam, I discover a commemorative plaque. It marks the grave of a dog that once served as a mascot to the Hoover Dam construction workers, stating that the animal was run over by a truck on 21 February 1941. But I do not find any plaque for the inhabitants of St Thomas at the Hoover Dam. Why not? And why not erect a plaque for the Lost City of the Puebloans whose settlements and burial sites endured for centuries?

A few hundred kilometres east of the Hoover Dam, on the upper reaches of the Colorado and its estuaries, Little Colorado River and San Juan River, the people on the Navajo reservation soon realized that a 180-kilometre-long dam was being constructed in Nevada. Filling Lake Mead, which holds as much water as the Colorado can transport in two years, marked the end of the Navajos' sheep and goat-herding culture as well as the ascent of agrobusiness in the American West. Even before Hoover Dam was completed, surveyors from the US Geological Society had warned that the Navajo's livestock were the cause of erosion and silting. According to the government's geologists, within a few years, this would lead to the silting of the Colorado River. To slow down the effects of erosion, the Navajo were required to reduce their herds of livestock, which had increased tenfold between 1870 and 1930 to over a million animals. At that time, half the Navajo's income came from this livestock, especially their trade in sheep-wool blankets. Regardless, they were forced by politicians in Washington and the Bureau of Indian Affairs to sell hundreds of thousands of animals to shore up the Colorado's water supply. No one in Washington imagined enlarging the Navajo reservation, which would have improved the ecological sustainability of the area and halted erosion. From the perspective of a policy primarily geared to economic factors, only sheep had a monetary value, but not the horses or goats that had no market outside the reservations. The radical reduction of goat and horse stocks was a simple solution to the complex problem of the silting Colorado.

Goat's milk and cheese, as well as goat and horse meat, were important subsistence foods on the reservations; but this played no part in the politicians' calculations. What mattered most was the water elevation in Lake Mead and the number of kilowatt hours that the Hoover Dam power plant could produce. The leaders in Washington did not even understand that Navajo women also had herds: they tacitly ascribed all animals to the male heads of the family, causing conflict between the sexes on the reservations. Ultimately, the Navajo did not stand a chance, whether male or female. In the tug-of-war between the reservation representatives and US Congress delegates, the balance of power was completely unequal. Within ten years, the Navajo had to give up more than half a million sheep, goats and horses, and drive them to the nearest railroad station. They received a ludicrously low compensation for this – between two and four dollars a horse, for example. Most of the goats that were confiscated did not even make it to the freight yard. Some were killed en route and returned to the reservation in the form of dried meat. Others were shot and rotted on the path, and still others were doused in gasoline and set on fire. From the Native American perspective, the US government's measures were scandalous and wasteful. After Washington had interfered with the Navajo's habitat, living conditions on the reservations became dire. The Navajo called this the 'Second Long Walk', the first denoting their forced resettlement from Arizona to New Mexico. The situation was extremely acrimonious. In hindsight, the coercive actions of the US government seem very cynical. After a short time, state-employed geologists and hydrologists had to admit that the reduction in herd numbers had not solved the problem: it was not the Navajo's grazing livestock, but climatic cycles with periodic high rainfall that were responsible for the silting of the Colorado River.[25]

## Ecological consequences

Engineers now estimate that the Hoover Dam has a maximum lifetime of just over 100 years. But the ecological consequences will endure far longer. Lake Mead has transformed the American Southwest but, contrary to its constructors' expectations, not in a positive way. The damage caused by dams is often only visible later on.

When President Roosevelt inaugurated the Hoover Dam in 1935 (calling it the Boulder Dam in an attempt to dissociate it from his Republican predecessor) during the aftershocks of the global economic depression, he declared that 'labor makes wealth'. To employ workers and materials, according to Roosevelt, was to translate the energy of the Colorado into a great national possession.[26] For the president and his contemporaries, the new dam was a concrete monument to human endeavour. Today, dams throughout the world have come under criticism. In the USA, there are more than 80,000 dam constructions. Only China has undertaken more dam-building. Economists, ecologists and politicians are increasingly questioning whether the benefits they offer outweigh the damage they cause. Some dams do make deserts habitable and prevent devastating floods to buildings and housing along riverbanks. In tandem with hydroelectric power stations, they also produce clean, renewable energy. But when dams change the course of a river, they interfere with a highly complex ecosystem with consequences that are difficult to calculate: they affect the tempo of the flow, the water level, the water temperature, the flora on the riverbank, the deposits on the riverbed and animal life below the water surface – something we notoriously know less about than life on land.

Larry Master, the chief zoologist of The Nature Conservancy, regards dams as the cause of the slow death of many American rivers. More than a third of all fish species and two-thirds of all crab species in the USA are already extinct, according to Masters, or are at risk of extinction. Dragonfly species are also threatened, as well as numerous types of birds and mammals whose natural habitat is the river shore.[27]

Before the Hoover Dam was built, the Colorado River Delta – the region where the river flows into the Gulf of California – was a biodiverse ecosystem roughly twice the area of Luxembourg. Besides the flourishing flora, it was home to deer, jaguar, beaver and coyote. However, for six years after the Hoover Dam was built, the lower reaches of the Colorado had almost no water because the entire water mass of the upper reaches was retained in Lake Mead. And, for an even longer period of twenty years, the lower reaches were dry when, in the 1960s, a second section was dammed to fill Lake Powell, east of the Grand Canyon. Today the ecological biodiversity of the Colorado Delta has been drastically reduced. In most years, the branches of the delta remain almost completely dry. At least four fish species native to the Colorado River are at risk or already extinct. The 'organic machine' metaphor for the Columbia River, coined by environmental historian Richard White, seems more apt here than ever before. The planners' technological dreams have transformed the Colorado into a cyborg-like artefact that is part nature, part technology. But we are only slowly becoming aware that human control over the river has its limits. The reservoir was supposed to benefit people, the river was supposed to be controlled and thus rendered useful; but the resulting ongoing destruction of nature inverts this dream into a nightmare. The dam is filling with sediment. Animal and plant species are becoming extinct. On the lower reaches of the Colorado, there is no water or agriculture. Nature has struck back with a warning that, in future, we should consider very carefully which spirits we summon.[28]

## The ascent of Las Vegas

To explore the area surrounding Lake Mead, I check into a slightly run-down motel in Overton, Nevada, just over six miles as the crow flies from the ghost town of St Thomas. The remains of the railroad to St Thomas are still visible. Overton is also home to the Lost City Museum which features replicas of indigenous Anasazi homes, utensils from the Pueblo period and historic documents. A typical desert town, it features a gas station, a post office, the County Sheriff's department, a Las Vegas Metropolitan Police station, two schools, three fast-food restaurants and three sports bars. In the evenings, locals and travellers passing through meet in the Red Rooster, a bar known for its smokers, gamblers and loud country music. The crowd is made up of billiard players and construction workers, as well as the wife of the local chief of police and people crossing the border from the Mormon state of Utah, where alcohol sales are restricted, and gambling is prohibited. In the Red Rooster, cash slips through people's fingers like water. There is a slot machine at every table. The Mormons of St Thomas would not have approved. And their descendants, of whom quite a few live in Overton, feel

Las Vegas, detail

the same. What would have happened to St Thomas, had the reservoir not been built? And what about Las Vegas?

One way of looking at it is that Vegas rose to the status of pleasure capital of the world because of St Thomas's demise. Without the flooding of St Thomas, or the water and electricity from Lake Mead, Vegas would have remained a village in the desert. Like St Thomas, Vegas was a town founded by Mormons. Thousands of years ago, the region was fed by artesian springs and inhabited by Paleo-Indians and later Puebloans. The Spanish christened the area 'Las Vegas', which translates roughly as 'fertile plains'. In 1855, the Mormons erected a fort halfway between Salt Lake City and Los Angeles, which they soon abandoned and whose ruins remain to this day. Mormon bankers, especially Parry Thomas, the President of the Bank of Las Vegas, played a central role in this story. Although the Mormons are forbidden from touching dice, this did not stop Thomas and his bank from granting 'character loans' – personal credits for gamblers and mobsters, who invested their money in dubious establishments and casinos.[29]

Las Vegas's ascent started slowly at first. According to the census of 1900, it only had 25 residents. Thirty years later, that figure had risen to more than 5,000. But, when Lake Mead was built, the town's population exploded: within thirty years, the population grew by a further 100,000, and today the city has 650,000 inhabitants alone while the area of greater Las Vegas comprises over two million people, making it the fastest growing metropolitan region in the USA.[30] In the twenty-first century, over seventy per cent of all Nevada residents live in or around Vegas. Today it seems as if Las Vegas owes its wealth to hotels and casinos. In fact, the origins of its 'Sin City' nickname go back to 1931 when Nevada eased its laws on marriage and divorce. A few years later, with the end of Prohibition, alcohol began to flow in large quantities.

## The nuclear wasteland and its casualties

The beginning of the region's meteoric rise took place in the 1940s and 1950s when the US military was stationed there. From the American government's point of view, remote desert areas were excellently suited to military projects. Scientists involved in the strictly confidential Manhattan Project were based in both Los Alamos, New Mexico and Las Vegas during the Second World War. This project aimed to drive forward the construction of nuclear weapons. The tempo at which the USA was militarised after the catastrophe

## St Thomas, Nevada. The Ghosts Return

of Pearl Harbor is utterly inconceivable today: in the 1940s, eight million workers moved from east to west in North America. Cheap hydroelectric power on the Colorado and Columbia Rivers facilitated the construction of aircraft factories and shipyards as well as production sites for aluminium, magnesium and synthetic rubber between Seattle, Washington and Phoenix, Arizona. The backward American West became a pacesetting region into which millions of dollars of state support flowed, forty billion dollars alone during the Second World War. Between 1951 and 1962, several hundred above-ground atom bomb tests were carried out on a military airstrip, some sixty miles from Las Vegas.

In Las Vegas, the A-bomb tests were marketed as a spectacle. The Las Vegas Chamber of Commerce published a calendar with the exact dates of Nevada Test Site detonations and gave locations for the best 'nuclear viewing'. Tourists packed 'atomic lunch boxes' and headed off for picnics at the detonation sites, known as Ground Zero, to watch the atomic mushroom clouds in the desert. Businesspeople celebrated with cocktails and 'Dawn Bomb Parties' on Vegas' rooftop decks. And when more than 200 journalists were invited in April 1952 to witness a particularly large detonation from a distance of only ten miles, images of the 'Big Shot', as the press nicknamed the bomb, were broadcast on national television. The whole of America was in the grip of atomic fever. 'Big Shot' was as powerful as the bombs dropped on Nagasaki and Hiroshima put together. The pictures from the Nevadan desert demonstrated the nation's atomic potency to a North American population intimidated by the Cold War. When a few individuals in Las Vegas expressed concern about these nuclear activities, a specially launched campaign of propaganda counteracted them with an array of 'alternative facts'. Many hoteliers seized the chance to market Las Vegas not only as the 'gateway to Hoover Dam', but also as the 'Atomic City'.[31] Hotels and casinos, especially the Sands and the Flamingo, offered 'atomic cocktails' and 'atomic hairdos', while 'Miss Atomic Bomb' was crowned in a beauty pageant contest. An advert still widely circulated today, shows Lee A. Merlin, Miss Atomic Bomb of 1957, a radiantly blonde showgirl, wearing a cotton dress in the form of an A-bomb cloud.[32]

But at the beginning of the 1950s, sheep herders in Iron County, Utah, noticed that their animals were contracting strange diseases and dying early. Several efforts were made to file lawsuits against the US government – without success. Conspicuously, the Atomic Energy Commission (AEC) refused to publish measurements, reports and eye-witness statements by veterinary surgeons who diagnosed the diseases and mass deaths of grazing livestock. Soon after the Iron County sheep, animals and people in other regions were also affected. Nearly all the reports came from areas northeast of the test sites in Nevada. In fact, to impact the densely populated regions around Las Vegas as little as possible, the AEC had given instructions to carry out the tests at times when the wind was not blowing in Vegas's direction. But, for this reason, the effect of the tests in St George, Utah was all the more devastating.

In the 1950s, St George was a pretty little town whose white Mormon temple rose against the backdrop of red cliffs in the desert. Most of its residents were orderly Mormons who abstained from alcohol, tobacco and coffee consumption. According to surveys from the 1950s, 55 per cent of the region's population drank milk produced by their own cow, 56 per cent fetched drinking water from the local well, and 65 per cent ate regional or homegrown vegetables.[33] This healthy lifestyle proved to be the undoing of St George's residents. Because, by eating local produce, they consumed radioactive isotopes that caused countless forms of cancer in the years to come – leukaemia, breast cancer, bone, stomach and bowel cancer, thyroid cancer, brain tumours and melanomas.[34]

Radio warnings were broadcast to St George residents of approaching radioactive clouds and children were advised not to eat snow; but not all warnings arrived in time. In internal memos, it was shown that the AEC understood nuclear fallout could cause skin burns – but it decided not to evacuate the population, so as to avoid alarm. One detonation in May 1953 was particularly fatal when an A-bomb was launched from a high metal tower. What happened on that day in St George played a decisive role for years during court proceedings that later took place. Agatha Mannering, for example, who was weeding her garden when the detonation went off and had not heard the radio warnings of an approaching radioactive cloud, suffered acute burns. A short time later, her hair fell out and soon her bones were as brittle as if she were an elderly woman suffering from osteoporosis. Elma Mackelprang Barnett, who was riding in a pick-up truck with her children to water her sheep, became feverish and dizzy, and later her hair and fingernails fell out. Her children, who were sitting in the driver's cabin and weren't directly exposed like their mother, remained unharmed at first. Miners from St George working in a nearby uranium mine vomited and came out in skin rashes. Many of St George's residents complained of a metal taste in their mouths. A man named Frank Butrico who was commissioned by the AEC to measure radioactivity levels on site was directed

## St Thomas, Nevada. The Ghosts Return

on the telephone to buy new clothes, dispose of his old ones and shower thoroughly. When he asked if he should pass on these instructions to the residents of St George, the authorities categorically forbade him to do so in case panic broke out. Only decades later in August 1980, did an investigative committee of the US House of Representatives admit that all the health hazards connected to atomic radiation had not only been ignored but had also been actively suppressed.[35]

The East Coast sees Nevada as an empty and barren place. This remote state seemed ideal for nuclear experiments. When above-ground detonations slowly met with resistance from the population, subterranean testing continued. Today the Nevada Test Site is a scarred wasteland, a moonscape full of detonation craters. With every explosion, more radioactivity seeped into the earth, sometimes directly into the groundwater. When nuclear testing stopped in Nevada in 1992 after the Cold War ended, more than eleven million terabecquerels of nuclear radiation had been released in the test zone – a level that surpassed the fallout from the atomic bombs dropped on Hiroshima by more than a hundred thousand times.

Nowadays, tourists with a morbid curiosity can visit the Nevada Test Site on selected days, provided they register nine months in advance and undergo a background check. A fully air-conditioned bus takes passengers from Las Vegas to the desert; short trousers and sandals may not be worn, and mobile phones and cameras may not be carried on the bus. The tour takes a route through the grounds of the nuclear site, past heavily armed sentries in the abandoned small town of Mercury; it stops at military training centres and formerly top-secret testing sites and gives nuclear nerds a close-up view of impact craters. A psyched tourist in a Las Vegas bar – a former GI from Colorado – tells me that, if you go on this tour, Stanley Kubrick's *Dr Strangelove* takes on a whole new meaning. He adds that he's also visited other 'military tourist sites' nearby, such as the simulated Afghan town of Ertebat Shar where US soldiers prepare for deployment in the Middle East. It's all really awesome, he claims, but nothing beats the crater tour. You can't fly to the moon, he says, but it's pretty close.[36]

Not until three decades after nuclear tests began, were plans made to build North America's (if not the world's) largest high-level nuclear waste repository in tunnels under Yucca Mountain just a few miles away from Nevada's Test Site. Today over a million cubic metres of 'low-level nuclear waste' are stored in Nevada's moonscape.[37] This quantity is enough to fill every one of the Empire State Building's 103 storeys. What's more, plans

109

were made to make underground deposits in Nevada's landscape of 98 per cent of the nuclear waste produced by over a hundred atomic reactors in the USA during the nuclear age. But violent protests by environmental activists and indigenous people – the areas in question belong to the heartlands of the Shoshone and Paiute peoples – dogged the government's plans. Corbin Harney, one of the spiritual leaders of the Western Shoshone, reminded the administration that Yucca Mountain actually belongs to his tribe. In speeches and publications, he called the Western Shoshone 'the most bombed nation in the world' and warned of the high risk from potential road accidents when transporting high-level waste through a total of 43 US states to the sacred grounds of his ancestors.[38] If a terrorist attack took place during the transport, the radioactive cargo on the trucks could turn into a 'mobile Chernobyl'. Almost more dangerous is the risk of an earthquake. Every year, hundreds of earthquakes with a magnitude of more than 2.5 on the Richter scale are recorded in the surroundings of Yucca Mountain. The probability that one of them could cause a leak in the metal containers of nuclear waste is therefore high. Seismic activity could destroy the dream of safe nuclear waste disposal with one blow. But water from flash floods penetrating the subterranean tunnels due to the area's geological nature also presents a danger. Who can be sure whether deserts are the ideal place to store radioactive materials? Who knows how the climate and geology of the Yucca Mountain region will develop over the next ten or hundred thousand years? Plutonium has a half-life period of 25,000 years, and the waste is likely to give off hazardous radioactive rays for at least 300,000 years. Who knows whether Nevada's desert will fully dry out by then, or transform into a rainforest? Who can be sure whether the centuries-old underground lake beneath the rocks of Yucca Mountain won't refill one day?[39]

## Gradual drought

No matter how the region surrounding Las Vegas develops in the distant future, the population in Nevada and the six arid neighbouring states are facing serious problems that are ignored by most: 2014 was the driest year in over 1,000 years. The average rainfall in Las Vegas is lower nowadays than in Kuwait or Oman. For years, the region's aridity has increased along with the number of inhabitants. If St Thomas had to be flooded for Las Vegas to flourish, what significance does it hold that the ruins of St Thomas are visible again today and its spirits have returned without being summoned?

## St Thomas, Nevada. The Ghosts Return

Since the beginning of the twenty-first century alone, the water elevation of Lake Mead has sunk by over forty metres. The white rings on the canyon's dark rockface, which locals jokingly refer to as 'bathtub rings', are due to mineral deposits; they unmistakably point to the sinking water level. For Las Vegas, this is a warning sign, similar to Echo Bay, Lake Mead's dried-up yacht harbour, because the desert city is drip-fed by the reservoir. If the water level sinks below 65 metres – a scenario that is no longer far from reality – there will be a water emergency and the adjacent states will throttle the water supply by four per cent. If it sinks below 58 metres, the residents will have to give up a further seven per cent. Ninety per cent of the water supply in the Las Vegas Valley comes from the Colorado River. Meltwater and rain in the Rocky Mountains have drastically sunk over the years and so has the level of water in Lake Mead. More than 22 billion litres of water are needed to fill the reservoir. Climate change and drought make the reversal of current developments highly unlikely.[40]

## Waterfalls in the desert

I have been to Vegas twice. Both times, I couldn't believe my eyes. The city is so much brighter and louder, glitzier and more bizarre than films or postcards suggest. Endless light strips and illuminations fill the place with neon and water everywhere. The fountains in front of the Bellagio Hotel dance to synchronised spotlights. Lit-up signs proclaim: 'Welcome to Fabulous Las Vegas'. Then there's the neon cowboy Vegas Vic and his partner, Vegas Vickie. Everywhere you look there are waterfalls and palm trees. A large lagoon with a tropical backdrop is located in front of the Mirage Hotel. The rumbling of the Mirage 'volcano' is accompanied by 130-foot-high 'lava' fountains. Everything is artificial and very colourful; it all flashes and whirrs at a hectic pace. Venice is simulated with a covered Canal Grande and gondolas. Light shows featuring two million lightbulbs take place on Fremont Street. There are hotels and gambling dens where Blackjack and roulette are played, and one-armed bandits stand. Finally, there is Insanity, a thrill ride suspended 300 metres above the ground.

Las Vegas is not good for everyone's health. The suicide rate is twice as high there as the national average.[41] One of its slogans is: 'Remember to Breathe'. And the city truly does seem breathless. Anything goes – as long as it is excessive. The constant neon and waterfalls fade into the background once you've been there for a couple of days. The contrast between the Mojave

Paradise Blues

A white 'bathtub ring' at Hoover Dam has bleached the rocks of Lake Mead. It shows how the water level has dropped over the last decades.

## St Thomas, Nevada. The Ghosts Return

Desert – a quiet, dry place – and Vegas could not be greater. Whose idea was it to build this pleasure capital right in the middle of the desert? And why does Vegas continue to grow at such an explosive pace?

The optimists refuse to see a problem: but in 2015, an extremely low-lying intake tunnel was created on the bed of Lake Mead. When the reservoir was built, no one ever thought that the water level could sink below the two higher intake points. The new tap aims to ensure that even the last drop of water can be sucked out of the reservoir and directed towards Las Vegas where the water level is constantly falling. The 'Third Straw', as this complicated technological process was dubbed by the press, cost over 800 million dollars and one human life.[42] And if, one day, the third and final straw is no longer effective because Lake Mead has completely dried up, then new pipelines plans in Las Vegas have long been made that will pump water from northern and eastern Nevada – without consideration for the livelihood of the local cattle breeders, Mormons or Shoshone people.[43] This is sheer blindness and ignorance.

In Las Vegas casinos, people have played away their savings and future for the past ninety years. Nowhere in the world is the hope of striking it lucky higher that in this desert city where everyone places bets. Here, luxury and bankruptcy, poverty and wastefulness live side by side. For the past two decades, the Vegas water authorities have put their money not only on tapping into new sources but also on economising – like a gambler trying to stop going broke before it's too late. The reason this strategy has worked so far is largely thanks to a civil servant called Patricia Mulroy. The daughter of a US soldier who grew up in Germany, Mulroy came to Vegas in 1974 to seek her fortune. After studying German literature, she began her career in the local administration of Clark County, became general manager of the Las Vegas Water District in 1989 and soon afterwards founded her own company, the central Southern Nevada Water Authority.[44] Mulroy's self-confident aura and insistence on new, radical regulations to reduce water consumption soon led to her nickname, the 'water czar' or even 'water witch'.[45] The 'cash for grass' programme, in which homeowners were financially compensated for every square foot of turf they gave up, made her a household name far beyond Nevada's borders. Almost three thousand soccer stadiums could be laid with the lawn that Las Vegas citizens have removed since then. 'Xeriscaping' (from the Greek word *xeros*, meaning dry) – or planting front gardens with local plants – was a hugely popular trend. Driving through the suburbs of Las Vegas, barely any lawns remain, unlike twenty years ago. They have been replaced by rock gardens of desert grasses, cacti, yucca and other plants suited to the arid climate. The water authority gives out coupons for 'smart' car washes that recycle water. The filling of ponds and fountains is severely restricted and watering of plants may only take place at designated times. 'Water police' (officially known as water waste investigators) uphold local laws.[46] If, for example, water flows from a front garden towards the street, the person responsible is automatically fined eighty dollars. And water consumption per capita has sunk drastically. Once, a green lawn was the pride and joy of every homeowner; now it is grounds for ostracism. Mulroy's strict regime is showing results. A large percentage of water used by hotels and casinos is recycled and reused. And quite a few mayors and city councillors in the American Southwest have adopted Las Vegas's water-saving measures as blueprints for their own regulations. What's more, smart businesspeople recently declared Las Vegas the 'Silicon Valley of water' – an innovative hub for hydro innovation. Today, water technology is big business and some ingenious devices have been developed in the desert city, such as washing machines with extremely low water consumption or computer-operated surveillance machines that register real-time leaks in subterranean water pipes.[47]

## Environmental roulette

Let's not kid ourselves: water consumption in Las Vegas is still significantly higher than in other northwestern American cities. The forty golf courses with their idyllic lakes in Las Vegas valley are as green today as ever and the evaporation in America's driest city undermines many of the authority's efforts. Almost twenty per cent of the water disperses in the air or via cooling towers. Las Vegas may have bought itself time in a game of water poker, but its future doesn't look rosy. Many things point to the fact that, in the short or long term, Vegas and Nevada will be overtaken by the problems caused by climate change. In the Red Rooster in Overton, the locals say: 'Vegas will never die. The city is ruled by the mob and the mob has money.' But money can't buy everything. Climate scientists predict that, in the future, there will be huge oscillations between heavy rainfall and dry spells. But in the long run, the American Southwest will continue to dry out. The creeping destruction of the environment will also prove problematic. Not only are water reserves threatened by contamination from radioactive waste from the atomic era, but also by decades of mining gold from the depths of the earth.[48]

## St Thomas, Nevada. The Ghosts Return

What made Las Vegas great was its remoteness. But the former habitat of mountain lions and coyotes, wildcats and owls has now given way to a 'new America of iron and concrete' which, according to the anarchist and author of *Desert Solitaire*, Edward Abbey, 'none of us can quite understand or accept or wholly love'.[49] The transformation of the desert – in which America's indigenous people for centuries (and the Mormons for decades) handled the sparse water reserves sparingly – into a region dominated by asphalt and casinos took place at a crazy pace. For the US government, the arid zone where no one wanted to settle was a sacrificial one where they deposited whatever they wanted to put out of sight: secret military operations, radioactive fallout, atomic waste, unpopular religious groups, gambling dens and prostitution. Vegas has become an ever-sprawling, water-and-energy-guzzling Moloch, a monster city with overcrowded prisons that lives beyond its means and where everything that makes cities liveable – from breathable air to public spaces – is missing, not least for the disadvantaged sections of the population.[50]

Seen through the lens of St Thomas's history, Las Vegas's attitude seems conceited and doomed. St Thomas may be dead: but its short life throws up more questions today than ever before. Should the unchecked diversion of water, described by the writer Wallace Stegner as an 'original sin', be stopped to restrict Las Vegas's growth?[51] Should the majority of people in America's Southwest be resettled? Or should the arid West be completely written off? The ruins of St Thomas are reminders of how difficult it is to live and survive in the desert, as well as of the vulnerability and resilience of human beings. These things remind us how precious limited resources are; but also how quickly those in power are prepared to sacrifice passed-on wisdom and heritage. This includes historical places, cultures, rivers, flora, fauna and a healthy environment. What's clear is that reducing lawn surfaces, using smart technological inventions or simply throwing a ball into the roulette wheel will not help secure people's future in America's Southwest. Very few societies in the course of history have been prepared to swallow a bitter pill to guarantee the welfare of the next generation. But in Nevada, more than anywhere else in the USA, a change in approach on a different scale is called for. Otherwise, playing roulette with nature will sooner or later drive the population out of their desert paradise.

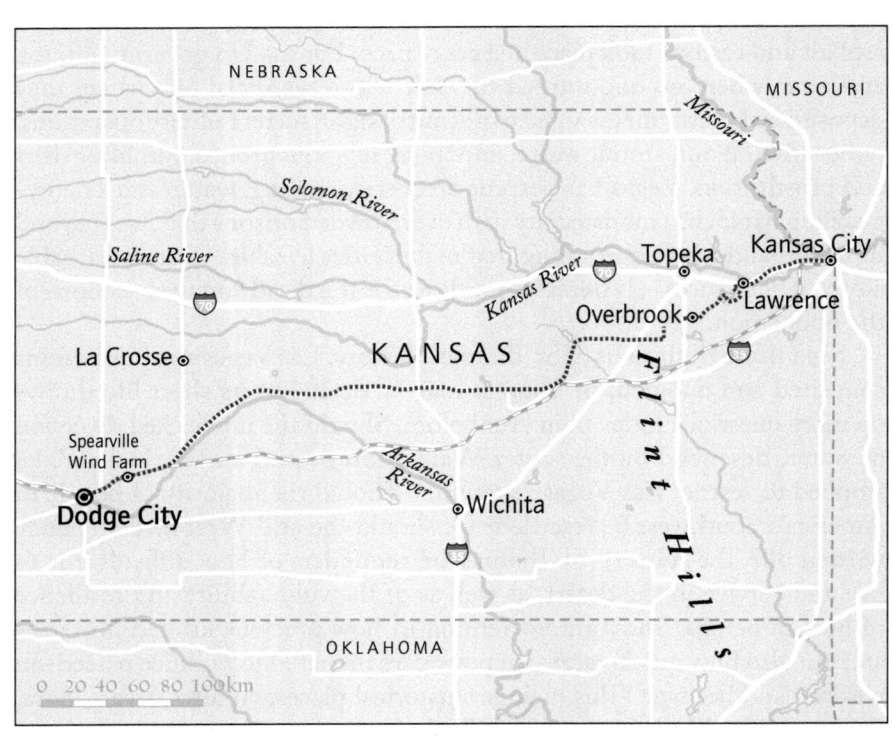

Dodge City, location map

# Dodge City, Kansas.
## The Windy Wild West

### The windy Wild West

Dodge City may be the best-known city in the Wild West. The TV series *Gunsmoke*, which was first broadcast in the United States in 1952 and has since been watched by viewers all over the world, sealed Dodge City's reputation as a cowboy mecca, which lives on today. On one hand, Dodge, as locals call it, stands for lawlessness and violence like no other US city. But, on the other, it represents a belief in progress and America's expectation of salvation, which led to the nineteenth-century philosophy of Manifest Destiny. Advocates of this belief thought the USA was destined to expand its dominion, spreading democracy and capitalism across the entire North American continent, even if this involved a bitter war against its indigenous peoples. No other city symbolises the myth of the Old West more perfectly than Dodge, which earned the label of 'Wickedest Little City in America' in the 1870s. Dodge stands for showdowns between gangsters and herders, sheriffs and bandits against the Hollywood backdrop of saloon bars, churches and law courts. Dodge City conjures up images of the covered wagons of settlers, traders and cattle drivers. And in Dodge City, the Wild West lives, on according to historian Andrew Isenberg. 'It has plenty of historic buildings and cattle feedlots', he tells me with a grin. 'If you want to experience the American West, go to Dodge.'[1]

### Not in Kansas anymore / storms

I start my trip at Kansas City airport where signs to the tornado shelter are hard to miss. The toilets on the lower floors are used as a refuge from these treacherous, destructive winds that form violently rotating columns of air and frequently lay waste to the landscape. One still notorious 1966 tornado sliced Topeka, the capital of Kansas, in two, causing over 200 million dollars' worth of damage – the highest sum to date in the USA. In the year 2007, the town of Greensburg, Kansas, was almost completely wiped out. Even a year after the storm, most of the 1,500 inhabitants were still living in trailer parks while the rebuilding of the town slowly progressed.

Since 1880, Kansas has endured more than 125 tornadoes on a Fujita scale of F4 and F5, killing a total of roughly 1,000 people. Kansas takes ill-fated second place (after Texas) in the tables of storm statistics. Tornadoes can occur whenever there is a thunderstorm. But on the Great Plains east of the Rocky Mountains, at the centre of which lies Kansas, the conditions for tornadoes are much more favourable than anywhere else in the world. Cool winds blowing in from the Rockies clash with warm air rising from the Gulf of Mexico. And on the prairie plains, they pick up full force and speed. No wonder the famous classic *The Wizard of Oz*, in which twelve-year-old Dorothy and her dog Toto are caught up in a tornado inside their wooden shack and thrown into the magical land of Oz, was set on a farm in Kansas.[2]

It's April and most tornadoes occur between March and September, so I decide to stay tuned to the weather channel while in Kansas. The quickest route from Kansas City to Dodge is five and a half hours but I plan to make quite a few stops along the way. The route is at least as interesting as Dodge itself – and the journey allows me to reflect on Kansas' history. I spend the first two days on historian Don Worster's small farm where his wife Bev keeps sheep. Don has dropped his full name since Trump came to power. He and Bev live half an hour from the small university town of Lawrence on the shore of Clinton Lake. When my satnav announces, 'You have reached your destination', there isn't a house in sight. I drive off the gravel track and carry on along a dirt path until I reach the farm. The Worsters live in absolute seclusion. To my amazement, a rafter of wild turkey wanders past the window while we drink coffee in the house. Don is used to it. 'They march past here every day now.' The Worsters' feathered neighbours include red-bellied woodpeckers, Zenaida doves, Swedish blue ducks, little blue herons, Canadian geese and hawfinches. The surroundings of Clinton Lake reservoir are home to squirrels, white-tailed deer, foxes, coyotes, mink, bobcats, beavers, striped turtles, glass creepers and bullfrogs. 'A Finnish friend of mine once counted forty species when he was visiting, not including insects', Worster tells me. The lake has a surface area of 55 square kilometres, a rarity in Kansas. And the fact that the Worsters own water rights on their farm makes their land valuable because, to build a house, you have to prove there is access to water.

Don recommends a few detours from my route to Dodge City that will take me along the Santa Fe Trail and through the Flint Hills, which he says is the most beautiful spot in the region. 'Kansas', he explains, 'is as flat as a pancake.' The further west you travel, the flatter it becomes. 'But here in the east, there are some amazing hills.' Don Worster knows what he's talking about. He grew up in the region – his parents were Dust Bowl refugees. And one of the books that has brought him fame is *Dust Bowl, The Southern Plains in the 1930s*. The succession of storms was one of the greatest environmental catastrophes in North American history. A particularly devastating tornado swept over the prairie in 1935 and turned an area almost twice the size of Germany into a barren desert. It was the result of an extremely dry period exacerbated by the profit-oriented, ruthless treatment of the land by farmers. The constantly soaring prices paid for wheat around the turn of the century, but especially from the First World War onwards, had turned the Great Plains into a paradise for cereal production. In 1888, only three per cent of the area affected by the Dust Bowl grew wheat; by 1930, almost ninety per cent of crops were 'King Wheat'. Gigantic combine harvesters, almost seven metres wide, destroyed the fragile earth by pulverising arable land, which then was swept away by the wind. John Steinbeck's novel *Grapes of Wrath* tells the story of people who lose their livelihood and then have to flee to California.[3]

I meet my colleague, Greg Cushman. When asked what he thinks Dodge City has to offer, he shoots back: 'The smell – sour and sharp.' Greg ought to know. He knows a thing or two about smells since his book about fertilisers made from bird excrement, *Guano and the Opening of the Pacific World: A Global Ecological History*, was published. Don Worster leans over the map before I leave and gives me some tips on what I should see on the way to Dodge City. His wife Bev says I should live it up there: 'Have a steak there tonight – and tomorrow night and the next.'

I'm not sure what to expect from the sight, sounds, and smells of Dodge. But first, I have to travel a whole day through Kansas, a state famous for its big sky.

## Santa Fe Trail

On my way to Santa Fe, I come across the first traces of the legendary Santa Fe Trail. A wall in a tiny little town called Overbrook is painted with a colossal mural by a local artist. It depicts the conquest of the American West, with symbols like the steam locomotive and a 'prairie schooner', as covered wagons pulled by oxen were called. A banner unfurls over the painted town

Paradise Blues

The Santa Fe Trail once ran through the area of Overbrook, a frontier town founded in 1886. Overbrook today has about 1,000 inhabitants.

hall and church with the words 'Don't overlook Overbrook. A Santa Fe Trail community, est. 1886.' Without the trail, this community, which has fewer than 1,000 inhabitants today, would never have come into existence. Before the railroad was built in the 1870s, the 1,300-kilometre-trail was frequented by a steady stream of settlers and traders transporting velvet, silk, cotton, lace, books and paper. Until 1846, Santa Fe was Mexican, and nationals paid for their wares in silver and gold.

The highway from Overbrook to Dodge City runs parallel to the old Santa Fe trail for long stretches. Wind and weather have erased almost all traces of its history but, in some places, the hooves of tens of thousands of cattle and wagon wheels dug so deep that you can still see them 150 years later. Back then, there were practically no navigable rivers or urban clusters west of the Mississippi. It's hard to imagine from our modern-day perspective how arduous it was for nineteenth-century people to cross the prairie. But, reading excerpts from the journal of George C. Sibley, a man commissioned in the 1820s by the governor of Missouri to survey the Santa Fe Trail so

120

that a tarred road could be built, there is no doubt that transport back then went hand in hand with huge exertion and danger. Had Sibley's journal been widely available back then, many a pioneer and settler would have thought twice about setting off across the prairie.

Sibley, an Indian agent who had conducted US government business for years with the Kansa and Osage tribes in Fort Osage near Kansas City, was already forty years old when he set off on his expedition. During his trip, he was attacked by Native Americans, plagued by sand and blow flies and bitten by rattlesnakes. One way to treat snake bites, as he described in his journal, was to apply the dried contents of a turkey vulture's stomach, ground into a powder, to the affected area. He also recommended digging wells because the streams were 'seasoned with buffalo urine'. The fate of George Sibley's journal, which he wrote in William Eckert's tavern in Saint Charles, Missouri, was tragic. After he'd checked the details of every entry and meticulously noted every freshwater source in Kansas' arid landscape, Sibley sent his manuscript to Washington for publication. After a long interlude, he received a telegram reporting that his text had been lost. A second version was also lost. But Sibley personally delivered the third and fourth versions, which he copied out himself, to the capital. His journal was never published during his lifetime, and the road he surveyed was never built. A good hundred years later, the manuscript was discovered in Washington and published in 1952, when the Wild West had long since disappeared.[4]

Even if you don't go looking for traces of prairie expeditions made by nineteenth-century Europeans, you come across their commemorations. Gigantic metal sculptures line the highway. Their silhouettes periodically appear on the horizon – farmers and oxen, covered wagons and cowboys. They suggest that the Kansas settlements took place peacefully; this was very far from the truth. Effectively it was a land grab that took away terrain from various Native American tribes who inhabited the prairie. For the Osage, Kiowa, Arapaho, Pawnee, and Kansa peoples (the latter are namesakes of the state of Kansas), the Santa Fe Trail signalled the end of their century-old way of life. The loss of their natural habitat, especially the decimation of the buffalo and wildlife populations, led to recurrent bloody warfare between different indigenous tribes. Greedy speculators and the antagonism towards Native Americans in Washington proved fatal for North America's indigenous population. At best, they could only survive in the reservations.

In 1846, the Kansa tribe was taken to a reservation near Council Grove, and this is where I make a stop. The small town was named after an agreement between the Osage tribe and European white settlers. The Europeans were granted the right to travel through the town in their wagon convoys and to gather as a council by a grove before their onward journey. Today the small town still basks in the glory of the Santa Fe Trail's history.[5] The jail that once housed 'desperados, border ruffians, and robbers' within its walls has been reconstructed. And in the Trail Days Café, built in 1860, making it the oldest stone house on the trail, there is even a small museum. It advertises that its 'Indian food' and dishes from the 'Old World', including German Schnitzel and strawberry rhubarb cake, will 'transport guests back to a time' when wagons rolled past the front door. Carved notches on the lintel of the back door allegedly go back to the Kansa tribe. In the town centre is a six-metre-high Madonna of the Trail memorial to commemorate the 'pioneer mothers': and the Rotary Club has reconstructed one of the 138 stone houses in which the semi-nomadic Kansa and Osage peoples once lodged. They had no choice, they were forced to move here. They did not like to live in stone buildings and used them as horse stables. When the Kansa people came to Council Grove in 1846 to sign the Mission Creek contract, their fate had long since been sealed. As the Methodist minister William Johnson reported at the end of the 1830s, smallpox, introduced to the New World by European settlers, massive floods that ravaged East Kansas' dry terrain in the 1830s (and later in 1844), and land grabs by immigrating pioneers, traders and settlers causing the displacement of native tribes had turned the indigenous population into 'pensioners of the United States, and beggars of the emigrants passing west, for clothing and food'.[6] For over 300 years, the Kansa people had primarily lived off hunting buffalo; but coming into contact with white settlers who tried to force them to hunt for furs and, later, settle down and convert to Christianity, delivered them a death blow. The Kansa, who were given a lasting monument in Council Grove in the form of reconstructed stone houses that did not represent their culture in any way whatsoever, never returned after they were driven out of their territories. At the start of the twentieth century, only 250 tribe members remained in Kansas. On 23 April 2000, their last full descendant, William A. Mehojah, died in Omaha, Nebraska.[7]

## The ecology of the Native Americans

For a century, US American history presented the settlement of the American West as a story of democratic triumph, social reform and economic progress. In doing so, it suppressed the sinister side – the destruction of indigenous

## Dodge City, Kansas. The Windy Wild West

cultures and ecological costs. Today we know that European expansion was met with a variety of resistance but that it was also based on cooperation between white settlers and Native Americans. French fur traders, for example, married Osage and Kansa women who ensured that their tribes adjusted their hunting to the market economy – for better or for worse.

The indigenous tribes were not 'noble savages', nor were they primitive peoples; they were a part of complex societies that had transformed the landscape of the Midwest over centuries. We know that they adjusted their agricultural methods to the prairie's specific environmental conditions and that they, too, had trouble holding its ecology in balance to ensure that people and animals could cohabit sustainably. The native people who lived in modern-day Kansas were not a homogenous group. Their culture combined nomadic hunting with sedentary farming. The farmers among them lived in mud huts or round houses, planted vegetables such as squash and beans, cultivated maize and used wild plants and herbs. They dug underground pits in which they stored surplus products and bartered with animal skins, furs and meat.

In the minds of many Europeans, the images of 'Indians' and horses are inseparable. But it wasn't until Columbus arrived in the New World that riding horses were introduced. The ancestors of modern horses already existed forty million years ago in America but, by the last Ice Age, these early horses had become extinct or migrated to Asia. The horses of the Spanish arrived in Kansas in the eighteenth century via trade routes from Mexico. They prompted some indigenous populations – especially in the far west – to reinvent themselves as nomadic horsemen. However, the assumption that horses adapted easily to the prairies is wrong. Native Americans soon proved to be excellent horse riders and the animals played an important role in indigenous ceremonies and as a form of bridewealth. But the social and ecological consequences of introducing horses to the prairie were far-reaching. It was not suitable to let the horses roam freely. Firstly, they might be stolen and, secondly, they were notorious for trampling the crops in gardens cultivated by the women. More than anything else, the presence of thoroughbred horses, as reported by the missionary Samuel Allis, contributed to quarrels, envy and family disputes.

The greatest challenge was the lack of animal feed during the winter months. The tallgrass in the prairie dried out as early as fall, and only contained nutrients underground in its roots. For this reason, the Pawnee in Kansas, whose habitat has been scrupulously documented in missionary reports, would drive their horses in winter to Grand Island on the Platte

River in modern-day Nebraska. They also made do with branches and bark from poplar trees, which were suitable replacements for hay. Mostly, however, the indigenous population in Kansas deliberately burned large areas of grass to revitalise the prairie. In the past, it was thought that this practice helped spot moose, white-tailed and mule deer, bears and antelope. But this makes no sense as the fires would not only have destroyed the grasses, but also wiped out trees and shrubs – the main food supply for wild animals. And the theory that the practice of burning areas of grass benefited the buffalo hunt is hardly tenable because the animals did not graze in the tallgrass, preferring the short grass areas of the prairie.

Today we know that the fires lit by indigenous nomadic horsemen primarily served as a way to secure food for their horses. Fire had greater significance for agriculture in Kansas than water. The complex interaction of heat, moisture and seed production had a grave impact on the grass of the North American prairie, as it did in other semi-arid regions of the world, such as the Central Asian steppe and the Namibian savanna. Fires made sure that older grass thickets and bark mulch were cleared. This way, the sun could warm the earth much earlier in the year and the yield was more plentiful. This was a subtle method used by the indigenous people, but of which the settlers from the Old World were ignorant. 'To make a prairie it takes a clover and one bee, One clover, and a bee', as Emily Dickinson wrote in a mid-nineteenth century poem.[8] Whether a clover and a bee were enough to *make* a prairie is up for discussion; but to *keep* one required more, such as unregulated fires which set the wheel of ecological succession in motion.

The ecology of North America's first settlers – farming and hunting – was not all positive. The indigenous people who once lived in Kansas were partly responsible for the eradication of great buffalo herds. Prairie fire sometimes raged uncontrollably across hundreds of kilometres and left behind irregular bare patches. It destroyed trees and bushes as well as grasses. Conflicts with the US settlers coming from the East were therefore inevitable especially once settlers immigrated in increasing numbers along the Santa Fe Trail in the second half of the nineteenth century.[9]

## The Flint Hills

Following Don Worster's advice, I drive from Council Grove towards the Flint Hills. It's raining – and rain is the biggest topic whenever I talk to people en route. Rain is rare and aridity is part of Kansas' history like snowfall

## Dodge City, Kansas. The Windy Wild West

in the Arctic. The weather has imposed limits on people in this region here since time immemorial. Extreme dry spells have driven them to leave the region more than once. The dry years of 1859 and 1861, for example, long before the 1930s Dust Bowl catastrophe, forced a third of the population of Kansas into exodus.

The Flint Hills are wilder and more rugged than the rest of Kansas. The steep slopes with their rough, drop-off edges tower more than fifty metres over the rest of the terrain. West of the Flint Hills, it rains less often than in the east. Instead of the high native bluestem grass, only the shorter grama grass grows in the west. The Flint Hills are named after the flintstones that punctuate the landscape. I'm here in April and broad swathes of the prairie grasses that would be over a metre high during any other season have been burned away. On the black areas left behind, on which new, wholesome grass is growing back, the flintstones are visible. Here and there a squirrel scampers across the rocky landscape. It's truly a feat that the grasses can pump up water in this terrain. Their roots wrap themselves around the stones and convoys of bugs and worms ventilate the earth.

Rock and soil formation,
Flint Hills, Kansas.

Three hundred million years ago, the Flint Hills belonged to a primordial sea. The movement of the water slowly created these enormous stone surfaces. It takes almost a hundred years for nature to deposit a centimetre of limestone. After the softer stone formations erode over time, flintstone remains. Within 20,000 years, this led to the creation of today's landscape scattered with flint. On the top of one hill, I find traces of a former indigenous quarry. Archaeologists estimate that it must be 2,000 years old. Flint was used by the native population to make arrows and spearheads, sharp blades and all kinds of tools. It was roughly hewn on site and later reworked. These early stone masons often had a long journey: this is shown by the shell and coral jewellery that archaeologists have discovered near the stone quarry.[10] The indigenous people used the prairie with its multitude of resources – grasses, animals and stones – in a similar way to how sea fishermen and seafarers use the ocean. Every time they made an excursion, they fetched what they needed, whether it was buffalo meat to eat, grasses to feed animals or flintstone to use as raw material. And for centuries, their lives flourished.

Native Americans adapted well to the nature that surrounded them, and the landscape only changed slowly under human influence. Almost 700,000 square kilometres of tallgrass were maintained for hundreds of years. Nowadays, only four per cent of this area is still intact – and nearly all of it is in the Flint Hills. Here, unploughed grass is making its last stand.[11] In the Tall Grass Prairie National Preserve, a nature reserve supported by US federal funds, park rangers are doing their best to win back part of this lost landscape and protect it for the future. In a two-square-kilometre area along Fox Creek, where the terrain is less stony than in the higher areas, tallgrass is being replanted. This small project is ambitious and complex. The grass first has to undergo a freeze/thaw cycle before it can germinate. Without herbicides, the first generation does not stand a chance of survival: and it still isn't clear whether the experiment will be successful, and the 'original' landscape can permanently gain ground in the long term.

Besides native flora, environmentalists at Kansas' Nature Conservancy want to bring original fauna back to the tallgrass preserve. In 2009, thirteen *ur*bison – the first animals to roam the Flint Hills – were transported from South Dakota to the preserve. Since then, the small herd has more than doubled in size. Efforts to 'restore nature', whatever that means exactly, are hopeful but also puzzling. Is the National Preserve a mixture of a zoo, botanical garden and natural history museum? Can the clock truly be turned back by conservationists reintroducing primeval flora and fauna into limited areas? People are expert manipulators of their environment. In the National Preserve, conditions that once reigned are being recreated; but at the same time, you can find 'beefalo' on menus and in American supermarkets – a hybrid meat made of beef crossed with bison, considered particularly healthy because of its low cholesterol and fat.[12]

It's windy and raining. The ground is wet, and the bison are far away; I'm still a few hundred kilometres from Dodge City. The flint boulders and the broad skyline are memorable sights. The nearer I get to Dodge, the flatter and broader the hills become. West of Kansas, the horizon dominates. Farms, windmills and trees jut into the air, visible for miles around, like monuments in the landscape. In Dodge City, I'm going to meet Rhonda Jeffries, a historian who works in the Kansas Heritage Centre and owns a small ranch with 500 cattle. 'If you think the landscape around Dodge City is empty', she says, 'you should have seen Kansas when I grew up here sixty years ago. When I was young', she adds, 'there were hardly any trees. "If you get lost, walk to the trees", my dad used to say to us when we were kids.' They were likely to be near farms where they were planted and watered or grew along creeks and rivers. In the East of the United States, they are part of the landscape; in the west, they are foreign entities. 'Every tree near Dodge that's over five feet was brought here', Rhonda explains, 'by birds, other animals, or settlers.'[13]

## Dodge – buffalo city, cattle town

Dodge City is smaller than I imagined. The streets are laid out in a series of rectangles, and it's inconceivable that anyone should lose their way here. The north section sits on a gentle slope, leading downtown to the restaurant area and, beyond the railroad tracks, the town opens out towards the mudflats of the Arkansas River. The city's topography has represented its social hierarchy for as long as people can remember. When Dodge was a cowboy town, the railroad tracks marked a boundary: women who crossed the line southwards lost their respectability. The wind, on the other hand, is a great leveller. No matter where you live, just as predicted, a 'sour and sharp' stench pervades. Thousands of cows are brought here on freight trains, month in, month out, and leave as meat. In huge feedlots, they are fattened on corn. The myth and history of Dodge are intricately linked to the shipment and processing of these huge animals.

Dodge City's career as a Wild West town began with hunting 'Indian

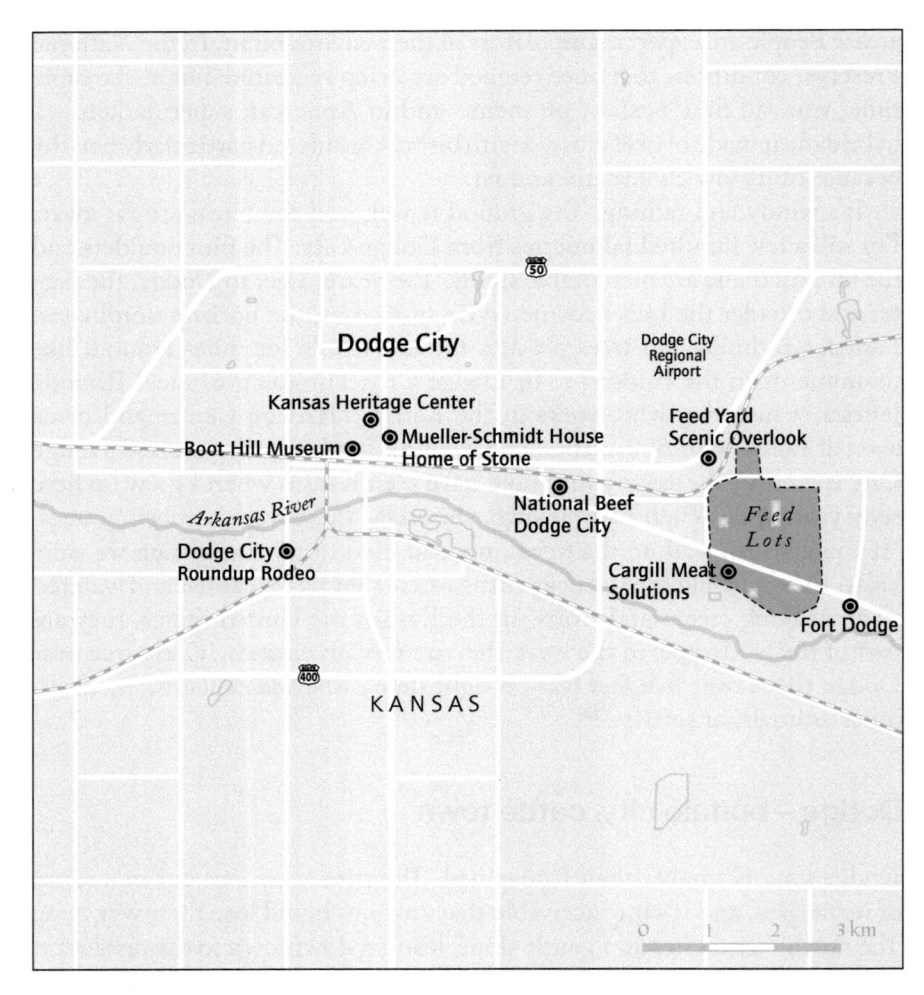

Dodge City

## Dodge City, Kansas. The Windy Wild West

buffalo' or, more accurately, bison, as these animals are related to European bison and not African water buffalo. But the American love affair with bison only lasted a short time: they loved them to death. One of the main culprits was the railroad. The workers who laid the tracks lived mostly off bison meat and, above all else, they loved bison tongue. William Frederick Cody, better known as Buffalo Bill, earned his nickname for hunting bison to feed meat to railroad workers. The deep gash in the prairie made by the Topeka & Santa Fe Railroad in the 1870s led to the division of bison herds into north and south; they in turn quickly divided into splinter groups that couldn't survive alone. Soon bison-hunting turned into a sport for hobby marksmen who would fire Colt shotguns and repeating rifles from train windows. When tanners discovered that bison hide could be cheaply turned into hardwearing driving belts for the industrial sector, the bison's death knell sounded. In contrast to the otter or beaver, bison were not eradicated by the fashion sector but by the industrial one.[14]

In 1872, when Dodge City opened its first ironware depot on a goods train, the town – a city only in the eyes of its barely 500 inhabitants – prospered almost solely from the bison trade. Cash was a rarity, bank credits unheard of and bison hide the most important currency. Any man with a decent rifle could shoot up to two dozen bison on a good day, and back then Kansas had almost 2,000 hunters. A bison hide sold for three dollars fifty, and those who had a few good days a week were 'stinking rich' in a very short space of time: thirty-five dollars is the modern equivalent of almost 500 hundred dollars. 'Stinker', as in Stinker Jim, or Dirty Ike were common ways to refer to hunters and skinners, who notoriously smelled of dead animals. Shooting and carting off bison could not happen fast enough. Photos dating back to the 1870s show dead bison in the snow, freezing more quickly than they could be skinned. And the most renowned buffalo photograph of Dodge City is of Charles Rath, a slick hunter, frontier trader, and businessman, dressed in a suit jacket and a bowler hat, sitting atop a throne of 40,000 animal hides waiting to be bundled by machine and sent to tanneries in the eastern states.[15]

In the 1870s, Buffalo City slowly became Cattle City, and the cowboy town of Dodge was born. Between 1875 and 1886 alone, cowboys herded more than five million Texan Longhorns – named for their horn spans of up to 1.8 metres – from Texas to Dodge. The open prairie whose fertile soils had once belonged to the bison and indigenous people was transformed at lightning speed from Texas to Saskatchewan into pastures for cattle grazing. During the American Civil War, the population of Longhorn cattle in southern Texas quickly increased because the northern states completely blocked export routes to slave states along the Mississippi and in the Caribbean. In Texas, Longhorns were worthless, but demand from slaughterhouses in Chicago, Detroit, Boston and New York was very high and these companies paid at least ten times the prices offered in Texas. In 1870, there were almost thirty million cows in the USA. This meant that there were roughly 770 cows to 1,000 people. Meat was therefore plentiful, but trading depended on being able to ship the animals to the right place at the right time. The USA, if letters written by German immigrants are to be believed, was already a country of bountiful beef in the nineteenth century. And before a railroad was built running from south to north (rather than east to west), the main facilitators of the beef supply were cowboys.[16]

Cowboys didn't own much besides a horse, a hat, a lasso and a revolver. Despite the enduring image of the lone cowboy riding off into the sunset, the job itself was anything but romantic. In the arid, treeless landscape, where temperatures rose to forty degrees Celsius in summer, there were no wooden huts to find shelter from the wind or other weather conditions. If they were lucky, cowboys might find a deep hole in the earth to shelter. Buffalo dung was used as fuel for campfires and cowboys got around the all-too-familiar shortage of water by camping at watering holes and along creeks and small rivers.[17]

Dodge City's cowboy era effectively began at the end of the Red River War of 1845–75 after various indigenous tribes from the southern prairie were beaten, restrained or driven out by the US Army. Dodge had a clear advantage on the cattle market thanks to its early railroad station, built in 1875, which was known for miles around. From here, livestock could be quickly sent to slaughterhouses in the east or to the plentiful pastures in Montana and Wyoming where decent prices were paid for Texan cattle. Almost every tiny locality in Kansas with a station shipped Longhorns north or east, even if only for a few months. But in the 1860s, when it was discovered that Texan cattle brought Texas cattle fever to Kansas (the Longhorns were immune to it but their ticks infected animals native to Kansas), politicians erected a quarantine zone where cattle trading was not permitted. At the start, Dodge, Abilene, Ellsworth and Wichita were all known as cattle towns. But the quarantine zone kept on expanding west; in the year 1883, Dodge City and Caldwell were the only towns outside it. Not long afterward, trading in Texan cattle was prohibited in Kansas and also came to a standstill in the rest of the USA.[18]

## Dodge City, Kansas. The Windy Wild West

The cowboy era, a topic that has given rise to countless cheap novels and popular Wild West films, only lasted a short time but the changes it caused were seismic. When cattle herds arrived in town to be sold and transported, dance halls, drinking dens and gambling saloons brimmed with visitors. Between June and October, Dodge's population swelled to well over 1,000 cowboys, of whom at least a third – unlike in Hollywood films that depicted them nearly all as white – were Mexican or Afro-American. Kansas was the birthplace of the cowboy and Dodge was the entertainment capital of the West. In 1878, the city had three dance halls, each with a bar, several gambling tables, orchestra music and, for a fee, paid female dance partners or sex workers. It also boasted almost two dozen saloons with long rooms, glitzy colours and large mirrors. These saloons opened in the late afternoon and truly came to life late at night and in the early morning. 'The *demimonde* are permitted to visit the saloons and gambling houses after midnight', a Kansas newspaper reported in 1885. 'And it is needless to add that they never permit an opportunity to slip by without embracing this golden privilege.' It was 'no wonder that the youth who comes is so soon estranged from the path of virtue and rectitude and falls an easy victim to the seductive ways of the unique and only Dodge'.[19] Dodge City had a reputation for being 'the wickedest town in the American West'. This was especially true of the establishments south of the railroad, but also for iconic Front Street: as rumour had it, there were more shoot-outs there than anywhere else in the Wild West.

Front Street's former splendour has been restored. It has saloons, bars and restaurants, and you can buy dry goods and textiles, groceries and cigars, hardware and tinware, lumber, firearms and munition; there's also a drugstore, a photographer, a barber shop, a farrier and a small jailhouse from 1865. Walking on the wooden boardwalk past rows of buildings covered by awnings is like being in a Wild West film featuring Marshal Matt Dillon, Miss Kitty and Sam the barkeeper. There isn't much to indicate it's a replica of the original Front Street, which was built in 1958 some hundred metres northeast. The original wooden buildings were destroyed in a fire in 1885. Front Street itself was replaced by a parking lot in 1970 as part of the city's extensive modernisation.[20] The mock-up of Front Street, which was carried out according to historic photographs, is part of the Boot Hill museum, whose entrance is in the historic Great Western Hotel.

When I enter the Long Branch Saloon on Front Street, there's not much going on. Three pensioners wearing cowboy boots and baseball caps

Replica of the original front street, Dodge City.

are standing at the bar drinking root beer. Someone is playing the piano. 'You have to come here in the summer', says the owner of the General Outfitting Store next door (a pensioner with a hearing aid and a cowboy hat). 'Then there are variety shows, can-can dancers, and horse races. And a High Noon Big Gunfight with stunts and armed robberies.' The man looks bored and explains that before Memorial Day, at the end of May, Dodge is pretty dead. Even the historic building of the Boot Hill Whiskey Distillery is still closed at the end of April. 'You're not from around here, are you?' calls out Mark Vierthaler, a distillery worker. 'Come on in!' Mark gives me a tour around the impressive building that once served as a town hall and was also home to the magistrate's office, local court, jailhouse, police and fire brigade. 'Dodge City was founded on alcohol. And we're keeping the tradition alive', says the distiller. Indeed, the history of Dodge began in the year 1872 when George M. Hoover, the first businessman and mayor of the city, opened a whiskey bar. He brought a truck full of bottles to Dodge and set up an inn in a sod building exactly five miles from the US military post in Fort Dodge – the minimum distance from it required for the public

## Dodge City, Kansas. The Windy Wild West

sale of alcohol. Mark Vierthaler pours me a glass of white whiskey and gives me a couple of miniatures to take with me. As if apologising for the quality, he adds, 'We're working on producing a real bourbon. It's going to take some time.'[21]

Dodge, its cowboys, sheriffs and fallen angels had a reputation for excessive drinking and gun fights. But, in reality, the Wild West was pretty tame. A large part of the poor repute of cattle towns came from sensationalist newspaper supplements that travellers sent as souvenirs and not quite as many fatal shoot-outs took place as the tabloid press would have people believe. Old stories were recycled and embellished. The sheriff's main job was to lock up drunks for a night or two. In Kansas's cattle towns, there were only three executions for murder or manslaughter in total; and none of the cowboy towns totted up more than five murders a year.[22] The Boot Hill Cemetery where, according to legend, boozing, gun-toting cowboys were hastily buried with their boots still on after wild shoot-outs, is part of the Boot Hill Museum. But neither the location of the cemetery nor the wooden crosses are authentic. Does anyone care? Hollywood constructed the myth of simple, badly paid Western cowboys, guns always at the ready. But these men only herded cattle from Texas northwards for two decades. After that, they were driven out and replaced by ranchers and the railroad. Yet, the USA fans the myth of the Wild West and its iconic cowboys to this day – not coincidentally, the gun lobby is more powerful here than anywhere else on the planet.

While walking in downtown Dodge, I run into Charlie Meade, a little old guy with a US Marshal star affixed to his shirt, and a revolver in his holster. 'Are you a real sheriff?' I ask. 'The only real sheriff in Dodge', he replies. On his business card, it says *Special Deputy US Marshal and Retired Deputy Marshal*. When Meade talks about his past, fact mixes with fiction: he remembers the actors from *Gunsmoke*, the Trail of Fame immortalised in bronze, and how he was born in a hearse. Here in Dodge, you can't escape the Wild West past, it seems. Even in the Best Western motel bar, there's an old jail where high-proof whiskies are locked away at night. And at the weekend I join the locals for a major team roping competition where cowboys and cowgirls show off their lasso skills by capturing calves.

133

Charles Meade, 'the only real sheriff in Dodge City'.

## Longhorns – biology makes history

It's a truism that there would be no cowboys without cows. Away from the glare of Hollywood spotlights, the real heroes of the prairie weren't men but animals. This is true of Dodge City too – like all cattle towns, it might have been pounded out of the earth by men, but it owed its momentum and survival to Texas Longhorns. Most of the work in the meat business was done, after all, by cows themselves. The nineteenth-century food revolution that saw Americans switch from grain to become the world's biggest meat eaters was in no small way down to these key protagonists.[23] Cows, like horses, were brought to the New World by Christopher Columbus on his second voyage. The cattle from the Canary Islands eventually spread under sixteenth and seventeenth-century Spanish rule to modern-day Texas and slowly changed from domestic to feral animals. As these cows gradually went native, they gained new characteristics: they learned to survive dangers such as fire and wolves and to endure harsh weather conditions. Their horns protected them from predators and could be used to dig for water or find food under thick snowfall. Unlike domestic cattle, they multiplied on the open prairie and took care of their calves. 'The habits of the half-wild cattle of Texas differ greatly from those of domestic cattle, wrote a Californian journalist in 1885. 'The latter are stupid, accustomed to depending on men who give them food and upon men for protection and food'. As reports from the time documented, more highly bred cows collapsed under the hardships of cattle farming after hours or days. But the Longhorns transformed the prairie grass into energy and meat and even carried themselves to market, like moving meat products – inconceivable for other commodities. In 1866, around 3,000 Longhorns were herded to cattle town railroad stations; in the following two decades, this number rose to a staggering five million.[24]

So, Dodge City's rapid rise is partly owed to the Longhorn's DNA and biotechnology. The creation of centres of power and economy and the ascent of elite groups is, according to a shrewd analysis by environmental historian Edmund Russell and his colleagues, tightly bound to the way people have manipulated the earth's finite resources to suit their interests, thus exerting influence and control over others. Seen this way, all power, whether social or physical, is nothing but transformed energy. When walking through Dodge, I come across an old house made of bright limestone, the Mueller-Schmidt House from 1881, and am reminded of Russell's theory. A plaque tells me that this impressive family home atop a hill is the oldest building in Dodge City still on its original site. It was built by the German-American couple, John and Karoline Mueller, along with its legendary walnut spiral staircase.[25] Even today, this house is the direct material result of the Longhorns' energy. Without cattle, John Mueller would never have come to Dodge and wouldn't have been able to start a cowboy boot business or invest in a saloon and three cattle farms. And the Mueller house would never have been built. From this perspective, the house is nothing but a symbol. When the Muellers left Dodge, Adam Schmidt bought the property in 1890; from then on it continued to be an emblem of social power. Now it functions as a museum – a memorial in stone to the economic significance of the Longhorns and Dodge City's cowboy era.[26]

## The railroad and barbed wire

Fights between cowboys and Indians, as peddled in picture books, pulp fiction and movies, never took place in the history of the American West. Towards the end of the nineteenth century, both factions were on the losing side. The disappearance of bison took away the Native Americans' century-old livelihood, and the cowboys' horses were replaced by wage labourers and locomotives. From the mid-1880s on, both had to make way for capitalist ranchers who secured ownership of creeks and rivers to the greatest possible extent, stored hay in winter, and fenced off their land. A wave of industrialisation, manifested in the linear route of the railroad, swept through the American West in a few decades. Tracks cut across the landscape with geometric precision without regard for the course of rivers or the migratory routes of prairie animals. In western Kansas, where railroad construction preceded communities, towns appeared at regular intervals like on a chain. It was in the interest of the railroad companies that traders and commissioners, vegetable processing plants, banks, inns and saloons were set up along their routes.[27] Not every town survived but the railroad route is still deeply inscribed into the map of the American West. Railroad stations always came with a windmill attached to pump clean water for locomotive boilers. Commercial businesses gradually appeared. And in the vicinity of these railway towns, farming geared towards surplus production and commercial profit was developed and expanded, which soon capitalised on specialties and monocultures, driving forward the delivery and marketing of single products, like wheat. Within a couple of generations, the railroad changed the face of western Kansas beyond recognition. Where hardy grasses, bison and indigenous people once lived, surveyors divided up the land based on train routes. Steel ploughs, barbed wire erected by cattle farmers, imported cereals, weeds and windmills created a radically new American landscape in which technology and capitalism reigned.

Barbed wire was invented by businessman Joseph F. Glidden in 1873 and it played a significant role in the transformation of the Old West into the New. Before it was invented, line riders would have to round up runaway cattle, driving them back onto the plains, often in extreme temperatures: wooden fences in arid regions like Kansas were too expensive. At the end of the 19th century, when fence posts and barbed wire could be easily transported in railroad wagons from east to west, cattle breeders began to fence in their ranches, access roads and water sources. In some parts of the USA, particularly in Texas, proper fencing wars broke out between ranchers and cattle drivers on one hand and cowboys on the other. The first fences caused serious injuries to those who tried to climb them. Fence-cutting gangs with names like the Hatchet Company, Blue Devils Knights of the Knippers, Javelinas and Land League wreaked havoc; and when cattle rustlers got mixed up, there was often real trouble. But in the end, wealthy ranchers managed to prevail over the Old West bandits.

In a few years, different types of barbed wire were developed. By 1900, there were as many as 400 patents for it in the USA. Varieties included lettered wire and types with small metal plates of all kinds. A piece of Glidden's original barbed wire could be bought in the 1970s for just 25 cents – but rare types have been sold for as much as a thousand dollars in recent times. Today, five-digit sums are paid for a collector's item as long as it is at least thirty centimetres long. There are barbed wire auctions and exchanges, not to mention a museum in La Crosse, Kansas. None of this is surprising when you consider that, besides the railroad, six-shooter and easily transportable windmills used to pump water for agriculture, barbed wire was the most significant invention for the taming of the American West.[28]

## Feedlots and slaughterhouses

Wyatt Earp Boulevard, formerly known as Front Street, is the name of the main drag in Dodge City, cutting a swathe between east and west. The name harks back to the legendary gunslinger, bison hunter, buddy of Doc Holliday, rancher and saloon- and brothel-owner who made a brief appearance in Dodge in the 1870s as deputy sheriff.[29] Driving eastwards up Wyatt Earp Boulevard, where the street and railroad tracks lead north, I come across an unusual vista. From a small hill, cattle are cooped up in three large feedlots divided into land plots. A sign informs me that these feedlots have 'a combined capacity of approximately 60,000 head', and 'Kansas feedyards market over five million fat cattle annually, around one-fourth of all the fed cattle in the USA'. One in three feedlots belongs to the Winter family. When I visit them unannounced, a shaggy dog sniffs me. 'Are you a good guy or a bad guy?' asks Joel Winter, the junior boss, by way of greeting as he sizes me up. 'A good one', I reply, 'not a journalist.' It seems I'm in luck. 'Didn't you have dinner in the Country Club the day before yesterday?' he asks. 'Didn't you order steak? Medium rare, on the rare side? We saw you. We knew you weren't from round these parts but definitely someone who knows how to

Corn feed mills and feedlot with cattle, Dodge City.

eat steak.' I had followed Worster's advice and ordered steak on arrival in Dodge City at the most expensive joint in town. It's something I rarely do but, as it turned out, it made Winter trust me.

Joel Winter and his father Ken take their time and show me historical photos and documents from their family archive. Back in 1956, Ken Winter and his father – Ken was six at the time – set up the first feedlot in Doge City with around 5,000 cattle. Twenty years earlier, Joel's grand-uncle Karl happened on the city by chance.[30] The weekly cattle auctions brought national fame to Dodge City. Its population, whose numbers had dropped after the economic crisis in the 1920s, rose steadily from then on. Two years after the outbreak of the First World War, according to the *Dodge City Globe*, 'five hundred farmers and ranchers' came to the cattle auctions of Karl Winter and his partner T.B. McKinley every Friday. Dodge City's cattle market soon became the largest in the American West. '126,949 head (cows) worth approximately 14 million dollars' changed hands in 1947 alone. Nowadays, numerous cattle are auctioned in Dodge and transported to markets all over the world. Japan is the chief importer, but the fastest-growing market is China.[31]

'It'd be great if the Chinese ate more meat', says Joel Winter. Does he know that export figures of US beef to China have skyrocketed since 2017? The wealthier it becomes, the more its population develops a taste for red meat.[32] With 10,000 animals, the feedlot is actually too small, Ken Winter explains. 'If we had 30,000 – if our farm was at full capacity, in other words, then we'd be a medium-sized business.' Joel explains that nothing has changed over the past sixty years. 'We have cell phones and a few more cattle', he says, but otherwise, things are just the way they used to be. 'The cows eat corn. Thirty pounds a day. They're fed twice a day. Dried corn is soaked and flaked. It's no different from cornflakes', Joel says. 'We feed the cows cornflakes.'

Unlike the tough Longhorns that were herded by cowboys to Dodge, these highly bred cattle arrive here in the twenty-first century by semitruck. 'Forty-five tons of animals are brought with each semi to Dodge, and forty-five tons are taken away', Joel explains. Some cows have travelled from afar – California, Ohio or Florida. The Floridian beef needs careful treatment because the Kansas winter is too harsh, despite being mild overall. Cattle auctions and feedlots have caused a small revolution in Kansas. Increasing numbers of cattle can be bought and sold at a dwindling number of places. And business is gradually more often done by investors from all over the USA rather than farmers. In the 1950s, farmers could still choose a slaughterhouse. These days, meatpacking businesses – a euphemism for slaughterhouses – are situated right next to enormous grain silos, the high temples of the modern agricultural industry, and feedlots that maintain their own feed mills. In meat production, nothing is left to chance, not even the size or shape of the cornflakes. After all, it's about fattening the cattle from 500–600 pounds to double that weight within 150 days. What counts is efficiency and speed. And because trains proved too slow and unreliable, the meatpackers in Dodge switched from rail to road decades ago.

Industrial cattle fattening and meat production have had a huge impact on professions, demographics, landscapes and eating habits in Kansas and far beyond. The times are over of Upton Sinclair, whose socially critical muckraking novel, *The Jungle*, exposed to a shocked US public the inhuman working conditions and abysmal hygiene of the biggest slaughterhouse in the world at the time, the Union Stock Yards in Chicago. In the slaughterhouses of Dodge City, the air is cooled to such low temperatures that the stench is not as foul as it was a hundred years ago. But the factory halls are loud, according to the Mexican assembly-line workers I talk to at the Tacos Jalisco and El Rodeo eateries in downtown Dodge. They aren't keen to talk, hardly speak English, and call the assembly line *la linea*. They sometimes use electric saws, they tell me, but mostly carry out the work by hand with knives – day in, day out, the same tasks, the same hand movements and the same thousand or so thrusts of the knife. In 2002, American journalist Eric Schlosser condemned the US meat industry, particularly McDonald's, when he claimed that meatpacking was the most dangerous job in the world. In no other sector were rates of work-related illnesses and accidents as high as in American slaughterhouses. Meat packers' wages in Dodge are below the national average. No wonder the workers in both Dodge's slaughterhouses, Cargill Meat Solutions and National Beef, are nearly all from Central and South America, while in neighbouring Garden City they're mostly from Somalia and Southeast Asia. In Dodge, you see countless Mexican flags and most workers send a portion of their earnings home.[33]

The Winters are not open to discussions about alternative forms of grazing. They think it's strange to hear about oxen in the Alps who feed on grass instead of cornflakes. Joel Winter says that beef doesn't taste good if it's not corn-fed. In Dodge City, where cattle have been transformed from social animals into mere precursors of steaks and burgers, I realise how inextricably linked the triumph of fast food and the industrialisation of cattle breeding are. Infrastructural and economic transformations, like McDonald's franchise system, for example, and technological innovations – from barbed wire to electric saws and refrigerated semi-trailers – have spawned the industrial burger and its distribution across America and the entire globe.

Dodge City is the epitome of a genuine American city: the cowboy is an American icon, and the hamburger is a quintessentially American product. But the rise of Dodge and the invention of the hamburger can only be understood on a global level. The European diaspora set off a radical transformation of the environment when it imported herbivorous animals into the New World, above all cows, sheep and horses; and this change also affected human eating habits. It happened gradually at first. The indigenous population – from the gauchos in South America to the horseback-riding, bison-hunting Comanche and sheep- and goat-breeding Apache in North America – profited at times from this slow agricultural-ecological revolution, as long as they adjusted to the new system. Together with the work done by hooves, manure and animal stomachs, European migrants turned unpalatable grazing animals into a seemingly infinite resource of energy which, in twenty-first-century Dodge City and other meatpacking capitals, is made fit for transport and processing by a new legion of migrants from Latin America and Asia.³⁴

## The answer is blowing in the wind

One day, I travel to Dodge City's immediate surroundings, first to the west and southeast, where I come across its recent history. In the west, the ruts of the Santa Fe Trail have been almost entirely eradicated and can only be seen when the sun is lying low. In the southeast, the freshly renovated Fort Dodge complex is a reminder of the presence of the US military, which was supposed to protect settlers and traders following the Civil War. But to the east on Highway 50, an entirely new world opens up to me. White windmills with a hub height of eighty metres stand in the middle of winter wheat fields, wet from the rain. The fact that wheat grows here in April is down to German Mennonites from Russia who imported this wheat type into the USA in the nineteenth century: it can stand the dry, cold winter and be harvested in spring. In the twentieth century, Kansas turned into a wheat state, known as the 'Breadbasket of the World' – and no one could have guessed this would happen back then. Industrial cattle rearing takes up less land than the old ranching system and corn and soya imports have increased the land used for wheat-growing. More wheat is cultivated here than in any other state.

What the future holds for Kansas and Dodge City is uncertain: no one knows how long the wheat fields, slaughterhouses and windmills will be around. The region, once home to prairie Indians and bison, is profiting from a brief moment in the earth's history when increasing numbers of people with growing wealth around the world are choosing a meat-rich diet. And the USA supports its global export of meat and cereals through modern technology, marketing, subsidies and surplus production.

But if the key to the future lies in the past, the Midwest will have to keep reinventing itself with increasing speed, if only because the people here are coming up against tight ecological boundaries; and because global interdependencies demand permanent adaption. It's common knowledge nowadays that industrial cattle rearing is anything but sustainable. The 'ecological hoofprint' of cattle is notoriously large. Quantities of energy and land used in meat production are several times higher than those used to produce plant-based foodstuffs. Cattle emit enormous amounts of highly flammable methane, contributing to a higher concentration of greenhouse gases in the atmosphere. And geographer Wolfram Mauser calculated that producing one single hamburger weighing 100 grams requires no less than 35 bathtubs of water. Highly fluctuating wheat prices are causing trouble for farmers on the former prairie. Over all of this hangs the Damocles sword of global warming and over-extraction, which threatens to dry up water reserves in the centre of the United States. In Florida, underground water reservoirs fill up of their own accord every time there is a storm. But the Ogallala Aquifer in the Midwest, which is fed by fossil groundwater from the earth's centre and is used by over a quarter of all agricultural irrigated land in the US, will need 6,000 years of rain to fill up again.[35] In the face of such challenges, will the No 1 global consumers of hamburgers change to vegetarianism or veganism in the twenty-first century? Eating habits and the power of the US beef and somatotropin lobby suggest otherwise. On the other hand, the number of vegans in the USA rose between 2014 and 2017 by no less than 600 per cent, mostly among young people.

What can be said for sure is that overgrazing and industrial farming decimate natural resources in the long term and burden the environment. Human intervention in natural environments, especially since the mid-twentieth century, has caused radical ecological changes. With this in mind, would it be better to let large swathes of land in the American West lie fallow and declare them areas of wilderness? Or would it make more sense to expand the experiment of Flint Hills – to restore archaic flora and prioritise the large-scale reintroduction of bison? For centuries, herbivores defined the prairie's ecology: after mastodons and giant sloths came bison and pronghorn antelopes. Environmental disruption caused by hooves, dung and urine was not the exception, it was the norm – with a positive effect on soil formation and the nutrient cycle. Perhaps, in the twenty-second century, the prairie will resemble how it looked in the nineteenth century.[36]

Or perhaps the answer is blowing in the wind. There are strong indications that, in the future, the surroundings of Dodge City will be turned into a wind farm of epic proportions. If its full capacity was exploited, Kansas could already cover 75 per cent of the electricity required in the USA. Dodge City's Economic Development director, Joann Knight, complains that Dodge doesn't have a four-lane highway or an institution of higher education, and that visitor numbers to the historic cowboy town have sunk from 300,000 to 80,000 in recent years. But she still predicts a rosy future

## Dodge City, Kansas. The Windy Wild West

for the city. The casino and waterpark are real attractions; the business sector is investor-friendly; and there are 350 windmills in the immediate vicinity which will soon be able to deliver wind energy to four other states.

Before I leave Dodge, I run into Charlie Meade once more, the town's 'real sheriff'. I ask him why he isn't wearing his cowboy hat today, but a baseball cap instead. 'So that my hat doesn't fly away', he explains. 'Didn't you know that Dodge is one of the windiest cities in the USA?'[37]

Niagara, location map

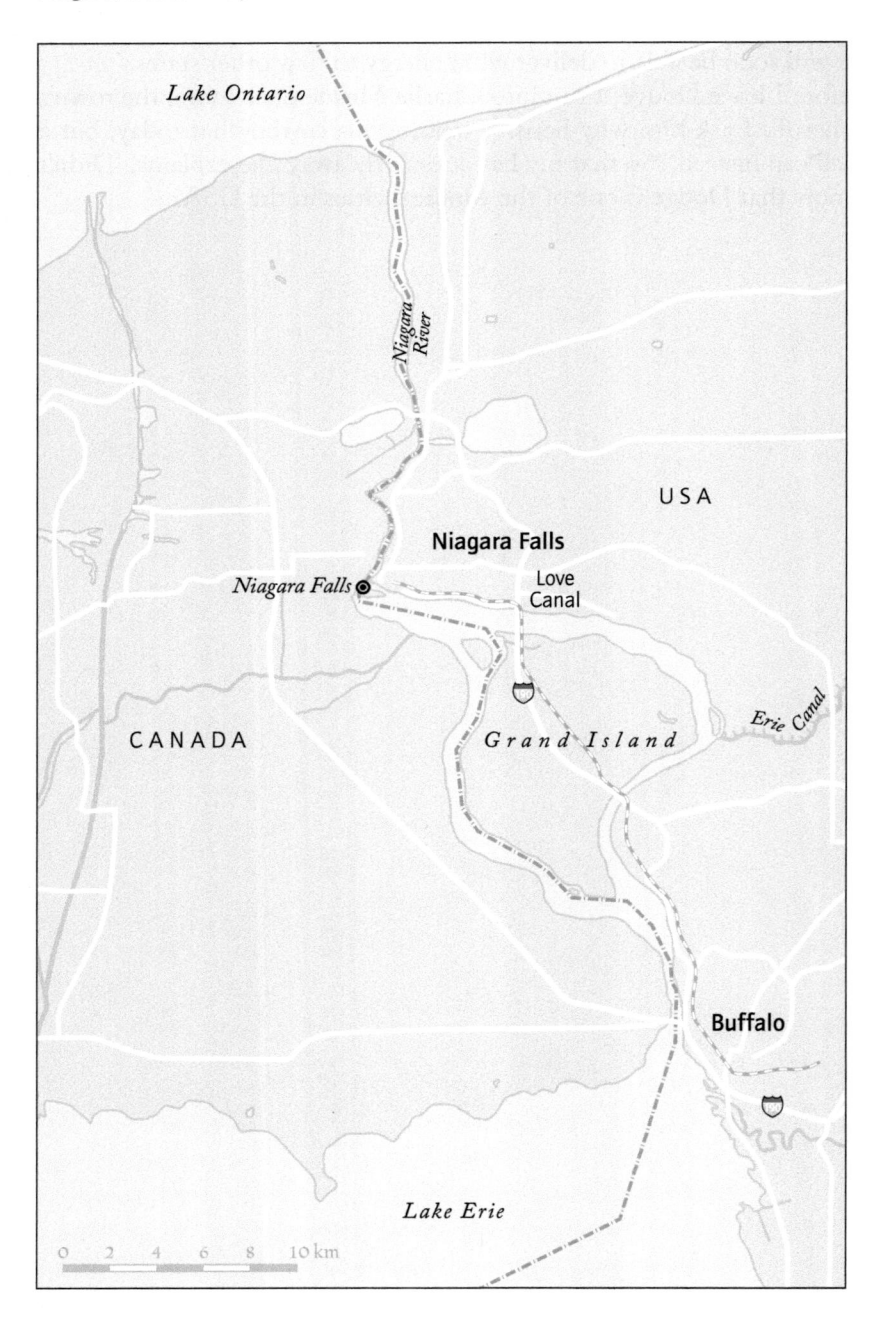

# Niagara, New York.
## The Second Greatest Disappointment

### The second greatest disappointment

Niagara Falls is the most renowned group of waterfalls in the world. Its name allegedly traces back to an indigenous tribe, the Niagagarega people, who populated the Niagara Peninsula over 600 years ago. The horseshoe-shaped gorge epitomises untamed nature for natives and tourists alike, with fathomless depths and thunderous rapids that exert a magnetic pull as well as induce horror. 'This surging foam for millions of years. This headlong death. This seething whirlpool. It's hell', wrote the Berlin author Alfred Kerr after his visit to 'Yankeeland' in 1924.[1]

Since the end of the American Revolutionary War in 1783, the border between the USA and Canada has run right through the middle of Niagara Falls. So the two countries compete in wooing visitors. In the early nineteenth century, the Falls were already a popular tourist attraction and towards its end, they'd even become the most popular honeymoon destination in the world. But they weren't always described in glowing terms. After his visit in 1882, Oscar Wilde is said to have called them 'the second greatest disappointment in married life'.

The geology of the Great Lakes, Erie Canal and Falls have defined the area around Niagara since time immemorial and added to its attraction. Niagara and neighbouring Buffalo's almost infinite supply of hydropower have made it one of the biggest industrial hubs in the USA. To push back against the increasing disfigurement of the landscape around Niagara caused by factory buildings and power plants, state parks were created on both the Canadian and American sides, with the explicit aim for the first time in American history of preserving the area's natural beauty.

In 1901, Buffalo hosted the spectacular Pan-American Exposition. Using millions of lightbulbs powered by electricity from Niagara Falls, the American 'Electropolis' turned night into day for all the world to see. The site was a symbol of optimism and national pride that fused the promise of utopia with natural beauty. But, since 1978, Niagara has also become a symbol for the toxic waste scandal in Love Canal that mobilised environmental activists across the country and signalled a new era of legislation in this field. And this is the place I will visit during my trip to Niagara – a place not marked on any map.

## Buffalo, New York

Like nearly every tourist who visits the Falls on the American side, I start my tour in Buffalo, New York. Fortune has not been kind to the city. Buffalo Central Terminal, with its seventeen-storey tower, has not been in service since 1979. The rails have long since been pulled up and the track marks are overgrown with weeds. Some striking buildings downtown, including the 150-metre-tall art deco town hall, and other sites designed by starchitects like Frank Lloyd Wright, Louis Sullivan and H.H. Richardson leave no doubt that Buffalo saw better times before the Second World War, better than in the early twenty-first century when I visit. The central square in Buffalo has been named after Niagara for over 200 years: if it weren't for the Falls, people would never have heard of Buffalo. Half a mile from Niagara Square, Buffalo Creek flows into Lake Erie. On this spot favoured by natural features, a trading post was set up in 1789, the first pioneer settlement on the site of present-day Buffalo. The colonists first named it after Lake Erie, then Buffalo Creek, soon shortened to Buffalo.[2]

The town's early history is complex because of various interests and claims to its ownership. It originally belonged to the land of Holland Purchase, an enormous territory west of New York State bought by thirteen Dutch investors who aimed to sell it quickly at great profit. The indigenous Seneca people also had rights to large sections of present-day Buffalo. In 1813, it was plundered and razed to the ground by British troops and their indigenous allies, then liberated a short time later by American militia.[3] Buffalo probably would have remained an isolated, provincial backwater had the inhabitants not recognised that the Erie Canal, which was built in 1817 to connect the Great Lakes to the Atlantic, was a one-off opportunity for its economic growth. Buffalo's greatest obstacle was its lack of a navigable port. A gigantic sandbank in the estuary of Buffalo Creek prevented ships from sailing to Lake Erie. My hotel concierge in downtown Buffalo tells me that every school kid learns about the sandbank that once blocked the port.

Although Buffalo had no serviceable equipment, no work crews, boats or barges in the nineteenth century, the river was excavated by its inhabitants, then a landing jetty was constructed and, within a few months, a working port was built. Events picked up speed once it was decided that the Erie Canal, which began in New York, should end in Buffalo and the 'artificial river' was inaugurated in 1825.[4] It was used to transport goods and industrial products from the Atlantic to the Midwest. New York became 'excessively rich' in Goethe's words, but Buffalo's rising prosperity was also boosted when the first ship sailed into its port.[5] Within five years, the population rose from 2,500 to 8,600, after which it doubled every decade for almost half a century. In 1860, it was listed as the tenth most populous city in the USA, then soon rose to the eighth, becoming New York's 'Gateway to the West'.[6] Most of all, this was facilitated by the grain trade. Enormous quantities of wheat were transported across the Great Lakes, via river, and through the Erie Canal to the Atlantic. And besides the waterways, the first grain silo with steam-powered lift and loading facilities, developed in Buffalo, and put in operation in 1843, played a decisive role in the city's growth. More than half the grain harvested in the USA found its way into Buffalo's grain silos until the early twentieth century. The former village on Buffalo Creek soon had the biggest grain port in the world and the biggest river port in the USA. In 1874, it was home to forty grain silos. The largest horse market on the North American continent was also located there, where more than ten million animals were bought and sold every year. In the nineteenth century, thanks to the Erie Canal, Buffalo already had two universities and an art and history association, and had become the first American city with widespread electric street lighting.

Wood and iron ore were first transported by sail and then steamship to Buffalo from the West.[7] Over the years, the town, therefore, became a centre for steel and railroad production.[8] But shipping in Buffalo didn't stop at grain, raw materials and metal goods. Its proximity to Niagara Falls soon made it an important gateway for middle-class American tourists. The equivalent for wealthy Americans in the 1820s of the Grand Tour for Europeans was a trip through New York State. Some of the attractions were the famous panoramic hotel in the Catskills Mountains, the Trenton Falls, Saratoga Springs, renowned for its mineral baths, and the Genesee River Aqueduct. Once the Erie Canal was completed, the fame and popularity of Niagara Falls soon surpassed all these other sights. Tourists travelled on 'packet boats' – postal ships – along the Erie Canal to Buffalo next to letters, packages and goods. Up to thirty passengers could travel for an affordable price on these package tours that included meals. The boats were surprisingly fast: they could cover up to 120 kilometres in 24 hours.[9]

The advent of good transportation along the Erie Canal and tourism around Niagara boosted the optimism of the young United States of America. But not everyone was happy about this technological progress, which radically changed the landscape in the Niagara region. For some, the upswing meant a decline.

## Niagara's indigenous population

The losers during this period of swift development were the indigenous people of Niagara, traces of whom can hardly be found in the region. Archaeologists assume that the small towns of Fort Erie, Niagara-on-the-Lake, Youngstown, Lewiston and Buffalo were all erected on the sites of Native American settlements. If you drive from New York City via Albany to Niagara Falls, you travel along almost the exact route used by the indigenous people of this region. In some parts of Mohawk Valley, the Iroquois Trail and the highway overlap. But this history remains hidden from drivers racing along the four-lane freeway. Names like Chippawa, Onondaga, Tonawanda, Cheektowaga, and Scajaquada testify to the fact that white settlers took over the sites of America's indigenous population.[10] The concierge of my hotel recommends that I go to Buffalo's cemetery. 'No one goes there. But believe me, it's one of the most beautiful places in this city and a treat for a historian like you.' At Buffalo's historic Forest Lawn Cemetery, with its picturesque hills, rivers and creeks, I spot a larger-than-life statue of the oratorically brilliant Seneca chief Sagoyewatha or Red Jacket – the last tribal leader to oppose the transformation of Niagara's landscape.[11] On my walk through the forested cemetery, I try to imagine how the indigenous population lived here, what it was like for them to experience the invasion of the white settlers and how quickly the culture of the colonisers changed their environment.

Up until around 20,000 years ago, the region around Buffalo and Niagara was covered by the immense Laurentide Ice Sheet. When changes occurred in the climate and the last Ice Age came to an end, an ice-free corridor was created in the Northeastern United States: here, rivers and lakes developed as well as vegetation populated by wild animals. In about 9,000 BCE, early stone-age people must have settled around the Great Lakes, Paleo-Indians who made serrated spearheads and tools and lived off fish as well as caribou. In the centuries that followed, when the water levels of the Great Lakes sank and large forests of oak, birch, pine and hemlock spruce spread, the nomadic indigenous population, who hunted all kinds of wild animals and gathered berries, also grew. Over time, starting around 3,000 years ago, this indigenous population settled and began cultivating field crops. There is evidence that maize has been grown in the Niagara region since 500 BCE and, when the first settlers arrived, they also found a variety of storable crops including squash and beans, as well as tobacco and sunflowers. The Native Americans hunted white-tailed deer and black bears, geese, turkeys, and waterfowl and supplemented their diets with fruit, nuts and berries. The Iroquois-speaking Wenrohronon in particular lived in the Niagara region. Iroquoians described themselves as Haudenosaunee (people of the long house); they lived in wooden buildings over thirty metres long with a fireplace and chimney. Every ten to twenty years, they would leave their dwellings and move to a new site a couple of days' journey away. In the past, historians assumed that they relocated because the soil was depleted. But, in truth, other factors likely played a role: the wooden palisades and huts rotted over time, firewood gradually became scarce and waste accumulated, causing hygiene to deteriorate.[12] Native Americans were constantly changing the environment in which they lived, not only through hunting and agriculture but also by using fire – to burn fields, clear thickets in the forest and scare off wild animals. The spread of hickory and walnut trees in the Niagara region also has its roots in the indigenous use of fire: besides maple and oak, nut trees are among the most fire resistant types of wood.

## Colonising the land

If it were possible to take a snapshot of Niagara's landscape when it was populated by Native Americans in 1700 and compare it to that of 1850 when it was colonised by white settlers, the contrast would be staggering. European wheat and rye gradually replaced the maize and beans originally grown on the land. The greatest difference, however, was how the two groups utilised animals. The Iroquois hunted game and beavers while the white settlers yoked oxen and horses to ploughs. While indigenous game hunting took place for a few months in autumn and winter, the domesticated animals of the white settlers were used all year round. Soon endless fences were erected across the Niagara region to enclose livestock and mark land ownership. The indigenous trails were turned into streets and boundary stones indicated property rights.

On fields planted by indigenous tribes, maize, beans and squash had grown close together for centuries. The 'three sisters' of indigenous American agriculture, as this triad of crops was known, grew high, kept weeds at bay, gave nutrients back to the soil and provided a diet rich in amino acids. For settlers, the advantages of ecological farming remained an impenetrable mystery. They were used to the aesthetic of European monocultures and the fields of the indigenous tribes seemed uncultivated, if not chaotic, to them. Most of the colonisers believed that they had come across 'virgin land' in the New World. Most were oblivious to the fact that it had been cultivated through the complex interaction between humans and nature.[13]

Most American history books ascribe environmental changes in the USA almost exclusively to the activity and power of white settlers. What's forgotten is that it was only possible to colonise the country by drawing on the extended experience of the indigenous population. The first white settlers took on their practices, such as trapping and hunting, 'ring-barking' trees to kill them off, extracting maple sugar and cultivating maize. They also adopted several indigenous means of transport, from canoeing to snow shows and runnerless toboggans.[14]

Yet, even though the indigenous people transformed the landscape of North America over time, the impact of their 10,000-year existence pales in comparison to white settlers' interventions in the century after the construction of the Erie Canal. The widespread belief that all American indigenous people were 'ecological natives' might be a myth, but it does have a kernel of truth. In their spiritual and religious concepts, animals, plants and unpopulated nature deserved the highest respect and their destruction was kept in check by some fundamental tenets. Other factors also reduced the indigenous impact on the natural environment, such as the relative scarcity of game, low birth rates, sparse population and preservation of forests – areas where crops were cultivated and that served as a natural barrier against enemy attacks.[15] Most importantly, unlike the white settlers, the indigenous population were not interested in accumulating wealth. Ownership was almost meaningless in their world. There was 'little social incentive to accumulate large quantities of material goods', explains environmental historian William Cronon. 'A wide range of resources furnished economic subsistence, while a narrow range of resources conferred economic status.'[16]

In this case, how did it happen that the Iroquois of the Niagara region became fur trade agents in the eighteenth century, ostensibly of their own free will? Was declining game responsible for an economic and spiritual crisis? Or were the temptations of the capitalist world, such as weapons, gunpowder, metalware and clothing, also a factor? What's certain is that the Native Americans were the outright losers in their culture clash with white settlers. By the early nineteenth century – decimated by epidemics, forcibly converted to Christianity, driven out of their lands and banished to the reservations – they were eking out a miserable existence. The Iroquois are mentioned in a letter written by Erastus Granger in 1817 to his superiors in the Indian Office: 'The situation of the Indians is truly deplorable. They have exerted themselves for the past year in trying to raise crops but have failed in their expectations. Their prospects have failed. Their hunting grounds are gone. They have availed themselves of their money arising from public funds, but they fall short. They are in fact in a state of starvation.'[17]

The introduction of European models of agriculture to the Niagara region, known for its harsh winters and dense forests, progressed only slowly at first. Farmers cleared two to four hectares of woodland per year on average and when the Frenchman Alexis de Tocqueville arrived in Niagara in 1831, around three-quarters of the area was still forested. He noted with astonishment that: 'Man [is] still making clearly ineffective efforts to master the forest.' In a rather laconic description of the farms, he added: 'Tilled fields covered in shoots; trunks in the middle of corn. Nature vigorous and savage.'[18]

Orsamus Turner, the editor of the daily *Niagara Democrat* and postmaster of Lockport – a town thirty kilometres east of Niagara Falls – wrote a series of monographs in the 1850s that documents in detail the history of the white colonisers and their disputes with the Native Americans in the region. A historical booklet, for example, features a three-part illustration that shows the breakneck transformation of the landscape during Turner's lifetime. In the first, a wooden hut stands in a clearing next to tree stumps; a settler leans on his axe while cows and sheep graze in the forest. The second picture, ten years later, shows geometric fruit plantations and a country road; the farm is fenced off and a horse-drawn wagon is bringing in the hay. The last, with the title 'Life's Work', shows an impressive farmhouse in New England Federal style in front of a winter landscape completely cleared of trees and a steam train running through.[19] Here, like elsewhere in the USA, the steam locomotive was a 'machine' that invaded the 'garden', in the words of the literary critic Leo Marx. It changed the landscape, values, and desires of people living in that era more drastically than ever before.[20] The Erie Canal provided the basis for the development of the area around Niagara and Buffalo, but the railroad sped it up to an unprecedented degree. Once the tracks were laid, nothing was the same.

## Miracles of technology – railroads and bridges

No sooner was the Erie Canal inaugurated than railroad tracks were built throughout New York state which competed with the shipping companies. The prominent British geologist Charles Lyell, who visited Niagara Falls in 1842, praised America's new transport routes. Several years ago, he noted, the trip to the waterfalls from Albany had taken several weeks. But now the railway moved at the rate of 16 miles per hour.[21] While the opening of the railroad from Buffalo to Niagara in 1834 introduced a fast connection to the Falls, a new line along the Erie Canal that opened a few years later made tourism possible in the Midwest in ways hitherto unimaginable. The number of 'summer migrants' who visited Buffalo between May and October rose rapidly. In 1840, some 20,000 tourists visited Niagara Falls but, by 1850, that figure had risen to over 60,000. The railroad's popularity not only impacted the leisure activities of America's middle classes; it also had a concrete effect on Buffalo's appearance. In the year 1875, a section of the 1,000 kilometres of railroad track cut through the city's urban area. New districts, as well as wheel, wagon and steam locomotive factories, sprung up along the tracks, often segregated according to ethnicity.[22] Tourism may not have been the only factor in the swift expansion of the railroad network: the description of travel destinations became part of the language of railroad advertisements as lakes, waterfalls, and other natural features could now be reached at 'railway speed' and at a much lower cost than by boat. Standing out from all of them was Niagara Falls, the eminent tourist highlight that could be explored even on a flying visit. Many tourists were day-trippers. They travelled up from Buffalo by train, quickly got out, marvelled at the Falls from close up, bought souvenirs, and rode back the same day.[23] From the second half of the nineteenth century, not only was the train journey to the Falls part of the authentic Niagara experience, the trip across one of the bridges that spanned the Niagara Gorge was a focal point. In less than fifty years, over seven bridges had been built, providing spectacular views of the waterfalls.

Probably no other bridge in the history of the USA has attracted so much public and engineering attention as the Niagara Falls Suspension Bridge, which was completed in 1855 by the German American engineer John August Roebling. Roebling's double-deck suspension and cable-stayed bridge on which both horse-drawn wagons and railroads could travel connected the USA with Canada and was justifiably considered a miracle of technology. At a height of seventy metres, it spanned a distance of 250 metres – over

## Niagara, New York. The Second Greatest Disappointment

twice the length of the world's longest railway bridge at the time. Only a suspension bridge was able to achieve this.[24] As soon as it was opened, the Niagara Falls Suspension Bridge became a tourist attraction. Some visitors might have been disappointed that the Falls lay some distance away from the bridge; on the other hand, they were compensated by the view down into the thundering gorge. Walt Whitman, who was not overly impressed by Niagara Falls, described the trip across the bridge as 'some lucky five minutes of a man's life'. Mark Twain, on the other hand, poured scorn on it, saying: 'Then you drive over to Suspension Bridge, and divide your misery between the chances of smashing down two hundred feet into the river below, and the chances of having the railway train overhead smashing down on to you. Either possibility is discomforting taken by itself, but, mixed together, they amount in the aggregate to positive unhappiness.'[25]

While tourists first visited Niagara for the Falls, the bridge soon competed for attention. In fact, Niagara Falls town, founded in 1848, was soon only called Suspension Bridge.[26] Countless postcards proudly displaying the American flag showed the bridge in the foreground, with the Falls merely providing a backdrop. Like no other construction in America, it symbolised technological triumph over untamed nature – the human equivalent to divine creation – and fulfilled the young American nation's eagerness for world recognition. Where it lagged in cultural assets, lacking Europe's grand palaces, museums, national literature and outstanding composers, it made up for it by laying claim to the best engineers worldwide.

The Niagara Suspension Bridge was more graceful, functional and, not least, much less expensive than Europe's heavy tubular bridges. In 1858, *Atlantic Monthly* took up the topic of America's railroad engineering feats. 'Mr Roebling's Niagara Suspension Bridge', it wrote, 'cost 400,000 dollars while a boiler-plate iron bridge upon the tubular system would cost for the same span about four million dollars'.[27] The Niagara Suspension Bridge was replaced in 1897 by a steel-arch bridge for heavier trains and soon other bridges were constructed in the area too, which slowly got nearer to the Falls and drew crowds. The rapidly expanding town of Suspension Bridge merged with an adjacent district at the end of the nineteenth century and was from then on called Niagara Falls. In 1890 it had approximately 5,000 inhabitants; ten years later, almost 20,000. Most passenger and goods trains that crossed the USA from east to west stopped in Niagara Falls. In summer of 1897, some 277,000 tourists came to Niagara by train. There they encountered a technological wonder world that had virtually nothing in common with Niagara's former landscape. Travellers drove through tunnels and across bridges, visited amusement parks and large hotels, waterworks and innovative heavy industry. The Falls provided enough electricity to power the city. It is where the first giant generators were built, and from where electricity was sent to far-off places.

## Arriving in Niagara

The route from Buffalo to Niagara Falls takes me through a steel pylon forest. I pass chemical and machinery plants, gas towers and chimneys, containers

Niagara Falls, Industrial Park.

## Niagara, New York. The Second Greatest Disappointment

and industrial warehouses along the highway. On the grassy verges between the highway exits, geese waddle.

A few minutes before I arrive in Niagara Falls, the skyline of the city on the Canadian side appears, with its 42-story Fallsview Tower Hotel. Signs to the Seneca Niagara Casino are reminders of who this land used to belong to. The Seneca Nation of Indians operates both a hotel and a casino here. I drive about aimlessly downtown and see signs everywhere that the place has seen better days. Along the streets, there are stacks of old tires, mounds of garbage, and abandoned gas stations. Smoke shops, liquor stores and discount household article shops, however, are thriving. In the 1970s, industries moved away, leaving behind a desolate wasteland, like in other Rust Belt areas of northern USA. I stop at an antique bookstore, taking a couple of dozen local history old books off the shelves. There is plenty on the Falls – but what I'm searching for is literature about the Love Canal toxic waste scandal. I turn to Henry, the bookstore owner, who also turns out to be an environmentalist. He asks why I'm interested in the Love Canal, and when I answer that I'm writing about it, he shows me to a pile of books in a back room. 'This is all on the Love Canal', he says, 'but it's all out of print because the topic was only of interest for a short period. Hardly any of them have been reprinted. I can't sell you any because some would cost a couple of hundred dollars. But you can make a note of the titles and borrow them from the library.' When I ask where Love Canal is exactly, he sends me over to the cash register to talk to his sixty-year-old African American colleague. Shirley grew up in Love Canal. She shows me a rash on her upper and lower arm. 'These are from the chemicals in Love Canal', she says. She tells me about birth defects and nervous breakdowns that her neighbours suffered and the greasy filth that rained down on her porch. By the end, she's told me a whole number of disturbing details. Then she tells me to go to 97th Street. 'That's where I used to live, but you won't find it in any travel guide', she adds.

I do the standard Falls programme for tourists before I head to Shirley's childhood district of La Salle, but all the time her stories are going through my head. I drive past chains of hotels, an aquarium and a waxwork museum. A friendly employee in the Niagara Fall Visitor Center recommends first going to Bridal Veil Falls then to the American Falls and, last, Goat Island. 'You can see all Niagara's sights in half a day. That's plenty of time.' She tells me that Prospect Point offers the best view of Rainbow Bridge facing Canada and that it's worth hopping over the border to see the Horseshoe Falls.

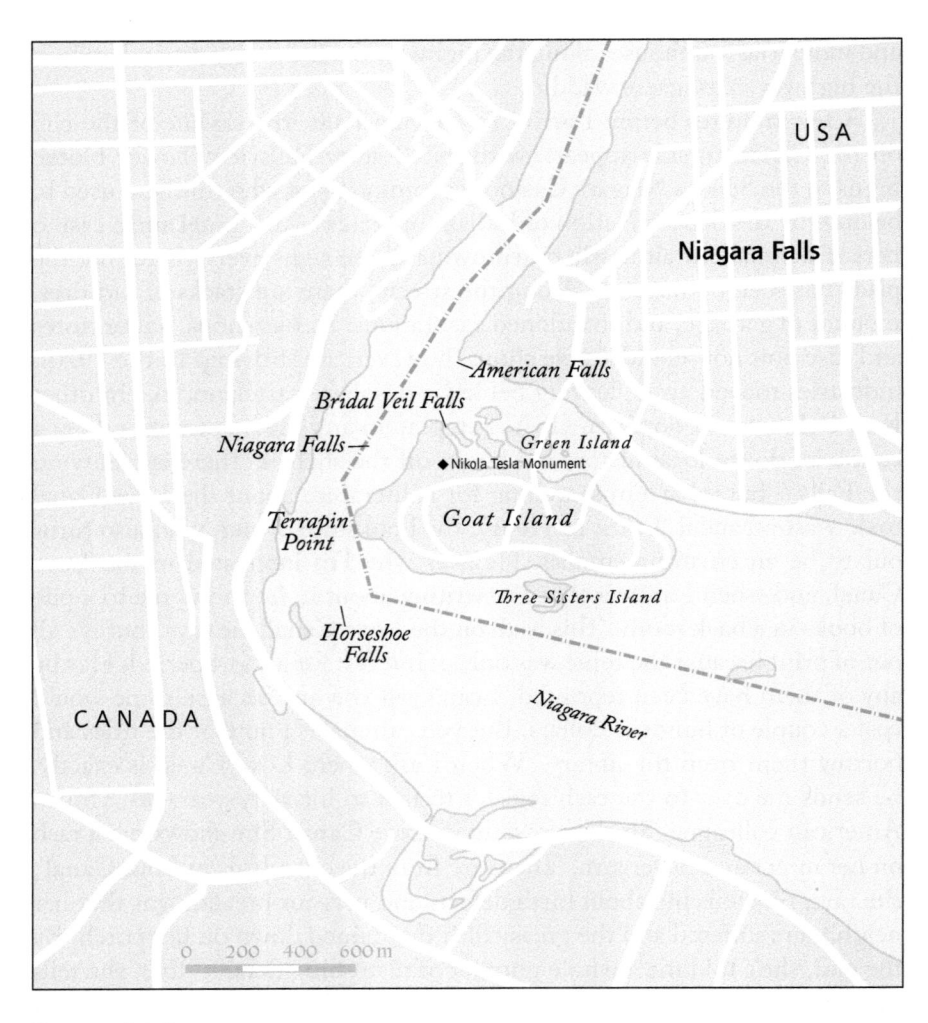

Niagara, detail

# Niagara, New York. The Second Greatest Disappointment

'Don't miss it! Go to the State Park – it's the oldest in the whole country.'

As soon as I enter the State Park, I leave the ramshackle town behind. I'm just one person in a tightly packed crowd of tourists, one of the thousands who take photos and film from the observation platform, Prospect Point, every day. I can see a rainbow and the American Falls from up here. In my mind, the pictures of Niagara are bigger than what I can see. A sign explains that the Falls are constantly moving back because the erosion rate of the rocks is very high: 'The American Falls began to form some 900 years ago.' It goes on to explain that they exist because of the last Ice Age 12,000 years ago, when glaciers caused Lake Erie to overflow, resulting in the short, fast-moving Niagara River that has thundered ever since over a high precipice into Lake Ontario. In geological terms, this precipice has eroded at unprecedented speed due to hard dolomite rock in the upper part and comparably soft shale further below. Because the force of the water hollows out the shale from the bottom up, the overhanging dolomite rock regularly crashes into the river. In the course of their existence, they have moved more than eleven kilometres towards Lake Erie.[28]

## Goat Island

To reach Goat Island, I have to first cross one footbridge to Green Island and then another to my destination, located between the Canadian and American Falls. In several thousand years, the river will probably have carried the island away, rock by rock. I wonder whether the town of Niagara Falls will still exist then too. Goat Island isn't spectacular, just an uninhabited, sparsely forested place with huge parking lots, footpaths and asphalt roads: its greatest attraction is the views it offers of the Falls. A park ranger diligently explains that its name dates back to the year 1778 when a Scottish officer, John Stedman, drove his goats onto it to protect them from wolves. But the harsh winter finished them all off except for his legendary Old Billy Goat. The island's name, however, stuck. At the far end, with a view of the Horseshoe Falls, stands a statue of Nikola Tesla, sitting in a reflective pose with a book in his lap as if he were a great philosopher. Tesla was in fact an engineer and the inventor of the AC motor and transmission technology. He was also Thomas Edison's rival and the namesake of Elon Musk's electric automobile enterprise. Nikola Tesla and George Westinghouse built the first hydroelectric power plant in Niagara Falls and from here, with Tesla's AC current, the electrification of the world began.

When walking across Goat, Green and Three Sisters Islands, I can barely imagine that today's State Park used to be an industrial zone. During the nineteenth century, the area around Niagara Falls, which belonged to the Senecas until 1802, was turned at turbo speed into America's number one hydropower site. The Falls, including the river shore, Goat Island and Green Island, were auctioned off to private investors in 1805 by New York State. At that time, the brothers Augustus and Peter Porter, and their business associate Benjamin Barton, purchased the land including water rights. In places like this, where profits and business lured investors, the young nation transformed more quickly than in other parts – more quickly, in fact, than any other country in the world. In 1818 the Porter brothers built a bridge from the mainland to Green Island. The public baths with hot and cold water they built there originally led to the name Bath Island. Besides this facility, they opened a billiard salon, various restaurants and a toll booth that charged a fee to walk around the island and observe the Falls. When Augustus Porter charged this fee even on Sundays, he was barred from the Presbyterian Church of Niagara Falls. Between 1820 and 1823 alone, the Porters had a wool factory, a forge rolling mill and a nail factory constructed. Bath Island was home to the biggest paper mill in the USA and a tannery, while Goat Island housed an iron factory.[29] None of these places exists today: and I'm off to find out why.

## Commerce and spectacle galore

In 1827, to attract wealthy capitalists from the East, the Porters came up with a unique, hitherto unseen spectacle called *The Sinking of the Michigan*. The *Michigan* was a disused ship on Lake Erie, partly owned by Peter Porter. The brothers decided to turn it into a 'pirate ship', loaded with all kinds of wild animals such as panthers, wildcats, bears and wolves. Nearby hotels were filled with tourists and these visitors could board the ship's zoo and sail upriver with the animals. On the morning of 8 September, the *Michigan* set off with a crew of bird scarers, including Andrew Jackson and John Q. Adams, who had fought an ugly election campaign three years previously. Not all the creatures advertised were on board; there were only bears and foxes, a buffalo, a raccoon and a dog that had allegedly bitten a reporter. These animals were set free from their cages as the *Michigan* careened towards the waterfalls, plunged down into the rapids and smashed to smithereens. Contrary to announcements by the event promoters, not all the animals survived. Only

## Niagara, New York. The Second Greatest Disappointment

a goose and a bear surfaced from the swirling depths of water. There is no mention of this callous spectacle in the tourist office today. But 200 years ago, *The Sinking of the Michigan* ushered in a new era of tacky commercial attractions in Niagara that gradually overshadowed its natural wonders. The area became the epicentre of entertainment tourism. Thrill seekers climbed into barrels and plummeted down the falls, or walked, did headstands and even pushed a wheelbarrow over a tightrope to the other side.[30]

The Porter brothers and like-minded investors provided the infrastructure for tourism generated by these kinds of schemes, which soon beat the awe of nature itself.[31] An observation tower was built near Horseshoe Falls, as well as steps that led from the cliff down to the Cave of the Winds behind the Bridal Veil Falls. Peter Porter developed a wildlife park, a fishpond and a poultry farm 'for the traveling gourmet' on Goat Island. He added

View from Niagara Falls State Park, New York, with Canada on the opposite side.

a romantic cottage that was soon transformed into a drinks and ice-cream stand. To compete with Canada's Clifton House in Ontario, large hotels such as Cataract House were built in New York state, and souvenir shops like Tugby & Walker were set up on the bridge to Goat Island. Striking Native American beads were hugely popular among big-city tourists from the East Coast. The Hülett brothers sold Seneca and Mohawk artworks in the Indian and Old Curiosity Shop, which, for advertising purposes, was renamed Dean's Metamora Indian Depot. A disappointed visitor in 1847 reported: 'Now the neighbourhood of the great wonder is overrun with every species of abominable fungus – the growth of rank bad taste, with equal luxuriance on the English and American sides – Chinese pagoda, menagerie, camera obscura, museum, watchtower, wooden monument, tea-gardens and old curiosity shops.' In a similar vein, the English American writer Henry James deplored the 'horribly vulgar shops and booths and catchpenny artifices' in *The Nation* magazine in 1871.[32]

## Free Niagara

No one seems to have mourned the transformation of Niagara more keenly than Frederick Law Olmsted. The pioneer of American landscape architecture and the chief designer of New York's Central Park visited the Falls as a little boy in 1828. When he returned forty years later, he remembered that trip with his father when 'hours were occupied, wandering about among the trees'. He described how 'people, then, were loath to leave the place; many lingered on from day to day after they had prepared to go.' This had all changed on his second visit; he lamented how the site was now dominated by all sorts of 'spectacular and sensational' attractions that visitors were forced to surrender to and pay for. More than the factories and power plants in the new milling district, he was disturbed by unsightly, cheap 'side shows', ugly signs, walls and fences around the site and the fact that tourists were charged admission to see the waterfalls.[33] After his visit, Olmsted took up leadership of the Free Niagara movement. Its name embodied its demands: free access to the waterfalls and the removal of unattractive facilities. His criticism was mostly directed at cheap souvenir shops and architectural eyesores. But he also rejected the installation of valuable artworks or statues on Goat Island, or introducing poison ivy, wolves and bears.[34] Olmsted was an aesthete but, above all, he was a moralist and his Free Niagara Movement had the fervour of a religious crusade.[35]

## Niagara, New York. The Second Greatest Disappointment

Among the members of the Niagara Falls Association around Olmsted was the landscape painter Frederic Edwin Church, whose legendary *Horseshoe Falls* oil painting of 1867 presents the site as dramatic, sublime nature – as if no people were living anywhere nearby. Olmsted and Church longed for the landscape to be unspoiled and natural. If possible, it should even appear untouched. In 1880, the Free Niagara group submitted a petition to the New York governor to turn the Falls and surroundings into a state park. It was signed by every important politician, scientist and cultural associate. These included not only the US Vice President, Secretary of State, all the US Supreme Judges, two governors and eight university presidents, but also the philosopher and writer Ralph Waldo Emerson, the poet Henry Wadsworth Longfellow, the British art and social critic John Ruskin, the Scottish essayist Thomas Carlyle, the editor of the *Atlantic Monthly* William Dean Howells and none other than Charles Darwin.[36] The Free Niagara group members referred to themselves as 'reservationists' because they wanted the nature of the Falls to be protected, and not an entertainment area.[37]

Their initial efforts were focused on expanding the planned reservation over the border to Canada. But, when these failed, the Free Niagara movement concentrated on an area that comprised Goat, Bath and Three Sisters Islands as well as a stretch of several kilometres of the Niagara River shore. On 30 April 1883, Governor Grover Cleveland, who was a passionate angler and later President of the United States, passed a law that not only left it up to New York State to determine the exact site of the reservation but also gave it the right to transfer it into private ownership. In 1885, the Niagara Falls Reservation was founded, the longest operating state park – and the first based on expropriation. Together with his business partner Calvert Vaux, Frederick Law Olmsted created a park that pursued three goals: to preserve the unique landscape of Niagara, to restore nature disfigured by human intervention and to create paths and an infrastructure to protect the site from damage inflicted by thousands of visitors. The old forests on Goat Island with their exotic tree population would be protected and bridges made of local natural rock were to be built. The meandering riverside paths would be reserved for pedestrians, and horses and carriages would be banned. Lastly, the walls in the observation areas would be replaced by more delicate parapets.

For Olmsted, the Niagara River rapids were more impressive than the Falls themselves, and these could be viewed from the islands. The French writer and politician François-René de Chateaubriand, who visited America in 1791, described the Niagara as 'not so much a river as a tempestuous sea whose hundreds of thousands of tides cascade into the gaping mouth of an abyss'. Other observers, such as the widely travelled George John Douglas Campbell, Duke of Argyll, a great admirer of Olmsted, described the view up the river from the islands as Niagara's most impressive sight because the 'foaming water of the rapids merged into the horizon' like the ocean.[38] One of Olmsted's most pressing concerns was to conserve vistas of unspoiled nature. For this reason, together with Calvert Vaux, he petitioned for the demolition of the paper mill and factory operations on Bath Island. Both planners also succeeded in abolishing tourist facilities such as pavilions, dance halls, art galleries, theatres and restaurants if they obstructed views. The steep railway on the waterfall hillside, as well as fences, toll booths, bathing resorts, souvenir shops and accommodation – a total of 150 buildings in total – were all razed to the ground, liberating the landscape of 'ugly parasites'.[39]

Where nature had been 'disfigured', it was not enough for Olmsted to restore it to its 'original state'. Paradoxically, he believed it should be 'improved' to create a much more natural impression.[40] Olmsted's ideal was a pastoral landscape with gentle hills, pleasant views, large grassy areas, old trees and untamed elements in the style he knew from Britain and New England. The American bourgeoisie who admired Olmsted's Central Park in New York believed that natural scenery could alleviate the stress of everyday life, quicken the imagination, evoke feelings and transform people into healthy, happy citizens.[41] In this spirit, *The New York Times* reported that the Niagara reservation represented 'a distinct step forward in civilisation'.[42] Essentially, Olmsted's Central Park barely differed from Niagara park, which employed 4,000 workers to excavate nearly four million square metres of earth, detonate rocks, heap earth to make hills, hollow out tunnels and lay drainage pipes. Every unsightly feature was removed, large boulders were hauled to the site and the surroundings of the Falls were levelled and artificially remodelled so that the landscape appeared 'more natural' than it actually was. In retrospect, it is fascinating that the visions of Church, an artist, and Olmsted, a landscape artist, were able to persuade New York State to buy up land with government funds for the first time in US history – with the sole purpose of making it more beautiful.[43] But, here, the story is far from over.

## Disappointments

On my walks across the island, I can understand Olmsted's passionate attitude towards the rapids. Not just planks but entire tree trunks are whisked

## Niagara, New York. The Second Greatest Disappointment

down the Niagara River at great speed. It is a slice of wild nature in a world that has been completely transformed by people. I spot Canadian geese and seagulls from afar. But, unlike in the Duke of Argyll's times, the Niagara River no longer meets the horizon. Instead, the view is overshadowed by high-rise buildings and pylons. What would Olmsted and Vaux have to say about modern Niagara? Goat Island, in their imaginations, was supposed to be accessible via a single bridge. But nowadays there is a second bridge for traffic from the mainland to the island. Olmsted gave priority to pedestrians, but these days enormous parking lots occupy both ends of Goat Island, and most visitors drive there. 'Any attempt to reduce parking spaces causes a protest', an employee at the visitor centre says ruefully as if to apologise for all the automobiles and asphalt. Olmsted wanted to maintain the old trees and forests on Goat Island – but these have long since disappeared. Instead of the meandering forest paths, there are now broad asphalt roads for buses to transport tourists who are either unable to walk or in a hurry. Olmsted and Vaux wanted 'untamed' nature, not a park; but now you walk into the Great Lake Garden next to the visitor centre with its large flower beds. Olmsted didn't want memorials, but now a larger-than-life statue of Nikola Tesla towers above the waterfalls. He turned his nose up at the electrical illuminations that were fashionable during his time, but now the Horseshoe Falls are illuminated every night with garish lights. He hated kiosks and picnic areas, but nowadays on Goat Island there are souvenir and snack bars galore, as well as the giant *Top of the Falls* restaurant near Terrapin Point. Terrapin Rocks, as it used to be called, which is located directly above the Falls and named after its shape, was unceremoniously connected to Goat Island by a series of footbridges. In 1983, to offer tourists on the American side the best possible view of the Horseshoe Falls, earth was piled up, the island enlarged, and the Niagara River redirected; 25,000 tons of unstable rock were blown apart with gunpowder and 120 metres of the waterfall on the American side were eliminated.[44]

The Niagara Falls Reservation proved to be a blessing and curse. In 1885, the year it opened, more than four times as many visitors came to Niagara as in the year before, a total of 1,000 to 6,000 every day. Hoteliers and railway companies drove the boom forward, but the relatively small reservation soon could not cope with the masses of people. Today, Niagara is suffocating in the hustle and bustle of tourism. Every year up to thirty million people visit the Falls. The reservation is far removed from the place Olmsted envisioned when he started the Free Niagara movement. Admission is free but parking and leasing fees are one of New York state's most substantial sources of income.[45]

It is astonishing, on the one hand, that a nineteenth-century landscape architect was able to turn back Niagara's industrialisation; on the other, it is remarkable how quickly a giant industrial world was winched into existence in the direct vicinity of the park. However, what appears to be a contradiction is due to very closely related circumstances. Kiosks, factories, mills and power plants were all removed because they did not fit Olmsted's idyllic, lush world of meadows, forests and waterfalls, or his aesthetic of renewed nature. Although he and his associates succeeded in hiding all traces of human presence, another industry sprung up in its place that produced much more dangerous substances than stinking, unsightly paper mills. Many of its entrepreneurs were prominent advocates of the Free Niagara movement and saw no conflict in giving support to both industry and landscape conservation. After all, both initiatives increased profits. What's more, the suggestion that the reservation contributed towards the environment allowed industrial leaders to carry out projects in a much more uncontrolled way than before. As the Falls soon produced vast amounts of surplus energy, electrochemical companies and aluminium shacks soon appeared as well as factories that produced silicon, chrome, tungsten, molybdenum, titan and carbon. On the surface, industry brought great wealth to the region and, for a long time, the damage it produced was invisible and little understood. But a century after the industrial boom had taken place, the environmental problems connected to the Love Canal scandal, wilfully concealed for a long time, suddenly surfaced into public awareness.

Before I drive to 97th Street on Shirley's advice, I take a detour to the Canadian side of the Falls. From here, I have the best picture-postcard view of the Horseshoe Falls. The masses of people and cars are almost as impressive as the waterfalls themselves. It takes me a quarter of an hour before I manage to get a sought-after spot at the railings. I skip a late lunch in one of the overflowing restaurants and walk past the Las Vegas-style attractions and side shows. Later I read about the casinos and 4-D cinemas I could have visited, the WildPlay Whirlpool Adventure Course for climbers, the White Water Walk by the river, the Whirlpool Aero cable car and the Mist Rider Zipline that lets you abseil to the foot of the Falls. While stuck in a long tailback on the way back to the American side, I'm glad I've brought along something to read. The US border control officer pulls me out of the queue and won't believe that I'm an academic who's writing about the Falls and has taken a few photos. Only when I show him the bill from the antique bookstore in Niagara with a list of titles, does his doubtful expression change to one of incomprehension and regret.

## Love Canal

Love Canal is less than twenty minutes from Niagara Falls. The district is the very antithesis of the tourist attractions just around the corner. At first glance, there is nothing to see here. The district on the outskirts of town looks like hundreds of other places all over the USA. Only an empty, fenced-off grassy area, a long street blocked to traffic and a few dilapidated bungalows stand out. Nothing points to the fact that I have ended up in a place that became the ambivalent icon of the environmental movement.

Its name goes back to William T. Love, who moved to a hitherto unknown area in Niagara Falls in 1892 to realise his dream of a model town with ideal working conditions and clean air. A manmade canal to divert water from the Niagara River would provide countless new factories with cheap energy. Niagara not only offered an outstanding backdrop of natural beauty but also a first-class railroad connection and limitless hydropower. Every company that would hire one person for every hp of power used should get the power for free. Unlike the East Coast cities that were burdened by high rent and energy costs as well as crowded living conditions, Love's utopian city offered an auspicious alternative that would also solve the 'social problems of our challenging times'. The necessary technological installations such as canals, water pipes and power cables were to be channelled out of sight through smaller roads. The leading architect, Nathan Franklin Barrett, was responsible for making the model city attractive and a specially established 'industrial university' would offer training in technical subjects and a practice-oriented training course. Every house and shop would have access to electricity, gas and water supplies as well as telephone lines. Pneumatic conveyor belts would transport the post. At the time of the turn of the century, these ideas were remarkable.[46] In his public appearances, Love himself praised his planned city with a rhyme that could be sung to the tune of 'Yankee Doodle':

> Everybody's come to town
> Those who left we all do pity,
> For we'll all have a jolly time
> At Love's new Model City.

> If you get there before I do
> Tell 'em I'm a-comin' too
> To see the things so wondrous true
> At Love's new Model City.[47]

Love's model city was not only a pipe dream: for a while, many factors indicated that it could become reality. 'We'll build a canal', Love explained, 'that redirects water from upper to lower Niagara [and] creates one of the biggest industrial towns in America'.[48] Using excavators, cranes and mules, huge teams of workers dug a canal over 25 metres wide, five metres deep and 1.6 kilometres long. But his dreams failed drastically when property prices rose, investors lost interest in Love's project and his money ran out. His utopia ended up buried in a ditch called Love Canal, which would become the site of another bitter story of failure.

One of the reasons for this was Nikola Tesla's AC technology. Towards the end of the nineteenth century, it seemed important, if not essential, to build big centres of industry directly next to water supplies. But when alternating current was transformed to a higher voltage through Tesla's invention, and could therefore be transported over wide distances, Love's spot near Niagara Falls lost its original attraction. When Love's organisation auctioned off the last of its land in the 1920s, the canal turned into a stretch of stagnant water along which children from the nearby housing estates played for decades. They swam and fished in it until the water was pumped off and the canal was turned into a disposal site for waste from one of the city's most important employers, the Hooker Chemical Company. From 1905 on, Elon Huntington Hooker's company produced chlor-alkali chemicals including a profusion of highly toxic substances. In the Second World War, the demand for lethal chemicals increased so rapidly that Hooker could no longer easily discharge the waste from his facility's production into the Niagara Falls wastewater system. So instead, he used William Love's canal. Between 1941, when the USA entered the Second World War, and 1953, Hooker's company dumped no less than 25,000 tonnes of chemicals into this landfill. Residents reported that members of the army wearing gas masks and with their weapons ready to fire lowered metal containers into the empty canal. When the suburbs of Niagara Falls continued to expand and spread out towards Love Canal – in the mid-1950s, the city numbered 100,000 residents – Hooker covered the disposal site with earth and sold the land to the state educational authorities for the symbolic sum of one dol-

## Niagara, New York. The Second Greatest Disappointment

lar. Hooker's company never made a secret of the fact that there were toxic substances on the site; in fact, he warned repeatedly and urgently against building on the land. He also obtained confirmation that any injuries that followed as a result, were solely the responsibility of the state.[49]

Nevertheless, the district of Niagara Falls had a school built on 99th Street in 1955 and a playground at the edge of the landfill. Bungalows were built on the land around Love Canal and, soon afterward, young working- and middle-classes families with children moved in. The story could have been set in a soap opera suburb and continued happily. But one day in the early 1970s, schoolchildren playing with chalk suffered burns to their hands and eyes. The fire brigade and security representatives from Hooker Chemicals analysed the substance and discovered it was Lindane – a highly toxic insecticide. In the years that followed, health complaints multiplied in the Love Canal district. A young mother, Lois Gibbs, who lived on 101st Street, was one of the first whose misgivings turned to suspicion, while Michael Brown, a reporter at the *Niagara Falls Gazette*, began to investigate the increasing flood of complaints. The number of nervous and blood disorders, miscarriages and congenital defects reached a frightening level in Love Canal. It was soon established that the groundwater level has risen as a result of rain and snowfall, and chemicals from the landfill had thus seeped into the surrounding houses and playgrounds. Environmental authorities carried out tests and found over eighty different toxic substances in the area, including hexachlorobenzene, chloroform and dioxin. In the summer of 1978, the New York State Health Commissioner ordered the closure of the school near Love Canal and pregnant mothers or those with young children were advised to leave the area. A few days later, over 55 residents founded the Love Canal Homeowners' Association, led by Lois Gibbs. Almost overnight, Gibbs became an icon of the US environmental movement. She and her fellow protestors demanded damages for all the families who no longer wanted to live in the Love Canal neighbourhood. When the governor of New York explained that only the residents in the two rows of houses around the landfill would be compensated and evacuated, Gibbs felt all the more compelled to continue her environmental protests and involve the press.[50] Soon, the risks and health hazards of the toxic waste in Love Canal were of interest not just to critical citizens but also journalists from publications like *Time* and *Newsweek*, the Phil Donahue talk show and NBC News. Suddenly, the entire country was caught up in the furore. In March 1979, the ABC TV broadcaster aired the documentary film *The Killing Ground* during a prime TV slot just when the

# Paradise Blues

US Congress had set up a hearing for the Love Canal case. The effect of the film was catalytic: it galvanised the American population with its footage of smoking dumps, ravaged areas of land, desperate people whose health was damaged and enraged activists from Love Canal and other areas, in particular the Valley of the Drums site in Kentucky.[51] Lois Gibbs' activism and the accompanying reports by the US media induced politicians in America to adopt completely new approaches to fight legal battles involving environmentally hazardous substances. In 1980 President Jimmy Carter signed the Superfund law that obliged regional authorities to report breaches of permissible limits to a national centre. Operators of waste landfills and chemical firms were not only required to clean up contaminated sites but also had to report where hazardous waste was stored or might leak. The new law stipulated that the perpetrators of environmental risks and damage should be criminally prosecuted 'for damage to natural resources'. As the lawmakers rightly assumed that the responsible parties could not always be identified or (owing to bankruptcy or refusal) would not pay, the government imposed a special tax on crude oil, oil products and other raw materials to fund 87.5 per cent of the Superfund, while the state contributed the rest.[52]

Abandoned house in Love Canal, New York.

Niagara, New York. The Second Greatest Disappointment

## Slow violence

I walk around the Love Canal district for a few hours; it's extremely quiet. The place where toxic chemicals were buried two generations ago on the site of the former school is now a large grassy area with some flowers dotted about. Barrels barricade the entrance to the streets. The asphalt is cracked, and weeds sprout through the crevices. Right next to the fence, isolated in the middle of the landscape, stands the red-brick Lodge No 132 of the Freemason's Organisation, founded in 1848. A traffic sign featuring a poodle indicates a dog exercise area. The bungalows that would have the best views across the fenced-in premises have their windows nailed shut and are stranded in overgrown gardens. I'm curious about who used to live here. The families who could afford the ranch-style houses and bungalows in the 1960s had every reason to believe in a prosperous future. In this community, there was not only a new school, but also excellent connections to the national road system and one of the country's greatest tourist attractions. The majority of the families who moved here were young and the average number of four people per household was higher than that in other parts of Niagara Falls. Not many elderly people lived here and income levels exceeded the national wage index by a few percentage points. Children could play in the nearby Little Niagara River and Black Creek.[53] It was certainly more pleasant to live in Love Canal's green neighbourhood than in downtown Niagara Falls or Buffalo. Those who lived here had moved closer to the American Dream: but they had no inkling of the nightmare it was about to become.

At the southeast end of the landfill for toxic waste on 95th Street and right next to the fence, I discover a row of attractive, medium-sized buildings with hipped roofs. Here, at Vincent Morello Senior Housing, new trees have recently been planted. When I take a photograph of the grounds, an elderly lady in a tracksuit waves me over with her stick. I apologise for taking a photograph without asking her, but she replies kindly, 'No, it's nice to see someone walking here.' I explain that I'm writing about the Love Canal catastrophe and ask if people still talk about the scandal – and whether she feels safe. 'My children say I shouldn't drink the tap water', she says. 'But we all know that there are toxic chemicals everywhere – here in New York and everywhere in America. The neighbourhood's pretty safe. They cleaned up the waste site.'[54] She's right: the Occidental Chemical Corporation, successors to Hooker Chemicals, was fined for contaminating Love Canal when the scandal came to light. The money was partly spent on sanitising the site;

in 2004, Love Canal was taken off the Superfund list of national priorities. Allegedly the toxins were no longer a danger to the health of residents. It surprises me that there is no commemorative plaque for the victims of the chemical scandal who were forcibly evacuated. The grass has literally grown over the toxic waste landfill.[55]

I wonder if anyone in these parts knows that, despite the clean-up operation, there are still 20,000 tonnes of toxic waste underground in Love Canal which may slowly be leaking. The longer I think about it, the more it strikes me that Niagara and Love Canal are complete opposites: one is dramatically on display, while the other is shrouded in secrecy and glossed over. At the Falls, care was taken so that the mass of water hurtling from the cliffs was plentiful for photo opportunities and the site did not pose any hazards or risks to visitors. But in Love Canal, the danger was belittled or ignored for years. Millions were spent on securing Niagara cliffs, but not on disposing of highly toxic substances. In fact, around the time the public became aware of the scandal, the rocks at Terrapin Point were being stabilised after a psychic predicted that a rockslide would swamp one of the boats below with a deaf child on board. Millions of dollars were spent on drillings, detonations and landscape remodelling to make the waterfalls safe and attractive to tourists. By contrast, it took many years for the complaints of Love Canal residents to be heard.[56] Out of sight, out of mind: as long as the lethal cocktail of chemicals in Love Canal remained invisible, no one seemed to take any action. In his books, the writer-activist Rob Nixon described how the slow violence of global warming and toxic substances disproportionately affects poor, disenfranchised and vulnerable communities. In Love Canal, this slow violence was able to spread until it became visible.[57]

## Disappointment and slow hope

Despite great differences, the history of the waterfalls and that of the chemical industry in Niagara Falls are closely bound and not only because toxic substances were discharged into the Niagara River.[58] In both places, the issues were the development of land and the commercial use of nature. The spectacular view of Niagara Falls and hydropower provided by the river were systematically exploited because good money could be made – both with the tourist industry, which encouraged people to treat the land as a consumer product, and in the industrial sector, which was very energy intensive. The first crowds of tourists were not only enthused by the beauty of the landscape in the area but also by technical sensations such as bold bridges and spectacular illuminations at night. The 'technological sublime' often caused great astonishment in the early days. It might not have exceeded the wonder of the landscape, but it certainly heightened it.[59] This transformation had its price, of course. The history of Niagara Falls is one of a dramatic landscape being destroyed. My disappointment, as with many other visitors over the past two decades, is largely due to how much the original beauty of the area has been lost because people have exploited its natural resources.

The history of Niagara also offers up some lessons that may be the reason for 'slow hope'.[60] In the nineteenth century, Olmsted and Church already realised that the romantic appeal of Niagara risked ending badly due to industry. Without this realisation, Niagara State Park would never have been built.

The American people became properly aware that the environment is more than the conservation of woods and landscape. In her bestseller *Silent Spring* of 1962 Rachel Carson demonstrated that water, earth and air, as well as all creatures on earth, are part of a vast interconnected system.[61] In it, she revealed the danger of environmental contamination through pesticides, which led to a ban on the use of DDT. Strident protests and striking footage of activists like Lois Gibbs in Love Canal led to the US federal government holding industry accountable in the long run, even if its commitment to the cause wavered.

Niagara Falls is still regarded as an unsurpassed national monument that most Americans want to visit once in their lives, preferably on their honeymoon. By contrast, Love Canal, which is hidden from the public, is a much more resonant national symbol. The fences secured by padlocks and the rest of this ghost community are a reminder of the fact that, behind the beautiful appearance of an intact landscape, in everyone's front gardens, hazards might lurk that have been imposed by modern industry, dangers that are a thousand times more lethal than the maelstrom of the Niagara River.[62] But despite all the deceptions and disappointments, Niagara and Love Canal are not only sites where crises have taken place; they are also places of hope. They help us appreciate that people can literally move mountains if they want to and that it's very important to remain alert in this complex and increasingly dangerous world.

Florida

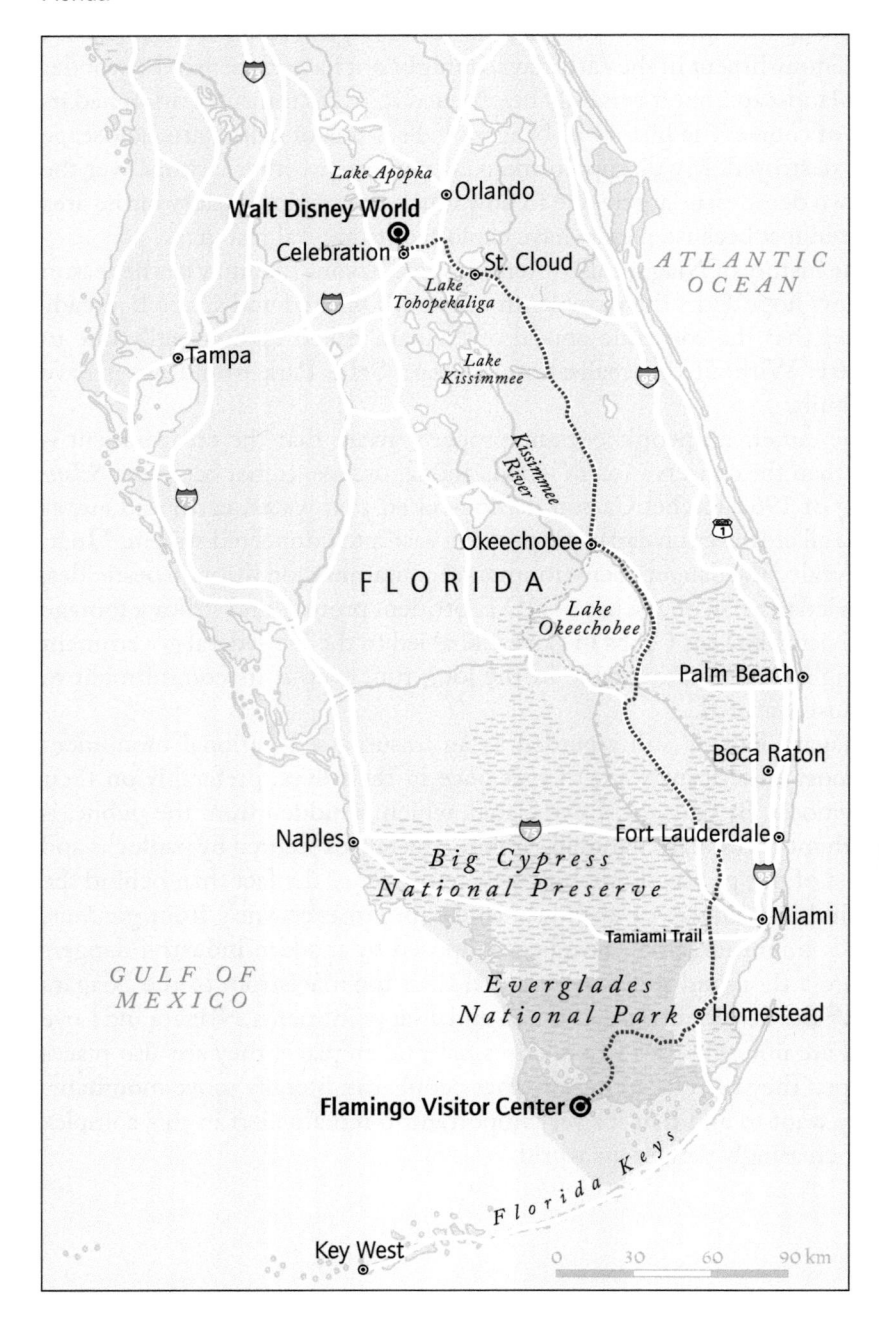

# Walt Disney World, Florida.
## At Least Two Natures

### At least two natures

Disney World in Florida is the biggest theme park in the world. Every year, more than twenty million visitors troop through the gates of the four parks: Magic Kingdom, EPCOT, Animal Kingdom and Hollywood Studios.[1] Without Walt Disney, Orlando might have remained an insignificant town. At the end of the 1960s, it had a population of barely 250,000; nowadays, that figure is two million. During a traffic census on Interstate Highway I-4 in 1971, the staff monitoring traffic fell asleep by the side of the empty freeway. A year later, a total of 22 million tourists visited Florida: nearly sixty per cent of them came to visit Magical Kingdom and Epcot, Disney's first two parks.[2] Fifteen years later, just as many made the pilgrimage to Orlando to visit Disney World alone.

Today, Orlando remains unbeaten as *the* US tourist mecca, with a total of seventy million visitors a year. A hundred years ago, only wealthy visitors came to Florida to sail along the coast and visit spa towns with their miraculous healing waters. Nowadays millions of people from all backgrounds make the trip to Disney's Cinderella Castle and the film world of *Avatar*. From an early age, nearly every American is familiar with Disney's version of nature and history. In Orlando, they can walk through this dream world in real life.

On the surface, there couldn't be a greater contrast between the artificial world of Disney and the natural region of the equally popular Everglades, the subtropical wetlands at the southernmost tip of Florida. But just how natural is this region? What kind of nature is native to Florida? How natural is Disney's Animal Kingdom? Is the Disney corporation justified in its claim to make a valuable commitment to the environment? And how does the proximity of Disney World to Lake Tohopekaliga, the region's headwaters, affect this?

To understand the environment and history of Florida, the Sunshine State's delicate ecosystem first has to be understood. The region is home to citrus fruit groves, snowbirds from the north and the fantasy worlds of Walt Disney, whose parks and films have become national attractions as well as global consumer goods.

## Orlando

From Orlando's international airport, I drive in a rental car to a garden house in the southern part of the city where I'm staying privately. If I'd chosen to stay at one of the expensive and exclusive Disney vacation resorts, the free shuttle, known as Disney's Magical Express, would have picked me up. As soon as I'm driving, I realise that Orlando is not so much a city as a car-friendly conglomeration of suburban estates. I motor past a hodgepodge of housing that lacks any centre, a fragmented, segregated world peppered with shopping malls and lakes, golf courses and gated communities, all loosely assembled around highways, avenues and winding streets. As late as the 1950s, African Americans were not permitted to take part in elections here.[3] The statistic that lists Orlando among the top 'murder capitals' of the USA clashes with Walt Disney's fantasy world.[4] Marginalisation and ostracism are themes I will frequently encounter here over the next few days.

Traditionally, Orlando, like many other southern states located at a crossroads, was a hub for transport and warehouse facilities. Citrus fruits and winter vegetables were delivered here and sent on by rail, as Orlando's railroad station started operating as early as 1880. In the Second World War, a military base was set up on the city's outskirts and, afterwards, the Martin Company – now Lockheed Martin – built a huge manufacturing plant for rockets nearby, which profited from its proximity to Cape Canaveral. New facilities and companies spawned suburbs and a commuter belt, and scattered estates increasingly mushroomed.[5]

I'm staying in a southwest neighbourhood of the city that is predominantly African American and Latino. I pull up outside a bright pink house surrounded by citrus trees, palms and other exotic plants. The rhyme 'Row, Row, Row Your Boat' suddenly starts playing in my head. It seems the perfect soundtrack to Orlando, a place where attractions include Harry Potter's Hogwarts, Legoland and Islands of Adventure, as well as trained belugas and killer whales at Seaworld. The city doesn't need a centre: it thrives on selling and consuming one vision – that 'life is but a dream'.

## Walt's vision

On 22 November 1963, the day that President J.F. Kennedy was assassinated, 61-year-old Walt Disney, the creator of Mickey Mouse and the most popular US film producer of his time, flew by private jet across Florida. He

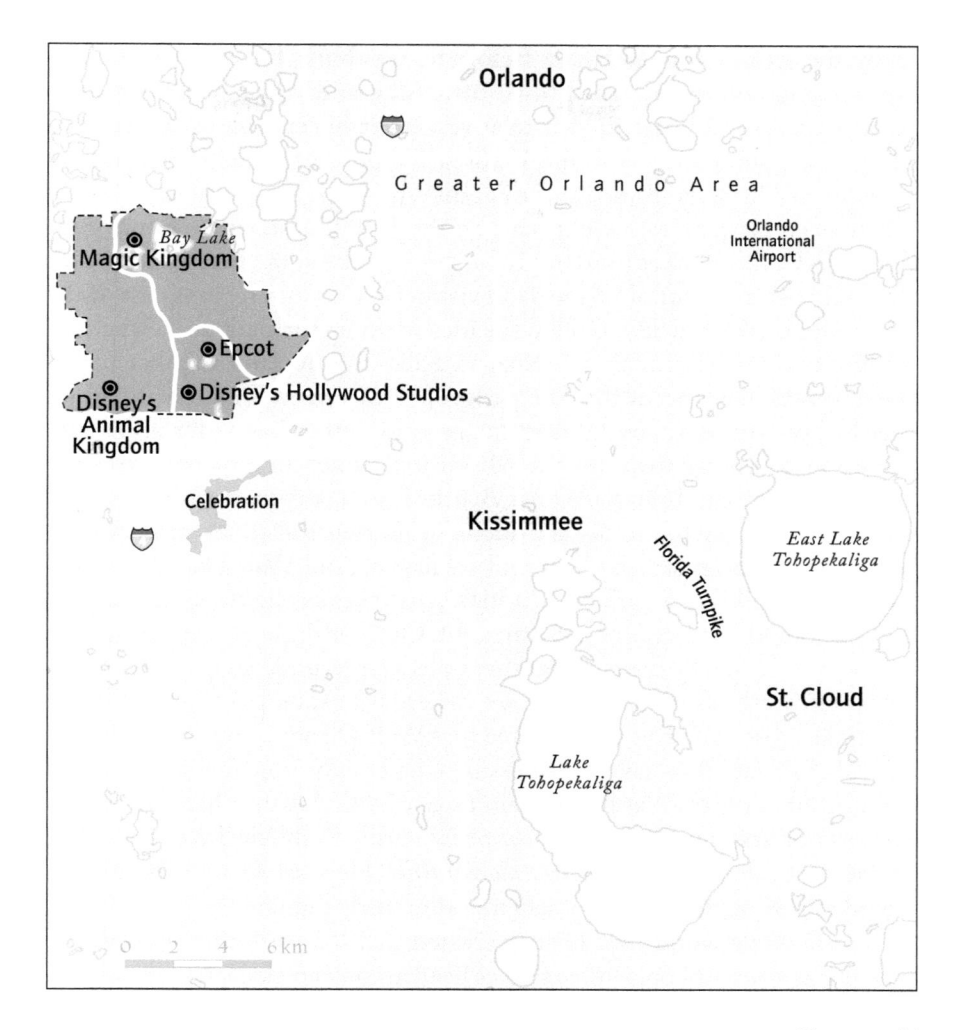

Disneyworld

knew the area around Orlando. Before he was born, his father had run a citrus plantation in the small town of Paisley, and young Walt had gone back there several times to visit relatives. After his enormous success as a Hollywood film producer in the 1920s, a TV pioneer of the 1950s and the founder of Disneyland in California, in 1955 Walt had wanted to set up a new, even bigger amusement park on the East Coast, and a 'future city'. Southern California was too densely built-up and, besides, surveys had shown that only two per cent of Disneyland visitors came from regions east of the Mississippi. Walt quickly rejected the idea to set up the park near America's leading vacation destination – Niagara Falls: the freezing weather in the north would have meant that the park could only open for a few months a year. St Louis in Missouri didn't make the grade either. Walt's flirtation with the up-and-coming town on the Mississippi ended in a quarrel with the German American brewer August Busch. Busch, a tycoon, philanthropist and leading citizen of the city considered it 'nonsensical' to set up an amusement park without serving beer and schnapps. And Walt Disney rejected the idea of building a park on Florida's coast because he thought the sand and sea would compete for the limelight. On that flight in 1963, however, Disney was struck by the fact that there was a large, undeveloped expanse of land southwest of Orlando, in the area where Interstate I-4 and the Florida Turnpike cross. And this was the area that Walt Disney homed in on for his 'Florida project'. As a savvy businessman, he bought up a few plots of land using front companies at the bargain price of 445 dollars a hectare to keep property prices low. One of the few people privy to the deal was the editor of the local newspaper, the *Orlando Sentinel*. He warned that the project would fall through if Disney's scheme were made public.[6]

The fairytale world that Disney created in 1965 was built on a swamp where alligators and poisonous snakes lived among creeks, lakes, grass- and scrubland, and dwarf cypresses. His realm extended over more than 100 square kilometres, making it as big as San Francisco and twice the size of Manhattan. In contrast to Disneyland in California, which was hemmed in by dense residential areas, he planned to remove any traces of urban life from Disney World, Florida – to create a world without visible boundaries and its own laws. Walt Disney's 'District' even had its own regional government, made up of his managers: he invested them with far-reaching powers that covered everything from infrastructure to energy supply, including water treatment, healthcare, fire and police services. Indeed, Disney, the futurist didn't simply want to build an amusement park in Orlando: he wanted to create a 'real' town that would 'never cease to be a blueprint for the future'. He christened it the 'Experimental Prototype Community of Tomorrow' or EPCOT for short.[7] Walt Disney passionately believed that a permanent flow of modern technology would secure progress and contribute to a healthy inhabitable, urban culture that would uphold traditional values and make people's everyday lives easier. His future city was not built straight away: instead, the name was used for the global amusement park EPCOT, which opened in 1982, and linked the theme of progress to an idealised global world exposition. Nevertheless, Orlando was perfectly suited to become an amusement park. In the 1960s, the region seemed worthless to most investors, nature was considered dangerous, the price of land was cheap and the purchase of an enormous area promised endless construction possibilities.

## Entering the kingdom

Disney World is a kingdom unto itself. Those who enter it leave behind highways and construction sites, traffic lights and signs, billboards and gas stations, fast food joints, malls and the hubbub of factories. To the left and right of the broad access road lies a green carpet: a meticulously mowed lawn, which gradually turns into flower beds and neatly clipped hedges near the hotels and park entrances. Over 3,000 kilometres of waterpipes supply the entire Disney domain and 65,000 sprinklers irrigate the expansive park.[8] Any element that might disturb the illusion of civilised nature or the aesthetic of the park is hidden from view. Staff accommodation and the backstage area are no-go zones. Aqua parks are hidden behind thick bushes and evergreen shrubs. The access road into this magical world evokes a feeling of freedom into which 'guests', as visitors are called in Disney-speak, are invited. There are no skylines on the horizon and no visible walls or fences. The streets themselves are meticulously scrubbed as if Disney World were expecting a royal visitor.[9]

When I reach the gigantic parking lot, from where I am ferried by Monorail to the entrance of the Magic Kingdom and can spy Cinderella's fairy-tale castle in the distance, I wonder for a moment if there is a way back. After all, the admission price is prohibitive. A day pass costs $207.68 including tax. But it's too late to turn back. In any case, I already paid a $25 parking fee at the entrance. Once I pass the cashier, I have to go through security, just like at an airport. The uniformed workers, who are called 'cast members' in Disney language, have permanent smiles plastered on their faces, even though they are notoriously badly paid. They inspect my rucksack and camera and take my fingerprints using a small gadget. So, this is how they treat 'guests' here, I think.

## The terrain is transformed

There is nothing to show how the land in the Reedy Creek Improvement District – where Disney World is located – looked only half a century ago. If the former swamplands, which lie twenty to thirty metres above sea level, had not been drained, the terrain would have been exposed to periodic, torrential floods. To counter future flooding, Walt Disney commissioned one of America's leading hydraulic engineers, a retired general major of the United States Army Corps of Engineers, William E. Potter, to 'improve' the land in 1965. Everything that seems so natural in Disney World – from its carpets of grass and wild thickets just outside the park's gates, to the dreams and lakes inside its walls – is in fact artificial and constructed. This is the result of full-scale drainage, landscape planning and terrain modelling. It took years to drain the swamp, excavate the mud and condense the soil. What no one suspects today is that under the porous limestone below Disney World, there were sinkholes, of which the largest measured almost 500 metres in diameter. Thousands of tonnes of concrete were poured into the ground to create today's Transportation and Ticket centre. Up to 4,500 people toiled in the damp Floridian heat so that the park could achieve its current look. More than four million cubic metres of earth had to be carried away, as well as 750,000 cubic metres of muck and incalculable quantities of sand. But most importantly, the workers were responsible for constructing an eighteen-kilometre-long canal system, thirty-kilometre-long dikes and thirty automatic sluices. The canals, whose function was to withstand constant rain and a fifty-year flood, were disguised in such a way that they resembled natural waters. Besides this, a large lake called Bay Lake was drained in December 1968 and kept dry until September 1970. In its natural state, Bay Lake's water was brownish in tone because organic substances had settled on its bed. But, because the colour brown did not fit Disney's fairytale concept, the Disney Corporation dug out the organic lakebed, cleaned it, covered it with sand, and then filled the pool with groundwater. Hidden sluices have kept water levels in the lake constant ever since – with fluctuations of up to thirty centimetres.[10]

Water is a vital resource in Disney World, and it needs to be preserved and kept clean. The theme park's water usage is immense and has constantly risen over the years. Between 1968 and 1973 alone, when water supplies were considered inexhaustible, levels sank by roughly 2.5 metres. In addition, wastewater produced by the amusement park's visitors contributed to the deterioration of water quality, due in part to an uptake in nitrate nitrogen.

The use of the land caused another problem. Disney's investments attracted the attention of property developers and speculators from the very beginning. Between 1968 and 1974 they bought more than 30,000 hectares of meadowland and citrus plantations from around Disney's complex, developed the terrain and then built one suburb after another. The area of greater Orlando grew rapidly, at times more quickly than any other metropolitan region in the USA. It spread more and more towards the southwest, and up to the edge of the ecologically precious Green Swamp region. The human thirst for water, which is anyway great in Florida, reached completely new dimensions in Disney's fairytale world with its tended lawns, irrigated golf courses, water slides and 260,000 park employees. In 2002, water usage by Disney was greater than in the entire country of Somalia which has over seven million inhabitants.[11]

## A world without a present

When you enter Disney's amusement park, there is no city or suburbs, no slums, no farming, no cars or multistorey parking lots and, of course, no sign of everyday life or work. Disney's 'imagineers' – a neologism crossing *imagination* with *engineer* – steer visitors' emotions towards a misty-eyed past, and a future brimming with optimism. The only aspect of time that is completely lacking is the present.

The Main Street I walk along in this magical realm evokes a time when the world was still in order: a strange mixture of urban cultures can be found here, a hybrid of colonial architecture reminiscent of the Old World and what could be called 'small-town America' – a barber shop and a candy store, a cinema and jeweller, a milliner, a tailor and an ice-cream parlour. Potted trees and lamps adorned with hanging flowers flank the boulevard in perfect geometry. The buildings, in historic or gingerbread styles with fake upper floors and façades, are home to stores hawking Disney merchandise: on the Main Street cinema, you can watch *The Art of Disney*, while The Chapeau milliner sells Mickey Mouse ears, The Clothiers stocks colourful sets of Disney T-shirts and The Uptown Jeweler is offering the latest Pandora collection.[12]

The oldest attraction in Disney World, the Carousel of Progress, can be found in a section of the Magic Kingdom called Tomorrowland, of all places. This mechanical attraction, which was originally presented at the New York world exposition in 1964 in collaboration with Walt Disney, shows in five episodes how the life of a typical American family has been improved throughout history by technology, from the invention of the lightbulb to voice-operated air conditioning (although only the last two newest episodes are ever swapped out). 'There is a great big, beautiful tomorrow/and tomorrow is just a dream away.' This is the chorus of the catchy song that a generation of visitors just can't get out of their heads. When the carousel – itself the expression of a past elevated by nostalgia and unwavering faith in progress – was supposed to be dismantled and disposed of at the turn of the twenty-first century, thousands of fans launched a successful protest.

Besides Tomorrowland, there is also a section called Frontierland. American progress, according to the Disney storyline, stems from the adventurousness and hard work of individuals. Frontierland tells the story of the conquest of the American continent, in which Western heroes like Davey Crockett played a decisive part. The park emphasises the ordering and civilising role of the army, which has a fort on Tom Sawyer Island, and the significance of natural resources like salt and gold, which can allegedly be found in the rollercoaster landscape of Big Thunder Mountain. The theme of the frontier, which was popularised more than a hundred years ago by the historian Frederick Jackson Turner, and which has represented America's optimistic self-image ever since, ultimately achieving what seemed to be an impossible dream – global dominance – correlates here with Disney's ideology of salvation and progress.

In the context of the Cold War, the period when Frontierland was conceived, the landscape here takes on a very special meaning. It conveys the notion that economy (exploitation of natural resources), order (the taming of the wilderness) and military security (Fort Langhorn) guarantee a life of freedom and wealth which Americans, in contrast to their Communist rivals, have already achieved. Interestingly, Disney, unlike Frederick Jackson Turner, did not address agriculture as a concept, as if America's resources could be excavated from the depths of the mountains without having to toil on the land. In Frontierland, like everywhere in the Magic Kingdom, the theme of democracy is also missing. For Frederick Jackson Turner, the frontier was the place where democratic structures had their origin. In Disney's world, by contrast, there are no controversies or democratic discussions. Everything that might evoke the reality of a conflict-laden or work-driven world has been eradicated. In Disney's 'frontier', there are neither immigrants nor Na-

## Walt Disney World, Florida. At Least Two Natures

tive Americans. An 'Indian village' only exists as a diorama, an idyllic genre painting, which the choo-choo train drives past on its way to Fantasyland. There is no reminder of the violence used to systematically persecute and destroy Native Americans. A lightness settles over everything, turning it into entertainment and spectacle in one.

The Magic Kingdom is the oldest of the four theme parks. There is a proud patina to everything. The cast members of the Jungle Cruise winkingly point to the 'wild animals' – pneumatic elephants, alligators and hippos made of fiberglass and plastic – which are showing their age. In the Magic Kingdom, everything is a mock-up, everything a joyful fantasy. The entire world around Cinderella's fairy-tale castle is one long distorted history, filled with copies of nature, and objects that imitate the real thing. In Umberto Eco's words, the Magic Kingdom is 'hyperreal', an 'authentic fake', and it is exactly this that exerts such fascination.[13] But Disney's Animal Kingdom could not be more different. The largest and newest of the four amusement parks, which was opened to a grand media circus on Earth Day in 1998, is flamboyantly dedicated to the trendy topic of the threatened animal world and environment.

## The great circus of the wild

In place of candy shops and crowds of people set in a fairytale world, when I walk into the Animal Kingdom, I enter a bucolic oasis filled with Chinese muntjac deer, flamingos, ibis, Australian wallabies, rocks and small waterfalls. It looks like unspoiled nature. Beyond the oasis, a new setting appears. From afar I spot the gigantic Tree of Life: the 42-metre-high baobab tree, with almost 9,000 shoots and branches, over 100,000 green plastic leaves and 400 wooden sculptures carved into its bark and aerial roots – by Native Americans, it should be noted – is the icon of the Animal Kingdom, the visual focus and the landmark of this section.[14] From here I first visit Dinoland USA. If I wanted to, I could meet Nemo, Pluto and Donald Duck & co. all 'live', and I could eat Dino-bite snacks and play with fossils in the Boneyard. Signs point from Dinoland towards 'Asia', 'Africa', and to Pandora, the world featured in the film *Avatar*.

Africa and Asia, in the Western imagination, are 'natural' continents of the highest order. We assume that what we will find there are wildly charismatic mammals, as well as jungles, impregnable mountains, safaris and adventures. Disney World does not disappoint its guests. In the Animal

## Paradise Blues

Kingdom, all of this and more can be 'discovered'. Tropical vegetation and mighty waterfalls, gorillas, elephants and lions, the Harambe fruit market with African drums, 'Kilimanjaro safaris' and 'Maharajah jungle treks', rundown shops selling equipment for high endurance Himalayan tours, a Bodhi tree with sacrificial garlands, ancient Indian palaces, and the Wildlife Express shuttle that ferries tourists from Harambe to the Conservation Station in the African jungle. Disney's exotic globe carries its guests off into a 'Third World', in which any trace of history has been wiped out. You won't find traces of colonial exploitation here, post-industrial slums or any lack of comfort. In Africa and Asia, adventure and wistfulness are connected. And whoever wants to can wash away their blues with a Victory Golden Monkey beer for a paltry ten dollars, an Adobo margarita for thirteen dollars, or any other Disney drink in one of the Animal Kingdom's outposts.

Harambe, a fictious African port city in Animal Kingdom designed by Disney's 'imagineers' who photographed landscapes on location to make their reconstruction look authentic.

## Walt Disney World, Florida. At Least Two Natures

Time and place simply do not exist here. I can walk from Asia to Africa in a matter of minutes, then into the Savannah without tedious preparation, or to the Serka Zong Bazaar without an airplane. Unlike at a zoo, the animals in Disney's kingdom are not kept behind fences but live in their 'natural' habitats. The landscape is reminiscent of pictures from the Discovery Channel, except that you can walk or drive through them. At safaris outside Disney World, tourists who have travelled long distances to be there wait futilely for big game to appear. In Disney World, these animals turn up 'spontaneously' and reliably. In the complimentary Wilderness Explorer's Handbook, all the animals and plants are registered that I can meet within a few hours if I so wish: from clownfish to macaque, warthogs to okapi, and anemones to the Tree of Life. As a visitor, I know what to expect. I need to do nothing more than wait my turn in line. Waiting times are displayed exactly: 25 minutes, 40 minutes, 95 minutes. The more popular the attraction, the longer the waiting time. The landscapes in the Animal Kingdom are 'real' – photographed on location by Disney's imagineers, and then reconstructed. The native tropical and subtropical flora of Florida has been turned into a jungle and its creeks repurposed as waterfalls or slow-flowing rivers. A hippo that we come across on the Gorilla Falls Exploration Trail seems about to ram our jeep but turns back just in time. An anteater appears at regular intervals and poses photogenically. These animals are real – made of flesh and blood. The photos I take in the Animal Kingdom look as if I have been on the set of *Animal Planet* or have been lifted from *National Geographic*. As a Disney tourist, I don't see the hidden ditches, concealed bollards, fences, dells or walls, nor the concrete buffer for the hippo set at a 45-degree angle, nor the air-conditioning that lures the lions into the open, nor the hidden feeding places for anteaters.[15]

In the Animal Kingdom, the animals are actors on an elaborately conceived set. In the clear light of day, the ecological park is one big circus in which animals and people move in prescribed, never-changing ways. Rather than trained tigers ruled by whip-crackers, engineers control and choreograph animal movements, create 'authentic' natural habitats and, through acoustic, olfactory and visual elements, manipulate the emotional perceptions of visitors down to the last detail. The buzzwords in 'Africa' and 'Asia' are *discovery* and *exploration*. But in Orlando's biggest open-air circus, there's nothing to discover or experience other than what thousands of others have already experienced that very day from the exact same angle. Every independent stab at exploration on the part of the visitor, and every attempt to stray from the beaten track ends in an impeccably hidden barrier. In the same way that the park's paths never deviate, diverging storylines have no place here either. There is a prescription for how visitors should interpret Disney World. The script offers everyone a chance to explore: from children to adults, and from Disney fans even to sceptical researchers like me. While waiting for the trip down the wild Kali River, for example, I am told how illegal deforestation in Asia is destroying nature and culture. And on the safari bus through the 'African' animal nature reserve of Harambe, we are instructed to keep a lookout for poachers, who, of course, will be stopped at gunpoint by a ranger at the end of the trip. Disney's African and Asian tourists can be sure that they are standing on the right side of history. On the way to the animal protection station in 'Africa', there are plenty of learning charts. We are reminded that Disney is dedicated to animal protection, 'through emergency rescue, scientific studies and education'. I learn that we should protect bats because they eat insects (mosquitos); and, paradoxically, that insects are our friends.

It is often reported that Walt Disney was a great friend of animals and protector of the environment. According to a memory he himself passed on, as a child, Walt seized a donkey in his family orchard in Missouri and, when the animal tried to fight back, he kicked it to death. This episode haunted and tortured him his whole life long – so much, in fact, that he made animals into the protagonists of his cartoons. But Walt Disney's attitude towards nature conservation had nothing to do with what it has evolved into today. For him, it only had one value: to be used and enjoyed by people. Incidentally, there is much to suggest that Disney World would not have been founded at all if David Brower, the head of the conservation organisation Sierra Club, had not prevented Walt Disney from realising a colossal Alpine ski and amusement project in the area of today's Sequoia National Park in California.[16]

## Pandora's world

The geographer Jan Eric Steinkrüger once described Animal Kingdom as a zoo and a safari park in one.[17] A widescreen cinematic experience is the ultimate aim here. Films are brought to life. This is more evident than ever in Pandora, the most elaborate and expensive attraction in the Animal Kingdom, costing around 500 million dollars, which turns *Avatar*, the most successful film of all time, into a multidimensional show.[18] In Pandora, nature communicates

## Walt Disney World, Florida. At Least Two Natures

Pandora, The World of Avatar at Animal Kingdom, Disneyworld.

directly with visitors via complex technology – through loudspeakers and electrode sensors, voice recognition systems and touchscreens. Pandora's plants can react and send out signals just like real plants. Artificial 'second' nature is in no way inferior to the first.

For two hours, I walk in a throng of people through a steep, hilly, futuristic landscape, at the foot of floating mountains supported by invisible steel struts, smelling damp earth and surrounded by real and imaginary creatures, as well as fantasy plants that are supposedly threatened with extinction (including the gigantic *flaska reclinata*). Horticulture and dramaturgy, original and imaginary animal noises, fake flora and Florida's plants are so indistinguishable from one another that even when I look more closely, I cannot tell them apart. Joe Rohde, the chief designer of the Animal Kingdom, who sports earrings from around the world in his left ear, described Pandora as an 'art form'. The point of it is not just technology and cognition, but principally the stimulation of emotions. Pandora is the result of an 'unusual creative process', which 'links the theatrical reality of an opera with the operative and design complexity of a power plant'.[19]

After walking along winding paths through abandoned bunkers and a lab where a frighteningly real-looking, extra-terrestrial Na'vi is floating in an enormous test tube, I am scanned with a 'hybrid digital scanner', and 'transformed' into an avatar that can fly. After putting on 3D glasses with a movable base, I start to race through the fantastical tropical world of Pandora on the back of a swift banshee dragon, feeling nauseous as we dip past waterfalls that spray me and zip through trees and branches, then across the ocean and steep cliffs.

According to the Disney storyline, the futuristic world of Pandora is about saving a fragile ecology, a rare and beautiful key species that has been almost destroyed by humans as well as protecting the indigenous population of the Na'vis from exploitation and violence. After the breakneck flight through Pandora, bio-luminescent drinks and snacks are on offer: for example, Night Blossom from Pandora's Sati'lu canteen or Pongu Lumpia, a sweet fried spring roll. As Instagram-worthy as these futuristic foods might be, I have no appetite for colourful fast food, although I know that you can't buy it anywhere else on the globe.

On my way back to Orlando – from the hyperreal to the real world – I go over Disney's ecological message in my head. I have been bombarded with a range of scientific and pseudoscientific information about real and fictitious plants and living creatures; I have come into close contact with 'wild' flora and fauna, time-travelled from ancient history to the future and was, even if only for a few minutes, concerned about the fate of animals in Africa. But above all, it has been drummed into me that the Disney Corporation is highly committed to global environmental conservation. Over and over again, it has been suggested that Disney World is an institution legitimised by science. This applies in equal measure to the Dino Institute (sponsored by McDonald's), and the greenhouses in EPCOT that celebrate the wonders of modern agricultural technology, from edible flowers to vertical farming. There was no time for reflection because one attraction followed the next at lightning speed. As Disney's guest, I leave the amusement park with the feeling that I have supported a good cause with my admission fee and have saved the planet from the worst. Interestingly, not much was expected of me in return. At the end of each attraction, I had little to do except treat myself – to an exotic snack, a replica of an unusual habitat, a Mickey Mouse safari hat, a Tree of Life snow globe, wilderness videos or toy animals – all souvenirs of my trip made of fake fur or plastic and designed to save the environment on distant continents. This is what it boils down to: I have not been asked to make a commitment to the environment, but to consume ecological kitsch. And instead of being enlightened about the ecology of the jungle, I have been given the impression that Africa's fauna has been accurately replicated and can be authentically experienced in Florida; and that engineers and artists can create fantastical, futuristic nature scenes, which are more miraculous than 'the world outside'; and that experiencing nature can be entertaining. How could anyone think otherwise! After all – according to the amusement park's propaganda machine – Disney works with the Audubon Society, which is committed to bird preservation, and with the Nature Conservancy, to which Disney ceded a nature reserve of 4,800 hectares of land. What no tourist finds out: establishing the nature reserve was the price paid by the Disney Corporation to be exempted from all environmental regulations when building a futuristic city in the direct vicinity of Disney World. Walt himself designed his experimental community of EPCOT on his deathbed. It is a circular-shaped settlement that takes up elements of Ebenezer Howard's Garden City plans and hides all traffic and garbage disposal underground. But after Disney's death in December 1966, the project was shelved for decades.[20] It was not until the 1990s that Walt Disney's dream of a future city was put into practice. The city now bears the utopian name of Celebration.

## Celebration

On my last evening before driving to southern Florida, I visit Celebration. It's a pretty little town with parks and lakes, tree-lined boulevards, downtown bookshops, boutiques, a Googie-style cinema, a postmodern town hall adorned with dozens of slim columns, a post office in the shape of a silo, a bank with an eccentric observation tower and even a private university. Wooden fences surround the front gardens of detached private houses. Order is everywhere and it all looks ostentatiously peaceful, like America before the fall from grace. I take a seat in the Columbia, a restaurant on Front Street that overlooks the city lake. It serves excellent Caribbean dishes. I'm served by a Venezuelan waiter. At first glance, Celebration has all the charm of Victorian England but, on closer inspection, there's something a little creepy about it. The architecture of the Columbia restaurant turns out to be a cheap imitation. The cinema has no programme and stopped operating over ten years ago. The boutiques are all identical. And while Orlando is teeming with people from all kinds of ethnic backgrounds, the only people you see strolling through Celebration are white.

Paradise Blues

The movie theatre in Celebration, Disney's real life town, outside of Magic Kingdom, was designed by star architect César Pelli. It has been closed since 2010.

## Walt Disney World, Florida. At Least Two Natures

It takes me a while until I can pinpoint what disturbs me about Celebration. The town is eerily tidy and perfectly styled: from the manholes to the road signs and the shop logos, everything follows an identical mono aesthetic. Houses can be ordered from a catalogue. They come in Classical, Victorian, Colonial and Revival styles. Even the design of the fireplaces, the colours of the façade, and the door and window handles originate from Celebration's very own catalogue. Along the streets, loudspeakers quietly ooze Fifties Muzak. Public buildings have been designed by the most renowned architects in the world – César Pelli, Michael Graves, Philip Johnson, Robert Venturi – but the whole town seems as artificial as one of Disney's kingdoms. Celebration celebrates the art of artifice. The lake and river are also artificial. Streetlamps pretend to be old. The 12-metre-high Christmas tree has plastic needles, and the ice-skating rink is synthetic. The snow that falls here in winter is not artificial – it's shaving foam. 'Feeding the alligators is forbidden', says a sign by the lake. Are there real alligators here? Or plastic animals like Disney's Jungle Cruise? Fantasy and reality blur into one here.[21]

I think back to my very first visit to Florida about fifteen years ago, with friends in Boca Raton. Every house had a simple and beautiful view of the artificial lake. 'You can't swim in the lake', my friends explained, 'there are alligators in there. And when a frog falls into the pool, it dies on the spot – because of the chemicals!' Later they told me that the height of palms was prescribed, that their crowns had to be cut into a certain shape, that all curtains had to be white, and that washing had to be dried in the dryer, never in the open air. Breaking these rules carried high fines. There are towns like Celebration everywhere in Florida.

Public controversies, differing values or diverging opinions on functionality or aesthetics are given as little airtime in most of Florida's gated communities as in the artificial town of Celebration. Disney's requirements for a functioning community, and those of his imitators, were a high measure of control and conformity, as well as the almost complete privatisation of polity. Amusement parks like Disney World and towns like Celebration are only minutely distinguishable from one another. The town, a scripted place run by managers instead of elected representatives, may be a particularly extreme example of polity that chooses planning over historical growth, prescriptiveness over democratic negotiation and artificiality over naturalness. But in Florida, hundreds and thousands of model towns and gated communities for the wealthy follow similar standards. Possibly, I think, people prefer the comfort of what is synthetic and controllable over the complexity of real life. Finally, after an overdose of artificiality, I'm drawn to an area in south Florida where nature is said to be at its wildest: the Everglades.

## An ocean of grass

The Everglades are probably the most renowned wetlands in the world. They are listed as an area of World Heritage, an international biosphere and a national park, and have attained a sacred status in the USA. Their long-legged birds and wide-mouthed alligators – for every eight residents in Florida there is one alligator – are among the most popular postcard themes in the Sunshine State. The Everglades appear in the opening credits of the crime series *CSI: Miami*, in Spiderman comics and films featuring swamp monsters, from *The Attack of the Giant Leeches* (1959) to *Mega Python vs. Gatoroid* (2011).

The Everglades ecosystem used to stretch from the suburban outskirts of Orlando to the Florida Keys. For centuries, the region that I can cross in my rental car by highways and secondary roads in just five hours was nothing but an enormous swamp and underwater prairie, an ocean covered in a river of grass. Up until the end of the nineteenth century, the geo-engineer, sportsman and scientist, Hugh Willoughby, who travelled around the area by canoe, was right when he claimed that the Everglades was as 'unknown to the white man as the heart of Africa'.[22]

Florida's extensive swamps, which used to begin right next to Disney World, were teeming with rats and snakes, cockroaches and scorpions, spiders and worms, sand flies and mosquitoes. The diversity of living creatures and plants was once breathtaking. Barely any people lived here. Instead, the region was inhabited by black bears and sponges, barracudas and painted storks, fox squirrels and minks, marsh rabbits and bottlenose dolphins, carnivorous plants and amphibian birds, tree-climbing oysters and ghost orchids, Royal palms and gumbo-limbo trees, swallowtail butterflies and manatees. One of the main reasons for the simply immeasurable diversity of species in this area is the ocean which means that, although the Everglades is on the same latitude as the Sahara Desert and receives as much sunlight, it has a very high rainfall and subtropical climate. Here, animals from the mild zones in the north live alongside tropical creatures. And it's the one place in the world where alligators from the north and crocodiles from the south live side by side.

Southern Florida emerged from the ocean in the last ice age, around 100,000 years ago. When dinosaurs were still roaming large expanses of North

America, the Everglades remained underwater for another 150 million years. The shells and skeletons of dead marine animals formed the porous layer of limestone; its cavities, channels, and gullies store today's drinking water in Florida. While rainfall ensures that the region is flooded all year round, limestone guarantees that water levels do not subside. About a hundred years ago, a 1.9-metre-tall man could have waded the route I take from Disney World to the southern tip of Florida without the water reaching his chin.[23]

A water engineer who was supposed to survey the area west of Miami in the spring of 1907 wrote in a particularly succinct way about the difficulties of crossing the Everglades: 'when one pulls one foot [out of the swampy mud], the other sinks in continuously, making it almost impossible to move forward'.[24]

## Invincible wilderness

For centuries, the flat swampy area of southern Florida was wild and merciless. Over 10,000 years ago, indigenous peoples might have lived on a few of its islets such as Horr's Island. They were all-year farmers and possibly the first sedentary Native Americans but, when the white settlers arrived, mostly the Calusa Indians inhabited southern Florida and made a living as coastal fishers. Juan Ponce de Léon – who accompanied Christopher Columbus on his trips to the New World and later became governor of Puerto Rico – went in search of the mystical island of Bimini and, at Easter 1513, over a hundred years before the Pilgrim Fathers, discovered mainland USA. He believed he had discovered a Caribbean island and christened it La Florida, which it has retained until this day.[25] The Calusa tribe drove out Ponce de Léon and his people and retained their lands in Florida for several hundred years. After the Calusa came the Seminole tribe, who battled against US military troops from 1816 to 1858, the longest period recorded.[26] These Native Americans defied any attempt by the military to tame them. For the rest of the USA, usable maps had already existed for a long time, but southern Florida remained unexplored.

Towards the end of the nineteenth century, the area south of Orlando was considered useless and full of danger. Cattle could not graze in the swamps, and the presence of freshwater, all the way to the south coast of Florida, remained a mystery until well into the twentieth century. Only a handful of visionaries were convinced that it was worth conquering the 'wild' southern region of Florida. One of them was Hamilton Disston, a businessman who had made a fortune producing iron swords and files in Philadelphia. Disston envisaged the draining of the Everglades as *the* business opportunity of a lifetime. In 1881, he bought 6,000 square kilometres of land from the deeply debt-ridden state of Florida for a rock-bottom price, probably setting a record as the largest area of land ever acquired by a private individual anywhere in the world. In a subsequent deal, Disston received an acre of land for himself for every two acres he drained. He also offered American and European investors from Scotland, Germany and Italy, to name a few, smaller tracts of land for purchase. In Disston's advertising copy, Florida was described as a winter paradise and breadbasket in one, a country with no frost, no illness and no mosquitoes, an orchard of fertile soil whose sun would yield sumptuous fruit and the best vegetables in the world. Disston had started his own farm in St Cloud, about a half-hour drive from Disney World. He experimented with growing rice, peaches, grapes and all kinds of vegetables, but sugarcane soon became his favourite crop. Many investors were enthused at the sight of his showcase orchards. Disston's water engineers boasted that the Everglades would be 'as dry as a bone' within a few years. The strategy behind this was blindingly simple: water from the Kissimmee Valley that flooded the river at irregular intervals would be diverted towards Lake Okeechobee which lay further south, while the river would be diverted from Okeechobee into the ocean. As long as the outflow was higher than the inflow rate, according to the bathtub logic used by the engineers, nothing could possibly go wrong.

To build the Erie Canal in the state of New York fifty years previously, people had relied on ox power but, in the meantime, amphibious excavators had been developed, gigantic steam vehicles driven by wood and coal (later, petrol and diesel) that emptied the swamp of around a hundred linear metres of dirt and mud a day using rotating steel buckets. Within a short time, large areas were drained. This success appeared to confirm Disston's assumptions – at least in the beginning. But after a series of exceptionally dry years, the area flooded like never before. Water inflow into Lake Okeechobee had increased but drainage work had stagnated. For twelve years, Disston's people managed to excavate canals along a length of 130 kilometres and drained the driest sections of South Florida. But, in the canals, the water almost stood still. They were shallow, narrow and no match for heavier floods.[27] When the whole of South Florida was affected by a torrential storm in September 1894, nature fought back. Between 1895 and 1896, frost destroyed large swathes of the fruit vegetable and sugarcane harvest. As if that wasn't enough, the US government revoked bonuses for cultivating sugarcane. Farmers whose fields had flooded turned in outrage against Disston. As for Disston himself, a capitalist and visionary who had once set off for Florida to tame nature and bend the Everglades to his will, in the spring of 1896, after having to lay off his canal workers, he put a gun to his head and took his own life.[28]

Henry Morrison Flagler stepped into the void that Disston left. His aim was to build a railroad line to southern Florida. Unlike Disston, oil magnate Flagler did not attempt to drain central Florida's lakes and rivers. Instead, he concentrated entirely on strips of land along the coast, had a dozen regional canals built, and constructed a railroad track along a narrow coastal ridge that was extended to Palm Beach, later Miami and then even the Keys within a few years. As early as 1894, Flagler opened the Royal Poinciana in Palm Beach, a six-storey grand hotel. More than 1,500 kilometres of wood were used in the construction. The hotel had 1,800 doors and 1,700 staff members to keep the business running. There was no bigger wooden building in the world, no bigger hotel, or nobler accommodation with a Mediterranean ambience. This place, and Flagler's other hotels along the Floridian coast, were meeting places for the rich, beautiful and famous, among them writers like Mark Twain and Somerset Maugham, US presidents from Grover Cleveland to Theodore Roosevelt, the baseball champion Babe Ruth, members of the Vanderbilt clan and many more.[29]

To build the railroad, pine groves had to be burnt down and tropical hardwood copses – known as hammocks – had to be felled. Mahogany and hornbeams, black poisonwood and palm trees made way for spanking new tourist lodges that sprang up out of nowhere. Along the sandy beaches, a paradise of parks and villas was created, while the lower classes were pushed further west. The railroad and new streets avoided central Florida, which was infested with mosquitoes and alligators. The Everglades were a long way from becoming a built-up residential area or even an agricultural oasis. 'Some people believe that the Everglades should be drained', commented a reporter drily towards the end of the nineteenth century, 'but others are demanding the annexation of the moon.'[30]

## A boom, a recession and another boom

What happened afterwards can be summarised by the following: first, the coast experienced a boom. Whatever direction Flagler's railroad and the new

Dixie Highway took, low-paid African American labourers were deployed to dig up entire mangroves including their roots, and to spread a layer of fine sand, like a carpet, all along the coast. The population of West Palm Beach quadrupled within five years and Miami's increased fivefold. Chic resorts like Hollywood-by-the-Sea, Coral Gables and Boca Raton were built, complete with country clubs. Golf courses and polo fields wooed the wealthy from the North, as well as con artists and swindlers. The Ku Klux Klan enacted its vicious rule, alcohol was plentiful in Miami despite prohibition, and Seminole attracted tourists to their villages, offering displays of alligator fighting, handmade baskets, jewellery and patchwork blankets.[31]

Secondly, nature tore through the countryside with unprecedented brutality. On 17 September 1926, a powerful hurricane, with winds of over 200 kilometres per hour, swept through southern Florida. Most residents in the new coastal towns had no experience with tropical storms whatsoever. When the eye of the storm passed directly over Miami, many thought that the worst was over; but, that evening, more than 200 people were killed. Damages to property reached sums of over $100 million, at the time higher than any other natural disaster in the history of the USA. In central Florida, dikes collapsed, the banks of Lake Okeechobee flooded, and tens of thousands of people were left homeless. Only two years later, another storm laid to waste the sun-drenched dreams of hotel owners and farmers. In Palm Beach, a wing of Flagler's Poinciana Hotel was destroyed. Five-metre waves broke a dam south of Lake Okeechobee and flooded the fields of nearby farms, submerging hundreds of predominantly African American migrant workers in their wake. The official death toll was around 2,000 – higher than the numbers killed during Hurricane Katrina – but the real figure was undoubtedly much higher. Even decades later, farmers came across skeleton remains when ploughing the fields, and human bones buried in blood-soaked earth.[32] In 1933, a catastrophic hurricane claimed the lives of war veterans who were building railroad and highway bridges to the Keys, also sweeping away their shacks. In a caustic essay, Ernest Hemingway, who lived in the Florida Keys himself at the time, accused those responsible of murder, saying that the workers had not been offered sufficient protection.[33] The devastation showed no sign of letting up. In the autumn of 1947, following a long period of aridity, two hurricanes ravaged businesses and crops, and turned the Dixie Highway into a river. Tens of thousands of animals – cows, panthers, and rattlesnakes – drowned or starved, while cesspits overran and the freshwater sludge of Lake Okeechobee, which entered the fishing territories of the ocean, drove away bluefish, snappers and tarpons, for which South Florida was famous.[34]

The two hurricanes of 1947 were probably what set in motion an agreement between farmers and fruit growers, environmentalists and city property developers, despite their different interests, to control the waters in central and southern Florida, which resulted in shovelling more earth than during any other project in US history, bar the construction of the Panama Canal. All the stakeholders were aware that Florida had enough water. It was the unpredictable cycle of flooding and aridity that prevented adequate water supplies from being in the right place at the right time. The United States Army Corps of Engineers tried to remedy the situation by coming up with a comprehensive plan for central and southern Florida. Between 1947 and 1965, the corps spent no less than 173 million dollars on building canals and dikes, pump stations and overflows, wastewater pipes and water purification sites. As a part of this scheme, the Kissimmee River was levelled, shortened by sixty kilometres, and transformed into a kind of water highway, known as Canal 38, or C-38.

Implementing these plans had far-reaching effects. The first was that the Everglades were transformed. Along the C-38, bird colonies were replaced by dairy farms and grazing pastures. South of Lake Okeechobee, a farm region was created, known as the Everglades Agricultural Area, which was protected by embankments for over 2,800 square kilometres, an area bigger than Luxembourg. In the east, suburban agglomerations spread along the coast and, in the far south, a national park was created that was supposed to protect the fragile wetlands. The second effect was that southern Florida experienced another economic upturn, this time more furious than the first. After the Second World War, when nature appeared to have been tamed, the Sunshine State grew four times as fast as the rest of the USA. Tourist figures exploded and agriculture flourished. The south eastern US states became the nation's 'sugar bowl', culminating in 1959 when Fidel Castro came to power and the USA banned the import of sugar from Cuba. Underpinning all these changes was the planners' conviction that they could change Florida's natural landscape as they saw fit with radical interventions – as if the whole of Florida were Disney World.

## Oranges and calves

During the transformation of its landscape, Florida was turned into a citrus paradise, whose residents, in the words of publicist John McPhee 'brush their teeth with orange juice'.[35] Along the highways from Disney World to southern Florida, enormous trucks laden with citrus fruit drive past me. Oranges adorn the car plates of the Sunshine State, and northwest of Lake Okeechobee, I drive past orange plantations that are several kilometres long. Caterpillar vehicles and trucks with loading hydraulics are used for the harvest. The workers pick fruit by hand, with or without a ladder, gathering at least 2,000 pounds of fruit per picker per day, as a Mexican explains to me in broken English. In the state's front gardens, limes, which are often wild, lemons and oranges grow in abundance. Nothing is so tightly interwoven with Florida's image as citrus fruit: around seventy per cent of America's national orange harvest comes, in fact, from there. Having said that – oranges are as foreign to the area as sugarcane and wild boar. For the Spanish, oranges from North America were unimpressive. It wasn't until the English occupation from 1764 to 1783 that oranges became one of the Old World's favourite export. Their juice was mixed with sugar, spices or alcohol because Florida's oranges were extremely sour before they were crossbred with sweet Chinese oranges.[36] In the nineteenth century, 'orange fever' seized parts of Florida. Harriet Beecher Stowe, the author of *Uncle Tom's Cabin*, who lived in a winter cottage in the village of Mandarin, Florida, and owned an orange grove from where she shipped fruit by steamer to the north, was the most prominent advertiser for orange-growing in Florida. For her, the orange tree was 'the worthiest representative of the tree of life'. Beecher Stowe was successful, but many orange growers who tried to make a living in northern Florida lost their harvest to frost. In the twentieth century, citrus plantations gradually wandered further and further south, where climate and geography promised greater yields. Farming, fertilisers and pesticides were perfected, and trees were cultivated to such an extent that, by the end of the twentieth century, the same area was producing at least ten to fifteen times as much fruit as a century before.[37]

I was expecting to see oranges in Florida. But I am overwhelmed by the diversity of crops and agricultural products that I see on my journey southwards. When I cross the district line of Okeechobee, I'm greeted by a sign saying 'Farming – welcome to the lifeblood of Okeechobee'. Apart from orange growing, Florida also ranks high in vegetable production, flower farming and mushrooms. I pass countless greenhouses and palm plantations. I see trucks laden with sugarcane and soil. Florida lies far ahead of any other state in the production of turf, thanks to its dark, damp earth. 'Be a man. Buy land', it says on some street signs. Here, you can still buy land cheaply, but the rows of derelict houses bear witness to broken dreams. What surprises me the most is the abundance of cattle along the highways.[38] In Okeechobee, a sign advertises a Cowtown Rodeo, and hamburger joints have names like Cattlemen's or Cowtown Café. The Wild Side Pawn and Gun Store in Okeechobee, a pawnshop that touts porn films, rifles and ammunition, evokes a time when Florida's ranchers drove their cattle across the open range without respecting farmers' enclosures and pulled their guns on anyone who dared stand in their way. A study at the University of Florida at the beginning of 2019 calculated that there were almost 1.7 million cattle in the state, taking up 15.6 per cent of the landmass – over ten times as much land as all the citrus plantations in the state taken together. Not only are milk and meat produced in Florida but, above all, it's a hub for calf-breeding – before the animals are transported to feedlots.[39]

I don't see any cowboys, but I've never seen so many Easy Rider lookalikes on Harleys in my life as on my way to the Keys – and never as many trailer parks, golf courses, mobile homes or retirement homes, churches or billboards for Jesus, the saviour. Florida's residents ironically call the state 'God's waiting room', due to the large numbers of elderly residents who flock to its mild climate, trying to escape the winter or plagued by arthritis. Many people in southern Florida are not just looking for citrus fruits but are following the example of the former 'Godfather of punk', Iggy Pop, who called it 'a kind of elegant coma, with a lot of peace and convenience'.[40]

## Okeechobee

On the shore of Lake Okeechobee, I make a stop; from the nine-metre Hoover Dike, erected in the 1960s as a barricade against hurricanes, I look across the water. It stretches all the way to the horizon as if the lake were the ocean. The dams and weirs, reservoir ditches and flood spillways show that it is, in fact, a huge hydraulic machine, a giant container filled with fish. The lake was once twice as large and known for its fifty-pound black bullhead catfish. Today, alongside smaller catfish, mostly blue spotted and black sunfish can be found here but also over a dozen exotic marine fish species that have lost their way and ended up here via the aquarium trade.[41]

Somewhere behind the scenes, nature is surveyed and controlled by the United States Army Corps of Engineers – a kind of full-scale Disney World that controls and serves the needs of sports and commercial anglers, farmers and tourists. At the start of every rainy season, the engineers simply lower the water level of the tenth largest lake in the USA, only to fill it back up again a few months later.

South of Lake Okeechobee, I drive past sugarcane fields. A complex system with sluices and canals zigzags throughout the area. The land is divided into squares on which beans and lettuce, celery and radish, and maize and rice are cultivated – although 65 per cent of the area is devoted to sugarcane. From far away, the sugar plants look like tropical sedge (*Cyperaceae*) but their appearance is deceptive. Sugarcane deprives the Everglades of water and nutrients and, in return, makes hundreds of millions of dollars in profit for large companies. Before the rainy season begins, enormous pump stations lower the water level of the irrigation canals by more than half a metre and raise them again in the dry period when the sugar plants require extensive irrigation. For decades the sugar industry has claimed more than half the water in the Everglades Agricultural Area but, at the same time, pays less than one per cent in regional taxes. The US Sugar and Flo-Sun lobby, alongside large real estate firms, are some of the most influential political powers in the southeast USA. Pesticides, which are used in large quantities, as well as surplus phosphorus and nitrogen, which are produced by microbe activity in the soil, are gradually destroying the environment. Initially, this 'sugar water' – with residues of pesticides and plant food – was fed back into Lake Okeechobee. From 1983, when sport fishing and activities by the local population started to cause the eutrophication of the lake, raising the alarm, farmers disposed of their brown by-product into the neighbouring nature reservations instead.[42] The use of heavy agricultural machinery has also had massive consequences for the environment. Under the weight of these machines, and in the process of harrowing the peaty soil, the earth oxidises and is gradually swept away by the wind. Air pollution is a consequence of the burning of sugar leaves and has been making headlines for years. In October when the harvest begins, soot or 'black snow' falls from the sky, but never in the areas where white people live. The Sierra Club is currently involved in a lawsuit challenging the regulation by Florida's Department of Agriculture that allows the burning of sugarcane leaves whenever the wind blows the ashes towards the poor homes of low-income sugarcane cutters.[43]

Walt Disney World, Florida. At Least Two Natures

## Towards Homestead

On the way towards Homestead, a town south of Miami, known as the 'Gateway to the Everglades', the highway takes me past dikes and canals, telegraph poles and electricity pylons. From the distance, I spot a few hills – excavation sites for Miami limestone which is used to produce cement and concrete. Florida has an abundance of everything required to produce construction materials: limestone, water and sand.

Over the decades, more housing complexes have been built here than in most other US states; after the First World War, more concrete was used in Miami's construction business than anywhere else in the world. A hundred years ago, the state had fewer than a million inhabitants, making it one of the least populated states; today, Florida takes the lead – after California and Texas – with 22 million inhabitants. Especially along the coast, despite the high hurricane risk, new concrete fortifications and bungalows are constantly being built.[44] Just before Homestead, the highway crosses the Tamami (Tampa to Miami) Trail, the first road for cars to cross from coast to coast

On the road to Homestead,
Southern Florida.

right through southern Florida. Construction began in 1915 and was carried out with floating dredgers in parallel to the canal, which delivered stone for the road's foundation. More than 2.5 million sticks of dynamite were used by the teams made up of groups of 25 workers that toiled away despite the heat, water, insects and reptiles. The road's maiden voyage featuring eight Ford Model Ts in 1923, however, turned into a nightmare. The estimated three days required by the 'Trailblazers', as they called themselves, to reach their destination became a laborious three weeks. Along the way, the drivers lived off wild game and turkey, only surviving because Seminole people waved them in the direction of Miami. The trail that eventually became Highway 41 was officially opened in 1928 and today effectively interrupts the flow of water from north to south.[45]

These days, the natural landscape of the enormous area from Orlando to the Keys, memorably referred to by the journalist and environmental activist Marjory Stoneman Douglas as a 'river of grass', has disappeared without a trace.[46] Native flora and fauna, which cannot thrive on drained soil, have all but vanished. Invasive Australian trees, of all things, survive best – Casuarina trees with their minute scale leaves, which Henry Flagler had planted during his time to decorate the streets of Palm Beach and Miami, and the Melaleuca tree, which John Clayton Gifford (the first American to obtain a Ph.D. in forestry) introduced to dry out the Floridian swamps from 1906 onwards. Melaleuca needs four times as much water as native plants. When scientists recognised the risks posed by these invasive Australian species two generations later, it was much too late. The thirsty plants had already interrupted the circulation of water, dried out the earth, caused massive forest fires and driven out native plants and animal species: in Melaleuca forests, the trees stand so close together that birds cannot land on them. A solution to stop the rampant proliferation of these trees, whose seeds were sown from aeroplanes in the 1940s, and which have no natural competitors in Florida unlike in Australia, has yet to be found.[47]

## Everglades National Park

From Homestead, I drive to the Everglades National Park, which was established in 1947 by Harry S. Truman. Right in front of the entrance to the park, there is an enormous fenced-off area that houses a prison, a fast-food joint (whose menu includes frogs' legs), and a reptile farm, whose owner breeds zoo animals and offers tourists alligator shows as well as Airboat tours

## Walt Disney World, Florida. At Least Two Natures

Inside a reptile farm, Everglades City, Florida.

through the Everglades. I'm interested in the latter. The propeller-driven boat is so loud that a tour is only possible using ear protection. However, it takes passengers through a fascinating water landscape with alligators and iguanas, herons, storks and ibis. The captain of the swamp boat, 'Psycho Paul', makes the obligatory jokes about tourists being eaten by alligators. In reality, people in Florida are not eaten by alligators, but alligators by people – hamburger style.

The Everglades National Park was the first in the history of the USA that was set up not for its scenery, but for its biodiversity. In the first three decades of the twentieth century, it was mostly mountain peaks and ranges that were declared national parks.[48] But in the 1930s, when environmentalists raise their voices and the significance of how nature is interconnected took centre stage, flora and fauna were viewed in a new light. From then on, landscapes no longer had to be spectacular to be considered worthy of protection; outstanding ecological significance was sufficient.

Despite oppositional voices from politicians that dismissed the project as a worthless 'park for snakes and swampland', in 1934, US Congress decided to set up a national park in the Everglades. Thirteen years later, after the state of Florida bought an area of over half a million hectares and put it into the hands of the government in Washington, there were no more obstacles to establishing the park.[49] I first stop at the Ernest F. Coe Visitor Center, named after a landscape architect who lobbied hardest for the park from 1925 on.[50] From there, it's a sixty-kilometre drive to the Flamingo Visitor Center in Florida Bay. The street winds through an abundance of diverse landscapes. Round tours encourage tourists to hike along wooden walkways across expanses of grass, or through cypress swamps to mangrove forests. Roseate spoonbills and wading birds stand in ponds in the middle of the grassy landscape; tropical islands of trees, made of limestone hillocks, covered in clusters of royal palms and black poisonwood trees, grow alongside wild coffee plants and vines, mastic trees and gumbo-limbos. In the brackish water of the south, mangroves and seagrass grow, while the dry coast is populated with cacti and agaves. Even levies of just a few centimetres lead to dramatic changes in vegetation in the flat, watery landscape of the Everglades. I can now fully appreciate how Ernest F. Coe managed to persuade decision-makers in Washington to protect this unique landscape by taking them on boat tours and Zeppelin flights. Although the area doesn't have an extraordinary topography – no mountains or canyons – the sounds of nature, the beauty of flocks of birds, the feeling of solitariness, the reflection of the sun in pools and the wide expanse of tropical wilderness have a distinctly magical effect. Thousands of people visit the Everglades; but this time, the guests barely leave a trace in this natural setting. Because the southernmost area of Florida is truly uninhabited.

## Flamingo

In Flamingo, the street ends at Florida Bay. Along the coast, even where today's campsite is located, tropical storms have piled up ocean sediments over the centuries – marl, sand and shells – and have built a natural dam. The indigenous population of the Tequesta tribe once lived here before fishermen founded a small village in around 1890, of which only ruins remain – because when the National Park was founded, the settlements were evicted and the houses demolished. Flamingo was never easy on its inhabitants. During a visit in 1893, the nature photographer Leverett White Brownell described the place as 38 'shacks on stilts', a squalid, motheaten, jerkwater town. The swarms of mosquitoes here were so thick that Brownell saw them

## Walt Disney World, Florida. At Least Two Natures

extinguish the light of an oil lamp. Flamingo achieved tragic notoriety by being regularly hit by devastating hurricanes and because 'America's first environmentalist', Guy Bradley, was murdered here. He lived in Flamingo and was originally an enthusiastic bird hunter, who made a fortune at the beginning of the twentieth century by selling exotic bird feathers, during the era when feather hats were in fashion. But he later did a 180-degree turn and became a game conservationist of the National Bird protection organisation, the Audubon Society. Bradley's murder, carried out by his former hunting companion Walter Smith in 1905, caused uproar throughout the country when Smith was let off; it also partially led to the decline in demand for fashionable feathers. From the First World War on, when sex workers in America began to decorate themselves with coloured feathers, the trend for feathered hats worn by upper-class women came to an end.[51]

Where fishermen, animal and reptile hunters used to live in huts, there are now parking lots and campsites, a canoe rental station, a restaurant, a shop for camping equipment, a public ramp for boats, a marina and a striking, flamingo-coloured, modernist building for the National Park administration. Flamingo is still stricken by terrible storms and climate change is also affecting its vegetation, a National Park employee tells me. A ranger reports on extensive renovation works: the buildings and compounds, including the remains of a hotel and gas station that were destroyed by a hurricane, were part of a large-scale project initiated by the National Park administration in the 1950s. The National Park Service director at the time, Conrad L. Wirth, saw the travel boom and the laws governing the construction of highways as a great challenge: mass tourism across the country was posing a threat to all national parks, which were in danger of being 'loved to death'. 'See the USA in your Chevrolet', proclaimed a famous TV ad from that time. At least eighty million automobile tourists were predicted in the year 1966, the fifty-year jubilee of the National Park Service. Instead of keeping the enormous crush of visitors in check, Wirth strongly advocated a huge extension of the National Park administration in keeping with the trends of the time. He applied for a budget of one billion dollars, oriented on those of large national institutions such as the Television Information Office and the US Army Corps of Engineers, and gained the support of the American Automobile Association which (assuming that more streets would translate into more cars sold) organised the launch dinner for the new initiative in Washington in 1955. More than 7,000 kilometres of streets were then either built or refurbished within the National Park and more than 1,500 parking spaces were created. 'Mission 66' was first and foremost a project to extend the infrastructure for cars within the national park, and the pink-coloured complex, with its bulky architecture, located along the drive from Homestead to Flamingo, was one of the proud model projects of the programme.

From a modern point of view, Flamingo is concrete proof of the slogan that the park was not only set up and then extended for nature's sake but also, as Harry S. Truman once emphasised, 'for the pleasure of Americans'.[52]

## A fragile dream

Driving back from Flamingo to Homestead, I stop at the Royal Palm Visitor Center. Here, in Paradise Key, I find the origins of efforts to conserve nature surrounding the National Park. In 1916, a group of environmental activists from the Florida Federation of Women's Clubs successfully protested to transform some 400 hectares of the Everglades into a state park. Interestingly, Mary Kenan Flagler, the wife of the railroad magnate, was one of them. Even Henry Flagler and speculative land developers like James Ingraham were convinced by the environmental activists' arguments. Although they considered Florida swamps useless, they were invested in conserving selected areas.[53] Developing natural habitats also had its limits. With this going through my mind, I am even more struck by the contrast between the seagrass prairie of the Everglades and the dark, fertile soils of vegetable and fruit fields as I drive back. Both landscapes share the same slow-flowing waters from north to south. The water that is redirected into the agricultural areas ends in the prairie at some point. The wild and tame worlds of Florida are very closely connected.

On my tour from the hyperreal fairy-tale world of Disney towards Flamingo, I had gone in search of Florida's original nature, knowing that it consisted of more than 3,000 plant species and more threatened bird species than any other US state.[54] But, at the southernmost tip, I discovered a richness of nature and a vast expanse of natural landscape, much like the one that dominated the peninsula long ago. In particular, animal species on the verge of extinction – from indigo adders to bush jays, smalltooth sawfish to North American manatees, Gopher tortoises to alligators and Florida panthers to Florida black bears – have all increased in number in the past few years. The Everglades' seagrass prairie with its orchids and tropical islands of trees is flourishing. But behind this impression hides another truth. Only one-fifth of the original Everglades swamp landscape still exists. Without

## Walt Disney World, Florida. At Least Two Natures

strict environmental laws, there would be no panthers in Florida. Without the pipe culverts and canals that punctuate the Tamiami Trail, there would barely be any water in the Everglades; and without complex controls that regulate the water flow along thousands of kilometres, Florida's 'wild' south would transform within a few years into a desert.[55] Disney's Magic Kingdom may well fool visitors into thinking they are in a dream world, whereas everything outside of it is real and natural. In reality, much of what people believe is real and natural in Florida is actually invasive and constructed, part of the second nature that is laid on top of its original one, as it were, like a camouflage.

And what is certain is that this second nature is the source of great hazards. Over 400 animal species are threatened with extinction. The beauty of the Everglades only exists because the dams and canals, positioned in the fragile world of the wetlands to make the dreams of millions of people come true, were destroyed. The water level in this state, which has more water than any other in the USA, is constantly sinking and, on the West Coast, seawater is being desalinated in some places because there is a lack of fresh groundwater. People will only be able to survive the next few hundred years in the unique world of Florida, a region threatened by hurricanes and climate change, if they learn from past mistakes. That requires the realisation that its second nature is dependent on its first and safeguards to ensure that Florida's 'river of grass' also flows in the future.

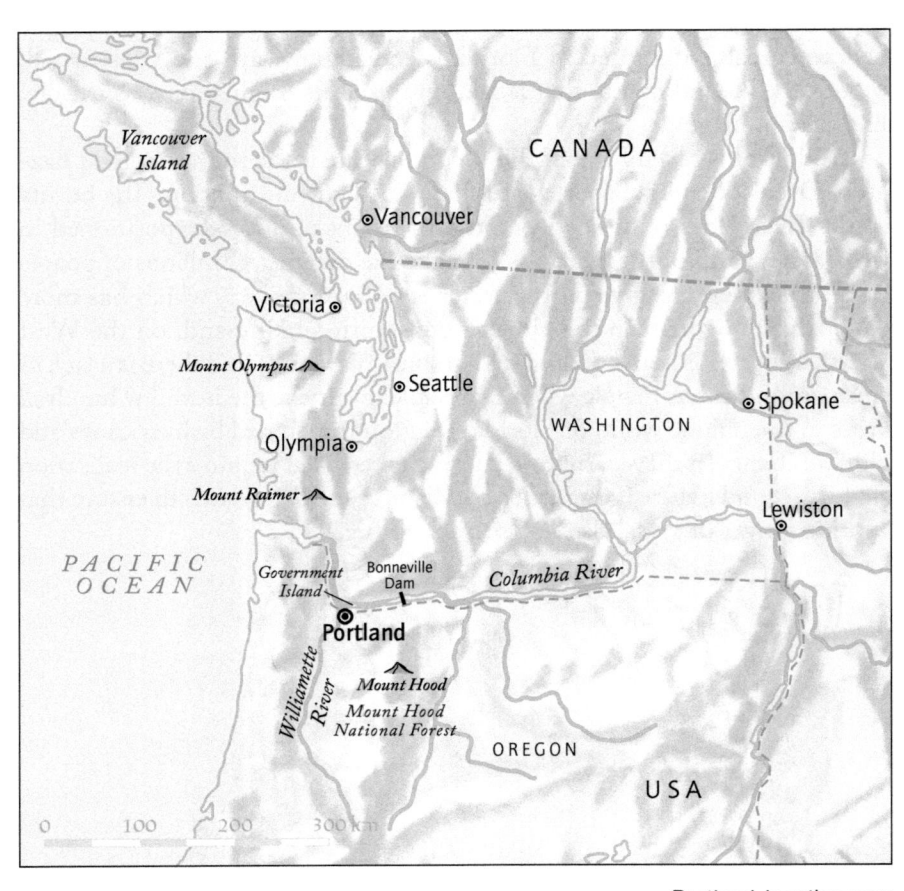

Portland, location map

# Portland, Oregon.
## Into America's Green Future

### Travelling through America's green future

Portland, Oregon, a city of half a million inhabitants in the northwest USA, is considered one of 'America's greenest cities' and an eco-friendly paradise. Large areas of the city are covered in parkland, its bridges are homes to peregrine falcons and more than half its energy comes from renewable sources. Portland's director of the Bureau for Sustainability is senior to its Bureau of Planning chief. For decades, $CO_2$ emissions in the city have been steadily declining despite its increasing population. Portland was the first major city in the United States to ban plastic, the first to convert its urban freeway into a park and the first to introduce a modern tram system. Here you will find the longest bridge closed to vehicle traffic in North America, the 520-metre cable-stayed Tilikum Crossing over the Willamette River. From bike manufacturers to craft breweries, the city has the most energy-efficient buildings per capita in the USA. More than a quarter of its residents cycle to work and use carpools, or public transport whereas the national US average is just under one per cent. And for years now, the quality of life in Portland has ranked among the highest.[1] The list could easily go on. Nevertheless, the history of Portland began with the radical erosion of the Pacific forests. Following this, shipbuilding, and the scrapping of wartime marine vessels during the Second World War, transformed the water of the Willamette River into a notorious toxic slurry. So, what brought about this fundamental transformation of Portland? What historic circumstances, planning visions and political factors resulted in its reinvention? And how did Portland's image as an ecotopia – a hip, progressive city – ultimately come about?[2]

### Bike City, USA

No other means of transport seems better suited for exploring Portland than a bike. This is not just because *The New York Times* described Portland as 'Bike City USA', but, as Hemingway noted, 'you learn the contours of a country best ... by riding a bicycle, since you have to sweat up the hills and coast down them'.[3] In Portland, the hills are not very steep. And the most scenic cycle paths run along the Willamette River.

If I'd known I could assemble my bike at Portland International Airport right after landing perhaps I'd have brought my own – there's a covered bicycle site next to the arrivals terminal with tools and a signposted cycle path to downtown Portland as well as a city train that lets you take bikes free of charge. Instead, I hire one from Waterfront Bicycles, one of over seventy similar outfits in the city. As I'm waiting, I read a sign that details the wide range of guided bike tours on offer – everything from the downtown tour (the cheapest at $59) to the brewery and marijuana tour, and even a canyon, coast and wine country tour ($99). A brochure tells me how bike-crazy people from Portland are. In May, they hold the Human Power Challenge – a festival of competitions for all kinds of human-powered vehicles; in August, the Bridge Pedal, a day on which some 20,000 cyclists get out and about across Portland's bridges; there are also events on 'the coldest day of the year' (in February) and 'the hottest day of the year' (in August). Whereas other cities organise their calendars around religious holidays, in Portland, bike events take priority. Since 2002, adults in Portland have been able to take part in 'zoobombing', which involves hurtling downhill from the zoo to the downtown area on disused children's bikes and do-it-yourself two-wheelers.

The wait at Waterfront Bicycles, which has a selection of over a hundred bikes, is well worth it. Employee Steve rents me a helmet, a lock, lights, a basket and even a bottle of water: 'So that you don't dehydrate.' When I mention that I'm writing about Portland, Steve takes a good quarter of an hour to draw all the places on the city map that he says are 'a must' for ecofreaks. I'm not an ecofreak, I think; even so, I follow Steve's route through the whole of Portland.

For a few kilometres, this takes me along the Willamette River. There are cycle paths everywhere, it seems, and the broad bike lanes on the roads are painted bright green with white bike symbols. For about two kilometres, the trail leads through the front garden of Portland's business district across a wide green lawn featuring varied foliage including about a hundred ornamental cherry trees. It is teeming with cyclists, strollers, joggers and skaters. A couple of teenagers are playing basketball and some elderly people are watching ships sailing down the river. In 1978, this area, the Tom McCall Waterfront Park, was inaugurated and later extended several times to include a small square with memorials on the edge of former Japantown

## Portland, Oregon. Travelling Through America's Green Future

Many motor vehicle lanes have been replaced by a seven-foot wide bicycle lane. More and more of these have an additional painted three-foot buffer on the traffic side.

or *nihonmachi*. Thousands of Japanese once lived in this district before they were forcibly evacuated as 'enemy aliens' and placed in detention camps.[4]

I make a stop a few blocks inland from the riverfront at the Keller Fountain Park in a redeveloped neighbourhood at the south end of downtown Portland. This legendary park with its monumental concrete fountains is a sight I've been wanting to see in real life for a long time, if only because the Portland historian, Carl Abbott, described it to me in a conversation in 2000 as 'a place emblematic of Portland'. This is where an urban planning revolution began in the 1960s, set off by Lawrence Halprin, a landscape architect whose office designed a quartet of parks in central Portland. For Halprin, modernism was not 'just a matter of cubist space'. For him, it was about 'a whole appreciation of environmental design as a holistic approach' and 'a matter of making spaces for people to live'. His fountains have almost nothing in common with traditional American design, but much more with the exuberant styles of Renaissance Rome, such as the Fontana di Trevi and the Piazza Navona. It comes as something of a disappointment when I finally set eyes on them: it's late March, still winter, and the taps are turned off. I try to imagine the water collecting in the narrow channels on the top of the fountain, swirling around the gigantic concrete blocks and plummeting down from the geometric rocks at a rate of 140,000 litres a minute.

When the fountain was inaugurated, young people, many of them anti-Vietnam War protesters, plunged into the water and took over the newly created cascades and park. The Ira Keller Fountain became a place where everybody and anybody felt welcome. Businesspeople started eating their lunch there, while hippies dipped in the water, smoked pot and drove the park attendants crazy. Over the past fifty years, it has been the site of many weddings and christenings, rock, pop and jazz concerts, and a colourful festival organised by the Portland Institute for Contemporary Art. The design of the fountain was inspired by the spectacular falls of the Columbia Gorge, a two-and-a-half-hour bike ride away. It is supposed to have the effect of a rallying cry on the people who see it, as if to say: 'Leave the city! Go forth into nature!'[5]

In talks with people I met in Portland, I realise how important the nearby mountains are, and how proud everyone is of their hiking boots and rain-proof gear. For many, the dramatic landscape is one of the main reasons to move to the Pacific Northwest. Mount Hood, the snow-capped mountain that towers above Portland at over 3,400 metres, is the highest elevation in Oregon and a semi-dormant volcano. This fiery mount is barely eighty kilometres from the city centre, and even though it hasn't erupted since 1865, every schoolchild knows that this peaceful era will at some point end. Perhaps for this very reason, Mount Hood exerts a great fascination over Portland's inhabitants. Most of them regard the area as an oasis for leisure activities, like hiking or climbing. Seen from the city hills, it looks like a white triangle that appears and disappears; and in films and on postcards, the mountain has long become an indelible feature.

# Portland, Oregon. Travelling Through America's Green Future

Vintage VW camper with Oregon landscape and Mount Hood.

## The natives of the Pacific Northwest

Like everywhere on the North American continent, there was once an indigenous population in the Portland region that has now almost slipped into oblivion. Even today, schoolbooks imply that the transformation of the American Northwest began with the white seventeenth-century discoverers who explored the coasts and later the rivers, notably the Spanish and British seafarers Bruno de Heceta, James Cook and George Vancouver, and, in the nineteenth century, the members of Meriwether Lewis and William Clark's overland expedition, who were commissioned by President Jefferson to map the lands of the American continent.[6] Accordingly, US and Canadian placenames abound that date back to these expeditions. Their written records formed the cornerstone of textbooks about US and world history. The fact that the indigenous population of the American West Coast had occupied, cultivated and forever changed the landscape across millennia before they arrived escaped the white travellers completely. They lacked an understanding of ethnology and archaeology, and often even of nature studies; after all, the purpose of their travels was to serve economic interests.

John Ledyard, an American-born explorer who accompanied James Cook on his Pacific expedition in the 1770s, was the first to extol the diversity of the landscape in the Northwest, some hundred kilometres north of Portland. Like many travellers, traders and settlers after him, he described the region from Oregon all the way to Vancouver as a new world 'of untouched nature'. There were no 'plantations' Ledyard explained, 'or any appearances that exhibited any knowledge of the cultivation of the earth'. John Work, who was a trader for the Hudson's Bay Company, described the area of modern-day Portland as a valley with neither 'a stone and scarcely a shrub to interrupt the progress of the plough'. Here, Work said, the conditions were like those of a 'stubble field'. Countless reports, diaries and letters by his contemporaries mention the Native Americans' annual fires. George Emmons, a surveyor on an official US expedition in 1841, described how, in the Willamette Valley thirty kilometres south of Portland, 'the prairie was burned for the purpose of drying the seeds of the sunflower' as a winter food supply. The forests, too, were often set on fire 'to entrap game'. Emmons' ecological observations were comparatively advanced but even he did not realise that, for centuries, these controlled fires had ensured the renewal of the savannah. Rather, he considered these burnings to be 'the greatest obstacle the travellers encountered in this country – one blocking up the way, and the other destroying the food of the animals [i.e., the expedition's horses]'.[7]

The cultivated land on the plains surrounding modern-day Portland in fact supplied the indigenous population with a diverse array of food. They hunted white- and black-tailed deer, elks, poultry and marine birds; and they supplemented their meat with camas and wapato roots, sword ferns, nuts, seeds and berries, while the horses – imported by the Spanish in the early eighteenth century by ship – grazed the savannah grass, causing it to grow rapidly.[8] Based on analyses of pollen as part of the settlement history of the region, we know that the ancestors of the indigenous Kalapuya population of the Pacific Northwest used fire clearing to keep their cultivated land in an ecologically stable condition for at least six if not ten thousand years.[9] But to the newcomers from Europe and the USA, the entire region up to southern Canada was a paradise of untouched nature. Those who traversed the continent in the footsteps of Lewis and Clark waxed lyrical when they approached the confluence of the Willamette and Columbia Rivers – in other words, modern-day Portland. The central and western areas of the vast North American continent always suffered from shortages of wood and water. By contrast, the Pacific West was a huge oasis with a wealth of natural resources, a land of great promise and potential riches, and a new green world whose purpose still lay in the future.[10]

As with the burnings, the new arrivals regarded the 'Indians' themselves as little more than an obstacle. They complained that the native population could not be enlisted for hunting beavers and otters. These animals were not eaten by the indigenous population and the British hype over beaver furs, because James Cook found out the Chinese in Canton were prepared to pay handsome sums for these, must have appeared utterly bizarre. Ultimately, the 'problem' posed by the Native Americans solved itself. Undetected viruses brought by the explorers turned out to be their allies. First, in about 1780, smallpox gradually spread. For a population that lacked genetic immunity, this was fatal. In August 1830, there was an outbreak of malaria, a parasitic disease transported by mosquitos from West Africa to America. Euro-Americans managed, for the most part, to recover from the severe fever of malaria infection; but, for the Native Americans, smallpox and malaria were almost always fatal. Within two generations, the indigenous population, who had largely welcomed the new arrivals with open arms, had been decimated. In some villages, these new viruses killed half the inhabitants; in others, the figure was up to ninety per cent. One catastrophe followed hard on the heels of the other and, by 1900, almost all the Native Americans in the region of modern-day Portland had been wiped out. They had either succumbed to fatal illness, had been driven out or were expelled to the reservations.[11]

The story of how the Northwest USA was 'discovered' is full of subplots in which the indigenous population played a tragic role. Many of them gave the new arrivals a helping hand at the beginning. Without the aid of young Sacagawea, a woman from the tribe of the Shoshone, for example, who accompanied Lewis and Clark on their trip in the Pacific West, the expedition would never have made it to its destination: she was knowledgeable about roots and healing herbs and protected the group from hostile attacks. And without the Native American woman Watkuweis, who had lived among white people in the past, Lewis and Clark were unlikely to have been warmly received by the Nez Perce tribe. But in the end, in this clash of two radically different views of the natural world, the clear losers were the indigenous people of America. The Euro-American gaze, which focused on material value, property and profit, failed to understand the world of the Native Americans. Explorers, traders and settlers, whether they were Spanish, Russian, English or American, had very different views: they saw beavers and otters as nothing more than fur and pelts, trees as building materials, mountains as ore and gold, and the savannah as winter feed. The dreams of the white man had a destructive edge.[12] A succinct summary of this one-dimensional, mission-conscious view of the Northern Pacific in the early nineteenth century was reflected in the words of the ageing former president, John Quincy Adams. In 1846, at the time Portland was founded, he used Biblical words to declare in Washington D.C.: 'We claim that country [Oregon] ... to make the wilderness bloom as the rose, to establish laws, to increase, multiply, and subdue the earth, which we are commanded to do by the first behest of God Almighty.'[13]

## Stumptown – Portland's makeover into a vibrant city

On my cycle ride through Portland, I try to imagine how the landscape must have looked when the first Europeans settled here. The region of the Willamette River must have been swampy in the 1840s when Portland's story was just starting. The first traders and settlers had ignored the small town; Fort Vancouver, a fur-trading post of the British Hudson's Bay Company on the Columbia River stole the show back then. Early immigrants preferred to settle in the lowlands of the Columbia or the surroundings of the Willamette Falls a few kilometres upstream where there were fewer mosquitoes, but plenty of salmon, and where the soil was best suited to cultivating crops. In Portland, in comparison, the Willamette was constantly threatening to burst its banks; and besides, a thick forest of fir, hemlock and maple trees first had to be cleared before house building could even be conceived. For years, inhabitants left the tree stumps in the middle of the dirt roads, literally stepping from one stump to another to avoid sinking into the wet soil. The stumps were whitewashed to make them more visible at night. It's no wonder, then, that the name 'Stumptown' for Portland has survived even to the present day.[14]

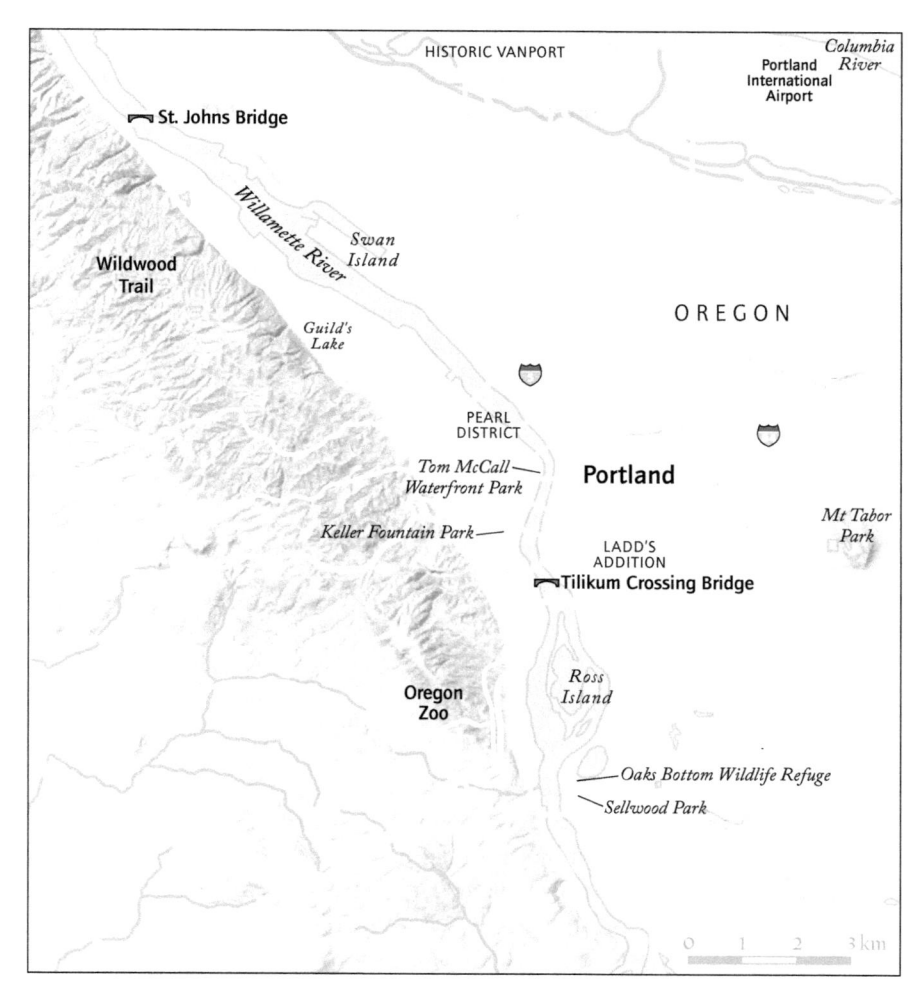

Portland

The majority of those who settled in the Pacific Northwest – from northern California to southern Canada – chose to live on a relatively narrow strip of land west of Cascade Mountain. Today, this is where all the larger towns are situated as if strung together on a chain: Medford, Eugene, Salem and Portland, Oregon; Tacoma and Seattle in Washington; and Vancouver in Canadian British Columbia.

Portland benefits from its geography. In hindsight, it seems inevitable that the town – at the confluence of two major rivers and within easy access to the ocean – has become a major city. Some say that it was 'a place produced by gravity': down the Columbia sailed grain, immigrants and riches from the Orient, and the Willamette brought farm products from the East. But in fact, it took half a century for the location to assert itself over other small settlements.[15]

In 1845, Portland was christened on the flip of a coin that beat the other contender, Boston. A year later, the region was given to the USA by the British. Back then, Portland consisted of between twelve and fifteen houses and sixty inhabitants, all but three of whom (if the sparse sources are to be believed) were caught up by the California Gold Rush in 1849 and thronged to San Francisco's hinterland. Paradoxically, after a minor downturn, the discovery of gold in California coincided with Portland's incessant growth: because in San Francisco, there was suddenly a massive demand for wood and grain. These could be found in abundance in the surroundings of Portland. Moreover, the Pacific Mail Steamship Company, which controlled the postal traffic from San Francisco, settled on Portland as its harbour, and Portland investors built the first 'Farmers' Highway' in the Northwest: a wooden plank road. Although the plank road was only a few kilometres long and very basic – just a few pieces of wood nailed onto crossbeams – it attracted farmers from the region, who brought their wheat to the Willamette for river transportation. Soon all roads led to Portland. A newspaper was set up, *The Oregonian*, which advertised the town and its business: between 1850 and 1855, a law was passed providing every man with 300 acres of land and married couples with 260 acres free of charge. Businesses sprang up everywhere; and, by 1853, four sawmills were already processing the wood from the surrounding forests, while fourteen steamships sailed daily from Portland toward the Pacific Ocean.[16] In short, there was money to be made in Portland. Businesspeople and investors settled there, and the Oregon Steam Navigation Company soon provided the town with a company that, in the words of its contemporaries 'was a millionaire-making machine': its ships transported cargo (grain, wood and coal) to California and across the Pacific to Asia.[17] Newly discovered gold deposits, such as in Idaho, and extensive wheat fields south of Portland also brought some wealth to the Northwest. By 1860, the population had grown to over 2,800 residents, exceeding all other settlements in the Pacific Northwest by a long chalk. In 1864, a telegraph line linked the city to the rest of the USA and, twenty years later, Portland was connected to the national railroad network. From then on, Portland's trajectory rose rapidly. At around the turn of the century, the population had already reached the 90,000 mark. There were docks and large warehouses in downtown Portland; more than a thousand factory workers produced iron goods and processed food. Mechanically driven streetcars crisscrossed the town centre and four bridges – masterpieces of modern engineering – spanned the Willamette.

During my cycle tour around Portland, I came across districts that have kept their early twentieth-century flair; one of these is Ladd's Addition. The neighbourhood is a listed area with historical detached houses, small public rose gardens and circular or diagonally arranged streets where liquor stores once operated before they were banned over a hundred years ago. Portland was made up of a strong middle-class population after the First World War – artisans and white-collar workers, who settled in the new outer districts that were linked to the centre by bridges and streetcars.[18] In short, at the turn of the century, Stumptown had been transformed into a vibrant city. Side effects of its success also materialised, not least of all in the Willamette. The river increasingly threatened to turn to mud and become blocked. The water drainage of the wheat fields carried silt; tree trunks floating upstream after a series of large-scale wood clearance measures were a hazard to the hulls of ships. Slowly, the Willamette lost its status as the most important connection inland. Just in time, the railroad was built, carrying cargo of goods and farming products all over the country.

## Downriver

On one of my first trips to Portland, I travelled downriver on the Willamette Star with a group of conservationists and environmental historians from St John's Bridge to Ross Island. We sailed past old ports and oil terminals, past the old classification yard of the Union Pacific Railroad and the pesticide producer, Arkema; we saw sand and gravel companies and grain silos. Here, industrial complexes were lined up, one after the other. Those who don't know

Portland's history might have a different impression of 'America's greenest city'.[19] The Willamette River of the twenty-first century is merely a shadow of its former self when Lewis and Clark discovered it in 1806. Without the aid of the indigenous people, the pioneers would never have discovered its lower reaches or 'Multnomah', which roughly translates as 'downriver'. They paddled twice past the confluence of the Willamette and Columbia in their canoes: small islets, overgrown with alders, poplars, willows and thick bushes obscured their view of the river. Nowadays, islands and sand reefs that stood in the way of industrial development have long since been replaced by a canal for shipping traffic. Swan Island has been connected to the mainland, a marshland prone to flooding has been transformed into what's now known as Swan Lake, and frog ponds and reed-covered wetlands have been filled in and fortified.

The changes to the river went hand in hand with industrial developments and Portland's resulting ascent. The city's growth and wealth were initially based on its natural resources, such as cattle, wood and grain, which could be shipped from Portland in all directions. The livestock sector attracted the meat and wool processing industries, while the wood sector saw the establishment of saw- and paper mills, as well as furniture companies; and, by 1910, Portland's enormous stocks of grain had turned it into the largest wheat port in North America. At the beginning of the Second World War, the city's growth continued unabated. The construction engineer, Henry J. Kaiser, who had already made a name for himself with large-scale projects such as the Hoover Dam, received an extremely lucrative commission from the Roosevelt government to build warships. More than a thousand modern Liberty Ships fit for the high seas were launched from Kaiser's Shipyards at unprecedented speed using quick construction methods. The defence industry drained the inland cities and villages of people, as Portland had a vast number of jobs to offer. Soon over 20,000 women were working at Portland's dockyards and the region's population grew in just three years from 1941, from 501,000 to 661,000 inhabitants. To ensure people moving to the region found homes, a separate town called Vanport was built in 1942; its name came from its location between *Van*couver in Washington State and *Port*land. It grew rapidly to a population of 40,000 – but was soon washed away in the Columbia River floods of 1948. Thousands of people, predominantly African Americans, lost their homes, and many of them moved to Portland.

After 1945, aeroplanes were still in demand in the USA, but warships became obsolete. As a result, Kaiser's Shipyards closed. Consequently, Henry

## Portland, Oregon. Travelling Through America's Green Future

Kaiser left Portland a twin legacy. Firstly, he made the city the headquarters of Kaiser Permanente, the health insurance company that he'd set up, especially for Kaiser's dock workers. Secondly, he bequeathed the Willamette River a wealth of hazardous chemicals and toxic substances that have affected the lives of Portland's people and its politics for generations.[20]

Even in the early twentieth century, untreated wastewater and sawmill refuse were already polluting the river's water and reducing fish stocks. But, with the outbreak of the Second World War, pollution took on completely new dimensions. Fossil fuels from oil terminals threatened to contaminate the water. Shipbuilders and scrappers, steel and gas producers, wood plants, and chemical manufacturers discharged environmentally hazardous waste into the river well into the 1970s, directly or via combined sewers. The contaminants settled in harbour sludge, seeped into the river sediment and sometimes penetrated the groundwater. The list of substances detected in the harbour of Portland is a deadly cocktail of toxic substances. It includes hexavalent chromium and arsenic; prohibited PCBs and DDT; polycyclic aromatic hydrocarbons that are released when fossil fuels are burned; carcinogenic dioxins and furans; and plasticisers that disrupt human and animal hormone levels. A decontamination study commissioned by several affected companies found no fewer than 29 contaminants that pose health risks to humans and 89 contaminants that affect the ecological functioning of animal habitats – in water, land and air.

Since at least the Second World War, the harbour of the 'eco-capital' Portland has been one of the most polluted environmental areas in the USA. In the year 2000, a length of over sixteen kilometres was therefore included in the Superfund Program of the national environmental protection agency, the EPA. Since then, some slow progress has been made: fourteen companies have started self-financed environmental decontamination programs and, in 2017, the US Congress approved the release of approximately one billion dollars for the removal of hazardous contaminated sites from Portland harbour. The clean-up work is anything but simple, firstly because the EPA has identified over 150 Potentially Responsible Parties (PRPs), some of which no longer exist while others try to shift responsibility as far away as possible. And secondly, because the spread of toxic substances can only be controlled to a limited extent. Some environmental cleanup initiatives over the past twenty years have only been partially effective; others were more for show than thorough sanitisations. For example, the public disposal of 11,000 cubic metres of tar in 2005 by NW Natural, a gas company with a slightly misleading name, represents only a tiny fraction of the tar stocks on the company's premises. And concrete walls anchored into the ground to block contaminated deep groundwater cannot prevent polluted shallow groundwater from spreading.

There is much to suggest that the removal of environmental pollution will take several decades, especially since many sites are affected. The particularly dangerous PCB toxins pose a risk to river otters and mink, common merganser, ospreys and others. However, the biggest health risks for humans do not come from river water itself, but from eating fish. This is especially true for non-migratory fish that spend their entire lives in Portland harbour (black bass and grouper, for example) and that feed directly or indirectly on worms, snails and crustaceans living in the contaminated river sediment. The concentration of chemical substances, which is still relatively low in direct food intake (bioconcentration), almost always increases dramatically throughout the food chain (biomagnification). The PCB contamination in Portland's local fish is up to 3.5 million (!) times higher than the contamination of river water itself, as the Oregon Health Department warns.[21]

Interestingly, you can swim in the Willamette again today. Swimmers should only be wary of blueish-green shimmering algae and contact with metal waste in the water, according to advice from Portland's environmental authority. Bacteria have posed a greater health risk to humans than chemicals in recent decades. However, since the city set up state-of-the-art sewage systems, following pressure from environmental activists and government authorities, including in late 2011 a ten-kilometre, multi-billion-dollar sewage pipe with a diameter of almost seven metres – affectionately called 'the Big Pipe' – *E. coli* pollution has drastically decreased.[22]

## Ecological transformation

Portland would not be Portland if the city's residents only used the Willamette River for commercial and industrial purposes. Formerly desolate industrial areas on the river have undergone a radical transformation in the past few decades. Abandoned industrial and warehouse buildings have been converted into upscale condominiums, galleries, studios, bars and restaurants. New building complexes interspersed with artworks and parks have sprung up alongside industrial relics; and a travel magazine named Portland's Pearl District, which stretches from the river to downtown, as one of the 'fifteen coolest neighbourhoods' in the world.[23]

## Portland, Oregon. Travelling Through America's Green Future

As we sail downriver with the *Willamette Star*, a contrasting landscape unfolds before us: distinctive high-rises and disused factory chimneys, canoeists and diesel tugs, anglers and herons, kingfishers and oil tanks; and all this against the backdrop of Forest Park. Portland's river may be a tamed body of water that rarely threatens to break out of its artificial bed – yet there is something wild about the Willamette. What other city in the world is home to so many bird conservationists and subjects for them to study? Two hundred and nine species were counted in the greater Portland area – from Great Blue Herons to rufous hummingbirds. The city of Portland has had a contract with the US Fish and Wildlife Service to protect migratory birds since 2003. For half a century now, people have been party to the spectacle of Vaux's swifts in the Northwest District near the Willamette where they amass and dive like flying acrobats into an old chimney at the beginning of

Many birds have returned to Portland over the last decades. They can even be found on building façades. In 1986 the Great Blue Heron (front center) was proclaimed Portland's official city bird by Mayor Bud Clark.

September before setting off for South America. If a species of bird were threatened with extinction or migratory birds in the Pacific Northwest changed their route, it would be registered by thousands of Portland birdwatchers. There has also been an overwhelming response to the Backyard Habitat Certification Program of the Portland Audubon bird protection association. Nowhere else in the USA are there so many amateur gardeners who replace invasive flora with native species (and receive a certificate for this). Unlike lawns, native flora does not need artificial fertiliser; it attracts regional insects, brings back native birds and contributes to species-rich ecosystems that are then woven into Portland's urban carpet in miniature, like green patches.

In her 1962 book *Silent Spring*, Rachel Carson conjured up the agonising silence of a world in which songbirds fell victim to the use of DDT. From the 1940s, ospreys, bald eagles and peregrine falcons, which are at the top of the food chain, increasingly produced eggs with such thin shells that they usually broke during hatching. The eradication of large birds of prey in the USA was thus inevitable. There was not a single peregrine falcon left in the state of Oregon in 1970. A large-scale programme to raise and release peregrine falcons in the Mount Hood and Columbia Gorge areas brought about a miraculous change. The peregrine falcon is once again native to Oregon, not least on high-rise buildings and bridges along the Willamette River. Even though its name reminds us that these lightning-speed hawks can travel long distances, six per cent of Oregon's peregrine falcons now nest in Portland, where they remain throughout the year.[24]

On my boat trip with environmental activists Mike Houck and Bob Salinger, I learned about Oaks Bottom, an urban nature reserve with small floodplains, forests and marshlands. Over a hundred different bird species live there – including such rare species as red-shouldered hawks and swamp sparrows.[25] At first, the city struggled to create a protected habitat for animals on the Willamette. Then, covert action by two activists in the 1980s turned out to be a decisive stage in the designation of Oaks Bottom as a wildlife refuge: 'My friend Jimbo Beckmann and I became active because the city wasn't doing anything', says Mike Houck, the director of the Urban Greenspaces Institute. 'We armed ourselves with forty bright yellow signs that said: "Wildlife Refuge". We took a hammer and a ladder along. Then we moved to Oaks Bottom and nailed the signs to telephone poles and swamp poles – pretty high up so no one would remove them anytime soon.' Soon afterwards, Oaks Bottom became a nature reserve. Recently, salmon from the Willamette have been given a 'rest spot' in a new specially constructed channel.[26]

At the end of the boat tour, we pass Portland's Memorial Mausoleum. The façade of the building – the last resting place of over 75,000 people – is covered in a huge green and blue artwork. At 4,000 square metres, it is probably the largest hand-painted mural in the USA. It features waterfowl and hawks, a monumental osprey with outstretched wings, and a twenty-metre heron – the bird that has officially emblazoned Portland's letterhead and the labels of local craft beers since 1986. The acrylic façade of the mausoleum serves as a warning. It reminds us that large birds on the Willamette were on the verge of extinction not so long ago.[27]

How has it happened, I wonder as we sail down the industrial river, that Portland has put nature first in so many ways? How has a city of two million people on the Willamette preserved its wildness? Where does the Portlanders' strong ecological interest come from? And their commitment to environmental justice? Where else do ship and bus tours expose 'the dirty side' of a city?[28] Is it because it was founded much later than New York and Boston and so early urban sprawl was prevented? Or has the attractiveness of the surrounding nature promoted environmental awareness? What is certain is that Portland did not become a green model city overnight. Quite the opposite. Enormous quantities of poison had to flow down the Willamette and Columbia Rivers before the green visions demanded by progressive urban and landscape planners in Portland at the beginning of the twentieth century became reality.

## The legacy of Olmsted and Mumford

In 1903, the city of Portland commissioned John Charles Olmsted, one of the most renowned landscape architects in the USA, to develop a pioneering concept for green spaces. John Charles was the stepson and longtime employee of Frederick Law Olmsted, the first landscape architect in the USA, who had made a name for himself throughout the world by planning New York's Central Park. At the turn of the twentieth century, parks were very fashionable in the USA. According to popular opinion, green spaces promoted the health of the population. They were considered the 'lungs of the city', capable of 'refining public tastes' and, by increasing a city's appeal, were able to attract powerful financial stakeholders who in turn boosted the economy. Portland was no exception. By giving Olmsted the commission, the city fathers (at the time, no women were involved in the administration) signalled that they wanted to leave the image of a frontier town behind and turn up-and-coming Portland into a respectable city that would attract investors.[29]

Portland was the first city in the western United States to host a world exhibition in 1905; John Charles Olmsted designed the plans for its site. The organisers quickly transformed a swamp and pastureland at the edge of the city centre into a glittering wonderland: around Guild's Lake, exhibition halls with turrets and domes in the style of the Spanish Renaissance, buildings made of fake marble, a 'cathedral' made of raw tree trunks (courtesy of the wood industry), and much more was built. For a few coins, you could marvel at 'the great wonders of the world' in an arcade. From a twenty-first-century perspective, it seems embarrassing that 25 half-naked Filipino people from the Igorot tribe were shipped specially to Portland and put on display. In 1905, human zoos were considered socially acceptable, and their racist character was not a subject of public discussion. And so, with the slogan 'Westward the Course of Empire Takes Its Way', the organisers celebrated the imperial triumph and expansion of the USA, which a few years earlier had annexed the Philippines. The official title of the exhibition – the Lewis and Clark Centennial Exposition and Oriental Fair – commemorated the centenary of Lewis and Clark's research trip in 1805 while propagating the proximity of the Pacific Northwest to Asia. Japan was the biggest exhibitor. Almost 1.6 million people, 400,000 of whom came from outside the region, attended the spectacle.

Not much was left of the world fair when it closed. John Charles Olmsted had hoped that Guild's Lake and the exhibition centre could become the core of a new park system. But, as early as 1904, United Railways acquired the exhibition site, unofficially used the lake as a landfill for garbage and debris, and eventually filled it in with soil. Nevertheless, Olmsted left a great legacy in Portland. In contrast to his famous stepfather, for whom England's pastoral idyll was the gold standard of park aesthetics, John Charles Olmsted believed in regionalism. He was fascinated by the tall trees of the Pacific Northwest, the native undergrowth, the mosses and the wild natural beauty he found in Oregon and Washington. In countless letters to his wife in 1903, he described horse-drawn buggy rides through Portland, long walks, the consistency of the soil and the smell of the vegetation. The gardens and parks that the New England architect planned for Portland were intended as 'clearings in the forest', offering carefully orchestrated views of the surrounding mountains and rivers.[30] Olmsted's recommendations were extensive. He proposed the acquisition of large undeveloped areas in several districts and along the Willamette, made proposals for the management of parks, and developed concrete plans and designs for facilities, boulevards and paths. His fundamental vision was to connect isolated parks in different parts of the city into a single system. The fact that only a fraction of these plans could be realised had to do with rapidly rising property prices and the city's unwillingness to pay. Olmsted's appeal to the superintendent of Portland's park administration, Emanuel Mische, and his warning that 'Boston could have saved millions if it had bought parkland when it was the size of Portland', was only partially heeded.[31] What remained of his recommendations was, firstly, a hitherto underdeveloped appreciation of the regional flora; secondly, the idea of an extensive system of connected parks (Sellwood Park, Mount Tabor Park, Rocky Butte, Ross Island and Terwilliger Parkway all go back to Olmsted's visions); and, thirdly, an urban wilderness called Forest Park, which extends over sixteen kilometres on a ridge above the Willamette. This area was supposed to be developed as a residential and business district, but geology thwarted the private owners because, when it rains, the clay literally slips down the hump of the underlying volcanic basalt, making any intention of building there unrealisable. In 1948, 28 years after John Charles Olmsted's death, the city decided to fulfil his landscape planning visions. Today, Forest Park is crisscrossed by fire breaks, paths and hiking trails. The longest, at 43 kilometres, is the Wildwood Trail. Over 110 bird species have been recorded in the park and, because the area is connected to the Pacific coastal forest, you can encounter cougars and lynxes, coyotes and wolves, bears, elks and red deer within walking distance of downtown Portland in Forest Park – although this is only conditionally recommended.[32]

In 1938, Lewis Mumford arrived in Portland. Until then, America's leading architecture critic had made a name for himself as a publicist. At the invitation of the Northwest Regional Council (NRC) non-governmental planning group, he accepted a consultancy contract for the first time. He was particularly impressed by the gigantic dam projects created on the Columbia River near Portland to generate energy. The power plants were regarded as marvels of modern engineering and the availability of hydropower offered the relatively sparsely populated region new perspectives. A few years after the Great Depression struck the nation and brought the US economic boom to a halt, causing hundreds of thousands of people to become homeless because of the environmental catastrophe of the Dust Bowl, planners turned their gaze to the northwest. 'This is the only place in the United

States new enough to become a land of milk and honey', said the Executive Director of the American Society of Planning Officials in 1937 at the inauguration of the Bonneville Dam, 65 kilometres from Portland. A few months later, Ben Kizer of the NRC, who invited Mumford to Portland, used a similar argument: 'Here', he wrote in May 1938, 'is a new land with new possibilities of development [and] natural resources'. In his book *The Culture of Cities*, published shortly before, Mumford explored the subject of historically grown cities. However, his ideal was a system of garden cities as organic components of a natural ecosystem.

By visiting the new town of Portland and the Pacific region, including a trip to Hawaii, Mumford was looking for completely new insights, because the northwest USA was still quite thinly populated and seemed in many respects more open than the area in which he had grown up.[33] In fact, like John Charles Olmsted 35 years before him, the architect was completely captivated by the landscape in the northwest of the USA: 'What I saw with my eyes was beautiful', he wrote in a letter to his girlfriend, Josephine Strongin. Although he criticised the 'massacre' caused by businesspeople 'out of greed for power', entailing the deforestation of the vast woodland areas, in the same breath he praised the snow-covered ridge of Mount Hood and the picturesque gorge of Columbia River, the sight of which reminded him of the great Chinese paintings of the classical era. 'Esthetically', he wrote, 'the greatest landscape I have ever seen, surpassing even Hawaii.'[34]

In a twenty-page memorandum, Mumford opposed 'false ambitions' and Portland's then-current urban planning concept, which he dismissed as a 'melancholy plan'. The availability of almost limitless reserves of hydropower would make it possible for Portlanders to go in completely new directions and build a chain of greenbelt towns instead of densely built-up spaces. A regional planning authority would have to be established that consistently pursued the goal of 'urban rehabilitation' and reforestation, creating near-natural spaces and averting 'social erosion'. Instead of grandiose, fashionable engineering projects, the first thing to do in the city itself would be to identify building areas that would give residents 'the greatest advantage without compromising the original beauties of nature'.[35] In front of the City Club of Portland, Mumford finally gave a speech that would go down in history, its rhetoric recalling the admonitions of Old Testament prophets: 'The Portlanders', he exclaimed, 'have the opportunity to do a job of city planning like nowhere else in the world.' But after seeing how the city had simply abandoned its beautiful land to third parties, he had doubts and asked: 'Are you good enough to

## Portland, Oregon. Travelling Through America's Green Future

keep it in your possession? Have you enough intelligence, imagination, and cooperation among you to make the best use of these opportunities?' [36]

For decades, Lewis Mumford's admonitions went unheard, and he never returned to Portland after his visit in 1938. Five years after him, New York city planner Robert Moses, perhaps the most consistent advocate of car-friendly cities to date, visited the northwest USA. Inspired by Moses' plans, Portland, like other emerging major US cities, decided to expand its highways and bridges systematically. It was not until Tom McCall was elected Governor of Oregon in 1966 that Mumford's green visions regained momentum. Right from the outset, the Republican maverick McCall consistently campaigned against urban sprawl and suburbanisation in Oregon. In his first term of office (1967–1971), he fought to pass a comprehensive regional planning law – the first in the USA. He also founded 1,000 Friends of Oregon, a non-profit organisation, which fought against urban sprawl and soon had more supporters than its name suggested.[37]

No unpaved part of the city is safe from Portland gardeners.

## Eco-culture and city politics

Environmentalists' voices grew louder across the country at the end of the 1960s; they joined the chorus of anti-war protesters, especially after President Nixon announced a US invasion of Cambodia in early 1970. In Portland, clashes threatened to break out between pacifists and war veterans when the American Legion organised a congress for tens of thousands of its members in Portland in August 1970. Like most Democrats across the country, McCall's rival Robert Straub supported the cause of the environment and peace movements in the election campaign for the governor's post. But Republican McCall pulled off a coup by state-sponsoring a rock festival – the only one in US history at that time – as a counter-event to the American Legion convention. The bread-and-circuses approach was a success: the left-wing supporters were fobbed off. With 35,000 visitors and the entire show that went with it – mud, loud music, hippies, hash and bare torsos – Vortex I became the West Coast's counterpart to Woodstock.[38] The week-long festival, which passed without police intervention, echoed the peaceful demonstrations by Portland's citizen movement, Riverfront for People. In the months running up to the festival, they had campaigned for the demolition of the highway along the Willamette. With sit-ins and a photogenic picnic, the young protesters had forced the city of Portland and Governor McCall to think about transforming concrete into grass and come up with alternatives to the downtown highway. Even if it took a few more years until alternative connecting roads were built, politicians in the city council were persuaded and the highway was demolished: the Riverfront movement had shown the yellow card to politicians who ignored grassroots interests. In 1974, the city highway was demolished, and a riverside park was set up in 1978, which was christened the Tom McCall Waterfront Park in 1984.

Meanwhile, the park movement was just one of many countercultural and neighbourhood initiatives that started around 1970.[39] *Terrasquirma* (Spanish for earthworm) was one of the grassroots organisations that had declared its mission to be nothing less than a worldwide 'non-violent revolution' and the radical transformation of communities and lifestyles. And with the Sunflower Recycling Cooperative, members of the *Terrasquirma* collective established one of the first household waste recycling companies in the USA. Others initiated a feminist publishing house (Olive Press), a district market (Fremont Community Market), a firewood cooperative and an alternative shopping circle. Still others participated in the Portland Com-

## Portland, Oregon. Travelling Through America's Green Future

munity Warehouse, where used furniture was collected and redistributed free of charge via the progressive radio station KBOO or a rape victim hotline. Not all projects lasted, but many grew beyond the districts in which they were created and, in some cases, beyond the borders of the city – such as *RAIN* magazine, which was founded in 1974 and links citizen groups and projects all over the world today.

The change in Portland's social landscape was radical. In the 1950s and 1960s the city had been a backwater and a food desert. The political leadership consisted of patriotic, Christian white men. Between 1966 and 1974, more civic initiatives suddenly sprung up there than anywhere else in the USA, which prompted sociologist Robert Putnam and his colleague Lewis Feldstein to speak of a 'positive epidemic of citizen engagement'. At the beginning of the 1970s, civic participation in Portland was still below the US average; in 1990 it was at least three to four times higher. One reason for the change was demographics. Between 1960 and 1970, the share of Portlanders aged between fifteen and 34 rose steeply from 22 to thirty per cent. Within a few years, interest groups that advocated quality of life and political participation had quashed the hitherto dominant traditional associations. The drastic nature of the change was also reflected in the changing group of Portland's leaders. According to the official Northwest Labor Press records, in 1975, only thirty per cent of the leaders from 1969 were still in office.

The spirit of optimism was mainly thanks to young citizens and neighbourhood movements. But it was also reflected in Governor Tom McCall's political determination and powerful rhetoric. In his mind, urban sprawl was not merely a local problem, but rather a challenge for the state as a whole. McCall's speech to Parliament on 8 January 1973 remains deeply engraved in Oregon's memory to this day. The governor cautiously urged to protect 'the interests of Oregon for today and in the future from the grasping wastrels of the land' and the 'condomania' of speculators. 'We must respect another truism', he went on: 'that unlimited and unregulated growth leads inexorably to a lowered quality of life. Our thoughts today, and our deliberations to come, must spring from our determination to keep Oregon lovable and to make it even more livable.'[40]

The effect of McCall's speech was like a beacon. Subsequently, the Oregon Congress passed Senate Bill 100, obliging the local governments of 24 cities in three districts to develop comprehensive Urban Growth Boundaries (UGBs). Portland presented its plan in 1979. One of the ambitious federal planning goals ('Goal 5') was the preservation of unbuilt space and the protection of natural and historical resources for future generations.[41] 'Goal 5' became a battle cry for conservationists who fought to protect the remaining natural areas in Portland from uncontrolled development by setting up a 65-kilometre loop. In addition to the argument of increased quality of life, landscape ecological demands have also been included in the activists' arguments since the 1980s. The Audubon Society has played a leading role in this process, and its Portland local group became far more than a bird conservationist club. The call for a green corridor was supported in particular by Portland's regional government. The political protagonists of the metropolitan region decided against Mumford's concept of an ensemble of satellite cities – instead, they relied on strengthening and revitalising the city centre and on expanding public transport. However, with the principles of regional planning, green corridors and urban growth limitation, they drew on Olmsted's and Mumford's ideas. Portland was well on its way to becoming a 'green city'. A group of dynamic and far-sighted politicians such as Governor Tom McCall, and the young mayor and later Governor Neil Goldschmidt played an important role in this. But also, Portland's committed population, young families and conservationists, forward-looking city planners and the politicians of the regional government (the only directly elected city government in the USA to date!) were involved in the changes. In 1992, an intensive period of civic participation began for a regional urban growth concept that extended into 2040 (the 2040 Growth Concept). Tens of thousands of citizens took part in urban planning through surveys, reviews, mailings, advertising and the involvement of focus groups. The preservation of open spaces and the expansion of public transport emerged as central concerns of the population. As the Portland region grew faster than all other major US cities in the 1990s, except for two cities in the US Sun Belt – Orlando and Atlanta – preserving green space was anything but a matter of course. Nevertheless, the regional government succeeded in pushing ahead with the establishment of urban nature reserves. A mixture of 'primitive', 'rural' and 'urban' landscapes established itself as a planning idea and as part of Portland's new collective identity.[42] The first official municipal publication on green spaces in 1991 described the underlying concept as 'a mosaic of natural spaces' intended to preserve the habitat of animals. The aim was to create 'greenways' – routes, paths and natural corridors – with ecological functions for animals, plants, and humans to counteract the 'loss of nature's most wondrous experiences', which John Charles Olmsted had advocated with his design of interconnected parks.[43] Two or three generations after

## Portland, Oregon. Travelling Through America's Green Future

the two landscape experts had visited, their ideas were on everyone's lips in Portland and their dreams were alive more than anywhere else.

## Utopia and parody – the myth of Portland

Portland's transformation is special. In a short time and with resounding success, politicians and citizens resisted the validity of planning assumptions that were considered irrefutable in the USA for decades after the Second World War. Instead of expanding suburbs in a car-friendly way, downtown and light rail transport were strengthened; instead of deifying 'free market forces', the city relied on municipal planning; instead of demolishing historical districts, they were revitalised; instead of strengthening the urban highway system, planners supported its demolition; instead of centralised government, Portland embraced regionalism and citizen participation; instead of gearing the city towards cars, they targeted alternative modes of transport and the ecological function of nature corridors.[44] The list of material changes to the urban landscape and organisational innovations is long. And yet Portland today differs more in degree rather than in principle from many large cities in the USA or Europe that have embarked on sustainable environmental policies. So where does its green image come from?

In dozens of conversations, I noticed how natural it is for the Portlanders to tell 'green stories' about their city, and how they are consistently told and retold. Olmsted and McCall feature in them; the demolition of the city highway, the importance of cycling (although it rains a lot), weed and coffee, the microbreweries, the recycling yards, Powell's (the largest independent bookstore in the USA), free tool rental, the light railway, the proximity to the mountains, neighbourhood initiatives, urban nature reserves, bird conservation, the heron as a city mascot. The stories about Portland are more than the sum of events: they convey values. And they constitute a myth – with heroes from the past and lessons for the future. Portland's myth strengthens the collective identity of the city's inhabitants and contains subtle guidelines and instructions for all those who are or want to become part of the community. The ecological exceptionalism that underlies the myth echoes the utopia that Ernest Callenbach invented in his bestselling 1975 novel, *Ecotopia*: *The Notebooks and Reports of William Weston*. This ecotopia has in fact found its way into Portland's pop culture, and half a century after it was published, some of it reads like a prophecy – as if Callenbach predicted Portland's ecoculture.[45] The plot of the novel, which gazes into the future set a quarter of a century away – 1999 – is easy to sum up. Investigative journalist William Weston is the first American to visit Ecotopia for a report in the fictitious *Times Post*. The country of Ecotopia, which includes Oregon, Washington and northern California, has split off from the rest of the US for ideological reasons. Through newspaper columns and private diary entries, readers learn from Will Weston's report on how people live in Ecotopia and how he experiences them on a personal level. Society is organised in a democratic, grassroots way with a president as head of state; it represents ecological principles, relies on solar energy instead of coal, uses bicycles and light rail systems instead of cars, builds sustainable houses, favours free love and lives in municipalities instead of nuclear families. Without using the term, which was not yet common at the time, *Ecotopia* advocated the principle of sustainability – in waste management, for example, and in the timber industry: everyone who buys wood must first plant and maintain trees. Property is frowned upon. What counts is not *having*, but *being*. Everyone shares everything, including partners. Ecotopians enjoy life, protect the environment, practise urban agriculture, consume cannabis and let their emotions run wild. They are interested in culture and creativity. They live a reflective and healthy life and swear by alternative education and healing practices, including sexual stimulation. In the novel, the reader learns how the narrator's resentment and scepticism increasingly fade, how he falls in love with a native Ecotopian called Marissa, and ultimately decides to stay in the region, a better alternative to the USA.

In the 1970s, Callenbach's novel read like a blueprint for a sustainable future based on ecological harmony. In Portland, people tried to put it into practice. To this day, 'America's greenest city' identifies more strongly with an ecological utopia than any other major city in the USA. The Portland myth contains in a nutshell the ideas and ideals, concepts and values of Callenbach's Ecotopia. In the novel, the future is not a non-place (u-topia), but a real, lived social utopia: a good place (eu-topia). This future has already begun in Portland, especially in the stories that Portlanders tell about their city.[46]

A series of literary utopias that emerged in close succession around the turn of the twentieth century (from William Morris' *News from Nowhere* to Theodor Herzl's *Old New Land* to H. G. Wells's *A Modern Utopia*) promised forms of progress and a rosy future, all of which ultimately proved to be unpracticable. *Ecotopia* is completely different. Callenbach's book is set in the future, but it's not too far removed from the present. The text is not instructive but satirical, similar to Thomas More's philosophical novel

## Portland, Oregon. Travelling Through America's Green Future

*Utopia*, which is set on a distant island rather than in the future. In More's and Callenbach's books – and especially the TV comedy *Portlandia*, which is certainly the most popular Portland utopia, everything should be taken with a pinch of salt. Between 2011 and 2018, *Portlandia* ran a total of 77 episodes on the US cable channel IFC.[47] The television series has made the clichés and lifestyle of Portland's ecofreaks and hipsters, artists and bohemians popular on a national level. Original film locations that alternate with studio shoots anchor individual episodes to Portland and, at the same time, give scope for caricature and satire. Real observation turns unexpectedly into exaggeration and wit, such as when two visitors to a restaurant in the first episode want to know whether the chicken they are eating was raised locally. Although the chicken turns out to have a name (Colin) and comes from a farm in the restaurant's neighbourhood, the protagonists decide to visit the farm to see if the chicken is worth eating. They end up living on the farm but reject the chicken when they go to the restaurant again. The episode is funny and absurd, not only because Portland has a lot of urban chickens, but also because Portlanders are extremely fanatical about food, and are known to push their ecological principles to the extreme.

In Portland itself, where bike tours tracing episodes of *Portlandia* are offered, satire is by no means frowned upon. Rather, the Portlanders have adopted the *Portlandia* fiction self-ironically and creatively. On my small tours, I sometimes feel like I'm cycling through a surreal world, not through Portland, but *Portlandia* – through an ecological counterculture that gives an impression of a life lived with incredible ease. The officials in the town hall wear sportswear. On private and public properties, there are rain barrels, rain gardens and 'bioswales' – vegetation-rich dips that naturally filter rain and wastewater. Wooden boxes with vegetables and herbs as well as borders with flowers can be found along traffic-calmed streets. Former wetlands – such as the seventeen-hectare Westmoreland Park – have been restored: where there used to be a wetland, then farmland, a golf course and an airfield, today there are natural playgrounds and streams and ponds where local fish swim. In some quarters, chickens cluck and goats graze behind the houses. Fittingly, the hotline of the municipal sustainability department explains what to take into consideration if you want to keep peacocks or cows, donkeys or bees, llamas or Vietnamese potbellied pigs.[48] The neighbourhoods where the *Portlandia* TV series is set abound with wellness, yoga and educational centres; bakeries and cafés and shops selling art supplies; vegan restaurants and cannabis shops. Christian Ettinger, the owner of Portland's Hopworks

Paradise Blues

One of many food stands that offer 'indigenous foods' in Portland. The city is home to an urban Native American population of 60,000 people from over 300 tribal nations.

Urban Brewery, rides his draft beer around the city on a self-styled bicycle with a built-in stereo system.[49] Uniformed female cyclists from the Portland Roasting Coffee Company chauffeur mobile coffee shops through the city; food trucks sell culinary snacks and fast food – from Buddha snacks to Thai pasta to native bowls.

Elsewhere, it would seem odd to see Zen being practised in silver Airstream buses. In Portland, they fit the picture. There are fitness centres that generate electricity from exercise energy and hundreds of shops with fantastic, curious and quirky names: I Am That, for example, Flying Cat Coffee, Barely Worn/Vintage Voodoo, or Freakybuttrue Peculiarium. The names of the breweries and microbreweries, of which there are 74 in Portland and over a hundred in the region, are similarly imaginative. Portland has the highest per capita density of microbreweries in the USA. Portland's culture and nature come together in the history of microbreweries: on the

## Portland, Oregon. Travelling Through America's Green Future

one hand, an urban economy that favours creative craft businesses; on the other, hops from the agrarian paradise of the Pacific Northwest as well as soft water from the surrounding mountains.[50]

In my conversations with Portlanders and during my bike tour through the city, I sometimes wonder whether I'm in the present or the future: whether Portland (like *Ecotopia*) is detached from global contexts, or whether it represents a perspective for the future. Urban sociologist Charles Heying, who has been scrutinising Portland's economic and cultural transformation for years at Portland State University, says it is both. For him, Portland embodies a 'cultural anomaly' because of the high level of political citizen participation and the minimal presence of large corporate headquarters. On the other hand, Heying credits Portland for having a model with future viability. For him, Portlanders are 'the Jetsons on bicycles', hip and homespun at the same time. He sees Portland as a post-industrial 'creative city', whose localism gets by without provincialism and whose organisational and economic forms prove to be sustainable because they are highly innovative and flexible. At the same time, however, by consciously rejecting the neoliberal model, they take the demand for humane working conditions seriously and are based on a comprehensive change in values that prefers and promotes local, sustainable do-it-yourself systems of production and use.[51]

Of course, Portland is not a perfect world. The history of America's greenest city also has its dirty, shady sides. For some Portlanders, the utopia has become a dystopia. The more attractive the city has become, the higher the rents have climbed; and the less its minorities have had a piece of its prosperity, as this demographic group has been pushed out of the city centre. The air is dirty, the water is still contaminated, the rich neighbourhoods are healthier than the poor, and former respectable heroes like Portland's mayor Neil Goldschmidt have lost their lustre and innocence.

But what Portland has shown is that a turnaround is possible: that even large industrial cities can reinvent themselves, not from one day to the next, but over time – not through regulation from above or by isolated actors, but through a variety of initiatives; that the radical increase in gross national product can be accompanied by a significant reduction in $CO_2$ emissions (very different from the rest of the USA); that a liveable future can draw on history – from past visions and plans that were thought to be almost lost, such as those of Olmsted and Mumford; that there is enough (and increasing) space, even in a rapidly growing city, for birds and fish, bees and chickens and game; that its radically democratic Metro government does not diminish urban identity but strengthens it; that citizens' initiatives and politicians can find a common cause in ecology and in the fight against urban sprawl; and that where the urban myth reaches the limits of feasibility, it can radiate beyond Portland. The migration of people and ecotopias from the Pacific Northwest to the shrinking cities of the rust belt – especially Detroit – is an example of this.[52]

Portland's transformation cannot be generalised. Unlike many major cities in the world, Portlanders benefit from proximity to the ocean and mountains that make the region worth living in. Unlike cities where multinational corporations are involved in politics, Portland's small-scale economy has proven less susceptible to major crises. Rents may rise steadily, but they rise more slowly than those of Los Angeles, San Francisco or Seattle; the gap between rich and poor is opening steadily, but not at the fast-forward pace of many other US cities.

What Portland's history shows above all is that it would be wrong to describe the USA as an all-round environmental offender. Although climate change is still 'debated' by many Republicans rather than stated as a fact, cities like Portland have shown impressive sustainability dynamics. Its interplay of social mobilisation, democratic transparency and ecological initiatives is unparalleled worldwide in comparison to cities with populations of its size. The success of the Portland Urban Laboratory shows that there are innovations in the US beyond Silicon Valley's (often self-loving and job-destroying) culture of creativity and enterprise. Portland is groundbreaking not because it wants to reinvent the world as quickly as possible with the help of devices and gadgets, but because it has relied on a social, ecological and planning philosophy of preservation and utopia. With Portland's ecotopia, a kind of green future has arrived that comes with a twinkle in its eye. How and where it spreads remains to be seen.

# Afterword

This is not a conventional history of the USA. It does not start with European-born settlers, and it does not follow a chronological order. This is a different kind of book. It starts in Alaska not New England and mixes subjective impressions and descriptions of nature with historical reconstruction. It is an unusual travel guide that retraces the paths of nature, history, and civilisation in the USA. And I have written my own perspective into the narrative – as an environmental historian, open-minded traveller and someone who reflects when walking.

Some historians have complained in recent times that history books sound increasingly sterile and passionless. In contrast to anthropologists and cultural commentators, historians try for the most part to erase themselves from their stories to achieve the required objectivity. But it has long been recognised that writing history 'as it actually occurred', as German historian Leopold Ranke aspired to do, is an impossibility.[1] That's why this book contains a mixture of verifiable facts *and* subjective descriptions: of events and experiences, analyses and anecdotes, interpretations and impressions. Seen this way, *Paradise Blues* is not just an environmental and cultural history. It also stands in the tradition of nature writing, a genre that combines natural history with personal observation and philosophical reflections on nature.

When writing, I had in mind an audience that knows the USA through movies, the media or vacations. I intentionally interwove in my writing places, objects, people and popular culture with a high degree of recognition worldwide: Hollywood and Disney, Niagara and Las Vegas, Inuit and gold seekers, Malibu wildfires and Mississippi blues, to name just a few. That's because *Paradise Blues* is a scholarly book in the guise of a road trip. The history of the environment, which is often unknown, is tightly interlaced with the American culture we are familiar with from the media. And this book tells its story with recent research in an accessible style.

My wish to write about the USA in a way that is different from my previous books came to me during a family vacation in the American West long ago. I didn't want to write about the USA as a whole, but about individual places instead – and about the relationship of people to their environment over long periods rather than about society and modern politics. On the last day of that memorable family trip, we came across three small towns in Colorado called Dinosaur, Rangely and Meeker and they could not have been more different. In Dinosaur, there was a museum with dinosaur skeletons and the streets were named after them – Brontosaurus Boulevard and Triceratops Terrace, to name just two. In neighbouring Rangely, we came across a desolate moonscape with no vegetation and endless rows of oil drilling rigs. This is where Chevron started production at the largest oil fields in the American West. Near the third town, Meeker, we drove through vast, dense forests. In Meeker itself, we stayed at the Meeker Hotel, a place whose walls were adorned with stuffed forest animals and irregular antlers. It seemed to have remained exactly as it had looked in the last century, as if the passionate hunter, Teddy Roosevelt, who founded several national parks, might march into the main suite any moment dressed in a suede outfit with a rifle slung over one arm. How did these three towns so close together develop completely differently?

Natural features played a decisive role, of course, as well as the ways in which people perceived and exploited those features over time. Long before the American continent was populated by humans, dinosaur skeletons were washed up and covered in silt in Colorado: geological movements and a mixture of lipophilic substances created a reservoir in the porous sand several miles away in which vast quantities of oil formed. The Native Americans in Colorado undoubtedly knew about the different aspects of nature in the area. However, it was the colonial gaze of European-born researchers, fortune-seekers and politicians that changed the fate of these three towns in one fell swoop – and, incredibly, all within a single year. In 1900, a palaeontologist from Pittsburgh discovered on the site of today's Dinosaur several dinosaur bones that he declared worthy of collection and put on show. In 1901, fortune-seekers found oil and built the first oil wells in modern-day Rangely. And, in the same year, newly elected President Roosevelt travelled to Meeker, stayed at the Grand Hotel, shot a couple of mountain lions and deer, and ensured that the area was turned into a national forest. What happened in northwestern Colorado did not much interest the politicians in Washington or the writers of history books. But for me, visiting these three far-flung towns threw up a series of unexpected questions: how many geological eras did it take to produce fossil liquids in Rangely? And what minuscule period will people take to consume this product that nature took millions of years to produce? Was the discovery of dinosaur bones and the foundation of

## Afterword

the museum a strong enough argument to prevent the planned reservoir in Dinosaur, which would have been flooded had it gone ahead? What would have happened to the forest if President Roosevelt, a hunting enthusiast, hadn't been so taken by it? At a glance, these three towns show that it is not just natural features – geology, flora and fauna – that have an enormous impact on environmental developments: our evaluations of nature count too. The way the world in which we live looks is linked to the kind of nature we find there – oil, bones or a forest – as well as what we know about our environment and the value we give to our discoveries: in other words, what we protect and what we exploit, and for which purposes.[2] My Colorado trip brought to light histories I would never have found in libraries, but which were highly pertinent to how people and nature interact while highlighting broader correlations too. It proved to me that it is worth discovering natural landscapes and their special features and that it's important to look at less significant places that aren't normally mentioned in national history books.

In *Paradise Blues*, I have not limited my exploration of the American outdoors to spectacular natural monuments or tourist attractions. Many of the places I have visited are so small that not even many Americans have heard of them, let alone foreigners. Wiseman, Alaska, only had thirteen inhabitants the last time I visited. St Thomas is a ghost town in ruins. Portland, Oregon, the largest city I explore in this book, does not even have a million people in its urban area. Just as I was fascinated on my trip through Colorado by the ensemble of towns and surrounding areas rather than just individual places, each chapter in *Paradise Blues* homes in on a single locality – but, from there, I pan out and take in a wider panorama to shed light on the many, often invisible, connections between the centres of places and the peripheries. We mark places on maps as if they were strictly separated from their surroundings. But if you take a trip to the outer limits of any city, you'll notice that there are no clear lines dividing urban and rural areas; each place is closely linked to its surroundings through infrastructure, migration, resources and the flow of goods.[3] That's why, for example, in the chapter on Disneyworld in Florida, I don't just focus on the amusement park and the futuristic town of Celebration, but also the entire southern tip of the state. After all, the source of the Florida Everglades, otherwise known as 'the river of grass', is very near the theme park. Similarly, in the chapter on Dodge City, I concentrate on the historic cattle trails from Mexico to Kansas and the wind energy produced by Kansas and delivered from there to faraway regions. In the chapter on Malibu, I look at the hinterland as much as the megacity of Los Angeles. And in the chapter on the desert, I not only concentrate on the ghost town of St Thomas, but also on Las Vegas because the two places are related to each other, and I want to reveal how.

## Walking and driving

The car is the most popular form of mobility among Americans. No other means of transport comes even close in terms of importance. And no other country in the world defines itself so strongly through automobile culture as America. Without cars, most places in the USA cannot even be reached. There are large towns, a prominent example being Arlington, Texas, with over 400,000 inhabitants, that don't have any form of public transportation at all – neither bus nor rail. And so in the USA, I rented a car, especially when I had a long journey to make. In Alaska, my route from Fairbanks to Prudhoe Bay took me to the northernmost part of the USA; in Florida, from Orlando to the southernmost corner of the mainland; and in Kansas from East to West straight through an ever-changing prairie landscape. In towns, I mostly covered everything on foot. The exception was Portland, Oregon, the self-proclaimed 'Bike City USA', where I used a bike. When I occasionally explored a town by car, I did it in a way similar to strolling, to allow chance discoveries. Rousseau and Wordsworth believed that we can reflect and take things in better when we move meditatively, that is, when we saunter and ramble, rather than having a specific goal in mind.[4] Those who *wander* have time to *wonder* – more easily than sitting at a desk. Everywhere I went, I consciously took up wandering and walking, and the resulting encounters with people and nature, as a form of exploration and a research method.

When bodies are in motion, they are in constant dialogue with their environment; in contrast to driving, our alertness and awareness are considerably heightened.[5] When we walk, as opposed to doing research at a desk, our immediate sensory impressions are the focus of our attention. I always took a camera with me and sometimes a recording device too.[6] It's interesting, as the British ethnologist Tim Ingold noted, that walking not only documents your sensory experience of your surroundings, it also offers you a deeper understanding of nature's temporality. This insight and the varying tempos at which landscape is transformed (by people and nature itself) accompanied me throughout my travels.

In Wiseman, Alaska, for example, at the northernmost tip of the USA, I became aware of what a huge role everyday, annual and intergenerational changes and continuities play in society and the landscape. The inhabitants in the past had been nomadic, many of them only settled when they attended missionary school. Hunting and gathering still play an important role in the partial subsistence economy of the former gold-mining village – even though satellite, computer and mobility technology have long since reached the region. The length of the seasons, the migration of huntable animals and the seasonal growth of flowers frequently came up in the conversations I had with those people. When I was walking through Alaska, I came across relics from the past ice-age glacial and earth movements. Every step of the way I also found traces of human intervention and cultural decline. Over time, the gold miners' ancient log cabins have begun to buckle under the snow load and sink into the tundra. Soon, remnants of the gold-rush era will have completely disappeared. In other words, observations made when walking not only create space but also time – past and future – in a way that is visible and tangible.

## Research and methods

I had conversations with all kinds of people everywhere I went. In Dodge City, I talked to a sheriff, the owner of a feedlot and a whiskey distiller; in Portland, to politicians and former hippies; in Malibu, to local historians and environmental conservationists; in Wiseman, to the entire village population; in the Everglades, to park rangers; in Niagara, to the employees of the visitor centre; in Love Canal, to the residents and many others. Besides these conversations, my research was done in libraries, archives and online. Among the sources I consulted for *Paradise Blues* were historic photographs, city and rural maps, autobiographies, newspaper articles, specialist geological and archaeological reports, TV footage and pop-culture objects.

We can't go back in time and relive the past. But, in contrast to other generations, we can survey the past from our present standpoint. We can portray history as if it were a landscape and, through our brushstrokes, evoke impressions and stories, much like painters or novelists evoke emotions that give the past a certain meaning. As John Lewis Gaddis once said, historical research is more than just time travel. He warned that 'being plunked down in some particular part of the past' in a time machine would mean losing control once we landed because we would be caught up in a completely new reality. Historical researchers, on the other hand, have a different set of capacities: 'They can be in several times and places at once, and they can zoom in and out between macroscopic and microscopic levels of analysis.'[7] In other words, they can choose where the journey goes.

When choosing my destinations in the USA, I was concerned with finding the greatest possible variety of natural features, as well as the greatest possible number of ways in which people have treated their environment. Every destination offers a unique aspect and, taken all together, they represent a broad swathe of natural regions and civilisations.

## Nature versus culture

In the humanities, distinguishing between nature and culture has fallen out of fashion with good reason. The term 'nature', as is constantly being explained, is nothing other than a cultural construction; there is no single place on earth that does not have 'traces of civilisation', or human culture. Whether it's the highest peak in the Himalayas or the deepest point in the ocean, every place has been changed by the presence of human beings. From the reverse perspective, humans are also not just *cultural* but also *natural* beings. Billions of bacteria and fungi – microscopic living creatures, known as microbes – make up the human body. Most of them aren't harmful; in fact, they're essential for our survival. If all multicellular creatures on earth disappeared, microbes would barely be affected. But if all microbial life were to become extinct, the planet and all its animals would die immediately. So, we humans only exist because we have found a way to co-exist with microscopic entities that are a constitutional part of our physical existence and our biosphere.[8]

In trying to understand a society or nation, we cannot help but integrate animals and plants alongside humans into our narrative. Can we imagine America without Native Americans on horseback or lasso-twirling cowboys? Or the Midwest without its immense fields of wheat? However, it was Columbus and his contemporaries who first brought horses to the New World, along with dogs, goats, sheep and pigs. And it was bluegrass inadvertently imported from Europe that spread across the Midwestern United States, displacing native canebrake that originally covered large areas of the continent and posed a real obstacle to the white settlers. Without the import of cattle or wheat seeds, which spread extensively via cow dung, the history of the North American continent might well have taken a completely different path.[9] Plants, mammals, epidemics and vermin are protagonists that need to be included in history as well as humans.[10] With this in mind, people are

## Afterword

not the only ones to play a central role in the chapter on Dodge City, for example, but also Longhorn cattle.

It is sometimes argued that nature only exists as something that is conceived and constructed through cultural practices like science and art. If this were true, all nature would also be culture because there would be no such thing as nature outside of cultural perceptions.[11] To escape this dilemma, some environmental historians use the term *natureculture*, introduced by ethnologist Donna Haraway to express the idea that the two are so tightly interwoven as to be inseparable.[12] Despite the obvious smooth transition between the two categories, in this book, I have mostly retained the terms *nature* and *culture*. Ultimately, the gulf between the two – culture being manmade and nature not – is manifested in environmental conflicts: when we protect natural resources or pollute the environment, we assume people's cultural or political interaction with nature. Besides this, the division of the two spheres is shown not least in people's alienation from and romantic yearning for intact nature, much like a long-lost paradise.[13] What's more, we perceive nature as something in opposition to us when it appears in the form of drought, epidemics, floods and volcanic eruptions that destroy or transform what is manmade and 'cultural'. In general, our way of thinking and acting, as well as our debates on social, political and technological topics, despite all theorising to the contrary, are shaped by a fundamental distinction between nature and culture. Human interests and ideologies, visions, and practices – culture, in other words – have long since influenced the non-human environment – or nature. Bearing this in mind, it seems reasonable to take the terms nature and culture as two categories that stand in a complex, ever-changing relationship to each other, however little they can be conclusively defined. Ultimately, the book's title *Paradise Blues* refers to the close intertwining of nature and culture and to the fact that the paradise of nature and what we have turned it into has a very melancholic side.

## The environment and history

If you go in search of North American nature, you find traces everywhere of past interactions between people and their natural surroundings – of insights into environmental history, in other words.[14] The environment played an important role in the writing of history even in ancient times. Hippocrates believed that what constitutes the environment – 'ignis, aer, aqua, terra, aether' (fire, air, water, earth, and ether) – was the cause of disease;

# Afterword

Herodotus referred to Egypt as a 'gift of the Nile' because of recurring flood disasters; and Pliny the Elder was convinced that the erosion of landscapes was reflected in the erosion of culture. Environmental history first gained new meaning, a certain contentiousness and its name in the late twentieth century, when the end of non-renewable resources, the boundaries between growth and people's destruction of their means of existence became largely visible.[15] The environment has surrounded people since the dawn of time but, in the twenty-first century, the term has become ubiquitous. Regardless of our political alignment, we all consider a healthy, intact environment as desirable, if not necessary, for our survival. From automobile engineers to health ministers, anti-nuclear activists to hiking organisations, the term 'environment' has been given a fundamentally positive connotation. And products or attitudes that claim to be 'environmentally-friendly' can be found wherever we look.

Rachel Carson's international bestseller *Silent Spring* (1962), a book that raised awareness of the environmental contamination caused by pesticides in regions across the world and which led to the prohibition of DDT in most countries, was probably the most significant catalyst in fostering present-day environmental awareness and movements, as well environmental history as a modern discipline.[16] It sees itself as an overarching field that integrates insights from natural science into historiography and examines human involvement in social and natural processes from a historical perspective. The environment has established itself as a concept that, on the one hand, describes the complex connections between living and inanimate instances and, on the other, under the heading of environmental justice, exposes striking inequalities in how different social groups are affected.[17]

On my travels through North America, I could not escape traces of the historic conflict between Americans and their environment. History is present everywhere, but it has to be perceived. The Australian historian Tom Griffiths once explained that it is possible to 'take history for granted' and for that reason 'overlook its power'. History can be constructed 'at the dinner table, over the back fence, in parliament and in the streets, not just in a tutorial room or at the scholar's desk'. And he added that 'it so seamlessly underpins everything we do that it can be hard, sometimes, to detect its daily revolutionary influence'.[18] That the world today is how it is can only be explained with history. The pressing questions of historiography – the hows and whys – indicate where we come from and where we are heading; and whether we exploit, destroy or sustainably secure the natural basis of our existence.

# Afterword

A series of ecological threads run through *Paradise Blues* that I did not consciously plan: almost all chapters deal with the American dream, in this case, utopias linked to unchecked economic risk that have led nowhere because nature 'struck back'. Unlike in Europe, many Americans adhere to optimism in the face of catastrophe, a desire to glean something positive from natural disasters. Lack of environmental justice is a further central theme running through American culture and history: in regions predominantly populated by Black Americans and other marginalised peoples, there is a higher likelihood of exposure to environmental toxins and pollution than in places, such as Malibu, where rich folk live. There has been tension and ambivalence in most Americans' attitudes towards their environment throughout history. Conservation and destruction often lie side by side. In America, people love nature, sometimes to death.

*Paradise Blues* makes it clear that the transformation of the American environment has increasingly intensified and accelerated since the nineteenth century. The famous hockey stick graph that shows $CO_2$ emissions, ozone levels and depletion of resources has its counterpart in increasingly radical and far-reaching environmental interventions. Technological progression afforded great comfort to the American people earlier than in other countries: tropical Florida was made inhabitable, streets were lit at night and the general standard of living in the USA was raised from an early stage. But, at the same time, consumer dependence and ecological destruction took a sharp upturn. The term 'Anthropocene', which was coined around twenty years ago by the chemist and Nobel Prize laureate Paul Crutzen, suggesting that human beings had gone from being historic protagonists to a driving force in planetary geology, provides an apt description for many of the environmental changes of the past decades. If you want to understand the Anthropocene, to study and analyse human intervention in planetary environments, it might be enough to take the USA as an example. In no other place in the world have human beings left such a heavy footprint on the natural world – at times, to conserve nature, but more often in a destructive manner. The scars from these interventions are sometimes highly visible, such as the disused goldmines in Alaska; in other places such as Love Canal, they can only be uncovered when we dig deep down into the history of the place. What's clear is that traces of the interaction between human beings and the environment have settled like sediment over centuries and stretch into the present – in the form of landscapes and collective memory, in bodies of water and the earth's strata, tree rings and human cells.

Afterword

## The stories we need

People in the USA and all over the world are more aware than ever that we need a different relationship to our environment.[19] Much too often, however, slogans and political demands are limited to global warming. Besides global warming, which lethally intensifies many existent problems, there are countless other ecological challenges, often in our immediate vicinity. To change our attitude towards the environment, we must urgently take a keen interest in and develop a sound grasp of our complex relationship with nature. That is precisely why environmental historians are so important. Published data and figures on our ecological footprint or global warming might temporarily shock the public. But do we change our everyday behaviour when we hear that one to two hundred animal species are permanently lost each day? A few hundred insects, birds and mammals every 24 hours? Doom-laden headlines often have a paralysing, not a motivating, effect on us. Rather than abstract figures or technological promises of the future, stories help us recognise that, in the relationship of human beings to nature, there is an infinitely large number of things to discover – in beautiful landscapes where danger lurks as well as in visions and behaviours that change the world and ecosystems. But, above all, stories demonstrate that where we come from and where we are going are intimately connected and therefore nothing has to remain as it is.

The search for nature in stories demonstrates that the beauty of landscapes and the natural foundation of our existence can only be maintained in the long run if we keep in mind that the future of people on earth depends on preserving soil, water, biotopes and ecological systems, of which we are merely a part. To this end, we should not act like parasites and permanently damage our host (our resources and the earth) but like organisms that feed off the earth's resources without inflicting lasting damage on it. The realisation that the status quo is precarious and requires improvement is just as important in this context as imagining a better world. *Paradise Blues* gives an insight into the vulnerability and beauty of nature. These stories demonstrate that vulnerabilities and pressures are almost always political constructions, and for that reason, they must be possible to deconstruct. Through a wealth of examples showing threats to the environment, I have demonstrated that even the greatest area of Arctic wilderness is not safe from destruction despite various efforts; that nature is a powerful protagonist we have to come to terms with, whether in the form of wildfires, earthquakes or hurricanes; that

# Afterword

there are regions whose long-term habitability we should seriously question; that toxic hazards might be lurking in the shadow of natural monuments; that some things labelled 'sustainable' make the gap separating rich and poor even greater; and that an adequate drinking water supply cannot be guaranteed without our intervention, even in subtropical wetlands. But I also offer a range of inspiring examples: for example, that activists are fighting for environmental conservation and against racism; that committed citizens can force big politics to its knees in the fight for environmental justice; that we can (and should) rewild archaic landscapes, flora and fauna; or that a contaminated city can be turned into a shining example of ecology, in the USA or beyond. In times of burnout, both social and planetary, passivity and deceleration are more useful when dealing with nature than action for action's sake and radical intervention. Small slices of inhabitable paradise can be found throughout the world. But we will lose them if we don't try to conserve them. Despite this recognition, this book is not a romantic plea to return to nature. It is a call to discover the beauty and imperilment of our environment. For those who are open to them, nature and history hold an almost infinite number of subversive observations, cultural finds, ecological insights and subtle political messages. This book is ideally an ongoing project that we all continue to write in some form or other: when we feel the urge to go exploring and to make our own findings either in the place where we live or in other places into which the stories of our lives may drive us.

# Acknowledgements

This book has a long history. Some of the ideas that went into it reach back about two decades. In reviewing the origins and evolution of *Paradise Blues*, I realise how fortunate I have been. During my time as director of the German Historical Institute (GHI) in Washington, D.C. (1999–2007), I had the opportunity to travel across the USA – to learn from colleagues when I attended conferences and to visit many diverse environments in North America, from New York to California and from Florida to Alaska. Colleagues have shaped my understanding of the US past and of the relationship between nature, culture and history; and friends and family have encouraged and supported me in many different ways.

I owe considerable thanks to various institutions and numerous people. They are too many to remember, let alone to list or properly acknowledge. Some of them, including librarians and conversation partners at various sites, are mentioned in the footnotes. Others, among them members of audiences who have patiently listened and commented on my presentations, must remain nameless even though I am very grateful to them because I know all too well that scholarly work never happens in isolation.

My explicit expression of gratitude begins with Lucy Jones, the translator of this book. It has been a true pleasure to work with her. I found Lucy to be both diligent and curious and, what matters most, Lucy caught my voice!

The translation of this book from its German original into English would not have been possible without funding that I received from the German Ministry of Research and Education (BMBF) through the Rachel Carson Center at LMU Munich. I am most grateful for the support of the ministry and my university.

As director of the GHI and of the Rachel Carson Center for Environment in Munich, I did not have regular semester breaks. I could only dedicate very few weeks per year to research and writing. I am therefore most grateful to Gregg Mitman and his colleagues in Madison who gave me a break in early 2020. They invited me to be the Carl Schurz Visiting professor at the University of Wisconsin. I enjoyed those two months before the pandemic

## Acknowledgements

immensely. They gave me a chance to do some final research for the book and to work towards finishing it.

In my scholarly career, I started out as a literary critic and a diplomatic historian but over the years the international community of environmental humanists has become something like my family, and the Rachel Carson Center has become my home. I have enjoyed thousands of conversations with colleagues and students from the environmental humanities. And I received significant impulses for this book from many of them. My particular thanks go to Carl Abbott, Matthew Booker, Dorothee Brantz, Erika Bsumek, J. Baird Callicott, William Cronon, Kyle Diesner, Wayne Dowdy, Jared Farmer, Dee Garceau, Robert Gioielli, Sara Gregg, Shen Hou, Andrew Isenberg, Tait Keller, Beth LaDow, Uwe Lübken, Cindy Ott, Jennifer Price, David Stradling, Louis S. Warren, Donald Worster and Thomas Zeller. There were many others, colleagues and friends at the RCC and all over the world, who have supported, helped and encouraged me. Among them I wish to thank in particular Jane Carruthers, Ranjan Chakrabarty, Tom Griffith, Johannes Heisig, Arielle Helmick, Shen Hou, Serenella Iovino, Ryan Jones, Sophia Kalantzakos, Thomas Lekan, Ann-Kathrin Mittelstraß, Katie Ritson, Libby Robin, Paul Sutter, Bron Taylor, Julia Adeney Thomas, Helmuth Trischler, Paula Ungar, Sabine Wilke, Verena Winiwarter, Mingfang Xia, and Frank Zelko. Thank you so much, dear friends!

I am also grateful for the generous assistance of my colleagues at the Carson Center – in particular that of Pavla Šimková who worked on the first German draft of this book and of Stefanie Schuster who provided the maps for the German edition. Special thanks also to Theresa Hilz who read the proofs of the English edition.

A manuscript is nothing without a publishing house. I had the immense pleasure of working with the incredible Sarah Johnson of The White Horse Press. Her dedication as a publisher is truly exceptional. Sarah and her cousin James Rice are great communicators, excellent editors and passionate publishers. In our increasingly anonymous world, it is a joy to know that there are editors who have an open ear for all kinds of authorial concerns, however outlandish these may be. It gives me much hope to see that The White Horse Press is doing well!

I cannot end the list of thanks without mentioning my students. Conversations in seminars and workshops with my students about past and future environmental challenges are among the most wonderful and rewarding things that I have experienced in my life. I am so pleased that I've had a

## Acknowledgements

chance to get to know the next generation of environmental humanists. The world needs them and I am very proud of them. I dedicate this book to my past and present students in Munich and elsewhere in the world!

# Notes

## Prologue

1. Perry Miller, *Nature's Nation* (Cambridge, MA: Harvard University Press, 1967); John Opie, *Nature's Nation: An Environmental History of the United States* (Fort Worth, Texas: Harcourt Brace, 1998).
2. Ted Steinberg, *American Green: The Obsessive Quest for the Perfect Lawn* (New York: W. W. Norton, 2006); Christof Mauch, *Amerikanische Geschichte: Die 101 wichtigsten Fragen* (München: C.H. Beck, 2016), p. 166.
3. See more recently Heike Bungert, *Die Indianer. Geschichte der indigenen Nationen in den USA* (Munich: C.H. Beck, 2020).
4. Christof Mauch and Kiran Patel, 'Umwelt: Naturschutz und Raubbau', in *Wettlauf um die Moderne. USA und Deutschland 1890 bis heute*, ed. by Christof Mauch and Kiran Klaus Patel (München: Pantheon, 2008), pp. 97–123.
5. Donald Worster, 'Doing Environmental History', in *The Ends of the Earth: Perspectives on Modern Environmental History*, ed. by Donald Worster (Cambridge: Cambridge University Press, 1988), p. 289.
6. Bill McKibben, *The End of Nature* (New York: Random House, 2006).

## Wiseman, Alaska. 'The Happiest Civilization'

1. Robert Marshall, *Arctic Village: A 1930s Portrait of Wiseman, Alaska* (New York: Literary Guild, 1933).
2. Fifty-five per cent of towns, according to official statistics from Alaska's Department of Commerce, Community, and Economic Development, had fewer than 500 residents. Alaska Mapping Business Plan. Appendix 2: An Overview of Communities in Alaska, 49: https://www.commerce.alaska.gov/web/Portals/4/pub/AKMBPA2.pdf
3. Stephen W. Haycox, 'The View from Above: Alaska and the Great Northwest', in *The Great Northwest: The Search for Regional Identity*, ed. by William G. Robbin (Corvallis. Oregon State University Press, 2001).
4. Roxanne Willis, *Alaska's Place in the West: From the Last Frontier to the Last Great Wilderness* (Lawrence, KS: University of Kansas Press, 2010), p. 4.
5. See Ibid., pp. 3–9.
6. We travelled there in August 2010. Since then, conditions have improved.
7. In a global comparison, the number of collisions in relation to kilometres driven is particularly high in Alaska. See 'Driving in Moose Country', Alaska Department of Fish and Game: http://www.adfg.alaska.gov/index.cfm?dfg=livewith.drivingmoosecountry (accessed 7 Oct. 2018).

# Notes

8   Cinema sales in the US reached $18.35 million, DVD sales $21.76 million, and worldwide sales $56 million. See *Into the Wild* (2007), The Numbers: https://www.the-numbers.com/movie/Intothe-Wild#tab=summary (accessed 22 May 2020); Diana Saverin, 'The Chris McCandless Obsession Problem', *Outside Magazine*, 18 Dec. 2013; Craig Medred, 'The Beatification of Chris McCandless: From Thieving Poacher into Saint', *Alaska Dispatch*, 28 Sept. 2016: https://www.adn.com/voices/article/beatification-chris-mccandless-thieving-poacher-saint/2013/09/21/. See also Susan Kollin, 'The Wild, Wild North: Nature Writing, Nationalist Ecologies, and Alaska', *American Literary History* **12** (1–2) (2000): 41–78, p. 41; Eric Heyne, 'The Last Frontier: Reinventing Alaska', in *Desert, Garden, Margin, Range: Literature on the Frontier*, ed. by Eric Heyne (New York: Twayne, 1992), pp. 3–15.

9   See Robert W. Service 'Spell of the Yukon' and 'The Cremation of Sam McGee', in *Songs of Sourdough* (Toronto: W. Briggs, 1907); and Jack London 'To Build a Fire', in *The Call of the Wild Collection: The Call of the Wild, White Fang & Other Tales from the Klondike* (independently published, 2020), pp. 193–202.

10  'History of Chena Hot Springs', Chena Hot Springs Resort: https://chenahotsprings.com/chena-history/ (accessed 7 Oct. 2018); 'History of Chena River State Recreation Park', Alaska Department of Natural Resources: http://dnr.alaska.gov/parks/aspunits/northern/chenariversra.htm (accessed 22 May 2020); 'Fascinating Tale: Pedro's Story of the Strike, and How Klondikers Won Out', *Dawson Daily News*, 16 Oct. 1906, n.p.; Ross Coen, 'Case Study: Chena Hot Springs' (Fairbanks, AL: University of Alaska/Alaska Center for Energy and Power, 2010); Willis, *Alaska's Place in the West*, p. 48 ff.

11  'Alaska Agriculture', Farm Flavor: https://www.farmflavor.com/alaska-agricultur (accessed 22 May 2020).

12  Clarence C. Hulley, 'A Historical Survey of the Matanuska Valley Settlement in Alaska', *The Pacific Northwest Quarterly* **40** (4) (1949): 327–40; Orlando W. Miller, *The Frontier in Alaska and the Matanuska Colony* (New Haven: Yale University Press, 1975), p. 66 ff.; Willis, *Alaska's Place in the West*, p. 48 ff.; Kathryn Taylor Morse, *The Nature of Gold: An Environmental History of the Klondike Gold Rush* (Seattle et al.: University of Washington Press, 2003), p. 183; Walter R. Borneman, *Alaska: Saga of a Bold Land* (New York: HarperCollins, 2003), p. 311–16.

13  Maria Reeves, *Alaska Gold: The History of Gold Dredge No. 8* ([Fairbanks, AL]: Gold Fever Press, 2009).

14  Harry A. Franck, *The Lure of Alaska* (New York: Frederick A. Stokes Co., 1939), p. 12. See also historical descriptions by Mary Lee Davis in 1930: Mary Lee Davis, *Uncle Sam's Attic: The Intimate Story of Alaska* (Boston: W. A. Wild Co., 1930), p. 138; Clark C. Spence, *The Northern Gold Fleet: Twentieth-Century Gold Dredging in Alaska* (Champaign, IL: University of Illinois Press, 1996), pp. 8, 98, 146.

15  Dermot Cole, *Historic Fairbanks: An Illustrated History* (San Antonio, TX: HPN Books, 2002), p. 21 f.

16  John Gunther, *Inside U.S.A.* (New York: Harper and Brothers, 1947), p. 159.

17  Jo Anne Wold, 'Digging the Davidson: An Engineering Marvel', *Fairbanks Daily News-Miner*, 14 July 1984. A historic 16mm silent film from the Alaska Film Archive (AFA) shows gold-dredging operations as well as the use of mercury. The film, with the signature AAF-1091, is in the AFA, Machetanz Collection, Alaska & Polar Regions

## Notes

Department, Elmer E. Rasmuson Library, University of Alaska Fairbanks. A small clip from the film was posted on YouTube on 31 Aug. 2012: https://www.youtube.com/watch?v=j74cIR1VAkA

18   *Alaska: The Complete Guide with Wildlife Viewing, Wilderness Adventures, Camping and Cruises* (New York/ Toronto: Fodor Travel Publications, 1998), p. 203; Bureau of Land Management, *The Dalton Highway: Visitor Guide* (Alaska Geographic, 2010).

19   Borneman, *Alaska: Saga of a Bold Land*, p. 303.

20   Willis, *Alaska's Place in the West*, p. 113–16. See also Peter Coates' classic book, *The Trans-Alaska Pipeline Controversy: Technology, Conservation, and the Frontier* (College, AK: University of Alaska Press, 1993); Tom Brown, *Oil on Ice: Alaskan Wilderness at the Crossroads* (San Francisco: Sierra Club Battlebook, 1971), p. 43.

21   *The Dalton Highway: Visitor Guide*, p. 3.

22   Conversation with George (anonymised) on 18 Aug. 2010 in Yukon Crossing.

23   Sundborg quoted in Dan O'Neill, *The Firecracker Boys: H-Bombs, Inupiat Eskimos, and the Roots of the Environmental Movement* (New York: Basic Books, 2007), p. 311; see also Willis, *Alaska's Place in the West*, p. 108; US Army Corps of Engineers, Alaska District, *Data on Rampart Canyon Project Studies* (Anchorage, AK: 1961); Lawrence Davies, 'Controversy Rages Over Plans for Big Alaska Power Project', *New York Times*, 22 Aug. 1964, p. 25; A. Starker Leopold and Justin W. Leonard, 'Alaska Dam Could Be Resources Disaster', *Audubon Magazine* 68 (1966): 176–78; Borneman, *Alaska: Saga of a Bold Land*, pp. 421–24.

24   'Alaska Native Claims Settlement Act (ANCSA)', Alaska Native Knowledge Network: http://www.ankn.uaf.edu/NPE/ancsa.html (accessed 22 May 2020).

25   In 1978, the Yukon Flats was conferred the status of National Monument. Two years later, it was downgraded to the protection status of a 'refuge' (Yukon Flats National Wildlife Refuge). 'Yukon Flats National Wildlife Refuge, Alaska', US Fish and Wildlife Service: https://www.fws.gov/refuge/yukon_flats/ (accessed 22 May 2020).

26   Interview by Marie Mitchell with Heidi Schoppenhorst, 16 Nov. 2006, Project Jukebox, Elmer E. Rasmuson Library, University of Alaska, Fairbanks

27   Conversation with Uta and Bernie Hicker, 20 Aug. 2010; interview by David Krupa with George Lounsbury, 17 Dec.1992, Ester Dome near Fairbanks, AK, University of Alaska Fairbanks Oral History Program. A digital version can be found at https://jukebox.uaf.edu/site7/interviews/316

28   Edwin Ardener, 'Remote Areas: Some Theoretical Considerations', *HAU: Journal of Ethnographic Theory* 2 (1) (2012): 519–33.

29   Information on the history, business operations and architecture of the Wiseman Trading Company can be found in archives in Anchorage, Alaska, and Washington, D.C.: Records of the Wiseman Trading Company: 1925–1999, Archives and Special Collections, UAA/ APU Consortium Library, Anchorage, Alaska. Wiseman Trading Co: Documentation, Historic American Buildings Survey: https://www.loc.gov/item/ak0060/ Library of Congress, Washington, D. C.

30   Marshall, *Arctic Village*, p. 140–41.

31   Conversation with Jack Reakoff, 20 Aug. 2010.

# Notes

32 Conversation with June Reakoff, 19 and 20 Aug. 2010.

33 Marshall, *Arctic Village*, pp. 83–85; conversation with June Reakoff, 19 and 20 Aug. 2010.

34 Conversation with Ruth and Francis Williams, 19 Aug. 2010. A photo of Florence Jonas (Kalhabuk) in front of her adobe house can be found in William E. Brown, *History of the Central Brooks Range: Gaunt Beauty, Tenuous Life* (Fairbanks, AK: University of Alaska Press, 2007), p. 149.

35 Susan M. Will and Pamela K. Hotch, *The Wiseman Historical District: A Report on Cultural Resources* (Fairbanks, AK: Bureau of Land Management/Yukon Resource Area. Fairbanks District Office, typescript, no date), pp. 10–11; Michael L. Kunz, *Cultural Resource Survey & Inventory of the North Fork Koyukuk, Middle Fork Koyukuk, Glacier, and Upper Itkillik River Drainages* (Fairbanks: NPS Draft Report I, 1985), p. 24 f., p. 160 f.

36 Conversation with Ruth and Francis Williams, 19 Aug. 2010; see also Tishu Ulen and Shirley English, 'Tishu's World', *Alaska Geographic* **10** (4)(1983): 40–69.

37 Marshall, *Arctic Village*, p. 42 f. There is also a table showing numbers of inhabitants and prostitutes: p. 38.

38 Conversations and interviews with Sheriar Erickson and Jeff Lund in Nolan, AK, 20 Aug. 2010.

39 Philip Caputo, *In the Shadows of the Morning: Essays on Wild Lands, Wild Waters, and a Few Untamed People* (Guilford, CT: Lyons Press, 2002), p. 95.

40 Interview with Jeff Lund in Nolan, AK, 20 Aug. 2010.

41 Leonard initially prospected in Gold Creek, 24 kilometres north of Wiseman, and later in Archibald Creek, a tributary of Nolan Creek. There he had a small log cabin in which he which he spent the summer months. Email from George Lounsbury to Christof Mauch on 20 Sept. 2019.

42 See interview by David Krupa with George Lounsbury, 17 Dec.1992. Email from George Lounsbury to Christof Mauch, 19 Sept. 2019. An 8mm-film *Living and Mining near Wiseman, 1930s*, can be found in the Alaska Film Archives, Elmer E. Rasmuson Library, and is on YouTube: https://www.youtube.com/watch?v=YN0VqeW03Fo. Harry Leonard Pictures, private property of Bernie and Uta Hicker. The inscription on Harry B. Leonard's grave in Fairbanks says: '10-27-1897, Lisbone Falls, Maine. 8-29-1989, Fairbanks, AK, 54 Yr Miner of Wiseman.' Irvine M. Reed met Harry Leonard in 1937: see *Report on a Reconnaissance of Upper Koyukuk Region Alaska* (Fairbanks, AK: Alaska Division of Geophysical Survey, 1937).

43 Borneman, *Alaska: Saga of a Bold Land*, pp. 34–89, 160.

44 The calculation of the volume of gold in rail wagons is based on the total production volume of 43.3 million troy ounces (1.35 million tons) of gold (from 1880 to 2017) and on the loading capacity of the most modern US freight cars (in 2018). These can each transport up to 125.5 tons of gold. The value of gold mined in 2013 was higher than in all other years, with the exception of the period around 1903. See Jennifer E. Athey and Melanie B. Werdon, *Alaska's Mineral Industry 2017* (Fairbanks, AK: Alaska Division of Geological & Geophysical Surveys (Special Report 73), 2018), in particular p. 61 ff.

## Notes

45  Jeff Lund also answers questions about subsistence in an interview with Carol Scott in Nolan, Alaska, 28 Jan. 1992 [2 audio cassettes], Oral History Collection, Alaska Polar Regions Collections and Archives, Elmer E. Rasmuson Library, University of Alaska Fairbanks. Thanks to Leslie McCartney (Oral History Curator) and Robyn Russell (Oral History Collection Manager) for their research assistance.

46  Long after my stay in Wiseman, I learned from George Lounsbury that Sheriar and Jeff, who have reached retirement age, have moved to Minnesota, Jeff Lund's home state. (Email from George Lounsbury to Christof Mauch, 20 Sept. 2019).

47  Joe Wilkins, *Gates of the Arctic National Park: Twelve Years of Wilderness Exploration* (Dallas, TX: Brown Publishing, 2018), p. 12–14. The six protected rivers are the Alatna, John, Nobuk, Noatak, North Fork Koyukuk and the Tinayguk.

48  Interview Bill Schneider and David Krupa with Sue Holly, 16 Sept. 1992, at the National Park Service Field Office in Bettles, Alaska, Project Jukebox, Elmer E. Rasmuson Library, University of Alaska Fairbanks; *Final Environmental Impact Statement Recommendation: Gates of the Arctic* (Fairbanks, AK: US National Park Service/ Alaska Regional Office, typescript 1980), p. 119.

49  Braun, *History of the Central Brooks Range*, pp. 191–204, 194. 'Hunting – Gates of the Arctic National Park', National Park Service/ Gates of the Arctic: https://www.nps.gov/gaar/planyourvisit/hunting.htm (accessed 22 May 2020).

50  See Ken Ross, *Environmental Conflict in Alaska* (Boulder, CO: University Press of Colorado, 2000), p. 317–27.

51  See O'Neill, *The Firecracker Boys*.

52  Ross, *Environmental Conflict*, p. 319; Robert Hunter, *Greenpeace* (Toronto: McClelland and Stewart, n.d. [= 1972]); Frank Zelko, *Make It a Green Peace! The Rise of Countercultural Environmentalism* (Oxford/New York: Oxford University Press, 2013), p. 65 ff.

53  Pamela King, 'Trump Administration Takes First Steps Toward Drilling in Alaska's Arctic Refuge', *Science* 19 April 2018.

54  Conversations with Jack Reakoff in Wiseman, 20 Aug. 2010, June Reakoff, 19 Aug. 2010, Heidi Schoppenhorst, 18 and 19 Aug. 2010; conversation with Uta and Bernie Hicker on 20 Aug. 2010.

55  William Cronon, 'The Trouble with Wilderness; or, Getting Back to the Wrong Nature', in *Uncommon Ground: Rethinking the Human Place in Nature*, ed. by William Cronon (New York: W.W. Norton & Co., 1995), pp. 69–90, p. 86.

## Malibu, California. Stranger than Paradise

1  For similar questions, but with a different focus, see C. Mauch, 'Unruly Paradise – Nature and Culture in Malibu, California', in *Unruly Environments*, ed. by Siddhartha Krishnan, Christopher L. Pastore and Samuel Temple (Munich: Rachel Carson Center, 2015), pp. 45–51; C. Mauch, 'Malibu, California: Edenic Illusions and Natural Disasters', in *A Field on Fire: The Future of Environmental History*, ed. by Mark D. Hersey and Ted Steinberg (Tuscaloosa, AL: University of Alabama Press, 2019), pp. 72–84.

## Notes

2   Frederick Hastings Rindge, *Happy Days in Southern California* (Cambridge, MA and Los Angeles: Rindge Family, 1972), p. 64.
3   'California Indian History', Native American Heritage Commission: http://nahc.ca.gov/resources/california-indian-history/ (accessed 24 Oct. 2020).
4   Luanne Pfeifer, ed., *The Malibu Story: The Saga of an Old Spanish Land Grant – Its Authentic Legends and the Colorful People Who Shaped Its History* (Malibu, CA: Malibu Lagoon Museum, 1985), pp. 13–18; Ben Marcus, 'Chumash to Hard Cash', *Malibu Magazine*, 20 April 2010.
5   An excerpt from Richard Gird's diary from 1882 is reprinted in Carolyn Merchant (ed.), *Green vs. Gold: Sources in California's Environmental History* (Washington, D.C: Island Press, 1998), p. 192.
6   Hazel Adele Pulling, 'Range Forage and the California's Range Cattle Industry', *Historian* 7 (1945): 113–29; 'The Story of Malibu: Chapter 3: The Fabled Ranch of the Rindges', City of Malibu: https://www.malibucity.org/106/History-of-Malibu (accessed 11 Sept. 2020).
7   Rindge, *Happy Days*, pp. 64, 129.
8   Isaac F. Marcosson, 'The Black Golconda – California's Oil Empire', *Saturday Evening Post*, 5 April 1924, p. 230, quoted in Nancy Quam-Wickham, 'Cities Sacrificed on the Altar of Oil: Popular Opposition to Oil Development in 1920s Los Angeles', *Environmental History* 3 (2) (1998): 189.
9   Quam-Wickham, 'Cities Sacrificed on the Altar of Oil', p. 200.
10  Rindge, *Happy Days*, p. 129.
11  See David K. Randall, *The King and Queen of Malibu: The True Story of the Battle for Paradise* (New York, NY: W.W. Norton and Company, 2016).
12  Ben Blow, *California Highways: A Descriptive Record of Road Development by the State and by Such Counties as Have Paved Highways* (San Francisco, CA: H.S. Crocker & Co. 1920); see Pfeifer, *The Malibu Story*, pp. 25–30; Mike Davis, *Ecology of Fear: Los Angeles and the Imagination of Disaster* (New York, NY: Metropolis Books, 1998), pp. 99–104; Rindge Co. et al. v. Los Angeles County. Rindge Co. v. Same, 262 U.S. 700, No. 237 (SC 1923).
13  Brian R. Jacobson, *Studios before the System: Architecture, Technology, and the Emergence of Cinematic Space* (New York: Columbia University Press, 2015), p. 168 f.
14  It is no longer possible to determine whether the spelling 'Malibou' or 'Malibu' was considered correct or whether the different names were the result of a simple spelling mistake.
15  Brian Rooney, *Three Magical Miles: An Appreciation of the Past & Present of Malibou Lake & Vicinity* (Malibu: R7 Media/Cornell Preservation Organization, 2009), pp. 7, 20–24 and 41–43; Cecilia Rasmussen, 'Malibou Lake Has Played Its Part in Movie History', *Los Angeles Times*, 4 Nov. 2007.
16  Joel Coen, *The Big Lebowski* (PolyGram Filmed Entertainment/Gramercy Pictures, 1998).
17  Justin Parkinson, 'The Perils of the Streisand Effect', *BBC News Magazine*, 31 July 2014; Mike Masnick, 'Since When Is It Illegal to Just Mention a Trademark Online?'

# Notes

*Techdirt*, 5 Jan. 2005, https://www.techdirt.com/articles/20050105/0132239.shtml; Frank Clifford, 'Streisand Donates Estate to Mountains Conservancy', *Los Angeles Times*, 18 Nov. 1993.

18  Jenny Price, 'Beyond the Gates, a Public Gateway', *Los Angeles Times*, 24 May 2005.

19  Bill Dowey, *A Brief History of Malibu and the Adamson House* (Malibu, CA: Malibu Lagoon State Beach Interpretative Association, 1995), pp. 27–36; Pfeifer, *The Malibu Story*, pp. 31–34; Ronald L. Rindge et al., *Ceramic Art of the Malibu Potteries 1926–1932* (Malibu: Malibu Lagoon Museum, 1988).

20  Numerous discussions with Jenny Price in 2008 and 2010 in Malibu and in 2013 at the Rachel Carson Center in Munich; see also David Ng, 'Urban Rangers on "Safari" in the City', *Los Angeles Times*, 16 Aug. 2009: http://articles.latimes.com/2009/aug/16/entertainment/ca-rangers16

21  '*Our Malibu Beaches: The Definitive Guide to the Public Beaches of Malibu*': https://ourmalibubeaches.com/ and https://apps.apple.com/us/app/our-malibubeaches/id565636167 (accessed 24 Oct. 2020); Adam Nagourney, 'In Battle Over Malibu Beaches, an App Unlocks Access', *New York Times*, 13 June 2013.

22  Dennis Green, 'After 32 Years of Headaches, David Geffen May Sell His Massive Malibu Beach House', *Business Insider*, 29 June 2015: https://www.businessinsider.com/david-geffen-to-sell-his-malibu-beach-fortress-for-100-million-2015-6

23  Chester D. King, *Evolution of Chumash Society: A Comparative Study of Artifacts Used for Social System Maintenance in the Santa Barbara Channel Region before A.D. 1804* (New York: Garland, 1990); Travis Hudson (ed.), *The Eye of the Flute: Chumash Traditional History and Ritual* (Santa Barbara, CA: Santa Barbara Museum of Natural History, 2nd ed., 1981); Campbell Grant, *The Rock Paintings of the Chumash: A Study of a California Indian Culture* (Berkeley: University of California Press, 1965); Michael A. Glassow, *Purisimeño Chumash Prehistory: Maritime Adaptations along the Southern California Coast* (Fort Worth: Harcourt Brace College, 1996); Ronald L. Rindge, *The Rediscovery of the Pueblo de las Canoas* (Malibu: Malibu Historical Society and Malibu Lagoon Museum, 1985).

24  Raymond F. Dasmann, 'Wildlife in Transition', in Merchant (ed.), *Green vs. Gold*, p. 27; Robert F. Heizer and Albert B. Elsasser, *The Natural World of the California Indians* (Berkeley: University of California Press, 1980).

25  Mike Sampson, 'Humaliwo. An Ethnographic Overview of the Chumash in Malibu', California Department of Parks and Recreation, 2009: https://www.parks.ca.gov/?page_id=24435 (accessed 24 Oct. 2020).

26  Pfeifer, *The Malibu Story*, pp. 10–12; further testimonies can be found in Joshua Paddison (ed.), *A World Transformed: Firsthand Accounts of California before the Gold Rush* (Berkeley: Heyday Books, 1998).

27  Sherburne Cook estimates that, between 1848 and 1860, the number of indigenous people fell from about 200,000 or 250,000 to between 25,000–30,000. Sherburne F. Cook, *The Population of the California Indians, 1769–1970* (Berkeley: University of California Press, 1976), p. 199.

28  Interview with Mati Waiya, 15 Jan. 2010. See also 'Nicholas Canyon Stream Restoration', *Wishtoyo Chumash Foundation*: http://www.wishtoyo.org/df-nicholas/; Resolution of the

# Notes

LA County Board of Supervisors Approving the Application, in Co-Sponsorship with the Wishtoyo Foundation for an Urban Streams Restoration Grant for the Nicholas Canyon Creek Habitat Restoration Project, 18 April 2002: http://file.lacounty.gov/bc/q2_2002/cm s1_002151.pdf

29 Francis M. Fultz, *The Elfin Forest of California* (Los Angeles: Times-Mirror Press, 1923), p. 26.

30 Old coral and flame trees as well as cape leadwort hedges (*Plumbago capensis*) can also be found in the Adamson House garden. When the flowers were imported from South Africa, so was their January flowering period. I would like to thank Prof. Jane Carruthers for this information.

31 Conversation with Andrew Gosser, 10 Feb. 2008.

32 Davis, *Ecology of Fear*, pp. 104–05; Brian Rooney, *Three Magical Miles*, p. 11.

33 'Official Report: Old Topanga Incident', County of Los Angeles Fire Department, 2–11 Nov. 1993: https://www.lafire.com/famous_fires/1993-1102_OldTopanga-Fire/19931102_OfficialReport_OldTopangaIncident.htm (accessed 11 Sept. 2020).

34 Barbara Marquand, 'The 10 Costliest Wildfires', *Insure.com*, 24 June 2013: https://www.insure.com/home-insurance/costliest-wildfires.html

35 Pearl Castillo, 'Los Angeles Fire Department Welcomes Back Super Scoopers, Helitankers', Los Angeles County Fire Department News Release, 12 Aug. 2016: http://www.publicnow.com/view/8F8F7101F2679EE8E5DF71DB5BB544E7047C49C0?2016-08-13-01:31:10+01:00-xxx8955

36 Bob Pool and Jason Song, 'Wind-Driven Fire Destroys 35 Structures in Malibu', *Los Angeles Times*, 24 Nov. 2007.

37 'Malibu Fire Claims 35 Homes, Forces 14,000 Evacuations', *KNBC*, 25 Nov. 2007.

38 Conversation with Andrew Gosser, 10 Jan. 2010.

39 Gil Segel quoted in Joe Mozingo, 'Officials Link Malibu Septic Tanks to Beach Pollution', *Los Angeles Times*, 13 Nov. 2000: https://www.latimes.com/archives/la-xpm-2000-nov-13-me-51196-story.html (accessed 27 Aug. 2015).

40 See, for example, '15 Green Actors', *Grist*, 2 June 2007: https://grist.org/article/celebs/; Frank Clifford, 'Streisand Donates Estate to Mountains Conservancy', *Los Angeles Times*, 18 Nov. 1993; 'Glitzy Giving: Donors', *Inside Philanthropy: Who's Funding What, and Why*: http://www.insidephilanthropy.com/glitzy-giving/leonardo-dicaprio.html

41 Dan Glaister, 'Why Septic Tanks Are a Washout in Malibu'; Arevalo, 'Beach East of Malibu Pier Named One of the Nation's Most Consistently Polluted'; Mark Dorfman and Angela Haren, 'Testing the Waters 2014'.

42 The environmental organisation Heal the Bay constantly carries out measurements. See the website https://healthebay.org/. However, since a high concentration of bacteria is not the same as a high risk of infection, the assessments are only of limited significance. About Legacy Park: 'Malibu Legacy Park Project', City of Malibu: http://www.malibucity.org/index.aspx?NID=427 (accessed 11 Sept. 2020).

43 Edward Humes, *Eco Barons: The Dreamers, Schemers, and Millionaires Who Are Saving Our Planet* (New York, NY: Ecco, 2009), p. 247; and, on the other hand, Jenny Price, 'Stop Saving the Planet! – and Other Tips via Rachel Carson for Twenty-First-Century

# Notes

Environmentalists', in *Rachel Carson's Silent Spring: Encounters and Legacies*, ed. by Lawrence Culver, Christof Mauch and Katie Ritson (Munich: Rachel Carson Center, 2012), pp. 11–30.

44  See Christof Mauch, 'Phönix und Mnemosyne. Katastrophenoptimismus und Katastrophenerinnerung in den USA. Von der Johnstown Flood bis Hurricane Katrina', in *Katastrophen machen Geschichte. Umweltgeschichtliche Prozesse im Spannungsfeld von Ressourcennutzung und Extremereignis*, ed. by Patrick Masius, Jana Sprenger and Eva Mackowiak (Göttingen: Göttingen University Press, 2010), pp. 133–51.

45  Jarmusch quoted in Vikram Murthi, 'Jim Jarmusch's "Stranger Than Paradise"', *IndieWire*, 24 June 2015; see also Roger Ebert, 'Stranger than Paradise', 1 Jan. 1984: https://www.rogerebert.com/reviews/stranger-than-paradise-1984

46  See Jared Farmer, *Trees in Paradise: The Botanical Conquest of California* (New York: W.W. Norton, 2013); Davis, *Ecology of Fear*.

## Memphis, Tennessee. Mississippi Blues

1  William Bearden, *Memphis Blues: Birthplace of a Music Tradition* (Charleston, SC: Arcadia Publishing, 2006); Beverly G. Bond and Janann Sherman, *Beale Street* (Charleston, SC: Arcadia Publishing 2006).

2  John E. Harkins and Berkley Kalin, *Metropolis of the American Nile: An Illustrated History of Memphis and Shelby County* (Woodland Hills, CA.: Windsor Publications, 1982); William Bearden, *Cotton: From Southern Fields to the Memphis Market* (Charleston, SC: Arcadia Publishing, 2005). I owe many insights to conversations with Jeffrey Jackson and Tait Keller in Memphis in October 2016.

3  Zack O'Malley Greenburg, 'America's Most Dangerous Cities', *Forbes*, 23 April 2009.

4  'Mighty, Mighty Mississippi', on the album *A New Kind of Blues* (Studio City, CA: Magnolia Gold Records [MGR-7181] 2008).

5  Mark Twain, *Life on the Mississippi* (New York: Penguin Books, 1984), p. 64

6  James M. Coleman, 'The Dynamic Changes and Processes in the Mississippi River Delta', *Geological Society of America Bulletin* 100 (1988): 999–1015; Christopher Morris, 'Only a River', *The Iowa Review* **39** (2) (2009): 149–65, p. 149 f.; John McPhee, 'The Control of Nature: Atchafalaya', *The New Yorker*, 23 Feb. 1987; Andrea Mustain, 'What Is to Blame for the Mississippi Floods?' *Live Science*, 11 May 2011.

7  Conversation with J. Baird Callicott, 8 Oct. 2017 in Memphis.

8  Jeannie M. Whayne, 'Cotton's Metropolis: Memphis and Plantation Development in the Trans-Mississippi West, 1840–1920', in *Comparing Apples, Oranges, and Cotton: Environmental Histories of the Global Plantation*, ed. by Frank Uekötter (Frankfurt/New York: Campus, 2014), pp. 49–84.

9  'Die Fahrt auf dem Mississippi: Wirklich erlebte Schrecksscenen [sic] nach Flint's Recollections etc., Newyork 1826', in *Columbus: Amerikanische Miscellen*, ed. by C.N. Röding (Hamburg: C.W.C Menk, 1827), pp. 18, 21.

# Notes

10  Floyd M. Clay, *A Century on the Mississippi: A History of the Memphis District, US Army Corps of Engineers, 1876–1981* (Memphis: US Army Corps of Engineers, 1886), pp. 24, 33–35; Whayne, 'Cotton's Metropolis', p. 52 f., p. 70 f.; Jeannie Whayne, *Delta Empire: Lee Wilson and the Transformation of Agriculture in the New South* (Baton Rouge: Louisiana State University Press, 2011), p. 63 ff.

11  On Hopefield, see Marion Bragg, *Historic Names and Places on the Lower Mississippi River* (Vicksburg, MS: Mississippi River Commission, 1977), David O. Demuth, 'The Burning of Hopefield', *Arkansas Historical Quarterly* 36 (Spring 1977): 123–30; James R. Fair, 'Hopefield, Arkansas: Important River-Rail Terminal', *Arkansas Historical Quarterly* 57 (Summer 1998): 191–204; Margaret Elizabeth Woolfolk, *A History of Crittenden County, Arkansas* (Greenville, SC: Southern Historical Press, 1993).

12  See Bill Dries, 'Mud Island Makeover: The RDC Wants to Nip Sags and Tuck Bags at a Park That's Seen Better Days', *The Memphis News*, 30 Nov. 2009.

13  Clay, *A Century on the Mississippi*, pp. 57–60.

14  Conversation with Wayne Dowdy on 5 Oct. 2016 in Memphis.

15  Mark Twain, *Life on the Mississippi* (New York & London, 1901), p. 207.

16  Charles H. McNutt (ed.), *Prehistory of the Central Mississippi Valley* (Tuscaloosa, AL: The University of Alabama Press, 1996): pp. 110–17, p. 247 f; 'Choctaws', *The Tennessee Encyclopedia of History and Culture. Version 2.0*: https://tennesseeencyclopedia.net/entry.php?rec=248 (accessed 25 Feb. 2020); Arthur H. DeRosier, Jr., *The Removal of the Choctaw Indians* (Knoxville: The University of Tennessee Press, 1970), p. 153 ff.

17  Christopher Juston Hartman, *An Assessment of the Mound Summit Investigations at Mound A (Unit 5), Chucalissa (40SY1) Shelby County, Tennessee* (Friends of Chucalissa Special Publication No.1, 2010), pp. 3–12; *Chucalissa: Outdoor Visitor's Guide and Trail Map* (Memphis, TN: C.H. Nash Museum Chucalissa/The University of Memphis n.d.); Gloria A. Young and Michael Hoffmann (eds), *The Expedition of Hernando de Soto West of the Mississippi, 1541–1543, Proceedings of the de Soto Symposia, 1988 and 1990* (Fayetteville, AR: University of Arkansas Press, 1999).

18  The herbs mentioned can still be found today in the herb garden of Chucalissa. See also David L. Lentz (ed.), *Imperfect Balance: Landscape Transformations in the Precolumbian Americas* (New York/Chichester: University of Columbia Press, 2000); and Christopher Morris, *The Big Muddy: An Environmental History of the Mississippi and Its Peoples from Hernando de Soto to Hurricane Katrina* (New York: Oxford University Press, 2012), p. 14–17.

19  See *Chucalissa: Outdoor Visitor's Guide*, n. p.

20  Charles H. McNutt (ed.), *Prehistory of the Central Mississippi Valley* (Tuscaloosa: University of Alabama Press, 2016), p. 241 ff.

21  Michael Conzen (ed.), *The Making of the American Landscape* (London: Routledge, 3rd ed. 1994); Morris, *The Big Muddy*, p. 85; Eleonora Rohland, *Cultural Adaptation from the French Colonial Era to Hurricane Katrina* (Dissertation, Bochum University, 2014).

22  Bearden, *Cotton*, p. 8

23  'Letter to Thomas Jefferson, 13 February 1789', *The Writings of George Washington; Being his Correspondence, Addresses, Messages, and other Papers, Official and Private*, ed.

# Notes

by Jared Sparks, Vol. IX (Boston: Russell, Odiorne, and Metcalf and Hilliard, Gray, and Co., 1835), p. 470.

24  Tim Flannery, *The Eternal Frontier: An Ecological History of North America and Its Peoples* (New York, 2002), p. 280.

25  *Historical Statistics of the United States, Colonial Times to 1970* (Washington, D.C.: Government Printing Office. Bicentennial Edition, 1975), p. 518.

26  See Constance MacLaughlin Green, *Eli Whitney and the Birth of American Technology* (New York: Longman, 1956); David A Hounshell, *From the American System to Mass Production, 1800–1822: The Development of Manufacturing Technology in the United States* (Baltimore, MD: Johns Hopkins University Press, 1984).

27  Sven Beckert, *Empire of Cotton: A New History of Global Capitalism* (London: Penguin/Random House, 2014), p. 104.

28  Whayne, 'Cotton's Metropolis', p. 59; Lynette Boney Wrenn, *Crisis and Commission Government in Memphis: Elite Rule in a Gilded Age City* (Knoxville, TN: University of Tennessee, 1998), p. 3. At the beginning of the 1940s, the share of the national cotton market even rose to 31 per cent: see Bearden, *Cotton*, p. 77.

29  Walter T. Durham, *Before Tennessee: The Southwest Territory* (Piney Flats, TN: Rocky Mount Historical Association, 1990), p. 218 f.; Robert Vincent Remini, *Andrew Jackson and the Course of American Empire, 1767–1821* (New York: Harper & Row, 1977), p. 332–40, Beckert, *Empire of Cotton*, p. 98–109.

30  Particularly decorative houses include the Woodruff-Fontaine House and the Mallory-Neely House. See Eugene J. Johnson and Robert D. Russell Jr., *Memphis: An Architecture Guide* (Knoxville, TN: University of Tennessee Press, 1990).

31  Donald E. Davis, 'Metropolis: Paradise Lost?' in Davis et al., *Southern United States: An Environmental History* (Santa Barbara, CA: nABC-CLIO, 2006), pp. 159–220, 160–66; Mikko Saikku, *The Evolution of a Place: Patterns of Environmental Change in the Yazoo-Mississippi Delta from the Ice Age to the New Deal* (Helsinki: Renvall Institute for Area and Cultural Studies, 2001), p. 246; Mikko Saikku, *This Delta, this Land: An Environmental History of the Yazoo-Mississippi Floodplain* (Athens, GA, et al.: University of Georgia Press, 2005); John Dougan, *Memphis* (Charleston, SC: Arcadia, 1998), pp. 19–30.

32  Dougan, *Memphis*, p. 22.

33  Morris, *The Big Muddy*, p. 153.

34  Ibid. 121 f., p. 176, 187; Peter Coates, *American Perceptions of Immigrant and Invasive Species: Strangers on the Land* (Berkeley and Los Angeles: University of California Press, 2006), p. 168.

35  Jimmy Carter, *An Hour Before Daylight: Memoirs of a Rural Boyhood* (New York: Simon & Schuster, 2001), p. 180; Deborah Blum, 'A is for Arsenic (Pesticides, if you Please)', *Wired*, 19 June 2012: https://www.wired.com/2012/06/arsenic-pesticides-in-our-food/ (accessed 25 Feb. 2020); Tom Charlier, 'As Insects Grow Immune, Pesticides Stay on Attack', *The Commercial Appeal*, 7 Nov. 2007; Rachel L. Carson, *Silent Spring* (Boston: Houghton Mifflin, 1962); Christof Mauch, 'Blick durch Ökoskop. Rachel Carsons Klassiker und die Anfänge des modernen Umweltbewusstseins', *Zeithistorische Forschungen* 1 (2012): 156–60.

## Notes

36  Pete Daniel, *Toxic Drift: Pesticides and Health in the Post–World War II South* (Baton Rouge/Washington, D.C.: Louisiana State University Press and The Smithsonian National Museum of American History, 2005).

37  David R. Goldfield, *Promised Land: The South Since 1945* (Arlington Heights, IL: Harlan Davidson, 1987), p. 211 f.; Robert D. Bullard, *Dumping in Dixie: Race, Class, and Environmental Quality* (Boulder, CO.: Westview Press, 1994), p. 26 ff.

38  Charlier, 'As Insects Grow Immune'; 'Superfund Site: North Hollywood Dump, Memphis, Tennessee': https://cumulis.epa.gov/supercpad/cursites/csitinfo.cfm?id=0403873 (accessed 25 Feb. 2020).

39  On the Superfund, see the Niagara and Love Canal chapter in this book.

40  Conversation with Wayne Dowdy on 5 Oct. 2016. Dowdy's most important Memphis books include G. Wayne Dowdy, *A Brief History of Memphis* (Charleston, SC: The History Press, 2011); and *Mayor Crump Don't Like It: Machine Politics in Memphis* (Jackson, MS: The University of Press of Mississippi, 2006).

41  Beckert, *Empire of Cotton*, p. 110 and f.n. 26, p. 481; *Population of the United States in 1860. The Eighth Census;* compiled from the original returns under the direction of the Secretary of the Interior by Joseph C.G. Kennedy (Washington, D.C.: Government Printing Office, 1864), pp. 17, 193, 269, 287, 465; 2010 census: https://www.census.gov/quickfacts/fact/table/memphiscitytennessee/PST045216 (accessed 25 Feb. 2020).

42  For broader context, see John R. McNeill, *Mosquito Empires: Ecology and War in the Greater Caribbean, 1620–1914* (Cambridge: Cambridge University Press, 2010). The specific figures on malaria mortality – supposedly 6 per cent for Blacks and 70 per cent for the remaining whites in Memphis in 1878 – mark a clear trend, but should be treated with caution on the whole because it can be assumed that older and less mobile whites remained in Memphis; see Whayne, 'Cotton's Metropolis', p. 65 f.

43  The Lee Wilson & Company Archives, Special Collections, University of Arkansas: http://libraries.uark.edu/SpecialCollections/ardiglib/leewilson/ (accessed 25 Feb. 2020), as well as an official documentary by the City of Wilson: 'Delta Empire': https://www.youtube.com/watch?v=sHB-amZG0Jc (accessed 25 Feb. 2020).

44  Bearden, *Cotton*, p.p 99, 102 f.; Flannery, *The Eternal Frontier*, p. 277.

45  Bond and Sherman, *Beale Street*, p. 7; Preston Lauterbach, *Beale Street Dynasty: Sex, Song, and the Struggle for the Soul of Memphis* (New York: Norton, 2015). On the significance of Beale Street in racial conflicts and on the role of the Ku Klux Klan in Memphis, see Sharon D. Wright, *Race, Power, and Political Emergence in Memphis* (New York and London: Garland Publishing, 2000).

46  On this and the following, see David Evans, *Big Road Blues. Tradition and Creativity in the Folk Blues* (Berkeley, CA: University of California Press, 1982), pp. 174–80; Jeff Todd Titon, *Early Downhome Blues: A Musical and Cultural Analysis* (Chapel Hill, NC: University of North Carolina Press, 2nd ed. 1994).

47  Sam Philipps, quoted in Douglas Martin, 'Sam Phillips, Who Discovered Elvis Presley, Dies at 80', *New York Times*, 1 Aug. 2003 and in Knox Philipps, foreword to Bearden, *Memphis Blues*, p. 6.

48  *Time Magazine* quotes from G. Wayne Dowdy, *Hidden History of Memphis* (Charleston, SC: The History Press, 2010), n. p.

# Notes

49    Bond and Sherman, *Beale Street*, p. 8.

50    David Garrow, *Bearing the Cross: Martin Luther King, Jr., and the Southern Christian Leadership Conference* (New York: Harper Collins Perennial Classics, 2004), p. 482.

51    Discussion with Prof. Dee Garceau at Rhodes College, Memphis, 7 Oct. 2016.

52    Conversation with Steve Reynolds near Wilson, Arkansas, on 9 Oct.2017; on the same topic, conversation with Bob Wenner, 6 Oct. 2017; Anheuser-Busch Budweiser Stein, 1993 Arkansas Brewed w/ rice N3940 Wildlife Edit. The beer stein can now only be found second hand. 'Budweiser rice contamination exposed', *Greenpeace International*, Feature story, 8 Oct. 2007: http://www.greenpeace.org/international/en/news/features/budweiser-rice-contamination071008/#more_story (accessed 25 Feb. 2020); 'Wassup with your beer?': https://www.youtube.com/watch?v=XPZlYmCqALY (accessed 25 Feb. 2020).

53    See 'Jericho (Crittenden County)', *The Encyclopedia of Arkansas History and Culture*: https://encyclopediaofarkansas.net/entries/jericho-crittenden-county-7170/ (accessed 25 Feb. 2020). For wider context, see Jeannie Whayne and Willard B. Gatewood (eds), *The Arkansas Delta: Land of Paradox* (Fayetteville, AR: University of Arkansas Press, 1993). On the flood of 2015, see Ryan McGeeney, 'Rising Mississippi will Likely Flood Thousands of Farmland Acres in Eastern Arkansas', *University of Arkansas Cooperative Extension Service*, June 2015: https://www.uaex.uada.edu/media-resources/news/2015/july2015/07-01-2015-Ark-Mississippi-Flooding.aspx (accessed 25 Feb. 2020).

54    Conversation with Wayne Dowdy on 5 Oct. 2016.

55    'President's Island', *Tennessee: A Guide to the State: Compiled and Written by Federal Writers' Project of the Work Projects Administration for the State of Tennessee* (New York: The Viking Press, 1939), n. p.; Nicholas Vrettos, *The Story of Presidents Island* (Memphis, TN: Presidents Island, Industrial Association, Inc., 2005); 'President's Island is "Going Concern. 19 Industries located there, says Report"', *The Commercial Appeal*, 1 Dec. 1956; 'Sites Last Sales Year $200000: Seven Firms Purchased 32 Acres Of Land', *The Commercial Appeal*, 10 Jan. 1957; Charles A. Brown, 'President's Island Facing Its Most Explosive Year', *Memphis Press-Scimitar*, 13 Jan. 1964; 'President's Island Enhances Transportation, Industry; Terminal Proving Big Help', *The Commercial Appeal*, 7 Oct. 1956; 'Port of Memphis', *World Port Source*: http://www.worldportsource.com/ports/USA_TN_Port_of_Memphis_1805.php (accessed 25 Feb. 2020).

56    Perre Magness, 'Island Grows from Bog to Boom', *The Commercial Appeal*, 1 Dec. 1991; 'President's Island: The County Workhouse as Managed by Gen. Forrest. To Admirably Conducted Institution', *Memphis Daily Appeal*, 5 May 1876 [The Lucille Webb Banks Historical Collection, Cossitt Reference Library, Memphis, TN].

57    Talk with Bob Wenner, 6 Oct. 2016 in Memphis. See also Meagan Nichols, 'See It Now: Wolf River Greenway Epping Way Trail Underway', *Memphis Business Journal*, 16 Nov. 2016; 'Stuttgart (Arkansas County)', *The Encyclopedia of Arkansas History and Culture*: https://encyclopediaofarkansas.net/entries/stuttgart-820/ (accessed 25 Feb. 2020). On Ell Persons, see Martha Park, 'Hard History: The Lynching Sites Project', *Memphis Flyer*, 4 May 2017. On the history of lynching in the USA, see Manfred Berg, *Popular Justice: A History of Lynching in America* (Lanham, MD: Rowman and Littlefield, 2011).

58    J. Baird Callicott, 'Bar-B-Que and a Side of Old Growth', *Center for Humans and Nature*: https://www.humansandnature.org/urban-land-ethic-j.-baird-callicott (ac-

# Notes

cessed 25 Feb. 2020); 'Finding The Park That Martin Luther King Riverside Park Wants To Be', *Smart City Memphis*, 25 May 2016: http://www.smartcitymemphis.com/2016/05/17428/ (accessed 25 Feb. 2020); John Linn Hopkins and Marsha R. Oates, 'Memphis Park and Parkway System', *The Tennessee Encyclopedia of History and Culture. Version 2.0*: http://tennesseeencyclopedia.net/entry.php?rec=897 (accessed 25 Feb. 2020); Josh Whitehead, 'Touring the Parkways, Our Emerald Necklace', *Smart City Memphis*, 1 Feb. 2010: http://www.smartcitymemphis.com/2010/02/4272/ (accessed 25 Feb. 2020); Whitehead, 'Tour of the Memphis Parkway System, Part Deux', *Smart City Memphis*, 9 March 2010: http://www.smartcitymemphis.com/2010/03/tour-of-the-memphis-parkway-system-part-deux/ (accessed 25 Feb. 2020); Whitehead, 'Touring the Parkways – The Finale: North Parkway', *Smart City Memphis*, 5 April 2010: https://www.smartcitymemphis.com/2010/04/touring-the-parkways-the-finale-north-parkway/ (accessed 25 Feb. 2020).

## St Thomas, Nevada. The Ghosts Return

1. G. William Fiero, *Nevada's Valley of Fire: The Story behind the Scenery* (Whittier, CA: KC Publishing, 2008).

2. The list of movies shot in the Valley of Fire is endless. Titles range from *The Black Cyclone* (1925) to the Westerns *Heldorado* (1946) and *The Dreaded Four* (1966) to *Wasteland: Tales from the Desert* (2015).

3. See F. Lynne Bachleda, *Dangerous Wildlife in California and Nevada: A Guide to Safe Encounters at Home and in the Wild* (Birmingham, AL: Menasha Ridge Press, 2002).

4. Joseph P. Sánchez, *Explorers, Traders, and Slavers: Forging the Old Spanish Trail, 1678–1850* (Salt Lake City: University of Utah Press, 1997); Ray Allen Billington and Martin Ridge, *Westward Expansion: A History of the American Frontier* (New York: Macmillan Publishing, 5th ed., 1982); LeRoy R. Hafen and Ann W. Hafen, *Old Spanish Trail: Santa Fé to Los Angeles* (Lincoln, NE: University of Nebraska Press, 1993).

5. On the history of the exodus of Mormons from Nauvoo to Salt Lake City, see Stanley B. Kimball and Violet T. Kimball, *Mormon Trail: Voyage of Discovery* (Whittier, CA: KC Publications, Inc. 1995).

6. Dan L. Flores, 'Zion in Eden: Phases of the Environmental History of Utah', *Environmental Review* 7 (4) (1983): 325–44; Lori M. Hunter and Michael B. Toney, 'Religion and Attitudes toward the Environment: A Comparison of Mormons and the General U. S. population', *The Social Science Journal* 42 (1) (2005): 25–38; Jeanne Kay and Craig J. Brown, 'Mormon Beliefs about Land and Natural Resources, 1847–1877', *Journal of Historical Geography* 11 (3) (1985): 253–67.

7. Parley P. Pratt, *Autobiography of Parley Parker Pratt*, ed. by Scot Facer Proctor and Maurine Jensen Proctor (Salt Lake City: Desert Book Co., 2000), p. 510. See also Terryl L. Givens and Matthew J. Grow, *Parley P. Pratt: The Apostle Paul of Mormonism* (Oxford, Oxford University Press, 2011).

8. Aaron McArthur, *St. Thomas, Nevada: A History Uncovered* (Reno, NV: University of Nevada Press, 2013). See also Marie Harrington, *On the Trail of Forgotten People: A*

# Notes

*Personal Account of the Life and Career of Mark Raymond Harrington* (Reno, NV: Great Basin Press 1985), pp. 141–91.

9    George A. Thompson, *Some Dreams Die: Utah's Ghost Towns and Lost Treasures* (Salt Lake City: Dream Garden Press, 1982), p. 90 ff.

10    'Historic Ghost Town', NAI South Utah: https://www.loopnet.com/Attachments/F/9/C/hF9C18F79-8FAB-4373-899E-A885C24CF926.pdf (accessed 28 Oct. 2020).

11    Frederick S. Dellenbaugh, *A Canyon Voyage: The Narrative of the Second Powell Expedition down the Green Colorado River from Wyoming, and the Explorations on Land, in the Years 1871 and 1872* (New York: G.P. Putnam's Sons, 1908), p. 175.

12    Henry Brean, 'St. Thomas Residents Knew Progress Doomed Their Town', *Las Vegas Review-Journal*, 26 Sept. 2010. The founders of St Thomas initially believed they had settled in Utah territory. When Nevada retroactively imposed taxes, some moved to Utah, but quite a few later moved back. See McArthur, *St. Thomas*, p. 50 f.

13    McArthur, *St. Thomas*, p. 89.

14    Jane Holtz Kay, *Asphalt Nation: How the Automobile Took Over America and How We Can Take It Back* (Berkeley, CA et al.: University of California Press, 1997), p. 141 ff.

15    McArthur, *St. Thomas*, p. 92.

16    Historic maps, plans and photographs can be found at the Lost City Museum, Overton, Nevada, on the website of photographer Kenneth Clarke, and in historical and contemporary travel diaries. See 'Ken's Photo Gallery': http://kensphotogallery.blogspot.de/ (accessed 28 Oct. 2020); 'Lloyd B Smith Sr.'s 1922 Trip Across the Country in a Model T', diary entry dated 30 Sept.1922, *Coast to Coast in 1922*: http://www.1922coast2coast.com/wp-content/uploads/2014/05/Sept29_30.jpg (accessed 28 Oct. 2020); Shirley Hatfield, 'When Dreams are Drowned: St. Thomas, Nevada', Zetta's Aprons, last modified 7 Jan. 2016, http://zettasaprons.blogspot.de/2016/01/when-dreams-are-drowned-thomas-nevada.html

17    McArthur, *St. Thomas*, p. 94.

18    See Harrington, *On the Trail of Forgotten People*, p. 158 f., pp. 184–86; Dena M. Sedar, *Nevada's Lost City* (Mount Pleasant, SC: Arcadia Publishing, 2012).

19    See Sedar, *Nevada's Lost City*.

20    'Chicago Was Built in Nevada 1500 Years Ago', *Los Angeles Times*, 27 May 1934.

21    McArthur, *St. Thomas*, p. 100.

22    Ibid., p. 116.

23    William D. Rowley, *The Bureau of Reclamation: Origins and Growth to 1945* (Denver, CO: Bureau of Reclamation, 2006); William E. Smythe, *The Conquest of Arid America* (New York: The Macmillan Company, 1905); Donald Worster, *Rivers of Empire: Water, Aridity, and the Growth of the American West* (New York/ Oxford: Oxford University Press, 1985), pp. 210–12; James C. Maxon, *Lake Mead and Hoover Dam: The Story behind the Scenery* (Whittier, CA: KC Publications, 2006), pp. 26–33; Brad Plumer, 'Lake Mead Helps Supply Water to 25 Million People. And It Just Hit a Record Low', *Vox: Energy and Environment*, 23 May 2016.

24    Marion V. Allen, *Hoover Dam and Boulder City* (Redding, CA: CP Printing & Publishing,1985); Mimi Garat Rodden, *Boulder City, Nevada* (Charleston, SC: Arcadia

# Notes

Publishing, 2000); Renée Corona Kolvet and Victoria Ford, *The Civilian Conservation Corps in Nevada: From Boys to Men* (Reno and Las Vegas: University of Nevada Press, 2006), pp. 98–103.

25   Peter Iverson, *Diné: A History of the Navajos* (Albuquerque: University of New Mexico Press, 2002), p. 137 ff.; Peter Iverson (ed.), '*For Our Navajo People': Diné Letters, Speeches & Petitions, 1900–1960* (Albuquerque: University of New Mexico Press, 2002), p. 250; Richard White, *The Roots of Dependency: Subsistence, Environment, and Social Change Among the Choctaws, Pawnees, and Navajos* (Lincoln, NE: University of Nebraska Press, 1983), p. 300 ff.; Patricia Nelson Limerick, *The Legacy of Conquest: The Unbroken Past of the American West* (New York and London: W.W. Norton & Co., 1987), p. 206 ff.; David Eugene Wilkins, *The Navajo Political Experience* (Lanham: Rowman & Littlefield Publishers, 2013), p. 85 f.

26   Franklin Delano Roosevelt, 'Address at the Dedication of Boulder Dam', 30 Sept. 1935, in *Public Papers and Addresses of Franklin D. Roosevelt. The American Presidency Project*: https://www.presidency.ucsb.edu/documents/address-the-dedication-boulder-dam (accessed 28 Oct. 2020).

27   Robert S. Devine, 'The Trouble with Dams', *Atlantic Monthly (Digital Edition)*, August 1995: http://www.theatlantic.com/past/politics/environ/dams.htm ; Lawrence L. Master, Stephanie R. Flack and Bruce A. Stein (eds), *Rivers of Life: Critical Watersheds for Protecting Freshwater Biodiversity* (Arlington, VA: The Nature Conservancy, 1998); Diane Raines Ward, *Water Wars: Drought, Flood, Folly, and the Politics of Thirst* (New York: Berkley Publishing Group, 2002), p. 72 ff.

28   William C. G. Burns u. a., *The World's Water, 2002–2003: The Biennial Report on Freshwater Resources* (Washington DC: Island Press, 2002), p. 139 f.; Carlie A. Rodriguez et al., 'Macrofaunal and Isotopic Estimates of the Former Extent of the Colorado River Estuary, Upper Gulf of California, México', *Journal of Arid Environments* **49** (2001): 183–93; Richard White, *The Organic Machine: The Remaking of the Columbia River* (New York: Hill and Wang, 1995). The four endangered species are the bonytail chub, the Colorado pikeminnow, the humpback chub and the razorback sucker.

29   Barbara Land and Myrick Land, *A Short History of Las Vegas* (Reno, NV: University of Nevada Press, 2004); Michael Green, 'How the Mormons Made Las Vegas: And Why We Need Their Engagement Now More Than Ever', *Vegas Seven*, 4 June 2014; David G. Schwartz, *Suburban Xanadu: The Casino Resort on the Las Vegas Strip and Beyond* (New York: Routledge, 2003).

30   'QuickFacts Las Vegas, Nevada', US Census Bureau: https://www.census.gov/quickfacts/lasvegascitynevada (accessed 28 Oct. 2020); Riley Moffat, *Population History of Western U.S. Cities & Towns, 1850–1990* (Lanham: Scarecrow, 1996); Jeff Burbank, 'Hoover Dam's Impact on Las Vegas', *Online Nevada Encyclopedia*, modified on 6 Sept. 2010: http://www.onlinenevada.org/articles/hoover-dams-impact-las-vegas

31   Gerald D. Nash, *The American West Transformed: The Impact of the Second World War* (Bloomington, IN: Indiana University Press, 1985); Nash, *World War II and the West: Reshaping the Economy* (Lincoln, NE: University of Nebraska Press, 1990); John Beck, *Dirty Wars: Landscape, Power, and Waste in Western American Literature* (Lincoln and London: University of Nebraska Press, 2009); 'Las Vegas – An Unconventional History: Atomic Tourism in Nevada', 17. The American Experience, *PBS Online*, last modified

# Notes

7 Nov. 2005: http://www.pbs.org/wgbh/amex/lasvegas/peopleevents/e_atomictourism.html ; Mark Ward, 'Tech Know: Carving an Atomic Bomb', *BBC Technology*, last amended 1 March 2011: http://www.bbc.co.uk/news/technology-12600177

32 'Miss Atom Bomb', *National Security Site History*, Las Vegas, NV: National Nuclear Security Administration (NNSA), Aug. 2013.

33 Philip L. Fradkin, *Fallout: An American Nuclear Tragedy* (Boulder, CO: Johnson Books, 2004), pp. 10–13.

34 Pat Ortmeyer and Arjun Makhijani, 'Worse Than We Knew', *The Bulletin of the Atomic Scientists*, Nov./Dec. 1997: http://www.ieer.org/latest/iodnart.html ; Carl Johnson, 'Cancer Incidence in an Area of Radioactive Fallout Downwind from the Nevada Test Site', *Journal of the American Medical Association* **251** (2) (1984): 230.

35 Sarah Alisabeth Fox, *Downwind: A People's History of the Nuclear West* (Lincoln, NE: University of Nebraska Press, 2014); Janet Burton Seegmiller, 'Nuclear Testing and the Downwinders', *The History of Iron County*: https://historytogo.utah.gov/downwinders/ (accessed 28 Oct. 2020); Glenn Alan Cheney, *They Never Knew: The Victims of Atomic Testing* (Danbury, CT: F. Watts, 1996).

36 Ralph Vartabedian, 'Nevada's Hidden Ocean of Radiation', *Los Angeles Times*, 13 Nov. 2009; 'Nevada National Security Site Tours', *Nevada National Security Site*: http://www.nnss.gov/pages/PublicAffairsOutreach/NNSStours.html (accessed 28 Oct. 2020). On Ertebat Shar, see Alan Taylor, 'A Replica of Afghanistan in the Mojave', *The Atlantic*, 18 Sept. 2013; Geoff Manaugh and Nicola Twilley, 'It's Artificial Afghanistan: A Simulated Battlefield in the Mojave Desert', *The Atlantic*, 18 May 2013.

37 Steve Kanigher, 'Yucca Mountain or Not, Nuclear Waste Resides Here', *Las Vegas Sun*, 13 Feb. 2011.

38 As of November 2015, 100 nuclear reactors in the United States were licensed: 'Map of Power Reactor Sites', United States Nuclear Regulatory Commission, last modified 13 Nov. 2015: http://www.nrc.gov/reactors/operating/mappower-reactors.html; Corbin Harney, 'Yucca Mountain: No Place for Nuclear Waste', *Nuclear Information and Resource Service*, Oct. 2000; Harney, *The Way It Is: One Water, One Air, One Mother Earth* (Nevada City, CA: Blue Dolphin Publishing, 1995), pp. 131–62.

39 Sean Davies, 'A Deeply Flawed Plan: Steve Frishman Discusses the Yucca Mountain Project', *Engineering and Technology Magazine*, 19 April 2010; Rebecca Solnit, *Storming the Gates of Paradise: Landscapes for Politics* (Berkeley: University of California Press, 2007), p. 132 ff.; Solnit, 'Tomgram: Rebecca Solnit on Nuclear Nevada', Tom-Dispatch.com, 10 Aug. 2004: http://www.tomdispatch.com/blog/1674/; Solnit, *Savage Dreams: A Journey into the Landscape Wars of the American West* (Berkeley et al.: University of California Press, 2014); *Yucca Mountain: The Most Studied Real Estate on the Planet*, Report to the Chairman Senator James M. Inhofe, US Senate Committee on Environment and Public Works, Majority Staff, Washington, DC: 2006.

40 Tim P. Barnett and David W. Pierce, 'When Will Lake Mead Go Dry?' *Water Resources Research* **44** (3) (2008); William DeBuys, *A Great Aridness: Climate Change and the Future of the American Southwest* (Oxford/ New York: Oxford University Press, 2012).

41 Matt Wray et al., 'Leaving Las Vegas: Exposure to Las Vegas and Risk of Suicide', *Social Science and Medicine* **67** (2008): 1882–88.

# Notes

42    Associated Press, 'Inside Lake Mead's Third Straw', *Daily Mail*, 6 July 2015.

43    'Groundwater Development Project', *Southern Nevada Water Authority*: http://water.nv.gov/hearings/past/Spring%20-%20Cave%20-%20Dry%20Lake%20and%20Delamar%20Valleys%202011/Exhibits/SNWA%20Exhibits/SNWA_Exh_191_2011%20Plan%20of%20Development.pdf (accessed 28 Oct. 2020).

44    'Into the Future', *Makers: Women in Nevada History*: https://womennvhistory.com/makers/ (accessed 28 Oct. 2020).

45    I was given the lead on the role of Pat Mulroy by Patricia Limerick. See also Abrahm Lustgarten, 'The "Water Witch": Pat Mulroy Preached Conservation While Backing Growth in Las Vegas', ProPublica, 2 June 2015: https://projects.propublica.org/killing-the-colorado/story/pat-mulroy-las-vegas-water-witch

46    'Frequent Questions About Water Waste', *Las Vegas Valley Water District*: https://www.lvvwd.com/conservation/water-waste/frequent-questions/index.html (accessed 28 Oct. 2020).

47    T.R. Goldman, 'Las Vegas Is Betting It Can Become the Silicon Valley of Water', *Politico Magazine*, 21 April 2016; Daniel Person, 'Water Conservation, Brought to You by Las Vegas', *Outside*, 22 Sept. 2015: http://www.outsideonline.com/2016686/water-conservation-brought-you-las-vegas

48    Bernd Schröder, 'Las Vegas – geht der Wüstenmetropole das Wasser aus?', *Telepolis*, 14 Dec. 2005; Robert Jerome Glennon, *Water Follies: Groundwater Pumping and the Fate of America's Fresh Waters* (Washington, D. C.: Island Press, 2002); James C. Warf, 'Radioactive Waste at Ward Valley', *Science* **269** (5231) (1995): 1653; Jeff Wheelwright, 'For Our Nuclear Wastes, There's Gridlock on the Way to the Dump', S*mithsonian Magazine*, May 1995: http://www.smithsonianmag.com/people-places/for-our-nuclearwastes-theres-gridlock-on-the-way-to-the-dump-1-32865155/

49    Edward Abbey, *Desert Solitaire* (Tucson: University of Arizona Press, 1988), p. 205.

50    Mike Davis, 'House of Cards. Las Vegas: Too Many People in the Wrong Place, Celebrating Waste as a Way of Life', *Sierra Magazine*, Nov./Dec. 1995: http://vault.sierraclub.org/sierra/199511/vegas.asp

51    Jackson J. Benson, *Wallace Stegner: His Life and Work*, (Lincoln: University of Nebraska Press, 2009), p. 399.

## Dodge City, Kansas. The Windy Wild West

1    Robert R. Dykstra and Jo Ann Manfra, *Dodge City and the Birth of the Wild West* (Lawrence: University Press of Kansas, 2017), p. 177 f. The expression 'wickedest town' came from a letter printed in the *Evening Star* (Washington, D. C.) on 1 Jan. 1878. See Tom Clavin, *Dodge City: Wyatt Earp, Bat Masterson, and the Wickedest Town in the American West* (New York: St. Martin's Press, 2017); Robert M. Wright, *Dodge City, the Cowboy Capital and the Great Southwest in the Days of The Wild Indian, the Buffalo, the Cowboys, Dance Halls, Gambling Halls, and Bad Men* (Dodge City, KS: 2nd Edition, 1913).

## Notes

2   Daniel C Fitzgerald, *Sound and Fury: A History of Kansas Tornadoes 1854–2008* (place not given: The Dan Fitzgerald Company, 2008), p. 16; Sue McKenna, 'One Year after Tornado, Greensburg Still Struggling to Survive', *Insurance Journal*, 9 May 2008; Lyman Frank Baum, *The Wonderful Wizard of Oz* (Chicago/ New York: George M. Hill Co., 1900).

3   Donald Worster, *Dust Bowl: The Southern Plains in the 1930s* (Oxford and New York: Oxford University Press, 1979); see also the book by eye-witness Lawrence Svobida, *Farming the Dust Bowl: A First-Hand Account from Kansas* (Lawrence, KS: University Press of Kansas, 1986) [original title: *Empire of Dust*, Paxton Printers 1940]. For information about Clinton Lake, see George Frazier, *The Last Wild Places of Kansas: Journeys into Hidden Landscapes* (Lawrence, KS: University of Kansas Press, 2016), pp. 21–22.

4   George Champlin Sibley, *The Road to Santa Fe: The Journal and Diaries of George Champlin Sibley and Others Pertaining to the Surveying and Marking of a Road from the Missouri Frontier to the Settlements of New Mexico, 1825–1827*, ed. by Kate Leila Gregg (Albuquerque: University of New Mexico Press, 1952); Sibley, *Seeking a Newer World: The Fort Osage Journals and Letters of George Sibley, 1808–1811* (St. Charles, MO: Lindenwood University Press, 2003); David Dary: *The Santa Fe Trail: Its History, Legends, and Lore* (New York: Alfred A. Knopf, 2001); Frazier, *The Last Wild Places*, p. 38–40; on Eckert's Tavern, see Justin Watkins, 'The Cooperage That Wasn't (and the Lime Kiln)', *Historic Saint Charles Preservation Journal* (2008): http://preservationjournal.org/properties/South/1106/1106-South.html (accessed 13 March 2020).

5   On the Kansa people, see William E. Unrau, *Kansa Indians: A History of the Wind People, 1673–1873* (Norman, OK: University of Oklahoma Press, 1971). On Trail Day Cafés, see Rawlinson-Terwilliger, Home Historic Site: https://www.travelks.com/listing/rawlinson-terwilliger-home-historicsite/14488/ (accessed 13 March 2020). In the USA twelve Madonnas of the Trail have been erected by the Daughters of the American Revolution. See Fern Ioula Bauer, *The Historic Treasure Chest of the Madonna of the Trail* (Springfield, OH: J. McEnaney Printing, 1984).

6   William Johnson, cited in Frazier, *The Last Wild Places*, pp. 184–85.

7   Frazier, *The Last Wild Places*, p. 185 f.

8   Emily Dickinson, *The Complete Poems of Emily Dickinson*, ed. by Thomas H. Johnson (Boston and Toronto: Little, Brown and Company, 1955), p. 710.

9   Dan Flores, 'Bison Ecology and Bison Diplomacy: The Southern Plains from 1800–1850', *The Journal of American History* **78** (2) (1991): 465–85; Rita Napier, 'Rethinking the Past, Reimaging the Future', in Rita Napier (ed.), *Kansas and the West: New Perspectives* (Lawrence KS: University of Kansas Press, 2003), pp. 1–40; Richard E. Jensen (ed.), *The Pawnee Mission Letters, 1834–1851* (Lincoln, NE: University of Nebraska Press, 2010); Ida M. Ferris, 'The Sauk and Foxes in Franklin and Osage Counties, Kansas', *Kansas Historical Collections* 11 (1910): 362.

10  Frazier, *The Last Wild Places*, p. 41 ff., p. 158; Huber Self, *Environment and Man in Kansas: A Geographical Analysis* (Lawrence, KS: The Regents Press of Kansas, 1978), pp. 40–46; Napier, 'Rethinking the Past', pp. 14–15.

## Notes

11  'Last Stand of the Tallgrass Prairie', Tallgrass Prairie National Preserve, National Park Service: https://www.nps.gov/tapr/index.htm (accessed 13 March 2020); Shirley Christian, 'A Prairie Home', *The New York Times*, 26 July 1998 (Travel Section).

12  'Tallgrass Prairie National Preserve Conducts First Roundup of Growing Bison Herd', *Lawrence Journal-World*, 27 June 2018; 'Beefalo Facts', *Mother Earth News: The Original Guide to Living Wisely*: https://www.motherearthnews.com/homesteading-and-livestock/beefalo-facts-zmaz81mazraw (accessed 13 March 2020).

13  Conversation with Rhonda Jeffries on 7 April 2017 in Dodge City.

14  Fredric R. Young, *Dodge City: Up Through a Century in Story and Pictures* (Dodge City: Boot Hill Museum, Inc., 1972), p. 15 ff.; Andrew C. Isenberg, *The Destruction of the Bison: An Environmental History, 1750–1920* (New York: Cambridge University Press, 2011); Christof Mauch, *Die 101 wichtigsten Fragen: Amerikanische Geschichte* (München: C.H. Beck, 2016), pp. 37–39.

15  Young, *Dodge City: Up Through a Century*, pp. 30–38. The photograph of Charles Rath, owner of Chas. Rath & Co. in Dodge City, is in the archive of the Kansas Historical Society. Call Number: FK2.F2 D.3 *2. KSHS Identifier: DaRT ID: 2088.

16  In the collection of letters written by German immigrants published by Wolfgang Helbich and others, there are many mentions of the American diet of meat. See Wolfgang Helbich, Walter D. Kamphoefner and Ulrike Sommer (eds), *Briefe aus Amerika. Deutsche Auswanderer schreiben aus der Neuen Welt, 1830–1930* (München: C.H. Beck, 1988); William Cronon, *Nature's Metropolis: Chicago and the Great West* (New York/London: W.W. Norton, 1991), p. 218; Joshua Specht, 'The Rise, Fall, and Rebirth of the Texas Longhorn: An Evolutionary History', *Environmental History* 21 (2) (2016): 343–63.

17  Geraldine C. Hearn, 'The Wire that Changed the West', *Persimmon Hill* (Summer 1984): 12; the best current depiction of cowboys' lives in the USA is by Christopher Knowlton, *Cattle Kingdom: The Hidden History of the Cowboy West* (New York: Houghton Mifflin, 2017).

18  Dykstra and Manfra, *Dodge City*, p. 53; Young, *Dodge City: Up Through a Century*, p. 19; Homer E. Socolofsky and Huber Self, *Historical Atlas of Kansas* (Norman, OK: University of Oklahoma Press, 1972), ch. 33; *The Globe Livestock Journal*, 17 March 1885, Kansas Heritage Centre Archives (KHCA), Cattle – Quarantine Lines, KHC Vertical Files.

19  *Kansas Cowboy* (Dodge City), 26 Sept. 1885, cited in Dykstra and Manfra, *Dodge City*, pp. 62–63.

20  Young, *Dodge City: Up Through a Century*, pp. 44, 181.

21  Ibid. p. 16; conversation with Mark Vierthaler on 6 April 2017.

22  Fredric R. Young, *The Delectable Burg: An Irreverent History of Dodge City – 1872 to 1886* (Dodge City, KS: Mennonite Press and Kansas Heritage Centre, 2009), pp. 36–81; Dykstra and Manfra, *Dodge City*, pp. 45–50; Richard White, *It's Your Misfortune and None of My Own: A New History of the American West* (Norman, OK: University of Oklahoma Press, 1991).

23  Timothy J. LeCain, 'How Did Cows Construct the American Cowboy?' in *Molding the Planet: Human Niche Construction at Work*, ed. by Maurits W. Ertsen, Christof

## Notes

Mauch and Edmund Russell (München: RCC Perspectives, 2016), p. 23. According to the 2015 OECD report, only the Australians consume as much meat as the US Americans, closely followed by the Argentinians and the Israelis. OECD (2015), Meat consumption (indicator): https://doi.org/10.1787/fa290fd0-en

24  LeCain, 'How Did Cows Construct the American Cowboy?', pp. 17–24; Specht, 'The Rise, Fall, and Rebirth of the Texas Longhorn', pp. 343–363; 'Texas Cattle: Peculiarities', *San Francisco Chronicle*, 7 July 1885, cited in ibid., p. 350. In the boom year of 1871 alone, 700,000 cows were herded into the Cattle Towns. Cattle – Quarantine Lines, KHC Vertical Files, KHCA.

25  The Mueller-Schmidt House has been a listed building since 1972. National Register of Historic Places, Kansas – Ford County: http://www.nationalregisterofhistoricplaces.com/KS/Ford/state.html (accessed 13 March 2020). Historical photos and materials can be found in the archive of the Ford County Historical Society. 'The Mueller-Schmidt House Museum': http://www.kansashistory.us/fordco/preview/preview.html (accessed 13 March 2020).

26  Edmund Russell, James Allison, Thomas Finger, John K. Brown, Brian Balogh and W. Bernard Carlson, 'The Nature of Power: Synthesizing the History of Technology and Environmental History', *Technology & Culture* **52** (2) (2011): 246–59. LeCain, 'How Did Cows Construct the American Cowboy?', pp. 17–24.

27  Napier, 'Rethinking the Past', p. 10 f.; T. Lindsay Baker, *American Windmills: An Album of Historic Photographs* (Norman, OK: University of Oklahoma Press, 2007), p. 28.

28  William Cronon, *Nature's Metropolis*, p. 221; Henry D. and Frances T. McCallum, *The Wire That Fenced the West* (Norman, OK: University of Oklahoma Press, 1965); John Franklin Vallentine, *Cattle Ranching South Of Dodge City: The Early Years (1870–1920)* (Ashland, KS: Clark County Historical Society, 1998); Carol Osman Brown, 'Barbed Wire: The Fence that Tamed the West', *Arizona Highways* **XLV** (10) (Oct.1969): 10–37; Earl W. Hayter, 'Barbed Wire Fencing – A Prairie Invention: Its Rise and Influence in the Western States', *Heritage of Kansas* (Sept. 1960): 7–16; Hearn, 'The Wire that Changed the West', pp. 8–17. Richard Holben, 'The Wire that Won the West', *Americana* (March 1974): 24–26. Vertical File Barbed Wire, KHCA. Kansas Barbed Wire Museum: http://www.rushcounty.org/BarbedWireMuseum/BWmuseum.html (accessed 13 March 2020); at first, the windmills were erected with the help of mules: T. Lindsay Baker, *American Windmills*, pp. 24–26, 54.

29  Andrew C. Isenberg, *Wyatt Earp: A Vigilante Life* (New York, NY: Hill and Wang, 2013).

30  The Winters came to Dodge because Dodge had a hospital and their 'great aunt with cancer could be treated in Dodge'. Conversation with Joel and Ken Winter on 5 April 2017.

31  'Cattle Empire: Dodge City Livestock Market Now Is 14,000,000 Institution', *Dodge City Globe*, 4 Sept. 1948; Arlyn G. Smith, 'Dodge City Still Cow Capital', *Hutchinson News*, 17 Feb. 1957; Newspaper Clippings. Cattle Files, KHCA. Historical population of Dodge City for period 1880–2014: http://population.us/ks/dodge-city/ (accessed 13 March 2020).

32  'U.S. Beef Exports by Country', *Beef2Live*: http://beef2live.com/story-beef-exports-country-yeardate-0–109756 (accessed 13 March 2020).

271

# Notes

33  Upton Sinclair, *The Jungle* (New York: Doubleday, Page & Company, 1906); Eric Schlosser, 'How to Make the Country's Most Dangerous Job Safer: The Power Lies with One Hamburger Vendor', *The Atlantic*, Jan. 2002: https://www.theatlantic.com/magazine/archive/2002/01/how-tomake-the-countrys-most-dangerous-job-safer/302395/. See Schlosser's critique: Sherwood Ross, 'Meat Industry Workers – "Most Dangerous Job In America"', *Rense.com*, 29 July 2001: https://rense.com//general12/job.htm. 55% of the residents of Dodge City have Hispanic backgrounds and, among elementary school children, the figure is as high as 85%. Interview with Joann Knight, Chamber of Commerce, Dodge City, 11 April 2017.

34  Natale Zappia, 'Revolutions in the Grass: Energy and Food Systems in Continental North America, 1763–1848', *Environmental History* **21** (1) (2016): 30–53; Harriet Friedman, 'Modernity and the Hamburger', not paginated.

35  Tony Weis, *The Ecological Hoofprint: The Global Burden of Industrial Livestock* (New York: Zed Books Ltd., 2013); Wolfram Mauser, *Wie lange reicht die Ressource Wasser? Vom Umgang mit dem blauen Gold* (Frankfurt a. M.: Fischer Taschenbuch, 2007), p. 184; David Biello, 'Farmers Deplete Fossil Water in World's Breadbaskets', *Scientific American*, 9 Aug. 2012: https://blogs.scientificamerican.com/observations/farmers-deplete-fossil-water-in-worlds-breadbaskets/; T. Gleeson, Y. Wada, M.F.P. Bierkens and L.P.H. van Beek, 'Water Balance of Global Aquifers Revealed by Groundwater Footprint', *Nature* 488 (Aug. 2012): 197–200.

36  'Why the Global Rise in Vegan and Plant-Based Eating Isn't a Fad (600% Increase in U. S. Vegans + Other Astounding Stats)', *Future of Food: Food Revolution Network*, 18 Jan. 2018: https://foodrevolution.org/blog/vegan-statistics-global/; Richard L. Knight, 'The Ecology of Ranching', in Richard L. Knight, Wendell C. Gilgert and Ed Marston (eds), *Ranching West of the 100th Meridian: Culture, Ecology, and Economics* (Washington/ Covelo/ London: Island Press, 2002), pp. 123–44.

37  Conversation with Joann Knight on 11 April 2017, Chamber of Commerce, Dodge City; Conversation with Charles Meade, 11 April 2017, Dodge City.

## Niagara, New York. The Second Greatest Disappointment

1  Alfred Kerr, *Yankee Land. Eine Reise* (Berlin: Mosse, 1925), p. 192.

2  Another name, New Amsterdam, which appears on city plans of the year 1804, was rejected by the town's population.

3  Orsamus Turner, *Pioneer History of the Holland Purchase of Western New York* (Buffalo, NY: Jewett, Thomas & Co., 1849), p. 401; Clara Davis Kirby, *The Early History of Gowanda and The Beautiful Land of the Cattaraugus* (Gowanda, NY: Niagara Frontier Publishing Company, Inc., 1976); Frank H. Severance, *Papers relating to the Burning of Buffalo* (Buffalo: Bigelow Bros., 1879 (Publications of the Buffalo Historical Society)); Mark Goldman, *High Hopes: The Rise and Decline of Buffalo* (Albany, NY: State University of New York Press, 1983), p. 21 ff.; John N. Jackson with John Burtniak and Gregory P. Stein, *The Mighty Niagara: One River – Two Frontiers* (Amherst, NY: Prometheus Books, 2003), pp. 105–11.

## Notes

4   Carol Sheriff, *The Artificial River: The Erie Canal and the Paradox of Progress, 1817–1862* (New York: Hill and Wang, 1996).
5   Johann Wolfgang von Goethe, Sämtliche Werke. Vol. 13: Sprüche in Prosa. Sämtliche Maximen und Reflexionen, ed. by Harald Fricke ( (Frankfurt a. M.: Deutscher Klassiker Verlag, 1993), p. 72.
6   For details, see Henry W. Hill, *Municipality of Buffalo: A History*, 4 vols (New York: Lewis Historical Publishing Company, 1923); Goldman, *High Hopes*, p. 25.
7   H. Jay Green, 'Buffalo's First Elevators and Mills', *The Northwestern Miller* 26 (1888): 437; Joseph Nathan Kane, Steven Anzovin and Janet Podell, *Famous First Facts: A Record of First Happenings, Discoveries, and Inventions in American History* (New York: H.W. Wilson, 4th edition, 1997), p. 4; William J. Brown, *American Colossus: The Grain Elevator, 1843 to 1942* (Brooklyn, NY: Colossal Books, new edition, 2015), p. 84; David Stradling, *The Nature of New York: An Environmental History of the Empire State* (Ithaca/London: Cornell University Press, 2010), p. 68 f.; Jackson, *The Mighty Niagara*, p. 176.
8   Goldman, *High Hopes*, p. 56 ff.
9   See Gideon Miner Davison, *The Fashionable Tour: An Excursion to the Springs, Niagara, Quebec, and Boston* (Saratoga Springs, NY: G.M. Davidson, 1825 [reprint, Miami, FL: HardPress, 2017]); Frances Wright anonymously published a series of letters about her travels in America during the years 1818–1820, *Views of Society and Manners in America: In a series of Letters from that Country to a Friend in England, during the Years 1818, 1819, and 1820* (London: Longman, Hurst, Rees, Orme, and Brown, 1821); John F. Sears, *Sacred Places: American Tourist Attractions in the Nineteenth Century* (New York: Oxford University Press, 1989), pp. 12–30; Stradling, *The Nature of New York*, p. 84 ff.
10  Jackson, *The Mighty Niagara*, p. 119.
11  William L. Stone, *The Life and Times of Red-Jacket* (New York/London: Wiley and Putnam, 1841); Goldman, *High Hopes*, pp. 28–33.
12  Arthur S. Dyke and Victor K. Prest, 'Late Wisconsinan and Holocene History of the Laurentide Ice Sheet', *Géographie physique et Quaternaire* **41** (2) (1987): 237–63; Francis Jennings, *The Invasion of America: Indians, Colonialism, and the Cant of Conquest* (Chapel Hill: University of North Carolina Press, 1975), p. 173 f.; Frederick Houghton, 'Indian Village, Camp and Burial on the Niagara Frontier', *Bulletin of the Buffalo Society of Natural Sciences* **9** (3) (1909): 367–74; Jackson *The Mighty Niagara*, pp. 69–74; Hans Läng, *Kulturgeschichte der Indianer Nordamerikas* (Bindlach: Gondrom Verlag, 1993), p. 118 f.; Stradling, *The Nature of New York*, pp. 15–23.
13  Kristen J. Gremillion, *Food Production in Native North America: An Archaeological Perspective* (Washington, DC: SAA Society for American Archaeology, The SAA Press, 2018), ch. 4; William Cronon, *Changes in the Land: Indians, Colonists, and the Ecology of New England* (New York: Hill and Wang, 1983), pp. 12, 128–130, 164 f.
14  Jackson, *The Mighty Niagara*, p. 94.
15  Shepard Krech III, *The Ecological Indian: Myth and History* (New York: W.W. Norton & Company, 1999); Christian F. Feest, 'The Greening of the Red Man: "Indians", Native Americans, and Nature', in *Nature's Nation Revisited: American Concepts of Nature from*

*Wonder to Ecological Crisis*, ed. by Hans Bak and Walter W. Hölbling (Amsterdam: VU University Press, 2003), pp. 9–29; Stradling, *The Nature of New York*, p. 19 f.

16   Cronon, *Changes in the Land*, p. 166.

17   Erastus Granger quoted in Carl Benn, *The Iroquois in the War of 1812* (Toronto/ Buffalo: University of Toronto Press, 1998), p. 123.

18   Alexis de Tocqueville, *Journey to America* (New Haven, Yale University Press, 1960), p. 129.

19   Turner, *Pioneer History of the Holland Purchase*; 'Obituary: Orsamus Turner', *The Buffalo Commercial*, 21 March 1855, 559–61.

20   Leo Marx, *The Machine in the Garden: Technology and the Pastoral Ideal in America* (New York: Oxford University Press, 2000).

21   Charles Lyell, *Travels in North America in the years 1841–2; with Geological Observations on the United States, Canada, and Nova Scotia*, vol. 1. (New York: Wiley and Putman, 1845), p. 16.

22   Jackson, *The Mighty Niagara*, pp. 163–67.

23   James Faxon, *The Niagara Falls Guide. WithFfull Instructions to direct the Traveller to all the Points of Interest at the Falls and Vicinity. With a Map and Engravings* (Buffalo: A. Burke, 1849), p. 7 ff.; Horatio A. Parsons, *A Guide to Travelers visiting the Falls of Niagara, Containing much Interesting and Important Information respecting the Falls and Vicinity* (Buffalo, NY: Oliver G. Steele, 1835), p. 82 ff.; Richard H. Gassan, 'Trains to Niagara: Railroads and the Culture of Tourism, 1820–1860', in *Exploring Travel and Tourism: Essays on Journeys and Destinations*, ed. by Jennifer Erica Sweda (Newcastle upon Tyne: Cambridge Scholars Publishing, 2012), pp. 169–90.

24   *Final Report of John A. Roebling, Civil Engineer, to the presidents and directors of the Niagara Falls Suspension and Niagara Falls International Bridge Companies*, 1 May 1855 (Rochester, NY: Steam Press of Lee, Mann & Co., 1855); *Report of John A. Roebling, Civil Engineer, to the presidents and directors of the Niagara Falls Suspension and Niagara Falls International Bridge Companies, on the condition of the Niagara Railway Suspension Bridge*, 1 August 1860 (Trenten, NJ: Murphy & Bechtel, 1860).

25   Walt Whitman, 'Seeing Niagara to Advantage', in *Specimen Days & Collect* (Philadelphia: Rees Welsh & Co., 1882); Mark Twain, *Sketches, New and Old* (Hartford / Chicago: The American Publishing Company, 1887), p. 64.

26   *History of Niagara County, N. Y., with Illustrations Descriptive of its Scenery, Private Residences, Public Buildings, Fine Blocks, and Important Manufactories, and Portraits of Old Pioneers and Prominent Residents* (New York: Sanford& Co., 1878), p. 323.

27   Author not named, 'Railway Engineering in the United States', *The Atlantic Monthly* 2, no. 13 (November 1858): 648.

28   Jackson, *The Mighty Niagara*, p. 55 ff.; *Great Lakes: An Environmental Atlas and Resource Book* (Chicago, IL: Great Lakes National Program Office, U.S. Environmental Protection Agency, 1987).

29   For more details, see Merton Merriman Wilner, *Niagara Frontier: A Narrative and Documentary History*, 4 volumes. (Chicago, IL: The S.J. Clarke Publishing Co., 1931); Laurence M. Hauptman, *Conspiracy of Interests: Iroquois Dispossession and the Rise of*

## Notes

*New York State* (Syracuse, NY: Syracuse University Press, 1999); William Wyckoff, *The Developer's Frontier: The Making of the Western New York Landscape* (New Haven: Yale University Press, 1988); Douglas Farley, 'Bath Island', *Niagara County Historical Society's Bicentennial Moments*: http://www.niagara2008.com/history54.html (accessed 1 Nov. 2020); William R. Irwin, *The New Niagara: Tourism, Technology, and the Landscape of Niagara Falls 1776–1917* (University Park, PA: Pennsylvania State University Press, 1996), p. 11 f.

30   Pierre Berton, *Niagara: A History of the Falls* (Toronto: McClelland & Stewart, 1992), pp. 242–75.

31   Berton, *Niagara*, p. 55 ff.; Ginger G. Strand, *Inventing Niagara: Beauty, Power and Lies* (New York et al.: Simon and Schuster, 2009), pp. 63–69.

32   Strand, *Inventing Niagara*, pp. 69-71. The blog of artist Gerry Biron shows a series of 19th-century daguerreotypes. See Gerry Biron, 'Niagara Falls and Tuscarora Beadwork', Historic Iroquois and Wabanaki Beadwork, last amended on 31 May 2011: http://iroquoisbeadwork.blogspot.com/2011/05/niagara-fallsand-tuscarora-beadwork.html; see also the photos in Paul Gromosiak and Christopher Stoianoff, *Niagara Falls: 1850–2000* (Charleston, SC: Arcadia Publishing, 1996), p. 10 and passim. Quoted from Frederic D. Schwarz, 'Niagara Falls: For Two Hundred Years It's Been Attracting Tourists – and Tourist Traps', *American Heritage*, **48** (5) (Sept. 1997); Daniel M. Dumych, *Niagara Falls*, vol. 2 (Mount Pleasant, SC: Arcadia Publishing, 1998), p. 11.

33   Frederick Law Olmsted, 'Notes', in *Special Report of the New York State Survey on the Preservation of the Scenery of Niagara Falls* (Albany: State of New York, 1880), pp. 28–29; Francis R. Kowsky, *The Best Planned City in the World: Olmsted, Vaux, and the Buffalo Park System* (Amherst, MA: University of Massachusetts Press, 2013), p. 153 ff.; Strand, *Inventing Niagara*, p. 141 ff.

34   Frederick Law Olmsted, *General Plan for the Improvement of the Niagara Reservation* (Niagara Falls: Gazette Book and Job Office, 1887), retrievable online: http://www.niagaraheritage.org/genplan.htm

35   Frederick Law Olmsted, 'Public Parks and the Enlargement of Towns', *Journal of Social Science* **3** (1871): 1–36.

36   Berton, *Niagara*, p. 112 ff.; Strand, *Inventing Niagara*, p. 142 f.; Kowsky, *The Best Planned City*, p. 164.

37   'An act to authorize the selection, location and appropriation of certain lands in the village of Niagara Falls for a state reservation and to preserve the scenery of the falls of Niagara'. *The General Statutes of the State of New York for the Year 1883* (Albany, NY: Weed, Parsons and Company, 1883), pp. 155–57.

38   F.A. de Chateaubriand, *Recollections of Italy, England and America*, vol. 1 (London: Colburn, 1815), p. 185; [George Campbell] Duke of Argyll, 'First Impressions of the New World', *Living Age* **144** (1) (1880): 38.

39   Strand, *Inventing Niagara*, p. 155.

40   Olmsted, *General Plan for the Improvement of the Niagara Reservation*; Strand, *Inventing Niagara*, p. 144 f.; Kowsky, *The Best Planned City*, pp. 168–77.

## Notes

41 Geoffrey Blodgett, 'Landscape Design as Conservative Reform', in *Art of the Olmsted Landscape*, ed. by Bruce Kelly, Gail Travis Guillet and Mary Ellen W. Hern (New York: New York City Landmarks Preservation Commission, Arts Publisher, 1981), pp. 111–39.

42 *The New York Times*, 15–16 July 1885, quoted in Stradling, *The Nature of New York*, p. 96.

43 Roy Rosenzweig and Elizabeth Blackmar, *The Park and the People: A History of Central Park* (Ithaca, NY: Cornell University Press, 1992). Interview by Christof Mauch with August Heckscher, 3 July 1997 in New York City; Christof Mauch with Elizabeth Barlow Rogers, 3 Dec. 2005 in Washington, D.C.; Irwin, *The New Niagara*, p. 86.

44 Dirk Vanderwilt, *Niagara Falls: With the Niagara Parks, Clifton Hill, and Other Area Attractions* (New York: Channel Lake, Inc., 2010), p. 35; Strand, *Inventing Niagara*, p. 146 f., p. 153.

45 Irwin, *The New Niagara*, p. 86; information from the Visitor Center, Niagara Falls State Park.

46 William T. Love, Model City: *The New Manufacturing Center of America* (Buffalo, NY: Niagara Power & Development Co., n.d. [1901]), pp. 5–11; Love, *Description and Plan of the Model City Located at Lewistown, Niagara County, NY. Chartered by Special Act of the New York Legislature, designed to be the most Perfect City in Existence* (Lewistown, NY: The Model Town Company, 1893), pp. 9, 22–24; Love, *Power Revolution: The Foreword of a Proposed World Movement to Solve the Labor and other Social Problems of Our Strenuous Times* (San Francisco: The Aragain Co., n.d. [1905]); Richard S. Newman, *Love Canal: A Toxic History from Colonial Times to the Present* (New York: Oxford University Press, 2016), p. 38 f.

47 *Love Canal, Public Health Time Bomb: A Special Report to the Governor and Legislature* (Albany, NY: The Office of Public Health, September 1978), p. 2. https://www.health.ny.gov/environmental/investigations/love_canal/docs/lctimbmb.pdf

48 William T. Love, *Model City: Niagara Power Doubled* (Lewistown, 1893), p. 1, quoted in Newman, *Love Canal*, p. 41.

49 Robert E. Thomas, *Salt & Water, Power & People: A Short History of Hooker Electrochemical Company* (Niagara Falls, NY: Hooker Chemical Co., 1955); Newman, *Love Canal*, pp. 66–90.

50 Those critical of Hooker Chemicals include Michael H. Brown and Lois Gibbs: see Michael Harold Brown, *Laying Waste: The Poisoning of America by Toxic Chemicals* (New York: Pantheon Books, 1980); Lois Marie Gibbs, *Love Canal: My Story, as Told to Murray Levine* (Albany: State University of New York Press, 1982); Critical of Niagara Falls city government or the Board of Education is Eric Zuesse, 'Love Canal: The Truth Seeps Out', *Reason*, Feb. 1981: https://reason.com/1981/02/01/love-canal/

51 See Newman, *Love Canal*, p. 178–84.

52 'Comprehensive Environmental Response, Compensation, and Liability Act', *Pub. L. 96–510*, 11 Dec. 1980. 42 U. S. C. § 9601 p. ff.

53 Newman, *Love Canal*, p. 102.

## Notes

54 Interview with anonymous resident of Vincent Morello Senior Housing, Niagara Falls in April 2012.

55 United States Environmental Protection Agency, *Superfund: National Priorities List (NPL)*: https://www.epa.gov/superfund/superfund-national-priorities-list-npl (accessed 1 Nov. 2020). The official records of the Love Canal Area Revitalization Agency (LCARA) are located in the State University of New York at Buffalo Manuscript and Library Collections, LCARA Records Collection, Box: 1–19, MC 4.12, MC 4.13; Newman, *Love Canal*, p. 189 ff., p. 252 f. There is no commemorative plaque but there is a granite stone several blocks from the former landfill to mark the success of the clean-up operation.

56 Ginger Strand, 'Designing a Natural Wonder': http://gingerstrand.com/niagara_designing.htm (accessed 1 Nov. 2020).

57 Rob Nixon, *Slow Violence and the Environmentalism of the Poor* (Cambridge, MA: Harvard University Press, 2011).

58 Even more so than for Love Canal, this is true for the landfill in Hyde Park, Niagara Falls, from which dioxin wastes from the Hooker Chemicals Company leaked into the Niagara Gorge via Bloody Run Creek. See Newman, *Love Canal*, p. 189.

59 See Irwin, *The New Niagara*, passim. The term 'technological sublime' goes back to Perry Miller but was popularised by David Nye. David E. Nye, *American Technological Sublime* (Cambridge, MA: MIT Press, 1994).

60 Christof Mauch, *Slow Hope: Rethinking Ecologies of Crisis and Fear* (Munich: Rachel Carson Center, 2019).

61 Former US presidential candidate George McGovern reported that piles of Rachel Carson's *Silent Spring* could be found in US bookstores and that the inadequacy of 'conservation' as opposed to 'environmentalism' slowly became apparent. George McGovern in conversation with Christof Mauch, Munich, 17 Oct. 2011; Rachel Carson, *Silent Spring* (Boston: Houghton Mifflin, 1962).

62 Both places are highly evocative and have captured the imagination of writers, including Joyce Carol Oates. In her novel *The Falls* a man on honeymoon plunges to his death in Niagara Falls. Later, the heroine's new husband acts as an attorney for the Love Canal plaintiffs. See Joyce Carol Oates, *The Falls* (New York: Ecco, 2004).

## Disneyworld, Florida. At Least Two Natures

1 These figures are valid for 2015 to 2019; there was a massive decline for 2020 and 2021 due to the COVID-19 pandemic. But numbers started going up again in 2022.

2 Mark Derr, *Some Kind of Paradise: A Chronicle of Man and the Land in Florida* (Gainesville, FL.: University Press of Florida, 1998), pp. 381–83.

3 Kevin Archer, 'The Limits to the Imagineered City: Sociospatial Polarization in Orlando', *Economic Geography* **73** (3) (1997): 322–36.

4 See Xander Peters, 'Orlando Ranked among Top Murder Capitals in America', *Orlando Weekly*, 14 Feb. 2018: https://www.orlandoweekly.com/blogs/archives/2018/02/14/

Orlando-Ranked-Among-top-murder-capitals-in-America. Depending on crime statistics, Orlando is sometimes lower in ranking, but always in the top twenty.

5   Archer, 'The Limits to the Imagineered City'.
6   Reinhold Reitberger, *Walt Disney. Mit Selbstzeugnissen und Bilddokumenten* (Reinbek: Rowohlt, 6th ed. 2010), 14 f.; Richard E. Foglesong, *Married to the Mouse: Walt Disney World and Orlando* (New Haven, CT: Yale University Press, 2001), p. 15; James Clark, 'The Day JFK died, Walt Disney Discovered Orlando', *Orlando Sentinel*, 21 Nov. 2013; John McAleenan, 'Building the New World', *Florida Magazine. Orlando Sentinel*, 10 April 1988.
7   Sam Gennawey, *Walt Disney and the Promise of Progress City* (Orlando, FL: Theme Park Press, 2011), p. xiii.
8   According to Disney management: 'What Happens After You Go to the Restroom at Walt Disney World is Pretty Amazing', Theme Park Tourist, 7 April 2016: https://www.themeparktourist.com/features/20160407/31864/what-happens-after-you-gobathroomy-walt-disney-world-pretty-amazing
9   See Chris Wright, 'Natural and Social Order at Walt Disney World: The Functions and Contradictions of Civilising Nature', *The Sociological Review* **54** (2) (2006): 303–17.
10  Arthur L. Putnam, *Summary of Hydrologic Conditions and Effects of Walt Disney World Development in the Reedy Creek Improvement District, 1966–73: Open-File Report 74-339* (Washington, D.C.: United States Geological Survey (USGS), 1974), pp. 3–7; Interview Martin Reuss with William E. Potter, Orlando, FL, Feb. 1981: *Engineer Memoirs: Major General William E. Potter* EP 870 1–2, Washington, D.C.: US Army Corps of Engineers. Office of the Chief Historian July 1983 (typescript), IX, 76, pp. 187–98; William Patrick Hightower, *Disney and the Domestication of Nature*. MA Thesis (Tallahassee: The Florida State University. College of Arts and Sciences, 2004), p. 39 f.; Steve Mannheim, *Walt Disney and the Quest for Community* (New York: Routledge, 2002), pp. 67–82.
11  Debbie Salamone, 'The Human Thirst', *Orlando Sentinel*, 7 April 2002; Edward R. German, *Summary of Hydrologic Conditions in the Reedy Creek Improvement District, Central Florida* (Tallahassee, FL: US Geological Survey Water-Resources Investigations Report, 1986); Ann Vileisis, *Discovering the Unknown Landscape: A History of America's Wetlands* (Washington, D.C.: Island Press, 1997), p. 226. The data disseminated via Disney media can only be verified to a very limited extent.
12  Visitors obviously contribute to Disney Corporation's sales of nearly ten billion dollars in 2019 with consumer goods alone, such as memorabilia and fabric figures. 'Revenue of the Walt Disney Company in the fiscal year 2019, by operating segment', Statista: https://www.statista.com/statistics/193140/reve nue-of-the-walt-disney-company-by-operating-segment/ (accessed 22 June 2020).
13  Umberto Eco, *Travels in Hyper Reality* (New York: Harcourt Brace Jovanovich, 1986), p. 43.
14  Melody Malmberg, *The Making of Disney's Animal Kingdom Theme Park* (New York: Hyperion, 1998), p. 38 f., p. 120. Malmberg's publication is a detailed, official presentation (approved by Disney Corporation).

## Notes

15 Malmberg, *The Making of Disney's Animal Kingdom*, p. 109. See also Susan Willis, 'Disney's Bestiary', in *Rethinking Disney: Private Control, Public Dimensions*, ed. by Mike Budd and Max H. Kirsch (Middletown, CT: Wesleyan University Press, 2005), pp. 53–74, p. 55. See also, below, Scott Hermanson, 'Truer than Life: Disney's Animal Kingdom', in ibid., pp. 199–230.

16 Richard Schickel, *The Disney Version: The Life, Times, Art and Commerce of Walt Disney* (Chicago: Elephant Paperbacks, 1997), p. 51; Hightower, *Disney and the Domestication of Nature*, pp. 28, 30–32; Tom Turner, *David Brower: The Making of the Environmental Movement* (Oakland, CA: University of California Press, 2015), p. 115 f.; *US Congressional Record: Proceedings and Debates of the 91st Congress, First Session*, 5 Feb. 1969 to 21 Feb. 1969, Volume 115, Part 3 (Washington, D.C.: US GPO, 1969), p. 3479.

17 Jan-Erik Steinkrüger, *Thematisierte Welten: Über Darstellungspraxen in Zoologischen Gärten und Vergnügungsparks* (Bielefeld: transcript, 2013), p. 279–85.

18 In 2011, the *Los Angeles Times* reported that *Avatar* had grossed $2.8 billion worldwide. 'Disney to license rights to *Avatar* for theme park attractions', *Los Angeles Times*, 21 Sept. 2011.

19 Rohde, quoted in 'Disney's Intergalactic Theme Park Quest to Beat Harry Potter', *Bloomberg*, 19 April 2017. See also *Pandora: The World of Avatar: A Complete Guide* (no author, n.d., Disney at Work); 'New Disney Patents Hint at Bioluminescent Plants in Avatar Attraction', *Entertainment Designer*, 11 Aug. 2016.

20 Hermanson, 'Truer than Life', p. 223; Jennifer Allen, 'Brave New Epcot', *New York Magazine*, 20 Dec. 1982, pp. 40–44.

21 John Beardsley, 'A Mickey Mouse Utopia', *Landscape Architecture Magazine* 87 (2) (1997), pp. 76–83, 92–93; Kevin Archer, 'Disneyfication of Central Florida', in *The New Encyclopedia of Southern Culture*, vol. 2, ed. Richard Pillsbury (Chapel Hill, NC: University of North Carolina Press, 2006), p. 48 f.; Tarpley Hitt, 'Celebration, Florida: How Disney's "Community of Tomorrow" Become a Total Nightmare', *The Daily Beast*, 26 Dec.2010; 'What Disney's City of the Future, Built to Look Like the Past, Says About the Present', *The Economist*, 24 Dec. 2016; *Celebration Florida Friendly Pattern Book* (Celebration, FL: Dix-Lathrop, July 2012); See also Frank Roost, *Die Disneyfizierung der Städte: Großprojekte der Entertainmentindustrie am Beispiel des New Yorker Times Square und der Siedlung Celebration in Florida* (Wiesbaden: VS Verlag für Sozialwissenschaften, 2000).

22 Hugh L. Willoughby, *Across the Everglades: A Canoe Journey of Exploration* (Port Salerno, FL: Florida Classics Library, 1992), p. 13.

23 David McCally, *The Everglades: An Environmental History* (Gainesville, FL: University Press of Florida, 1999); Thomas E. Lodge, *The Everglades Handbook: Understanding the Ecosystem* (Boca Raton, FL: CRC Press, 2017).

24 John T. Stewart, *Report on Everglades Drainage Project in Lee and Dade Counties, Florida. January to May 1907* (Washington, D.C.: US Department of Agriculture, 1907), p. 68.

25 Robin C. Brown, *Florida's First People: 12,000 Years of Human History* (Sarasota, FL: Pineapple Press 1994), p. 31–38; Darcie A. MacMahon and William H. Marquardt, *The Calusa and Their Legacy: South Florida People and Their Environments* (Gainesville, FL:

University Press of Florida, 2004), p. 1 f., p. 69 ff.; Frederick T. Davis, 'Juan Ponce de Leon's Voyages to Florida: Source Records', *Florida Historical Society Quarterly* **14** (1) (1935): 3–70. After being expelled by the Calusa during his first visit, Ponce de León returned in 1521 to colonise Florida. Instead, he was hit in the thigh by a poisonous arrow, fled to Cuba and died shortly afterwards as a result of the injury.

26  John Missall and Mary Lou Missall, *The Seminole Wars: America's Longest Indian Conflict* (Gainesville, FL: University Press of Florida, 2004). See also Robert H. Keller and Michael F. Turek, *American Indians and National Parks* (Tucson, AZ: The University of Arizona Press, 1998), pp. 216–31.

27  'Buying Four Million Acres: An Immense Sale of Land by the State of Florida', *The New York Times*, 17 June 1881. A separate chapter on Hamilton Disston can be found in Jack E. Davis, *An Everglades Providence: Marjory Stoneman Douglas and the American Environmental Century* (Athens, GA: University of Georgia Press, 2004), pp. 81–89; Michael Grunwald, *The Swamp: The Everglades, Florida, and the Politics of Paradise* (New York et al.: Simon and Schuster, 2007), p. 89 ff.; Karl Hiram Grismer, *The Story of Fort Myers: The History of the Land of the Caloosahatchee and Southwest Florida* (St. Petersburg, FL: St. Petersburg Printing Co., 1949), p. 105; Christopher Knowlton, *Bubble in the Sun: The Florida Boom of the 1920s and How It Brought on the Great Depression* (New York: Simon and Schuster, 2020), p. 343, fn. 23.

28  Disston's suicide is considered controversial. I follow the research and opinion offered in Davis, *An Everglades Providence*, p. 88.

29  For hotels, see the richly illustrated publication by R. Wayne Ayers, *Florida's Grand Hotels from the Gilded Age* (Charleston, SC: Arcadia Publishing, 2005); for Flagler's biography, see Les Standiford, *Last Train to Paradise: Henry Flagler and the Spectacular Rise and Fall of the Railroad that Crossed the Ocean* (New York: Broadway Books, 2002).

30  Charles Torrey Simpson, *In Lower Florida Wilds: A Naturalist's Observations on the Life, Physical Geography, and Geology of the More Tropical Part of the State* (New York, London: G. P. Putnam's Sons, 1920), p. 45; Davis, *An Everglades Providence*, pp. 120–22. The quote on the annexation of the moon can be found in many places in secondary literature, e.g. in Samuel Proctor, *Napoleon Bonapart Broward: Florida's Fighting Democrat* (Gainesville. University of Florida Press, 1993), p. 230; an original source could not be found.

31  McCally, *The Everglades*, p. 168. On Miami, see J. Kenneth Ballinger, *Miami Millions: The Dance of the Dollars in the Great Florida Land Boom of 1925* (Miami, FL: The Franklin Press, 1936); on Hollywood, see in particular the website of the Hollywood Historical Society: http://www.hollywoodhistoricalsociety.org/; Susan Gillis, *Boomtime Boca: Boca Raton in the 1920s* (Charleston, SC: Arcadia Press, 2007); Donald W. Curl, 'Boca Raton and the Florida Land Boom of the 1920s', *Tequesta* 46 (1986): 20–33; on Coral Gables, see Linda K. Williams and Paul S. George, 'South Florida: A Brief History', Historical Museum of Southern Florida: https://web.archive.org/web/20100429002717/http://www.hmsf.org/history/south-florida-brief-history.htm (accessed 22 June 2020); Keller and Turek, *American Indians*, p. 226 f.; Robert S. Carr and Timothy A. Harrington, *The Everglades* (Charleston, SC: Arcadia Publishing, 2012), pp. 17–26.

## Notes

32  Raymond O. Arsenault, 'The Public Storm: Hurricanes and the State in Twentieth-Century America', in *Paradise Lost? The Environmental History of Florida*, ed. by Jack E. Davis and Raymond O. Arsenault (Gainesville, FL: University Press of Florida, 2005), pp. 201–32, p. 210; Jay Barnes, *Florida's Hurricane History* (Chapel Hill, NC: University of North Carolina Press, 1998), pp. 111–26, 363–426; Carr and Harrington, *The Everglades*, p. 74.

33  Ernest Hemingway, 'Who Murdered the Vets?' *New Masses*, 17 Sept. 1935, pp. 9–10; Standiford, *Last Train to Paradise*, pp. 225–54.

34  Grunwald, *The Swamp*, p. 218 f.

35  McCally, *The Everglades*, p. 150; Vileisis, *Discovering the Unknown Landscape*, pp. 231–35; Derr, *Some Kind of Paradise*, p. 316 ff., p. 357; John McPhee, *Oranges* (New York: Noonday Press, 1991), p. 17 ff.

36  I found large orange plantations north and west of Lake Okeechobee. On the history, see Christian Warren, 'Nature's Navels: An Overview of the Many Environmental Histories of Florida Citrus', in Davis and Arsenault, *Paradise Lost?*, pp. 177–200; harvest figures can be found in the statistics of the United States Department of Agriculture – see the summary by Mark Hudson (Florida State Statistician), 'Agriculture in the Sunshine State', *National Agricultural Statistics Service in Research and Science*, 15 Oct. 2019: https://www.usda.gov/media/blog/2019/10/15/agriculture-sunshine-state

37  Harriet Beecher Stowe, *Palmetto-Leaves* (Gainesville, FL: University of Florida Press, 1968), p. 18; Shana Klein, 'Those Golden Balls Down Yonder Tree: Oranges and the Politics of Reconstruction in Harriet Beecher Stowe's Florida', *Southern Cultures* 23 (3) (2017): 30–38; Warren, 'Nature's Navels', p. 185 f.

38  Hudson, 'Agriculture in the Sunshine State'.

39  Derr, *Some Kind of Paradise*, pp. 97–100, 320. Alan W. Hodges, Christa D. Court, Mohammad Rahmani and Caleb A. Stair, *Economic Contributions of Beef and Dairy Cattle and Allied Industries in Florida in 2017. Sponsored Project Report to the Florida Cattlemen's Association and Florida Dairy Farmers* (Gainesville, FL: University of Florida-IFAS, Food and Resource Economics Department, 2019), p. 5. On citrus production, see Adam Putnam, *Florida Citrus Production 2016–2017* (Tallahassee, FL: Florida Department of Agriculture and Consumer Services, 2017), p. 6.

40  Mark Tutton, 'Iggy Pop: "I Was Looking for an Elegant Coma"', *CNN*, 3 Dec. 2008: https://edition.cnn.com/2008/TRAVEL/12/03/iggy.interview.miami/index.html

41  Lodge, *The Everglades*, p. 157 f.

42  Mark Derr, 'Redeeming the Everglades', *Audubon* 95 (1993): 48–56; Vileisis, *Discovering the Unknown Landscape*, p. 312 f.; Grunwald, *The Swamp*, pp. 281–83; Lodge, *The Everglades*, p. 331 f.

43  J.S. Adams, 'The Case Against "Black Snow": Chronic Health Problems Force Residents to Take a Stand Against Florida's Sugar Industry', *Florida Courier*, 21 July 2019. On the working conditions of the cane cutters from a historical perspective, see McCally, *The Everglades*, pp. 164–70.

44  J.E. Hoffmeister, K.W. Stockman and H.G. Multer, 'Miami Limestone of Florida and Its Recent Bahamian Counterpart', *Geological Society of America Bulletin* 78 (2) (1967): 175–90; Grunwald, *The Swamp*, pp. 179, 229 ff.

# Notes

45  Joseph Reese, *History of the Tamiami Trail and a Brief Review of the Road Construction Movement in Florida* (Miami, FL: Tamiami Trail Commissioners Movement of Dave County, FL, 1928), pp. 4–7, 13 ff.; Gary Garrett, 'Blasting Through Paradise: The Construction and Consequences of the Tamiami Trail', in Davis and Arsenault, *Paradise Lost?*, pp. 260–79.

46  Marjory Stoneman Douglas, *Voice of the River* (Sarasota, FL: Pineapple Press, 2011), p. 191.

47  John C. Gifford., *The Everglades and Other Essays Relating to Southern Florida* (Kansas City, MO: Everglade Land Sales Co., 1911); Derr, *Some Kind of Paradise*, pp. 57–58; Lodge, *The Everglades*, pp. 352–56.

48  Mount Rainier National Park was established in 1899 and Grand Teton National Park in 1929. Hal Rothman, *America's National Monuments: The Politics of Preservation* (Lawrence, KS: University of Kansas Press, 1994), p. 171.

49  US Congress, Congressional Record, 73rd Congress, 2nd session, 23 May 1934, p. 9497; Luther J. Carter, *The Florida Experience: Land and Water Policy in a Growth State* (New York: Johns Hopkins University Press, 2011), p. 110.

50  Marjory Stoneman Douglas, 'The Forgotten Man Who Saved the Everglades', *Audubon* 73 (1971): 79–95.

51  Lodge, *The Everglades*, p. 132; Kyle Pierson, 'The Flamingo Lodge: Florida's Mission 66', *Journal of Florida Studies* 1 (8) (2019): 1–19; Carr and Harrington, *The Everglades*, pp. 70–71; Stuart B. McIver, *Death in the Everglades: The Murder of Guy Bradley, America's First Martyr to Environmentalism* (Gainesville, FL: University Press of Florida, 2009); Charlton W. Tebeau, *They Lived in the Park: The Story of Man in the Everglades National Park* (Coral Gables, FL: Everglades Natural History Association, 1963), p. 107.

52  Richard West Sellars, *Preserving Nature in the National Parks* (New Haven and London: Yale University Press, 1997), pp. 180–84; Harry S. Truman, 'Address on Conservation at the Dedication of Everglades National Park', The American Presidency Project: https://www.presidency.ucsb.edu/documents/address-conservation-the-dedication-everglades-nationalpark (accessed 22 June 2020); *US Congressional Record: Proceedings and Debates of the 91st Congress, First Session*, 13 Aug. 1969 to 10 Sept. 1969, Volume 115, Part 18 (Washington, D.C.: US GPO, 1969), p. 24690.

53  Vileisis, *Discovering the Unknown Landscape*, pp. 157–59

54  Conversation with the ornithologist Richard ('Nels') Nelson, 15 Feb. 2016 in Pennyroyal, Australia. 'Florida Nature: Endangered Birds', 19 Aug. 2020: http://www.floridiannature.com/Florida Endangeredbirds.htm; Zenaida Kotala, 'Florida Declared a Global Biodiversity Hotspot', *UCT Today*, 26 February 2016.

55  'Top Ten Florida species that could have gone extinct without the Endangered Species Act, Florida Conservation Voters Education Fund, 22 Aug. 2017: https://www.fcvedfund.org/2017/08/22/top-ten-endangered/'

# Notes

## Portland, Oregon. Travelling through America's Green Future

1. The expression 'America's Greenest City' referring to Portland is widely used, and also features in *The Portland Song* by Jewel Kilcher. Statistics and data on Portland can be found in the online resource library of the website Prosper Portland https://prosperportland.us/resource-library/ (accessed 16 June 2020); information on breweries can be found in Charles Heying's introduction to *Brew to Bikes: Portland's Artisan Economy*, ed. Charles Heying (Portland, Oregon: Ooligan Press, 2010), pp. 13–22. In 2015, there were 78 bicycle manufacturers in Portland according to 'The Economic Impact of the Bicycle Industry in Portland: Technical Report' (Portland, Oregon: Bureau of Planning and Sustainability, 2015): https://www.portland.gov/sites/default/files/2020-02/bicycleindustrytechnical report_2015.pdf (accessed 16 June 2020). Information on its green urban spaces can be found in Michael C. Houck and M.J. Cody (eds), *Wild in the City: Exploring the Intertwine. The Portland-Vancouver Region's Network of Parks, Trails, and Natural Areas* (Corvallis, Orgeon: Oregon State University Press, 2011). I am grateful to Kyle Diesner, Bureau of Planning and Sustainability, City of Portland, for important references he gave me during an interview on 29 March 2016.

2. All the chapters in this book represent particular moments and the author's perceptions at those moments. All the places visited will have changed since these encounters; however, it is worth acknowledging that the situation in Portland has altered drastically since the chapter was conceived in the spring of 2016. After 15 straight years of growth, Portland's population began declining in 2020. It is in 2023 one of the fastest shrinking cities in the USA. For recent developments, see Bill Conerly, 'Death Of A City: The Portland Story?', *Forbes* 18 Jan. 2021.

3. Ernest Hemingway, 'Battle for Paris', *Collier's*, 30 Sept.1944, cited in *By-Line, Ernest Hemingway: Selected Articles and Dispatches of Four Decades*, ed. by William White (London: Collins, 1968); William Yardley, 'In Portland, Cultivating a Culture of Two Wheels', *The New York Times*, 5 Nov. 2007.

4. 'Governor Tom McCall Waterfront Park: Portland, Oregon', Great Places in America, American Planning Association: https://www.planning.org/greatplaces/spaces/2012/tommccall.htm (accessed 16 June 2020); Connie P. Ozawa (ed.), *The Portland Edge: Challenges and Successes in Growing Communities* (Washington, D.C.: Island Press, 2004), pp. 152, 156; Henry Sakamoto, 'Japanese American Historical Plaza (Portland)', *The Oregon Encyclopedia*: https://oregonencyclopedia.org/articles/japanese_american_historical_plaza_portland/ (accessed 16 June 2020); Sakamoto, 'Japantown, Portland (Nihonmachi)', *The Oregon Encyclopedia*: https://oregonencyclopedia.org/articles/japantown_portland_nihonmachi_/ (accessed 16 June 2020).

5. Randy Gragg (ed.), *Where the Revolution Began: Lawrence and Anna Halprin and the Reinvention of Public Space* (Easthampton, MA: Spacemaker Press, 2009); Randy Gragg, 'Urban Plazas that Set Portland's Modern Landscape Get Some TLC', *The Oregonian*, 29 June 2003, A01; Peter Walker and Melanie Simo, *Invisible Gardens: The Search for Modernism in the American Landscape* (Cambridge, MA: The MIT Press, 1994), p. 9.

6. Gary E. Moulton (ed.), *The Lewis and Clark Expedition Day by Day* (Lincoln, NE: University of Nebraska Press, 2018). The over 5,000-page diary of Meriwether Lewis

# Notes

and William Clark is available online: 'Journals of the Lewis and Clark Expedition': https://lewisandclarkjournals.unl.edu/ (accessed 16 June 2020).

7   John Ledyard, cited here in William G. Robbins, *Landscapes of Promise: The Oregon Story 1800–1940* (Seattle, WA: University of Washington Press, 1997), p. 52; see also James Zug (ed.), *The Last Voyage of Captain Cook: The Collected Writings of John Ledyard* (Washington, D.C.: National Geographic, 2005); John Work, quoted from Leslie M. Scott, 'John Work's Journey from Vancouver to Umpqua River, and Return in 1834', *Oregon Historical Quarterly* (1923): 238–68, p. 242; George Emmons quoted from Robert Boyd, 'Strategies of Indian burning in the Willamette Valley', *Canadian Journal of Anthropology* 5 (1986): 65–86, p. 71.

8   Paul Alaback, Joe Antos et al. (eds), *Plants of the Pacific Northwest Coast: Washington, Oregon, British Columbia & Alaska* (Redmond, WA: Lone Pine Publishing, 2004), p. 53; Kathryn Anne Toepel, 'Traditional Lifeways: The Western interior', in *The First Oregonians: An Illustrated Collection of Essays on Traditional Lifeways, Federal-Indian Relations, and the State's Native Peoples Today*, ed. by Carolyn M. Buan and Richard Lewis (Portland: Oregon Council for the Humanities, 1991), pp. 15–20; Robbins, *Landscapes of Promise*, p. 35.

9   Boyd, 'Strategies of Indian Burning', p. 67 ff.

10  Robbins, *Landscapes of Promise*, p. 68.

11  Melinda Marie Jetté, 'Beaver are numerous, but the natives ... will not hunt them: Native-fur trader relations in the Willamette Valley, 1812–1814', *Pacific Northwest Quarterly* **98** (1)(Winter 2006/2007): 3–17; David Peterson del Mar, *Oregon's Promise: An Interpretive History* (Corvallis, Oregon: Oregon State University Press, 2003), p. 36 f., p. 42. On disease: Robert T. Boyd, *The Coming of the Spirit of Pestilence: Introduced Infectious Diseases and Population Decline among Northwest Coast Indians, 1774–1874* (Seattle, WA: University of Washington Press, 1999); del Mar, *Oregon's Promise*, p. 27–29; Carl Abbott, *Greater Portland: Urban Life and Landscape in the Pacific Northwest* (Philadelphia: University of Pennsylvania Press, 2001), p. 33; on the global context of malaria: John R. McNeill, *Mosquito Empires: Ecology and War in the Greater Caribbean, 1620–1914* (Cambridge: Cambridge University Press, 2010).

12  Moulton, *The Lewis and Clark Expedition Day by Day*; on Watkuweis, del Mar, *Oregon's Promise*, pp. 36–37; Richard White, 'Discovering Nature in North America', *The Journal of American History* **79** (3) (1992): 874–91, p. 888.

13  *Congressional Globe*, 29th Cong., 1st Session (1845–46), pp. 338–42 (9 Feb. 1846). See also Adams, *Memoirs* 12: p. 259, 27 April 1846.

14  Bethany Nemec, 'Early Towns and Cities: From Robin's Nest to Stumptown', *Oregon Trail History*, 23 Nov. 2016; Carl Abbott, *Portland in Three Centuries: The Place and the People* (Corvallis, OR: Oregon State University Press, 2011), p. 20.

15  See Dorothy O. Johansen and Charles M. Gates, *Empire of the Columbia: A History of the Pacific Northwest* (New York: Harper and Row, 2nd ed., 1957), p. 279

16  On Portland's early history, see Abbott, *Portland in Three Centuries*, p. 20. In 1846, Oregon comprised three later states: Idaho, Washington and Oregon.

17  On 'Oregon's first millionaire-making machine', see Abbot, *Portland in Three Centuries*, p. 36 f.

## Notes

18  Unlike other cities in the Northwest of the USA, with the exception of San Francisco, Portland's population around 1900 had a high proportion of Chinese and Europeans. Businesses were firmly in the hands of people from Eastern or Midwest USA, Great Britain and not least from Germany. Germans even maintained two newspapers in Portland in their language: the *Deutsche Zeitung* and the *Staatszeitung*. 'Mining in Idaho' (Boise, ID: Idaho State Historical Society, 1985 [ISHS Reference Series 9]); on the telegraph and the railroad: Abbott, *Portland in Three Centuries*, pp. 38–39; on population. ibid, p. 49; Flora Belle Ludington, 'The Newspapers of Oregon. 1846-1870', *The Quarterly of the Oregon Historical Society* **26** (3) (1925): 229–62; *Pacific States Newspaper Directory* (San Francisco: Palmer & Rey, 6th edition, 1894), p. 97.

19  River tour on board the *Willamette Star* from St John's Bridge to Ross Island during the ASEH conference with Carl Abbott (Portland State University), Jorge Guadalupe Lizárraga (Washington State University – Vancouver), Mike Houck (Urban Green Spaces), Steven Kolmes (University of Portland), Bob Salinger (Audubon Society) and Joseph Taylor (Simon Fraser University / University of Portland), among others, Portland, 10 March 2010.

20  Florence Riddle, 'The Changing Fortunes of the Lower Willamette River', in Houck and Cody, *Wild in the City*, pp. 35–37; Abbott, *Greater Portland*, pp. 42–45; George Kramer, *It Takes More than Bullets: The WWII Homefront in Portland, Oregon* (Eugene, OR: Heritage Research Associates, 2006); Amy Kesselman, *Fleeting Opportunities: Women Shipyard Workers in Portland and Vancouver During World War II and Reconversion* (Albany, NY: SUNY Press, 1994); Manly Maben, *Vanport* (Portland: Oregon Historical Society Press, 1987).

21  Julia Rosen, 'A City's Lifeblood', *Oregon Humanities*, 22 Aug. 2017: https://oregonhumanities.org/rll/magazine/claim-summer-2017/a-citys-lifeblood/ (accessed 17 June 2020); 'Portland Harbor Superfund Site: Health Assessment Summary', Public Health, Oregon Health Authority, 7 July 2014 (=OHA 8618): https://www.oregon.gov/oha/PH/HEALTHYENVIRONMENTS/TRACKINGASSESSMENT/ENVIRONMENTALHEALTHASSESSMENT/Documents/PHarbor-RecreationalUserSummary_2014.pdf (accessed 17 June 2020); Cassandra Profita, 'A Guide to the Portland Harbor Superfund Site', *Ecotrope*, 26 Sept. 2012.

22  'Ready for Willamette River Swimming, Boating, and Playing?' *The City of Portland Oregon: Environmental Services News Release*, 18 June 2018: https://www.portlandoregon.gov/bes/article/688669 (accessed 17 June 2020); Beth Slovic, 'Portland's $1.4 Billion Big Pipe Project Comes to an End after 20 Years', *The Oregonian*, 27 Nov. 2011, https://www.oregonlive.com

23  'The 15 Coolest Neighborhoods in the World in 2018', *How I Travel*, 10 March 2016: https://www.howitravel.co/the-15-coolest-neighborhoods-in-the-world-in-2016/ ; 'The Pearl District: An Urban Development Case Study of the Pearl District and Brewery Blocks in Portland, Oregon' (CBC's Green and Smart Urban Development Guidelines) Oct. 2015, unpublished manuscript.

24  *Resource Guide for Bird-Friendly Building Design* (Portland, OR: Audubon Society of Portland, 2012); 'Swift Watch', Portland Audubon: https://audubonportland.org/local-birding/swiftwatch (accessed 17 June 2020); 'Backyard Habitat Certification Program', Portland Audubon: https://audubonportland.org/issues/backyardhabitat (accessed 17

June 2020); Rachel Carson, *The Silent Spring* (Houghton & Mifflin, MASS., 1962); Katy Muldoon, 'Once Endangered, Peregrine Falcons Thrive in Portland's Urban Landscape, Audubon Says', *The Oregonian*, 16 April 2011: https://www.oregonlive.com/portland/2011/04/peregrine_falcons_find_portlan.html

25  Houck and Cody, *Wild in the City*, pp. 68–73.
26  Conversation with Michael C. Houck in Portland, Oregon 23 March 2010. The Oaks Bottom Habitat Enhancement Project, City of Portland Environmental Services, has information on the 9-million-dollar project to build a canal for salmon, jointly funded by the US Army Corps of Engineers and the City of Portland: https://www.portlandoregon.gov/bes/76508 (accessed 16 June 2020).
27  Michael C. Houck, 'Portland, City of Herons', in Houck and Cody, *Wild in the City*, pp. 78–80; Carl Abbott, 'Urbanism and Environment in Portland's Sense of Place', *Yearbook of the Association of Pacific Coast Geographers* 66 (2004): 120–27, p. 121; Joe Fitzgibbon, 'Native Birds Take Wing in a Mammoth Mural', *The Oregonian (Special Issue)*, 27 Sept. 2009: https://www.oregonlive.com/portland/2009/09/native_birds_take_wing_in_a_ma.html
28  See also the street magazine *Streetroots News*, which is firmly committed to social and ecological justice and exposes discrimination against minorities. 'This Land is your Land … The Efforts to make Portland's Brown Fields Viable', *Streetroots*, 27 Aug. 2014: https://news.streetroots.org/2014/08/27/land-your-land-efforts-make-portlandsbrownfields-viable
29  Mansel G. Blackford, *The Lost Dream: Businessmen and City Planning on the Pacific Coast, 1890–1920* (Columbus, OH: Ohio State University Press, 1993), p. 129 f.
30  David C. Streatfield, 'John Charles Olmsted's Northwest Legacy', in Joan Hockaday, *Greenscapes: Olmsted's Pacific Northwest* (Pullman, WA: Washington State University Press, 2009), pp. 139–42; Joan Hockaday, 'Introduction: A Life in the Shadow', in ibid., pp. 1–7; on the world fair, Hockaday, *Greenscapes*, pp. 13–16 and illustrations following p. 20; Abbott, *Portland in Three Centuries*, pp. 71–76; Riddle, 'The Changing Fortunes of the Lower Willamette River', p. 36.
31  Hockaday, *Greenscapes*, p. 21.
32  *Report of the Park Board. With the Report of Messrs. Olmsted Bros., Landscapes Architects, Outlining a System of Parkways, Boulevards and Parks for the City of Portland* (Portland, OR: Park Board, 1903); Marcy Cottrell Houle, *One City's Wilderness: Portland's Forest Park* (Portland, OR: Oregon Historical Society, 1988), pp. 36–49; Florence Riddle, 'Forest Park', in Houck and Cody, *Wild in the City*, pp. 117–20.
33  Walter Blucher, quoted from R. Bruce Stephenson, 'A Vision of Green: Lewis Mumford's Legacy in Portland, Oregon', *Journal of the American Planning Association* **65** (3) (1999): 259–69, p. 261; Ben Kizer, quoted from ibid., p. 261; on Mumford, see Donald L. Miller, *Lewis Mumford: A Life* (New York: Weidenfeld and Nicolson, 1989).
34  Lewis Mumford, *The Culture of Cities* (New York: Harcourt, Brace, and Company, 1938); letters from Mumford to Josephine Strongin, 17 and 29 July 1938, here quoted from Stephenson, 'A Vision of Green', p. 262.
35  Lewis Mumford, *Regional Planning in the Pacific Northwest: A Memorandum* (Portland, OR: Northwest Regional Council, 1939), pp. 7–20. See also R. Bruce Stephenson,

## Notes

'Regional Planning and Growth Management in Portland, Oregon', in *Regional Government Innovations: A Handbook for Citizens and Public Officials*, ed. by Roger L. Kemp (Jefferson, NC and London: McFarland & Company, 2003), pp. 179–91.

36 Lewis Mumford, 'Are You Good Enough for Oregon?' *Portland City Club Bulletin* 18 (1938): 26.

37 Sy Adler, 'The Oregon Approach to Integrating Transportation and Land Use Planning', in *Planning the Oregon Way: A Twenty-Year Evaluation*, ed. by Carl Abbott, Deborah Howe and Sy Adler (Corvallis, OR: Oregon State University Press, 1994), pp. 121–46.

38 Floyd J. McKay, *Reporting the Oregon Story: How Activists and Visionaries Transformed a State* (Corvallis, OR: Oregon State University Press, 2016); Martha J. Bianco, 'Robert Moses and Lewis Mumford: Competing Paradigms of Growth in Portland, Oregon', *Planning Perspectives* 16 (2) (2001): 95–114; also biographies such as Tom McCall, *Maverick: An Autobiography* (Hillboro, OR: Binford and Mort, 1977); Charles K. Johnson, *Standing at the Water's Edge: Bob Straub's Battle for the Soul of Oregon* (Corvallis, OR: Oregon State University Press, 2012); Brent Walth, *Fire at Eden's Gate: Tom McCall and the Oregon Story* (Portland, OR: Oregon Historical Society, 1996); Matt Love, *The Far Out Story of Vortex I* (Pacific City, OR: Nestucca Spit Press, 2004).

39 Abbott, *Greater Portland*, pp. 144–48; 'Terrasquirma', in Steven Reed Johnson, *Civic Portland: Specific Institutions*: http://stevenreedjohnson.com/stevenreedjohnson/pdx.Terrasquirma.html (accessed 17 June 2020); Putnam and Feldstein quoted in Steven Reed Johnson, 'The Myth and Reality of Portland's Engaged Citizenry and Process-oriented Government', in Ozawa, *The Portland Edge*, pp. 102–39, at p. 102; on the evaluation of the Labor Press and its leading personalities, see E. Kimbark MacColl, *The Growth of a City: Power and Politics in Portland, Oregon, 1915–1950* (Portland: The Georgian Press, 1978).

40 The original manuscript and an audio recording of the speech are available online: 'Tom McCall's copy of his speech to the Oregon Legislative Assembly, 1973', The Oregon History Project: https://oregonhistoryproject.org/articles/tom-mccalls-copy-of-his-speech-to-the-oregonlegislative-assembly-1973/ (accessed 17 June 2020).

41 See Stephenson, 'A Vision of Green', p. 264; Carl Abbott and Joy Margheim, 'Imagining Portland's Urban Growth Boundary: Planning Regulation as Cultural Icon', in Carl Abbott, *Imagined Frontiers: Contemporary America and Beyond* (Norman, OK: University of Oklahoma Press, 2015), pp. 36–55.

42 Houck and Cody, *Wild in the City*, p. 100 f.; Joseph Poracsky and Michael C. Houck, 'The Metropolitan Portland Urban Natural Resource Program', in *The Ecological City: Preserving and Restoring Urban Biodiversity*, ed. by Rutherford H. Platt, Rowan A. Rowntree and Pamela C. Muick (Amherst, MA: University of Massachusetts Press, 1994), pp. 251–77; Amanda Suutari, 'USA – Oregon (Portland) – Sustainable City', *The EcoTipping Points Project: Models for Success in a Time of Crisis*, June 2006: http://www.ecotippingpoints.org/our-stories/indepth/usa-portland-sustainable-regional-planning.html

43 *Metropolitan Greenspaces* (Portland: Metro, 1991).

44 Bradshaw Hovey, 'Building the City, Structuring Change: Portland's Implicit Utopian Project', *Utopian Studies* 9 (1) (1998): 68–79.

## Notes

45   Ernest Callenbach, *Ecotopia: The Notebooks and Reports of William Weston* (Bantam, Toronto 1975).

46   David Landis Barnhill, 'Conceiving Ecotopia', *Journal for the Study of Religion, Nature and Culture* 5 (2) (2011): 126–44; on the larger context, see James J. Kopp, *Eden Within Eden: Oregon's Utopian Heritage* (Corvallis, OR: Oregon State University Press, 2009).

47   Eleanor Courtemanche, 'Satire and the "Inevitability Effect": The Structure of Utopian Fiction from *Looking Backward* to *Portlandia*', *Modern Language Quarterly* 76 (2) (June 2015): 225–46; James D. Proctor and Evan Berry, 'Ecotopian Exceptionalism', *Journal for the Study of Religion, Nature and Culture* 5 (2) (2011): 145–63.

48   'Raising bees and livestock animals in Portland', The City of Portland, Oregon. Sustainability and Planning: https://www.portlandoregon.gov/bps/article/362065 (accessed 17 June 2020).

49   Laura Cesafsky, 'Brew', in Heying, *Brew to Bikes*, p. 72.

50   'Brewery Count by District and City', The Oregon Brewers Guild: https://oregoncraftbeer.org/facts/ (accessed 17 June 2020).

51   Charles Heying, 'Introduction' and 'Conclusion: Further', in Heying, *Brew to Bikes*, pp. 20, 295–97; Charles Heying and Marianne Ryder 'Genesis of the Concept', in ibid., pp. 23–29. On 'creative city', see Allen J. Scott, 'Creative Cities: Conceptual Issues and Policy Questions', *Journal of Urban Affairs* 28 (1) (2006): 1–17; Charles Landry, *The Creative City: A Toolkit for Urban Innovators* (London: Earthscan, 2001).

52   Elena Torres Ruiz, *The Invention of Urban Farming: How the Food Reform Movement Came to Detroit, 1893–Today*, Inaugural dissertation (Munich, Ludwig Maximilian University 2020).

## Afterword

1   Leopold von Ranke, *Geschichten der romanischen und germanischen Völker: von 1494 bis 1535* (Leipzig: Reimer, 1824, 6th ed.): https://reader.digitale-Sammlungen.de/de/fs1/object/display/bsb10408217_00010.html

2   Christof Mauch, *Notes from the Greenhouse: Making the Case for Environmental History* (Munich: Rachel Carson Center, 2013), pp. 21–23.

3   See William Cronon, *Nature's Metropolis: Chicago and the Great West* (New York/London: W.W. Norton, 1991) 16th ed.

4   See the chapters on Rousseau and Wordsworth in Solnit, *Wanderlust*, p. 14 ff., p. 104 ff. See also Christof Mauch, 'Walking – Driving – Traveling or Why There are no Walkers in America', in *Microlandscapes – Landscape Culture on the Move*, ed. by Brigitte Franzen and Stefanie Krebs (Münster: Westfälische Landesmuseum für Kunst and Cultural History, 2006), pp. 88–100.

5   Hannah Macpherson, 'Walking Methods in Landscape Research: Moving Bodies, Spaces of Disclosure and Rapport', *Landscape Research* 41 (4) (2016): 425–32; Edward Relph, *Place and Placelessness* (London: Pion, 1976); Tim Ingold, 'The Temporality of the Landscape', *World Archaeology* 25 (2) (1993): 152–74. Psychogeography also took a similar, avant-garde approach at the end of the 20th century, including the now

## Notes

discontinued journal *Transgressions: A Journal of Urban Exploration*. See Iain Sinclair and his subversive observations and walks in *London Orbital: A Walk around the M25* (London: Penguin, 2003).

6   Since I sometimes only found sufficient time to write a chapter years after my trip, the visual and acoustic records of the walks and encounters proved indispensable.

7   John Lewis Gaddis, *The Landscape of History: How Historians Map the Past* (Oxford/New York: Oxford University Press, 2002), p. 22 ff

8   Myra J. Hird, 'Volatile Bodies, Volatile Earth: Towards an Ethic of Vulnerability', *RCC Perspectives* 29 (2012): 67–71, p. 69.

9   See also Mauch, *Notes from the Greenhouse*, p. 19 f.

10  See Mary E. Wharton and Roger W. Barbour, *Bluegrass Land and Life: Land Character, Plants, and Animals of the Inner Bluegrass Region of Kentucky, Past, Present and Future* (Lexington, KY: The University Press of Kentucky, 1991), p. 27 f.; Virginia DeJohn Anderson, *Creatures of Empire: How Domestic Animals Transformed Early America* (Oxford: Oxford University Press, 2004); Alfred W. Crosby, *Ecological Imperialism: The Biological Expansion of Europe, 900–1900* (New York: Cambridge University Press, 2nd ed., 2004); Crosby, *The Columbian Exchange: Biological and Cultural Consequences of 1492* (Westport, CT: Praeger, 2003).

11  William Cronon has argued that nature, even in its supposedly most original form, 'wilderness', is a profoundly culturally constructed concept. See William Cronon, 'The Trouble With Wilderness, or, Getting Back to the Wrong Nature', in *Uncommon Ground: Toward Reinventing Nature*, ed. by William Cronon (New York: W.W. Norton, 1995), pp. 69–90.

12  See Donna Haraway, *The Companion Species Manifesto: Dogs, People, and Significant Otherness* (Chicago: Prickly Paradigm Press, 2003). In 2012, the international online journal *NatureCulture* was founded in Japan, combining ethnology with science and technology studies in particular.

13  See also Mohamed El-Kamel Bakari, 'Sustainability and Contemporary Man-Nature Divide: Aspects of Conflict, Alienation, and Beyond', *Consilience: The Journal of Sustainable Development* 13 (1) (2014): 195–216; Franz-Josef Brüggemeier, 'Natur und kulturelle Deutungsmuster. Die Kulturwissenschaft menschlicher Umwelten', in *Handbuch der Kulturwissenschaften Band 1: Grundlagen und Schlüsselbegriffe*, ed. by Friedrich Jaeger and Burkhard Liebsch (Stuttgart: J.B. Metzler, 2011), pp. 65–78.

14  John R. McNeill, 'Observations on the Nature and Culture of Environmental History', *History and Theory* 42 (4) (2003): 5–43; Donald Worster, 'Transformations of the Earth: Toward an Agroecological Perspective in History', *Journal of American History* 76 (4) (1990): 1087–106.

15  Mauch, *Notes from the Greenhouse*, pp. 34–41; Etienne S. Benson, *Surroundings: A History of Environments and Environmentalisms* (London and Chicago: University of Chicago Press, 2020), pp. 1–3; Paul Warde, Libby Robin and Sverker Sörlin, *The Environment: A History of the Idea* (Baltimore, MD: Johns Hopkins University Press, 2018).

16  Rachel Carson, *Silent Spring* (Boston: Houghton Mifflin, 1962).

## Notes

17  Benson, *Surroundings*, pp. 1–5, 193–96; Warde, Robin and Sörlin, *The Environment*. See also Verena Winiwarter and Martin Knoll, *Umweltgeschichte. Eine Einführung* (Cologne/ Weimar/ Vienna: UTB Böhlau, 2007); Bernd Herrmann, *Umweltgeschichte: Eine Einführung in Grundbegriffe* (Berlin: Springer, 2016).

18  Tom Griffiths, *The Art of Time Travel: Historians and their Craft* (Carleton, VIC: Black Inc., 2016), p. 4 f.

19  Sandra Rousseau, and Nikk Deschacht, 'Public Awareness of Nature and the Environment during the COVID-19 Crisis', *Environ Resource Econ* 76: 1149–1159 (2020). https://doi.org/10.1007/s10640-020-00445-w; see also Harald Lesch and Klaus Kamphausen, *Die Menschheit schafft sich ab: Die Erde im Griff des Anthropozän* (Munich: Komplett-Media, 2016).

# Index

**A**
Abbey, Edward 115
Abbott, Carl 210
Abilene, KS 130
Adams, John Quincy 158, 214
Adamson House, Malibu, CA 50, 56
Albany, NY 148, 152
Allegheny Mountains 65
Allis, Samuel 123
Anchorage, AK 14, 27, 33, 38
Anheuser-Busch 84
Ardener, Edwin 26
Arkansas River 127
Arrowhead Trail 97

**B**
Barrett, Nathan Franklin 165
Barton, Benjamin 158
Baxter, Warner 46
Bayer Crop Science 84
Beale Street, Memphis, TN 63, 78–82, 87, 88
Beckmann, Jimbo 222
Beecher Stowe, Harriet 196
Bettles, AK 35
Big Lake, AK 28
Blues Highway 82
Boca Raton, FL 189, 194
Bonaparte, Napoleon 71
Bonneville Dam, OR, WA 226
Boot Hill Museum 131–33
Boreal Mountain, AK 34
Boulder City, NV 100
Boulder Dam 103
Bow, Clara 46
Bradley, Guy 203
Bramlett, Delaney 65
Breck, Charlie 31
Brockman, Ross 31
Brooks, Alfred Hulse 34

Brooks, Mel 46
Brooks Range, AK 10, 14, 28, 33–35
Brosnan, Pierce 57–58
Brower, David 184
Brownell, Leverett White 202
Brown, Michael 167
Buffalo Bill 127
Buffalo, NY 145–48, 151–52, 154, 169
Bunkerville, NV 97
Burnett, Chester Arthur *see* Howling Wolf
Busch, August 176
Butrico, Frank 108

**C**
C-38 (Canal 38), FL 195
Callenbach, Ernest 231–33
Campbell, George John Douglas (Duke of Argyll) 162
Cape Canaveral, FL 174
Caputo, Philip 31
Carlyle, Thomas 161
Carmichael, Stokely 82
Carson, Rachel 9, 76, 171, 222, 244
Carter, Jimmy 23, 34, 76, 168
Cascade Mountain 216
Cash, Johnny 63
Castaic, CA 53
Castro, Fidel 195
Celebration, FL 187–97, 239
Central Park, New York City 160, 162, 223
Chaplin, Charlie 47
Charleston, SC 72
Chateaubriand, François-René de 161
Cheektowaga, NY 148
Chena Hot Springs, AK 17–20
Chickasaw Bluff 66
Chickasaw Nation 70, 73
Chippawa, ON, Canada 148
Chucalissa Site 69–71

291

# Index

Church, Frederic Edwin 161–62, 171
Clark, William 211, 213, 214, 218, 224
Cleveland, Grover 161, 193
Clinton, Hillary 78
Clinton Lake, KS 118
Cody, William Frederick *see* Buffalo Bill
Coe, Ernest F. 202
Coen brothers 48
Colman, Ronald 46
Colorado River 116, 119–123, 126, 132
Columbia River 99, 101–04, 107, 111
Columbus, Christopher 123, 135, 191
Cook, James 211, 212
Cooper, Gary 46–47
Coral Gables, FL 194
Council Grove, KS 121–22, 124
Crespí, Juan 53
Crockett, Davey 180
Cronon, William 39, 150, 249
Crutzen, Paul 245
Cushman, Gregory T. 119

## D

Dalton Highway 15, 15, 20–22, 24, 34, 36–38
Dalton, James W. 22
Darwin, Charles 161
Deadhorse, AK 22
Dellenbaugh, Frederick S. 96
del Río, Dolores 46
DiCaprio, Leonardo 58
Dickinson, Emily 124
Dinosaur, CO 238–39
Disney, Walt 173–76, 180, 184, 187, 189
Disston, Hamilton 191–93
Dockery Plantation, MS 80
Donahue, Phil 167
Doroshin, Peter Petrowitsch 32
Dowdy, Wayne 78, 85, 249
Downey, Roma 46
Dylan, Bob 82–83

## E

Earp, Wyatt 137
Eckert, William 121
Eco, Umberto 181
Edeson, Arthur 47

Edison, Thomas 157
Ellsworth, KS 130
Emerson, Ralph Waldo 161
Emmons, George 212
Erickson, Sheriar 30, 33
Erie Canal 145–48, 150–52, 192
Erie, Lake 146, 157–58
Eugene, OR 216
Everglades 173, 190–95, 198–99, 201–02, 204–05
 Everglades National Park 200–02

## F

Fairbanks, AK 15–21, 28, 32–33, 240
Feldstein, Lewis 229
Flagler, Henry Morrison 193–94, 200, 204
Flagler, Mary Kenan 204
Flamingo, FL 202–04
Flint Hills 118, 124–25, 142
Florida Bay 202
Florida Keys 190, 193–94, 197, 200
Font, Pedro 53
Forest Park, Portland, OR 221, 225
Forrest, Nathan Bedford 86, 88
Fort Erie, ON, Canada 148
Fort Osage, MO 121
Fort Vancouver, WA 214
Franck, Harry A. 19
Frigid Crags, AK 34
Fultz, Francis M. 54

## G

Gaddis, John Lewis 241
Garceau, Dee 82, 249
Gates of the Arctic National Park 13, 33–36
Geffen, David 50–51
Germantown, TN 78, 87
Gibbs, Lois 167–68, 171
Gifford, John Clayton 200
Giles, UT 95
Gird, Richard 44
Glidden, Joseph F. 136–67
Goat Island, Niagara Falls 155, 157–63
Goethe, Johann Wolfgang von 147
Goldschmidt, Neil 230, 235
Gosser, Andrew 55–57
Grand Canyon 65, 96, 104

# Index

Granger, Erastus 151
Graves, Michael 189
Great Plains 70, 86, 118, 119
Green Island, Niagara Falls 157–58
Greensburg, KS 117
Griffiths, Tom 244
Gunther, John 20

## H
Hagman, Larry 46
Halprin, Lawrence 210
Hammond River, AK 30
Handy, W.C. (William Christopher) 79
Hanks, Tom 46, 59
Haraway, Donna 243
Harney, Corbin 110
Harrington, Mark Raymond 97–98
Harris, John S. 75
Harvard, John 44
Heceta, Bruno de 211
Heisig, Johannes 15, 20, 23, 39, 249
Hemingway, Ernest 194, 207
Herodotus 244
Herzl, Theodor 232
Heying, Charles 235
Hickel, Walter 21
Hicker, Bernie 24, 34, 38
Hicker, Uta 24, 34, 38
Hippocrates 243
Hoffman, Dustin 57
Hogan, Mary E. 77
Holliday, Doc (John Henry) 137
Hollywood-by-the-Sea, FL 194
Hollywood 41, 43, 46–48, 51, 55, 58, 60, 92, 117, 131, 133, 134, 173, 176, 237
Homestead, FL 199–200, 204
Hooker, Elon Huntington 166–67
Hoover Dam 92, 99–104, 107, 112, 218
Hoover Dike, FL 197
Hoover, George M. 132
Hopefield, AR 67–68
Horr's Island 191
Houck, Mike 222
Howells, William Dean 161
Howling Wolf 63, 80
Hudson Bay Company 212, 214
Humes, Edward 60

## I
Iggy Pop (James Newell Osterberg Jr.) 197
Imperial Valley, CA 100
Ingold, Tim 240
Ingraham, James 204
Iroquois 149–51
Iroquois Trail 148
Irving, Washington 86
Isenberg, Andrew 117, 249

## J
Jackson, Andrew 73, 86, 158
James, Henry 160
Jarmusch, Jim 60
Jefferson, Thomas 70, 72, 212
Jeffries, Rhonda 127
Jericho, AR 83–84
Johnson, Philip 189
Johnson, Robert 80
Jonas, Florence *see* Kalhabuk
Jones, Art 46
Juneau, AK 32, 35

## K
Kahanamoku, Duke 46
Kaiser, Henry J. 218–19
Kalhabuk 27–29
Kansas City 117–18, 121
Keller, Tait 64, 81
Keller Fountain, Portland, OR 209–10
Kenai Peninsula, AK 16, 32
Kennedy, John F. 174
Kerr, Alfred 145
King, B.B. (Riley B.) 63, 81
King, Martin Luther 63, 80, 82, 89
Kissimmee River 192, 195
Kizer, Ben 229
Knight, Joann 142
Kowee, Tlingit Auke chief 32
Koyukuk River 14
Krakauer, Jon 17

## L
Las Vegas, NV 7, 31, 91–93, 97, 100, 104, 106–15, 164, 237, 240
Lawrence, KS 118
Ledyard, John 212

293

# Index

Lee, George W. 80
Leonard, Harry 32
Lewis, Jerry Lee 63
Lewis, Meriwether 211, 213–14, 218, 224
Lewiston, NY 148
Little Niagara River 169
Lockport, NY 151
Lompoc, CA 53
London, Jack 17
Longfellow, Henry Wadsworth 161
Lord, Hugh 99
Los Alamos, NM 106
Los Angeles, CA 41–45, 50, 52–53, 55, 56, 59, 97, 98, 100, 106, 236, 240
Lost City, NV 97–98, 101, 104
Lounsbury, George 32
Love Canal, NY 8, 145, 155, 164–71, 241, 245
Love, William T. 165
Lund, Jeff 31, 33
Lyell, Charles 152

## M

Mackelprang Barnett, Elma 108
Malibou Lake 47
Malibu Lagoon 46
Mandarin, FL 196
Mandle, Harry 46
Mannering, Agatha 108
Marshall, Robert 13, 26–27, 29–31, 34–35
Martin, Strother 47
Marx, Leo 151
Master, Larry 103
Matanuska Valley, AK 18, 39
Maugham, Somerset 193
Mauser, Wolfram 142
McCall, Tom 227–31
McCall Waterfront Park, Portland, OR 208
McCandless, Christopher 16–17
McKinley, T.B. 138
McPhee, John 196
Mead, Lake 93–94, 100–06, 111–13
Meade, Charlie 133–34, 143
Medea Creek, Malibu, CA 47
Medford, OR 216
Medred, Craig 17
Meeker, CO 238
Mehojah, William A. 122

Mercury, NV 109
Merlin, Lee A. 107
Miami Beach West, FL 59
Miami, FL 191, 193–94, 199–200
Mische, Emanuel 225
Mississippi River 8, 9, 63, 65–76, 78–80, 84–87, 120, 130, 176
Mississippi River Delta 70, 72–73, 80
Mississippi Valley 65, 69, 71–72, 75, 77–78
Mohawk Valley 148
Mojave Desert, CA 61, 111
Morris, William 232
Moses, Robert 227
Mount Hood, OR 210–11, 222, 226
Mount Tabor Park, Portland, OR 225
Muddy River Valley 92, 94–98
Mud Island, Memphis, TN 66–68
Mueller, John 135
Mueller, Karoline 135
Mulroy, Patricia 113–14
Mumford, Lewis 223, 225–27, 230, 235
Murray, Bill 46
Musk, Elon 157

## N

Napoleon *see* Bonaparte, Napoleon
Navajo 101–02
Nevada Test Site/Nevada National Security Site 107–09
New Orleans, LA 69, 86
New York City, NY 59, 72, 74, 75
Niagara Falls 7, 8, 145, 147, 148, 151–59, 161, 163, 165–67, 169–71, 176
Niagara Falls Reservation 161–64
Niagara River 157, 161, 163, 165, 169
Niagara State Park 171
Nicholas Canyon Creek 53–54
Nixon, Richard 228
Nixon, Rob 170
Nolan, AK 30–31, 33–34
Nome, AK 33
North Hollywood, Memphis, TN 77
North Slope, AK 33

## O

Oaks Bottom Wildlife Refuge, Portland, OR 222

# Index

Ojai, CA 53
Okeechobee, FL 192, 196–97
Okeechobee, Lake 192, 194–98
Old Topanga Canyon, CA 55
Olmsted, Frederick Law 160–64, 171 230, 235
Olmsted, John Charles 223–26, 231
O'Neal, Tatum 46
Onondaga, ON, Canada 148
Ontario, Lake 157
Orlando, FL 173–77, 179, 183, 186, 187, 190, 191, 200, 230, 240
Overbrook, KS 119–20
Overton, John 73
Overton, NV 97–99, 104, 114
Overton Park, Memphis, TN 88

## P

Pacific Coast Highway 50–51
Paez, Juan 53
Paisley, FL 176
Palm Beach, FL 193–94, 200
Paradise Key, FL 204
Patton, Charlie 80
Pelli, César 188–89
Penn, Sean 17
Persons, Ell 88
Philipps, Sam 80
Phoenix, AZ 100, 107
Pilz, George 33
Piru, CA 53
Pismo Beach, CA 53
Pitt, Brad 59
Platte River 123
Pliny the Elder 244
Point Hope, AK 36
Point Mugu, CA 53
Ponce de León, Juan 191
Porter, Augustus 158–59
Porter, Peter 158–59
Potter, William E. 178
Powell, John Wesley 99
Powell, Lake 104
Pratt, Parley P. 95
President's Island, Memphis, TN 85–88
Presley, Elvis 63, 88
Price, Jenny 50–51

Prudhoe Bay, AK 14–15, 20–21, 23, 37–38, 240
Prudhomme, Leon Victor 43
Pueblo Grande de Nevada *see* Lost City, NV
Putnam, Robert 229

## Q

Quigualtam, Chief 70

## R

Rachel Carson Center 248–49
Ramírez Canyon 48–49
Rangely, CO 238
Ranke, Leopold 237
Rath, Charles 129
Reagan, Ronald 47
Reakoff, Jack 24, 27, 34, 38,
Reakoff, June 24, 27, 28, 38
Redford, Robert 57–58
Red Jacket *see* Sagoyewatha, Seneca chief
Reynolds, Steve 83
Richardson, H.H. 146
Rindge, Frederick 43–45, 55, 61
Rindge, May Knight 43–47, 50, 55
Roberts, Julia 58
Rocky Mountains 34, 65, 97, 111, 118
Roebling, John August 152–53
Rohde, Joe 185
Ronstadt, Linda 46
Roosevelt, Franklin D. 103, 218
Roosevelt, Theodore 193, 238–39
Ross, Harry 25
Ross Island, Portland, OR 217, 225
Rousseau, Jean-Jacques 240
Ruskin, John 161
Russell, Edmund 135
Ruth, Babe (George Herman) 193

## S

Sacagawea, Shoshone tribe 213
Sagoyewatha, Seneca chief 148
Saint Charles, MO 121
Salem, OR 216
Salinger, Bob 222
Salt Lake City, UT 94, 97, 106
San Francisco, CA 41, 45, 176, 216, 236
San Juan River 101

295

# Index

San Luis Obispo, CA 53
Santa Fe Trail 118–22, 124, 141
Santa Monica Mountains 47–48, 59
Saratoga Springs, NY 147
Saticoy, CA 53
Savannah, GA 72
Scajaquada Creek, NY 148
Schlosser, Eric 140
Schmidt, Adam 135
Schoppenhorst, Heidi 24
Scrugham, J.G. (James Graves) 97
Seattle, WA 14–15, 19, 26, 107, 216, 236
Segel, Gil 57
Service, Robert W. 17
Seward, AK 33
Seward, William H. 14
Sibley, George C. 120–21
Simi Valley, CA 53
Sinatra, Frank 57
Sinclair, Upton 139
Smith, Joseph 94
Smith, Walter 203
Smythe, William E. 99
Soto, Hernando de 69–70
Spielberg, Steven 57
St Cloud, FL 192
St George, UT 108–09
Stedman, John 157
Stegner, Wallace 115
Steinbeck, John 119
Steinkrüger, Jan Erik 184
Sting (Gordon Sumner) 46
Stoneman Douglas, Marjory 200
Stonewall, James 84
Stonewall, Stephen 84
Straub, Robert 228
Streisand, Barbra 47–49, 59
Strongin, Josephine 226
Sullivan, Louis 146
Sundborg, George 23
Swan Island, Portland, OR 218
Swan, Robert 17
Swan, Thomas 17
Swanson, Gloria 46
Sweetwater Canyon, Malibu, CA 50

**T**
Tacoma, WA 216
Tall Grass Prairie National Preserve 126
Tamiami Trail 205
Terrapin Point 163, 170
Terwilliger Parkway, Portland, OR 225
Tesla, Nikola 157, 163, 166
Theron, Charlize 59
Thomas, Parry 106
Tocqueville, Alexis de 151
Tohopekaliga, Lake 173
Topeka, KS 117, 129
Torrance, CA 44
Trenton Falls 147
Triunfo Creek, Malibu, CA 47
Truman, Harry S. 200, 204
Trump, Donald 37, 78, 118
Turner, Frederick Jackson 180
Turner, Orsamus 151
Twain, Mark 65, 69, 153, 193

**V**
Valley of Fire, NV 91–92
Vancouver, BC, Canada 216
Vancouver, George 211–12
Vanport, OR 218
Vaux, Calvert 161–62
Venturi, Robert 189
Vierthaler, Mark 132–33
Virgin River, UT, NV, AZ 99

**W**
Waiya, Mati 51–54
Walt Disney World 173–205
    Animal Kingdom 173, 181–85
    EPCOT 173
    Hollywood Studios 173
    Magic Kingdom 173, 177, 179–81, 188
Ward, Rachel 46
Warner, Jack 46
Washington, DC 121
Washington, George 72
Wells, H.G. (Herbert George) 232
Wenner, Bob 87–88
Westinghouse, George 157
West Memphis, AR 65, 82, 84
West Palm Beach, FL 194

# Index

Whales, James 47
White, Richard 7, 104
Whitman, Walt 153
Wichita, KS 130
Wilde, Oscar 145
Willamette River 207–08, 212–14, 216–23, 225, 228
Willamette Valley 212
Williams, Francis 28
Williams, Ruth 28
Willis, Roxanne 15
Wilson, AR 79, 82
Winter, Joel 137–40
Winter, Karl 138
Winter, Ken 138
Wirth, Conrad L. 203
Wolf River, TN, MS 66, 68, 77, 87–88
Wordsworth, William 240
Work, John 212
Worster, Don 118–19, 124, 138, 249
Wright, Frank Lloyd 146

**Y**

Yellowstone National Park 35
Young, Brigham 94
Youngstown, NY 148
Yucca Mountain, NV 109–110
Yukon River 21–23, 33, 37